CH00919224

BRITAIN AND THE END OF THE ROMAN EMPIRE

BRITAIN AND THE END OF THE ROMAN EMPIRE

KEN DARK

TEMPUS

First published 2000

PUBLISHED IN THE UNITED KINGDOM BY:

Tempus Publishing Ltd
The Mill, Brimscombe Port
Stroud, Gloucestershire GL5 2QG

PUBLISHED IN THE UNITED STATES OF AMERICA BY:

Arcadia Publishing Inc.
A division of Tempus Publishing Inc.
2 Cumberland Street
Charleston, SC 29401
1-888-313-2665

Tempus books are available in France, Germany and Belgium
from the following addresses:

Tempus Publishing Group	Tempus Publishing Group	Tempus Publishing Group
21 Avenue de la République	Gustav-Adolf-Straße 3	Place de L'Alma 4/5
37300 Joué-lès-Tours	99084 Erfurt	1200 Brussels
FRANCE	GERMANY	BELGIUM

British Library Cataloguing in Publication Data.
A catalogue record for this book is available from the British Library.

ISBN 0 7524 1451 8

Typesetting and origination by Tempus Publishing.
PRINTED AND BOUND IN GREAT BRITAIN

Contents

List of illustrations

Text figures

Colour plates

Acknowledgements

I would like to acknowledge the continual and invaluable help and encouragement of my family and my colleagues at the University of Reading. The Ashmolean Library in Oxford and the libraries of the Universities of London and Reading have proved an invaluable assistance, as has the ability to visit most of the sites and see most of the artefacts discussed here, whether they are in Britain or elsewhere. Many friends and colleagues have provided unpublished data or produced draft maps and illustrations for this book, and even more have discussed specific issues with me in detail, both directly in relation to the book or while I was working on it. I would especially like to thank Diane Brooke, Ewan Campbell, Hilary Cool, Mark Corney, Sally Foster, Anthea Harris, John Hines, Heather James, David Longley, Chris Lowe, Ros Niblett, Oliver Padel, David Petts, Jude Plouviez, Mark Redknap, Carol van Driel-Murray, Colin Wallace, Roger White, Howard Williams, Tony Wilmott, and Susan Youngs. Heinrich Härke and Edward James both kindly read and commented on the text. Lastly, the interest, support and discussion afforded by the Late Antiquity Research Group has been of much value.

Introduction

In the late seventh century, Christian Anglo-Saxon kings ruled great kingdoms with newly emerging towns, trading with France and beyond. These kings were patrons of the Church, granting land to many small monasteries, commissioned written laws, and had just begun to issue coins copying their Continental counterparts. By this time, the Anglo-Saxons understood their identity in terms of a 'North Sea' community of Germanic peoples, speaking Germanic languages (of which 'Anglo-Saxon' was one), ruled by a largely illiterate warrior aristocracy. The other peoples of Britain had been relegated to a peripheral role in political, military, economic, and even linguistic, terms. The pattern of political, cultural and economic change that was to develop into a single English-speaking 'Kingdom of England' in the tenth century, and a Gaelic-speaking 'Kingdom of Scotland' in the ninth, was already set in motion (**colour plates 1 & 2**).[1]

This pattern might be traced, at least in part, to the political and cultural links between eastern Britain and France during the mid- to late sixth century. These led first to the adoption of Continental concepts of government and then to the conversion of Anglo-Saxon kings to Christianity. In this way, the seventh century can be viewed as a prolonged phase of profound political, religious, cultural and economic change, characterised by the growth of royal control, the conversion of the Anglo-Saxons to Christianity, and associated with the new Continental linkages. This affected many aspects of everyday life. So, for example, long-established burial customs of depositing objects with the dead ('accompanied burial') reach their 'Final Phase' in the seventh century, and artefacts indicate a growing emulation of Continental, and perhaps particularly Mediterranean, dress fashions.[2]

Two hundred years before 597 (when the Papal missionary St Augustine arrived in Kent to begin the conversion of the Anglo-Saxon kings) a wholly different religious, political, cultural and economic situation prevailed in Britain. In 397, Britain was a part of a Europe-wide state, the Roman Empire, with a single currency, a centralised military and legal system, and an elite connected to a transnational culture spanning western Europe and the Mediterranean with Latin as its official language. While the Roman Empire itself was officially Christian by this date, most of the ruling elite of Britain remained pagan, and temples rather than churches dotted the late Romano-British landscape. The population as a whole appears to have retained pre-Roman, 'British', tribal and cultural identities, and to have spoken a 'Celtic', not Germanic language.[3]

The centuries between 397 and 597 witnessed the collapse of the Roman Empire in western Europe and the establishment of states governed by non-Roman ('barbarian') kings, mostly derived from peoples immediately beyond the northern frontiers of the Roman Empire ('Germania'). These centuries saw linguistic and cultural transformation

1 'Anglo-Saxon' cemeteries in Britain. This is usually taken to represent the extension of 'Anglo-Saxon' political control and culture across Britain (illustrations 1-3 are based on Hines):

   1 Fifth-century sites, open circles represent sites with evidence of mid-fifth-century or earlier date: filled circles represent mid- and later fifth-century sites.

   2 Early sixth-century sites.

   3 All sites from the fifth to the seventh centuries.

   4 Middle Anglo-Saxon cemeteries of the seventh and eighth centuries (after Geake)

across Europe, the establishment of Christianity as the principal European religion, and the origins of medieval and later European literacy, literature and law.

Without exaggeration, the fifth and sixth centuries saw the formation of many of the central aspects of what might today seem the basis of European culture and identity. This was the background to the 'seventh-century transformation' in Britain and elsewhere. In this sense, the 'seventh-century transformation' was merely the outcome of a process of political, cultural, religious and economic transformation beginning in the fifth or even fourth century, and defining a distinct period of European and Middle Eastern history, called by scholars 'Late Antiquity'.[4]

These transformations, from the fourth or fifth to seventh centuries, show many similarities across regions and peoples, but the conventional view is that Britain is an exception to all of these. Indeed, the term 'Late Antiquity', while widely used when discussing Europe as a whole, is seldom applied to Britain. Instead, the 'end of Roman Britain' is frequently interpreted as, in many respects, a uniquely catastrophic aspect of early fifth-century European history.

Post-Roman cataclysm remains the conventional picture of the end of Roman Britain for many professional archaeologists and historians, although interpretation of the end of Roman Britain has become a field of heated debate since at least the beginning of the 1990s. Four main alternative interpretations, other than that first proposed for western Britain by the author in 1994 and developed in this book for the whole of the island, are currently available. It will put the present work in perspective to outline these alternatives very briefly.

In one, once the 'establishment' view, Roman Britain 'wound down' slowly in the fifth century. No trace of its political or economic institutions and culture (except possibly for the Christian Church) survived after 450, but these were gradually declining from the 360s until that time. Fifth-century British history was dominated by the Anglo-Saxons, who migrated into eastern Britain in increasingly large numbers from the early fifth, or even late fourth, century from their homelands in modern Holland, Denmark and Germany. The Britons (that is to say, the descendants of the former Roman citizens in Britain) gradually returned to a 'Celtic Iron Age' way of living in western and northern Britain, apart from holding Christian beliefs. So that 'Britons' and 'Anglo-Saxons' lived in very similar ways, in warring tribal kingdoms, from the mid-fifth century onward, and after the mid-sixth century the Anglo-Saxons gradually conquered the 'Celtic West', leading to the dominance of Anglo-Saxon kingdoms in the seventh century.[5]

This first view held sway until at least the late 1970s, coexisting for much of that decade with the so-called 'Continuity Debate' over whether continuous patterns of political, cultural, economic and geographical development could be traced in Britain from prehistory to the twentieth century. In particular, many archaeologists hoped to discover evidence that the histories of specific towns and rural settlements could be traced back to the Roman period and beyond. The possibility of a late fourth- or early fifth-century phase of overlap between Anglo-Saxon migration and a functioning Romano-British society, seemed to hold out hope of this. This stage of investigation might be said to have come to an end with the highly-influential 'End of Roman Britain' conference, when a series of (then apparently strong) arguments against such continuities were proposed.[6]

The main alternative — favoured by several of the scholars who spoke at the 'End of Roman Britain' conference, and then developed by others through the 1980s — was to argue for dramatic discontinuity between 'Roman Britain' and 'Anglo-Saxon England'. This contrasting perspective could be termed the 'new establishment' interpretation, because by the early 1990s it had largely replaced the former as the conventional interpretation held by professional archaeologists. The most complete and forceful expressions of this interpretation were proposed in Simon Esmonde-Cleary's book *The Ending of Roman Britain*, and in a volume of papers edited by Steve Bassett entitled *The Origins of Anglo-Saxon Kingdoms*, both published in 1989.[7]

According to the 'new establishment' view, Roman Britain flourished until *c*.AD 400 but then dramatically collapsed, leaving almost nothing of its way of life after the early fifth century (*c*.430 is often mentioned). The pagan Anglo-Saxons migrated into eastern Britain during the early to mid-fifth century, probably in lesser number than scholars holding the former view believed. There was no phase of overlap between a functioning Roman Britain and Anglo-Saxon settlement. The Britons were extremely similar to the Anglo-Saxons in social, economic and technological terms, except in so far as the former were mostly Christian and had an archaeologically invisible material culture. Both groups had kings controlling small territories who competed in a 'knock-out competition' of political and military action, leading to Anglo-Saxon political and economic dominance by the seventh century. Intermarriage and cultural dominance by Anglo-Saxon rulers led to those Britons living inside Anglo-Saxon controlled territories gradually adopting Anglo-Saxon culture and language.

Another option had been suggested at the same conference, and was subsequently developed, by Richard Reece. This too has been very influential in shaping perceptions of the end of Roman Britain, although it has seldom been supported wholeheartedly. Reece argued that Roman Britain was transformed not in the fifth but in the third and fourth centuries. In his view, Romano-British towns ceased to survive the fourth century as more than mere 'administrative villages', because Roman urbanism could not 'take hold' in Britain. In Reece's opinion, the countryside saw the growth of village-sized settlements around Romano-British villas, so that before 400 the landscape was full of 'villages' of roughly similar size. Reece argued that Romano-British culture was little more than a 'façade', dropped when the imperial bureaucracy departed or even before. The Anglo-Saxons did not migrate in any substantial numbers, but 'Anglo-Saxon' fashions became popular in eastern Britain during the fifth century. 'Anglo-Saxon England' was a consequence of fashion-changes in eastern Britain not affecting the 'Celtic West'. This 'short-chronology' for Roman Britain has recently been revived by Neil Faulkner, who argues for much the same picture, largely based on statistical studies of Roman-period construction work.[8]

Finally, in the 1990s Nicholas Higham suggested a version in which most of the 'new establishment' view is retained, but the fifth-century Britons are credited with retaining aspects of Roman-period administration into the late fifth century. Higham divides late fourth-century Roman Britain into two zones, one in the east with a 'highly-Romanized' Christian elite, and the other with a pagan and 'un-Romanized' upper class. In the former, he argues, early fifth-century defence depended on the use of Anglo-Saxon mercenaries, and when these rebelled (still in the early fifth century) the Britons there were unable to defend themselves. So the whole of what had been eastern Roman Britain passed very rapidly under Anglo-Saxon rule. In the latter zone, tribal kingship kept the Britons free of direct Anglo-Saxon rule, but their rulers were politically and militarily subordinate to Anglo-Saxon kings before 500. In Higham's opinion, after the mid-fifth century all Britons were governed by rulers who, while Christian, acknowledged the overlordship of pagan Anglo-Saxon kings. Anglo-Saxon culture was rapidly adopted by the Britons in emulation of their new masters, while pagan Anglo-Saxon kings attempted to retain aspects of the former Roman administrative framework.[9]

We shall see that none of these four views offers an adequate interpretation of the end of Roman Britain or of the origin of the seventh-century political, cultural and religious landscape of Britain. This being said, each contains important contributions and each highlighted interesting problems regarding the study of this period. It is equally important to note that these interpretations all have a number of key points in common regarding the late fifth and sixth centuries:

1 Fifth- and sixth-century Britain was divided into two largely homogeneous cultural zones, approximately the east ('the Anglo-Saxon area') and (the 'Celtic') west of what had been Roman Britain. These were to become 'England' and its 'Celtic periphery' of Wales, Cornwall, and Cumbria.

2 The whole of the British Isles, from at latest the mid-fifth century onward, was ruled by kings.

3 All of the fifth- and sixth-century peoples of Britain were similar in social, economic and technological terms.

4 Romano-British material culture was not produced after the early fifth century, and was not used after the mid-fifth century at latest.

5 Anglo-Saxon paganism was the dominant religion in eastern Britain from the mid-fifth to late sixth century, although small isolated Christian communities might have survived from Roman Britain.

6 Town-life ended in Britain before the mid-fifth century, and did not re-emerge in Britain until the seventh century.

7 After the mid-fifth century at latest, people employing Anglo-Saxon culture and religion were in political control throughout eastern Britain.

8 Britain was 'different' from the rest of Europe, so that the concept of 'Late Antiquity', however useful elsewhere, is irrelevant to any part of fifth- and sixth-century Britain.

Here, I shall argue that *all* of these points are misconceptions, and argue for a very different interpretation of fifth- and sixth-century Britain. This new interpretation places Britain in the mainstream of European religious, cultural, political and economic development. It reasserts the similarity between Britain and other parts of what had been the Roman Empire, throughout the fifth and sixth centuries. It proposes that most of fifth- and sixth-century Britain shared the same 'Romano-Christian' culture of Late Antiquity as developed in other parts of the former Roman world from the fourth century AD onward. In so far as most of Britain was different from other Late Antique western European societies at all, we shall see that this was often because *more*, not less, of its Roman heritage survived and because the Britons were particularly effective in spreading their version of the Late Antique Romano-Christian culture to neighbouring peoples. What enabled these differences to occur was the ability of the Britons to retain their political independence longer than any of their Western provincial counterparts, and this was related to differences between the Britons and the other peoples of fifth- and sixth-century Britain.

In order to explain why it is possible to propose such a dramatic alternative, one which contradicts many of the most deeply-held preconceptions about the British 'Dark Ages' (as the period AD 400-600 has often been termed) it is necessary to begin by looking — very briefly — at some aspects of Roman Britain in the late fourth century, before moving forward in time to examine these themes.

Roman Britain in the late fourth century

South of Hadrian's Wall (the northern Roman frontier line in the fourth century) Britain was wholly part of the Roman Empire and officially referred to as the Diocese of Britanniae ('the Britains'). A 'diocese', in this sense, was a Late Roman administrative unit made up of a group of related provinces. The Diocese of Britanniae comprised four or five provinces (hence the term 'Britains' — 'British provinces'), with the diocesan capital at London. In the east lay the provinces of 'Maxima Caesariensis' and 'Britannia Secunda'. To the west of these lay 'Britannia Prima' and, to the north of all of these, 'Flavia Caesariensis'. Another province, 'Valentia', is known but may have been one of the former provinces re-named. The capitals of the provinces were large Roman towns, all apparently occupied throughout the fourth century.[10]

Within these provinces were smaller political divisions: *civitates* (singular *civitas*), about the size of modern English counties. Each had its own capital, in some respects like a 'county town' today. Again, these were major Roman towns, provided with walls, public buildings and at least one market place and with a central 'forum-basilica' complex. In the early to mid-fourth century these towns had shops and private houses, and services were provided by specialists resident in them, such as lawyers and doctors. By the end of the fourth century, many Romano-British towns had many of their public buildings converted to other uses, especially basilicas, which became metalworking establishments at Silchester, Caerwent and perhaps elsewhere. However, the towns seem to have retained political, economic and administrative functions and were still centres for elite residence, with 'town-houses' being both used and built in the late fourth century.

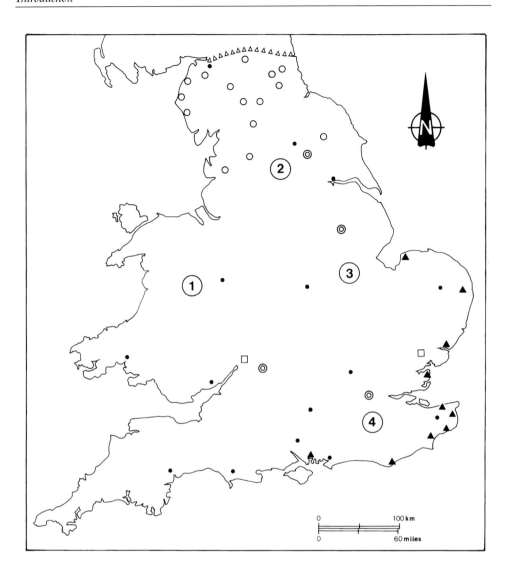

2   *Roman Britain in the fourth century, showing provinces, centres of civilian administration and military commands. Circled numbers 1-4 indicate the approximate locations of the four Late Roman provinces. The location of the fifth province, Valentia, is uncertain. (Based on Jones and Mattingly and Frere.)*

Civilian administrative centres:

Double circles = Provincial capitals

Filled circles = Civitas *capitals*

Squares = Coloniae, not also provincial or civitas *capitals*

Military commands:

Open circles = Forts of the Dux Britannarium *certainly identified in the* Notitia Dignitatum

Filled triangles: Forts of the Saxon Shore

Open triangles indicate the line of Hadrian s Wall, part of the command of the Dux Britanniarum

In the fourth century, another 'tier' of towns existed, known by modern archaeologists — but not Romano-Britons — as 'small towns'. These were provided with fewer public buildings and often had a less 'Roman' looking plan, at least as it appears to us today. They seem to have served as market-centres and administrative foci for the surrounding areas, and also had shops and private houses inside them. In the late fourth century, several were closely connected to large-scale production, such as pottery-making and iron-production. The products of such 'industries' could travel widely in their own provinces and sometimes to other parts of the diocese, but were not exported in large quantities outside Britain.[11]

The fourth century was the heyday of Romano-British villas (country residences 'built to impress'), suggesting a wealth-producing agricultural economy. Although the number of Romano-British villas may have declined in the later fourth century, many were still occupied up to and beyond the end of the century, and most people in the countryside were engaged in farming, either for themselves or working estates owned by the wealthy. Both single farms and small farming villages are known in addition to villas, and villages also grew up along the principal paved roads ('Roman roads') linking the major towns and other important locations. The occupants of roadside villages seem to have provided goods and services to travellers, and also took part in farming.

The majority of farming communities of whatever sort had some access to manufactured goods, especially pottery, glass and metalwork. This shows that these communities were producing a sufficient surplus both to feed themselves and participate in commerce, despite a very harsh taxation system known from written sources relating to the Late Roman Empire. Rural buildings were generally well-constructed of wood or mortared stone, often with thatched or tiled roofs, and villas would often also have some rooms with mosaic floors, hypocausts providing under-floor heating, and private sets of 'Roman baths'.

A particular indication of the wealth of fourth-century Roman Britain is the construction of 'palatial' villas, especially in the West Country (defined here as modern Somerset, Dorset and Gloucestershire). These sites appear to represent a very high rank of villa-owning aristocrats; for example that at Woodchester has the largest Roman mosaic north of the Alps. Although elsewhere in western Europe a minority of villa owners fortified their estates, in Britain there is no undeniable case of fortifications at even these luxurious villas, and one gains the impression that the countryside as a whole was considered free from regular violence. The wealth of their owners may also be indicated by the large number of hoards of silverware from Late Roman Britain. Although arguably eventually buried for safekeeping in times of risk, these attest some very wealthy people in fourth-century Britain, willing to commission elaborately decorated display items.

This impression of relative security in the west of Britain is emphasised by the disposition of the Roman army in Britain. In the late fourth century almost all imperial troops in Britain were located in one of two places: either they were on Hadrian's Wall and in the forts of the north, supporting it; or they were positioned on the east coast. In the north-east there was a network of coastal signal stations probably affording advance warning to a cavalry unit at Malton. On the south-east coasts were a group of strongly defended Late Roman enclosures. These are called by a Continental inventory (the *Notitia*

Dignitatum) the *Litus Saxonicum* ('the Saxon Shore'), but this command may not have come into existence until the 390s, and possibly not until 400-8. Before that these forts may have defended the military transport network along the Channel coasts, and while the name 'Saxon Shore' may attest raiding (by 'Saxons') by that time, there is no hint that eastern Britain was provided with other forts, nor that 'Saxon' settlement was taking place. So before the 390s most of southern Roman Britain lay undefended and perhaps vulnerable to coastal raiding. These raids were a prelude to subsequent developments, as too was the religious composition of Late Roman Britain by 400 (**colour plate 3**).[12]

Fourth-century Britain contained both Christian and pagan communities. There is currently much debate about the relative size of these, their social composition, and distribution, although recent work suggests that Christianity was 'a major religion of fourth-century Britain'. Textual evidence informs us of bishops in the provincial capitals (London, York, Cirencester and Lincoln) from the early fourth century onwards, but there are strong hints from archaeological data that Christianity, an 'urban religion' in many parts of the fourth-century West, was unusually popular in the fourth-century Romano-British countryside.

A serious difficulty in detecting Romano-British Christians is that there are also hints that they were particularly conservative with regard to religious matters, and that Christianity may have been more widespread among the poor than the landowning elite. In the fourth century, religious conservatism could have affected a willingness to employ Christian symbols (such as the Chi Rho symbol or the cross), as there was still strong reluctance to use religious symbolism among some Christians. The rich also tend to have more purpose-made religious objects, religious buildings and elaborate tombs than the poor, rendering their religions more 'visible' to archaeologists.[13]

It is reasonable to expect urban bishops to have had purpose-built churches (their 'cathedrals') as elsewhere in the Late Roman Empire, although only one possible structure of this sort has been found, and what might be church buildings are known elsewhere from fourth-century Britain, as at Colchester and Icklingham. More conservative Romano-British Christians might have worshipped in 'house-churches' and these could be simply a room used occasionally for Christian services or prayer. The only known 'house-church' identified in Roman Britain is the painted chapel in Lullingstone villa, but this may relate to the unusual elite context or to the lack of specific decoration in such rooms, rather than their absence. A sixth-century Continental text refers to Breton clergy using portable altars to serve Communion in the homes of their flock. As sixth-century Bretons were either the descendants of migrants from Britain or such migrants themselves, this may be relevant to the British Church at that time also. The relevance to Britain may be supported by the observation that portable altars became popular in the seventh-century British and Irish churches, where many aspects of practice derived specifically from the Romano-British past. If fourth- and fifth-century British Christians used portable altars and employed their homes for worship, places of Christian preaching and prayer would be extremely difficult to recognise archaeologically.

Christianity and paganism are also differentially visible in the archaeological record because pagan practices involved more distinctive artefacts — votive objects, cult statues, 'curse-tablets' and regalia all characterise fourth-century paganism. Votive hoards (those deposited as offerings) also indicate the existence of wealthy fourth-century pagans, as at Thetford, where the 'Thetford Treasure' contained a gold buckle set, 22 gold finger rings and other items, buried *c*.390. But the richest Christian artefacts known from fourth-century Britain — those in the 'Water Newton hoard' — are likely, as Kenneth Painter has suggested, to be liturgical (objects used in church services).

That is, Christianity may be less easily 'visible' in the archaeology of fourth-century Britain than paganism because of differences in religious practices. Conversely, paganism is likely to be more archaeologically 'visible' than Christianity because of these differences in religious practice, and the number of fourth-century Christians in Britain remains difficult to estimate. It may well have been higher than often supposed, at least by the late fourth century.[14]

As a consequence of this 'visibility' we know a lot about fourth-century Romano-British paganism from archaeological evidence. Paganism in late fourth-century Britain was very diverse. A large number of pagan cults existed and no one pagan religion predominated, although almost all were polytheistic, employed sacrifice, and venerated statues of their deities. Temples were still used in the late fourth century across most of southern Britain, and there is a particularly large concentration of such sites in the West Country, but the old interpretation of a 'pagan revival' in the late fourth century no longer has anything to support it. The key site — Lydney — has been re-dated by John Casey following excavation in the 1980s. Casey finds no evidence to support a new impetus of religious activity at Lydney in the late fourth century, and this was a period at which other temples were closing across the whole of southern Britain.[15]

Conversely, there are hints that paganism was beginning to decline rapidly in the late fourth century. While large numbers of pagan temples are known from fourth-century Roman Britain, few survived until the 390s. In a recent catalogue of these, Dorothy Watts could list only 20 possible examples. Not all of these were definitely temples or certainly in use in the 390s, and of those that were, only 12 (Bath, Bourton Grounds, Carrawburgh, Farley Heath, Frilford 2, Henley Wood, Lydney, Maiden Castle, Nettleton, Pagan's Hill, Witham and Woodeaton) were still in use by 400. Even if Uley can be added to this list, it leaves only 13 temples from the whole of Roman Britain in use *c*.400, and only four of these were outside the West Country.[16]

The reason for the number of temples in the West Country may be the location of the Late Romano-British rural elite, as this is an area with an exceptional number of rich fourth-century villas. Temples were architecturally related to the villas of the rural elite of fourth-century Britain, and the artefacts deposited at temples attest patronage by the same social group. Late fourth-century villas often have pagan mosaics and artefacts suggesting that their owners remained pagan until this time. Villas and temples were often the only, or main, contexts in which new substantial masonry buildings were constructed in the countryside of fourth-century Britain, again perhaps implying some connection between them. The temples were perhaps linked to a rural villa-owning pagan elite, rather than to rural paganism more generally, and the absence of a 'pagan revival' should not be taken as evidence for the absence of a pagan landowning class. The decline of temple numbers by *c*.400 may suggest that this group was no longer able to support these establishments or no longer found it expedient to patronise them.[17]

3 Tutulus brooch from Kirmington, Lincolnshire. Reproduced with the kind permission of Kevin Leahy

Thus, in *c*.400 the Romano-British population apparently included both substantial (and growing?) Christian and (declining?) pagan communities. There were probably bishops and churches in the major towns, but pagan landowners still predominated in the countryside, although there are suggestions of unusually early rural Christianity.

Whether Christian or pagan, by the fourth century the whole free population of the Diocese were considered citizens of the Empire at birth, and any division between 'Romans' and 'Britons' had long disappeared. There is no evidence for large numbers of Germanic immigrants in fourth-century Britain and, if born free in Britain, the children of Germanic migrants were Roman citizens.[18]

Identifiable Germanic communities in Late Roman Britain include military units and, especially perhaps in East Anglia, civilian women. 'Tutulus' and 'supporting arm' brooches — characteristic of people from beyond the northern Roman frontiers — have been found in a thin scatter across Norfolk, Suffolk, and into Lincolnshire. That Germanic migrants existed in a wholly Late Roman context seems likely from the lack of distinctively 'Germanic' settlements of this date, and finds of 'supporting arm' brooches at sites with no other indications of Germanic occupation.[19]

Perhaps the most evocative instance is the discovery of a woman's body in a late fourth-century pit at the Romano-British 'small town' of Scole. She was wearing a string of beads held in place by two brooches: one was a late fourth-century 'supporting arm' brooch, the other a second-century Romano-British example. This may indicate not only how Germanic and Romano-British elements could be combined in the multicultural synthesis of the late fourth century, but also how long Roman-period material culture remained in circulation. The latter point inevitably affects how we regard the transition from 'Romano-British' to 'post-Roman' material culture in the fifth and sixth centuries, as we shall see later.[20]

Only a few fourth-century Germanic brooches have been found in Britain in contexts where they are certainly not heirlooms kept by much later generations, and there is no reason to suppose that late fourth-century Germanic communities represent the first 'Anglo-Saxons'. Nor were they the only immigrant group in Late Roman Britain: in keeping with the Late Roman world in general, people from across the Empire settled and lived in the Diocese, for example the Arab (probably Syrian) soldiers at South Shields.[21]

Roman Britain did not include all of the island of Britain. North of Hadrian's Wall there were Britons living outside of Roman rule. No towns, forts or villas existed in this area, and it was a wholly agricultural community with no evidence of mass production. Romano-British manufactured goods were widely available, but these occur on hill-forts and settlements of essentially 'Iron Age' appearance. Nevertheless, the Britons in this area probably shared some form of common identity with those south of the Wall, and both were probably encompassed in the term *Combrogi* ('people of the same country'), the origin of later *Cymru* (the Welsh name for Wales) and *Cumbria* (an English county name) alike.[22]

To the north of these 'intermural' Britons, in what is today north-east Scotland, were the Picts, who came to the notice of Roman observers as seaborne raiders, also living in an 'Iron Age' manner. Whether or not their later neighbours, the Irish-speaking Dalriadan Scots, had already become established in Argyll will be discussed later.[23]

Continental Roman writers tell us that the Picts and Scots, the latter probably from Ireland, and the 'Saxons' (the term 'Anglo-Saxon' is a much later invention), raided Roman Britain. However, outside Romano-British contexts, Germanic settlement is unattested in the fourth century and there is no evidence that any of these other peoples settled in Roman Britain.[24]

By 400, then, the stage was set for the developments of the fifth century, but there was little trace that Britain was about to undergo dramatic change, apart perhaps from the increasing size of the Christian Church. In order to introduce these changes, we may first glance at the rest of the Roman Empire. This will, in turn, highlight current peculiarities regarding interpretations of the end of Roman Britain, and suggest new ways of thinking about Britain in the fifth and sixth centuries.

Western Europe 400-500

The late fourth and fifth centuries were a period of crisis and political collapse throughout the Roman West. In Italy, the very core of the former Western Empire, Roman rule was replaced at the end of the fifth century by that of the Ostrogoths, a Germanic 'barbarian' people from beyond the northern frontier of the Empire who had been converted to a heretical form of Christianity, Arianism. In Gaul, after a period of political and military turmoil, a pagan Germanic people (the Franks) came to hold political control, and were eventually converted to orthodox 'Catholic' Christianity from the late fifth century onward. In Spain too, Arian Goths — there the Visigoths — took control. Smaller areas of the former Roman West were ruled by other 'barbarian' peoples whose origins lay (or were claimed to lie) beyond the Roman borders, such as the Burgundians, Alans and Alemanni. The part of North Africa belonging to the Western Empire passed under the control of another Arian barbarian group, the Vandals.[25]

By 500, the whole West was ruled by Germanic kings, whose religious beliefs were often at great variance with those of their western Roman subjects, mostly Catholic Christians, with a perhaps substantial pagan minority. Further east, the Eastern Roman (or 'Byzantine') Empire remained in firm control from the Balkans and Egypt to the Danube and Caucasus. There, the fifth century saw an economic boom, and a period of social and cultural consolidation, reformulating the secular culture of the Greco-Roman world into a new Christianised form: their own version of the Romano-Christian culture of Late Antiquity seen among former provincials in the West. For this Eastern Roman world, 'the Empire' had not fallen, merely the West had been (perhaps temporarily) lost. There, a Roman emperor still ruled from a Roman capital city, Constantinople (modern Istanbul).

The Germanic 'barbarians' who entered the West were not wholly untouched by 'Roman' provincial culture, as the conversion of the Goths and Vandals to Arianism demonstrates. Nor were they unfamiliar, as a whole, with Roman provincial material culture. Pottery, glass, metalwork, and even Roman coinage and weapons, are widely found in northern Europe beyond the imperial frontiers in the fourth century. This material may have arrived partly in the form of trade and partly as a result of imperial diplomatic gifts and payments to 'barbarian' rulers or warriors for service to the Empire. Some may have come as booty from 'barbarian' raids, but this is unlikely to account for much of the material given the composition of the assemblages recovered from so-called 'free Germania' (that is the Germanic areas east of the Rhine).[26]

An eminent twentieth-century historian of the Germanic barbarians of this period, E.A. Thompson, suggested that the level of contact with the Roman world experienced by the people of 'free Germania' enables one to divide them into two groups, comprising roughly concentric zones. In the first zone, 'Inner Germania', contact with the Roman world was long-standing and intense, and a high degree of mutual understanding was achieved. Peoples, such as the Franks, who lived within this zone were well-acquainted with the way of life of Roman provincials and the institutions of the Roman state long before they came to rule part of the former Empire. The other zone, 'Outer Germania', contained peoples who had little or no direct experience of the Roman world, and a far lower understanding of its ways of life and mode of government. Peoples in this outer zone included those ancestral to those Germanic migrants who settled in fifth-century Britain. Thus, one would expect quite different experiences of the Empire would result in different responses to the changed circumstances of the late fourth and fifth centuries.[27]

The familiarity of the peoples of 'Inner Germania' with the structures of imperial life might well account for the nature of the new social, cultural and economic circumstances of the fifth century in the formerly Roman provincial areas in which they settled. In Frankia, formerly most of Roman Gaul, the Franks ruled a mixed population of Germanic migrants and former western Roman provincials. Yet there was a synthesis in administrative terms of the Frankish and provincial elite. For example, the Church structures of the Roman state were preserved and presided over by the descendants of the former Roman provincial upper classes, while the ruler was a Frankish 'barbarian' king, whose style of government owed little in other respects to the Roman past. In this context, we find Late Romano-Gallic art and culture surviving throughout the fifth century, and well into the sixth, with Latin literacy, and the carving of sculptured tombstones and sarcophagi, widespread.[28]

The 'sub-Roman' elites who governed the bureaucracy and Church lived, it seems, in their ancestral villas in a 'Roman' way well into the fifth century. Ironically, perhaps the most evocative description of life in a 'Roman villa' in the West is by a writer from late fifth-century Gaul, Sidonius Apollinaris. Some towns, too, continued to act as administrative centres in the fifth and sixth centuries, although the extent to which they still contained concentrations of population, secular public buildings or shops is unclear. In many, 'episcopal complexes' (a group of buildings comprising a cathedral church and sometimes other churches, bishop's residence, administrative offices and guest house) which characterised Late Roman provincial towns in the West continued in use throughout the period. Written and archaeological sources attest the continuing significance of trade in at least a few Gallic towns, including long-distance trade with the Mediterranean, bringing amphorae of wine and other goods to Gaul from North Africa and the Eastern Mediterranean.[29]

This society developed the distinctive 'Romano-Christian culture' — one combining 'Roman' and Christian elements — that was mentioned earlier as characteristic of 'Late Antique' societies. The same type of combination is also found in Italy and Spain, and typifies the emergence of 'Byzantine' culture in the East. Alongside this, we find a quite different — Germanic — way of life. Sites such as Brebières and St Martin-de-Mondeville, Neerhaven-Reekem, show that timber post-built rectangular houses, and sunken-featured buildings, of Germanic style were in use contemporary with the Roman-style episcopal complexes, towns and villas already mentioned. When the Frankish king Childeric was buried at Tournai in the late fifth century, his funeral appears to have been wholly pagan and Germanic in character, with accompanying horse-sacrifices placed in nearby pits, as one could expect from a pagan Germanic barbarian people.[30]

From the late fifth century onward, Frankish burial practice, in particular accompanied inhumation burial in approximate rows (*Reihengräber* or 'row-graves'), soon became standard throughout the whole Frankish kingdom. While burial at churches and in cemeteries with Latin-inscribed tombstones, and even sculptured sarcophagi in the most 'Roman' of contexts, coexisted with this custom, *Reihengräber* apparently encompassed burials of both the Frankish and provincial Roman population, and both pagans and Christians. *Reihengräber* were — it seems — about status and political affinity, not religion and ethnicity.[31]

This observation emphasises that it would be mistaken to draw a hard-and-fast division between the world of the 'sub-Roman' and Frankish elites. This division was further eroded after the 490s by the Conversion of Frankish rulers to Catholic Christianity, rapidly followed by the Frankish aristocracy. Henceforth, Frankish aristocrats began to found their own churches, and were buried inside them. Yet, the *Reihengräber* burial tradition continued, and graves are found under churches of patrons buried in this manner. So, Frankish and sub-Roman Gallic populations, identities and cultures converged to form a new synthesis around the Romano-Christian culture of the latter.

Elsewhere, a similar pattern can be observed. In Italy, the adoption of 'Romano-Christian' cultural features by the Gothic aristocracy appears to have begun immediately. Although, as in Gaul, 'Romans' and 'Goths' long remained distinct (here aided in this by fundamental religious differences and legal restrictions against inter-marriage), and these populations show a degree of increasing cultural convergence as time goes by. When the Byzantines re-invaded Italy in the early sixth century, it was sometimes hard to tell the two populations apart, and popular sympathies were not necessarily with the eastern Roman imperial forces. As in Gaul, town-life, the occupation of villa sites in a 'Roman' manner and the local agricultural economy all seem to have continued throughout the fifth and sixth centuries, with long-distance trade based at Roman-period ports maintained into the sixth century.[32]

Similar religious divisions, and political ideology, also maintained the separation of former provincials and Visigothic rulers in Spain. Yet, once again, the Visigoths and the sub-Roman population display many of the same characteristics as seen in Gaul. Accompanied clothed inhumation became a widespread burial practice regardless, it appears, of ethnicity or religion, and communities coexisted despite their deep-seated religious and political differences. As in Gaul and Italy, urban life survived, albeit in a reduced form, and trade with the Mediterranean was maintained throughout the period, as evidenced at a series of southern coastal trading centres. Once again, by 600 Romano-Christian culture, including orthodox Catholic Christianity, had begun to form the focus for a new national culture and identity.[33]

The key point here regarding these changes is that a common pattern of sub-Roman survival and the adoption of a Romano-Christian culture can be seen in all these cases. Town life, villa occupation and long-distance trade all survived in some — often rather attenuated — form. The institutions and centres of Church life were maintained, and the church buildings themselves were both refurbished and newly constructed. Roman coinage continued to be used, Roman-period technologies were frequently preserved, and Roman-style education and literacy survived. Artefacts similar to those used in the fourth century were still manufactured and traded. Yet, alongside these survivals, there were new 'Germanic' elements, notably furnished clothed inhumation burial, Germanic-style artefacts and buildings, kingly government and the coexistence of Germanic as well as Roman law codes.

Central both to the fusion of Germanic and local ways of life and to the longevity of sub-Roman communities was the emergence and growth of their Romano-Christian culture. The latter is evidenced from every Continental area of what was the Roman Empire in AD 400, from western Gaul to Armenia, and from the Rhine to the Sahara. Moreover, it spread at varying rates to all the Germanic successor states of the fifth century and later. This culture was, quite literally, the basis of later European culture and identity, as it remains today.[34]

The apparent generality of this pattern throughout the former Roman West might well make one suspicious of the suggestion that Britain was the lone exception to all of this. Was the end of Roman Britain really uniquely cataclysmic, rapid and absolute?

The concept of Late Antiquity and the end of Roman Britain

This highlights the way in which concepts and frameworks of analysis are central to the study of Britain in the fifth and sixth centuries. Preconceptions and artificial boundaries have cast very long shadows over the study of the Late Roman Empire and 'Dark Ages' alike. Imagined divisions between 'Roman' and 'medieval' archaeology and history have hindered studies ranging across the fourth to sixth centuries. Even more damaging has been the desire to create accounts based on 'pure' archaeology or 'pure' history, deliberately excluding all the available sources for this period. While some issues are likely to remain largely the province of the historian (studying the past through its written remains) or the archaeologist (studying the past through its material remains), because the majority of the evidence is probably going to be archaeological or textual in those particular cases, to exclude wilfully one source or another on the grounds of disciplinary purity or ignorance is obvious folly. Yet this is an approach advocated by some historians and particularly some of the leading archaeologists of this period. Needless to say, it will not be the approach adopted here.

Imagined contrasts between 'Celts' and 'Anglo-Saxons' (and so between 'Celtic' and 'Anglo-Saxon' archaeology or history) have also long confused the study of Britain during the fifth and sixth centuries. These ethnic labels lie loaded with underlying assumptions about the relationship of past peoples to modern nations and of the relative origins and ethnicity of the inhabitants of fifth- and sixth-century Britain. For example, 'Celt' is not a term found in fifth- and sixth-century British or Continental sources — let alone those from Late Roman Britain — to refer to the Britons.[35]

'Anglo-Saxon' might be felt more valid as an archaeological term for the study of this period than 'Celtic', but is equally anachronistic for the fifth and sixth centuries. However, there is no reason to suppose any concept of a common 'Anglo-Saxon' identity existed before the late sixth century at earliest, and the term is unknown in fifth- and sixth-century (and earlier) texts. To their contemporaries the peoples who are today usually called the 'early Anglo-Saxons' were 'Saxons', 'Frisiones', 'Angli' or 'Germani', but not 'Anglo-Saxons'. So, while 'Anglo-Saxon' might be used in a conventional manner to describe their archaeology or history, only as a modern term, we should not confuse this with past perceptions of identity.[36]

However, these 'labels' need not have been wholly arbitrary. The clearest hint that the term 'Saxon' was not always applied to whatever group of north Germanic barbarians it seemed to suit (from the viewpoint of a particular Roman provincial writer) comes from Sidonius Apollinaris. Sidonius is seldom mentioned when discussing fifth-century Britain, but he and his family had long-standing connections with eminent fifth-century Britons. His grandfather, Apollinaris, had been an appointee of the British usurper Constantine III in the first decade of the fifth century, and Sidonius himself was a friend of Constantius (who wrote an account of Britain in his *Vita Germani*) and was both baptised by, and corresponded with, the British bishop Faustus of Riez. Another of his correspondents, Riothamus, was also a Briton.[37]

Sidonius attributes several specific characteristics to fifth-century 'Saxons', about whom he appears to have eyewitness information. Sidonius' 'Saxons' are the most vicious raiders of the coast of Gaul, who characteristically launch surprise attacks using hide-covered sailing ships with curving prows, also equipped with oars. They are pagans, who cast lots and practice human sacrifice and, he says, have blue eyes and a distinctive haircut: the front of the head shaved and the hair grown long at the back so as to make the face look larger. These sound like actual descriptions, not rhetoric or fancy alone, and seem to imply Sidonius had a 'culturally-distinct group' in mind. As Sidonius was well-acquainted with the terminology of barbarian ethnicity (he refers on other occasions to the details of Frankish and Gothic appearance for example), it may well be valid to take this as the one genuine description of fifth-century Saxons.[38]

However, to juxtapose 'Celts' and 'Anglo-Saxons' as two ethnic groups or 'nations' is misleading, and by no means all Germanic immigrants into fifth-century Britain need have been what Sidonius would have called Saxons, nor all 'Roman Britons' what many modern scholars call 'Celts'. Although it is possible to write of 'Germanic' populations in fifth- and sixth-century Britain (that is those who were descended from people from the area called 'Germania' by Roman observers) by no means all of these need have been either 'Angles' or 'Saxons'. It is more legitimate to write of 'Britons', given that we know this was a contemporary name employed by these people themselves. But 'Anglo-Saxon' should be understood as an archaeological or conventional term here. It is placed in inverted commas when used in this way in this book, and 'Celtic' is used only as a linguistic term throughout.

Disposing of all these preconceptions as far as possible, this book will present an alternative view of the archaeology and history of Britain in the fifth and sixth centuries. This is not to say, of course, that it is the only possible interpretation or that it lacks any preconceptions, and (like all interpretation) it can only be a product of its own time and circumstances, not least of the data available at the time of writing. However, the starting points here are contemporary evidence (whether written or material) demonstrably deriving from the period under study — and logic. In future years, an archaeologist or historian would doubtless write this work in a different way, using different evidence, and perhaps even in a different medium.

The theme of this book is that Britain during the fifth and sixth centuries is best understood in terms of the concept of 'Late Antiquity'. It will be argued that we can identify a local version of the same Romano-Christian culture we have found shared across Europe in the fifth to seventh centuries among the majority of the inhabitants of fifth- and sixth-century Britain. In Britain too, this produced a way of life that was dissimilar both to that of the early Roman world (before *c.*AD 250) and that after the 'seventh-century transformation'. Although the origins of these cultural transformations lay within the fourth century, it is their continuation in the period 400-600 that concerns us here.

The Roman past formed a set of linkages and pathways for new beliefs and values to spread and be transformed. But the 'seventh-century transformation' — the widespread rejection of existing ways of life current in 600 in favour of new forms of social, political and religious organization — brought the world of Late Antiquity to its end, and is the basis for ending the chronological scope of this work in *c.*600.

As we shall see, at least in those areas which remained in the control of the Britons, and probably more widely, this concept enables us to understand political, cultural and religious change in new ways. Interpreting Britain in relation to the broader processes attendant upon the end of the Western Roman Empire also explains the title of this book.

1 Beyond Roman Britain

Written evidence is of very limited use in reconstructing fifth- and sixth-century Britain and its relationship with processes of political, cultural, religious and economic change taking place in the wider European world. But the importance of the scanty evidence which may be gleaned from texts is sufficient that we may begin by examining what they may tell us about the fifth and sixth centuries. As we shall see, they may well help illuminate the formal end of Roman imperial rule in Britain, the origins of British monasticism, the arrival of the Germanic immigrants known later as the 'Anglo-Saxons', and aspects of the politics, society, culture, religion and economy of the Britons.

Until the end of the fourth century the political and military history of Roman Britain is outlined by written evidence, although in an incomplete manner. Occasionally, more detailed evidence about social, cultural and economic circumstances survives. After 400, until the seventh century, we have far fewer written sources, and fewer still offer reliable assistance in reconstructing political or military developments. These sources may be divided into two groups: Continental sources (wholly in Latin and Greek languages) which refer to Britain, and sources produced in Britain in Latin, Anglo-Saxon, Welsh and Irish languages. The Continental texts only offer much help for the early fifth century and thereafter provide no more than a few incidental details. Sources produced in Britain are more plentiful, and cover a longer time-span, but sadly many problems exist with these, and many texts are inadmissible as evidence for a variety of compelling reasons. Let us examine each of these categories of evidence in turn.

Written evidence for Britain 400-600: the Continental sources

The main Continental sources mentioning Britain in the fifth and sixth centuries are Procopius, Orosius and Zosimus (all historians writing broadly in the Classical Roman tradition,) the *Gallic Chronicle* (a list of events of dubious credibility in relation to Britain) and the *Vita Germani*, written in what is today France, by Constantius of Lyon, and describing St Germanus of Auxerre's mission to Britain in the early fifth century (perhaps specifically 429).[1]

There are some other sources that have occasionally been discussed by scholars in this context. One has already been mentioned, a quasi-official or official list of troop-dispositions and imperial posts, the *Notitia Dignitatum*. This is incomplete (the western part of this list may be missing) and it could include material of various fourth- and early fifth-century dates combined. As an indication of the location and units of the Roman army in Britain at the end of the fourth or early fifth century it may be reliable and useful.

But it is unlikely to afford direct information about Britain later than 408. Less reliable is the chance mention of troop withdrawals in 401/2 under the imperial military commander Stilicho, by Claudian, in his poem *De Bello Gothico* (416-8). Although often taken to be a historical source for early fifth-century Britain there is no reason to suppose that it is anything other than pure panegyric (praise poetry) directed at Claudian's patron.[2]

None of the writers who produced even the more potentially reliable of these texts need ever have visited Britain. Moreover, hardly any of them lived at the same time as the events they describe. For example, Zosimus wrote a century later than the 'history' he recounts and on the 'other side' of the Empire. This does not necessitate disbelief in his testimony, because later sources might themselves use reliable earlier material — including the lost writings of earlier and reliable historians. For instance, Zosimus probably based his account of the early fifth century on another historian in the Classical Roman tradition, Olympiodorus, whose historiographical (history-writing) skills seem, from the surviving fragments of his work, to have been considerable. Zosimus might well, on these grounds, represent a reliable source for early fifth-century Britain.

Only Procopius's account purports to tell us anything about sixth-century British history, but it contains mythological elements and could well have been a compilation of travellers' (perhaps merchants') tales. To give an example, the writer believed that the isle of Thanet in eastern Kent was so named because the souls of the dead were taken there: presumably a misunderstanding of the name Thanet itself by Greek-speaking Procopius (*thanatos* is Greek for death). To get a flavour of his other shortcomings as a source for Britain, one might look at another of Procopius' major works, the *Secret History*. While this is not about Britain, it shows him to have been a credulous, extremely biased and sensationalist writer. For instance, in the *Secret History* he seems to want the reader to believe that the Byzantine emperor was literally a monster![3]

An uncritical approach to his sources affects potentially credible parts of Procopius' references to Britain, even his name for the island. He appears to have become confused by hearing of 'Brittia' and 'Britannia' from different informants, and believed that Britain was two islands instead of one. It seems his 'Brittia' was eastern Britain, while 'Britannia' was the west of Britain. This may represent no more than the two quite separate trade-networks which linked the Byzantine Empire (in which Procopius lived) and Britain in the sixth century, reconstructable from archaeological evidence. One of these brought metal objects to eastern Britain up the river systems of western Europe, the other pottery and glass via the straits of Gibraltar to western Britain.[4]

The *Vita Germani* is potentially very useful, in that it is the only fifth-century Continental account of a visit to Britain. It was written 480-90 by Constantius of Lyon, at least 50 years later than the events described, and its utility is reduced by the lack of detail it contains. The *Vita* claims that Germanus made two visits to Britain which sound so similar that they probably, as Nora Chadwick argued, derive from differing accounts of a single visit, probably in 429. In fact, even the date is uncertain — only Prosper of Aquitaine's *Chronicle* dates Germanus' visit, not the *Vita*.[5]

After 429 (if that was the date of Germanus' visit) we have no description of another visit to Britain until St Augustine's mission in 597. Nor do Continental sources, except perhaps Procopius, seem to have recorded the stories of merchants or others who had been to the British Isles. Otherwise Britain no longer appears in Continental sources, although texts refer to Britons elsewhere. For example, we find British pilgrims in fifth-century Syria (in the Life of St Simeon Stylites), a passing reference to a sixth-century British harpist, and correspondence between Sidonius Apollinaris and the British bishop Faustus of Riez, referring to books carried to Britain in the mid- or late fifth century by a British priest and monk, Riochatus.[6]

Continental sources are, in general, of little direct help in reconstructing fifth- and sixth-century British history. However, they provide crucial information about the formal end of Roman rule in the Diocese and refute the suggestion that Britain was isolated from Continental Europe and the Mediterranean in the fifth and sixth centuries.

Continental written sources and the formal end of Roman rule in Britain

The first few decades of the fifth century were a crucial time for the transformation of the formal relationship between Roman Britain and the remainder of the Empire. Many of these sources purport to give us dates for the 'loss' of Britain by the Empire in the fifth century, but they neither define what they mean nor concur upon the date at which this happened.

For example, the *Gallic Chronicle* tells us that Britain (perhaps meaning only part of Britain) 'passed under the control of the Saxons' in the 440s, but this is a highly questionable source and exactly what the entry means is extremely unclear. According to the sixth-century British writer Gildas, who might have been better informed, the Britons (probably again, those of a particular area) still felt it possible to appeal to Aëtius, a Roman military official in Gaul, in the mid-440s. So, one could claim that the island was not wholly independent of the Roman Empire politically even then. It is more likely that there were still people in Britain as late as the mid-fifth century who held hopes of 'Roman' intervention, but these hopes were unrealized.[7]

Both Zosimus and Gildas refer to the 'Rescript of Honorius', a letter in which the Western Roman emperor told the British *civitates* to see to their own defence. This was, effectively, granting them independence from Rome, and must be counted as the formal end of Roman rule whatever the lingering aspirations of some Britons may have been. That Honorius wrote to the *civitates* might imply that diocesan government had already collapsed, or that the imperial authorities did not recognise the legitimacy of whatever diocesan government there was in 410 in Britain.[8]

Written sources appear to provide an impression of the prelude to this decision. The first aspect of the background they sketch for us is a sequence of barbarian raids on Britain and coups by would-be Roman emperors in the island. The latter began with Magnus Maximus in 383-8 (later celebrated in Welsh legend as 'Mascen Wledig'), and continued with Marcus in 406-7 and Constantine III in 407-11. Evidently, Roman Britain was under military pressure in the last decades of the fourth century, and looked to the elevation of its 'own' Western Roman emperor to solve the problem. But the stresses of external attack and the hopes for a 'quick fix' by promoting a domestic candidate to the throne are insufficient to explain the timing of the Roman 'retreat from Empire' in Britain.[9]

Hints of other factors may be provided by sources relating both Continental and British events. Potentially the most important evidence concerns the *bacaudae* — provincial rebels — and the earliest western monasticism. These were both movements sweeping Gaul from the last decade of the fourth century into the fifth, and that may have affected Britain. The *bacaudae* included discontents of low social status, although not all *bacaudae* were necessarily low-status, who took part in violent opposition to what they saw as the oppressive circumstances of their lives. It is not clear what their aims were, perhaps 'self-help' groups might be an accurate characterization, or how they were organised, although Greg Woolf has pointed out that the names of their leaders hint that these were of low-status background.[10]

This rebellion affected Gaul in the early fifth century and north-west Spain in the fifth. While it is unclear whether the bacaudic rebellion as such included Britain, Zosimus tells us that Britain and Armorica (approximately modern Brittany and Normandy in western France) revolted against Roman rule in 409. The rebels — perhaps either *bacaudae* or in imitation of them — expelled Roman administration and ceded from the Empire while Constantine III was in Gaul. The 'Rescript of Honorius' might then be read as a recognition of this de facto political independence by the imperial government, unable to recover the situation but unwilling to recognise any authority in Britain above that of the *civitates*.[11]

This revolution suggests that the Britons (or some of them) no longer considered that Constantine III might secure Britain from external attack. Constantine III, like Magnus Maximus before him, had crossed to Gaul in an attempt on the Western imperial throne, and although at first his campaign was successful, by 409 it was already in difficulties. A major 'Saxon' attack on Britain in 408/9 may have acted as the direct stimulus to the British to adopt an alternative 'self-help' strategy. This proved disastrous for Constantine, whose campaign ended in his own capture and execution by imperial forces in 411, but not for Britain as we shall see later.

A second factor that may have affected the political and cultural consequences of the revolution may be the monastic movement. Whereas earlier Christian missions had been primarily urban and tolerant of coexistence with paganism, the new monasticism current in Gaul in the late fourth century focused on the countryside and adopted a more strident approach to the elimination of paganism. This movement, pioneered by a former Roman soldier — St Martin of Tours — took monasticism into what is today north-west France. Its aggression was not directed toward people, rather it targeted the temples and idols of pagan worship — an efficient strategy of conversion as pagans believed in the actual presence of their deities in the statues erected to them, and the vengefulness of the deities they believed present in these statues toward their enemies. A Christian holy man who broke statues and denounced the gods, yet did so unharmed, effectively refuted a principal tenet of pagan belief. Unsurprisingly, Martin and his followers were astonishingly successful at converting the Romano-Gallic countryside to Christianity.[12]

There is no direct evidence undeniably connecting Britain with Martinian monasticism. Martin never visited Britain, and no text tells us of Martinian monasteries in the British Isles. Nevertheless, there are hints that this monasticism did spread across the Channel in the very early fifth century. As Jeremy Knight has noted, the ecclesiastics who travelled between Britain and the Continent up to the time of Germanus had strong Martinian connections, and a version of the *Vita Martini* (the 'Life of St Martin') dating from before 460 was known in Britain. Anthony Birley observed that St Martin's pupil, Victricius, wrote to Ambrose that he had 'taken the precepts of the martyrs to Britain' — by which Victricius probably meant spread the message of Martinian monasticism there. Interestingly, Victricius — a rare name in the Late Roman world — occurs on a late fourth- or early fifth-century pewter bowl with a Christian Chi Rho symbol, from Appleshaw. It is at least possible that this attests the spread of Victricius' fame to Britain in the late fourth or early fifth century.[13]

Martinian monasticism in early fifth-century Britain might bear some relation to the events already discussed. If a substantial part of the population of Roman Britain was Christianised in the late fourth or very early fifth century, then many or all of the rebels may well have been Christians. If so, then Martinian concepts of militant Christianity — associated in Gaul with 'anti-establishment' leadership — might well have played a part in this rebellion. Whether or not this contributed to the instigation of the British revolution against Roman rule, it could well have coloured the character of the resulting society. For example, this could explain why, after the revolt, there is no evidence whatsoever of Romano-British paganism, although this still existed *c*.400. When Constantius, Patrick and Gildas describe fifth-century Britain it appears wholly Christianised, and St Germanus visited the island to combat Pelagian Christian beliefs, not paganism. Perhaps this is also why Gildas seems to have associated militant Christianity with social revolution.[14]

The 'British revolution' may, therefore, have been primarily a strategy of desperation following the failure of Constantine III to deliver Britain from external threat, and could have had both low-status and militant Christian associations. We may even see the beginnings of this trend in the elevation of Constantine III, as remarkably, among the few things we are told about him by potentially reliable sources (in this case by Orosius) are that his son Constans was a Christian monk, and that Constantine III himself was, immediately prior to his elevation, a devout Christian and private soldier. That is, immediately before the 'British revolution' (with perhaps militant Christian and low-status associations) a low-status Christian with monastic connections was promoted as Britain's 'last chance'. This might well seem too much of a coincidence, but not all scholars would agree.[15]

John Drinkwater, in particular, has recently argued that because one of Constantine III's sons was called Julian this excludes the possibility that his rise was associated with growing Christian militancy in Britain. Constantine I's nephew Julian (now called 'Julian the Apostate') renounced Christianity and tried to re-establish paganism in the Roman Empire. But this is to assume that a late fourth-century Christian Briton would have understood the significance of the name Julian in the same terms as a twentieth-century Ancient Historian such as Drinkwater. We do not know what associations the name 'Julian' carried in early fifth-century Britain, nor where Constantine III got the name 'Julian' from. For example, he might have copied the names from a still-circulating coin, or an inscription he had seen in military service, and have known nothing more about him.[16]

Nor should we assume that everyone in fourth- or fifth-century Britain knew as much about Late Roman imperial political history as a whole as we might derive from texts. If Constantine III really was a 'private' Late Roman soldier immediately prior to elevation, he is hardly likely (at this time) to have been well-read in the available histories of Constantine I's reign or that of Julian. Moreover, if we believe Orosius' testimony that Constantine III was elevated because of his name, then we must also credit that this was due too to his Christian devotion, as Orosius also tells us this. If so, as naming one's son 'Julian' evidently did not pose a religious problem to Constantine III himself, it seems much more likely that the naming of Constantine III's sons is more problematical to a modern Ancient Historian than it was to a fifth-century low-status British Christian.

Countering Drinkwater's objection in these ways, an outline sequence of the events leading to the formal independence of Britain from the Roman Empire may be reconstructed from textual sources alone. Less certainly, hints of the possible motivations of those involved may be recognised. The sequence is that an intensification of barbarian raids in the last half of the fourth century produced repeated attempts to secure Britain through the promotion of a 'British' Western emperor. The culmination of these attempts was the reign of Constantine III, whose failure to secure Britain from barbarian attack led to popular rebellion against his rule in 409, following a major raid in the previous year. The election of Constantine III and the rebellion of 409 were connected with the emergence of a new elite in Britain, although the exact relationship between these two events is unclear. This elite was perhaps closely connected with militant Christianity of the type associated in Gaul with St Martin, and may have had partly (or entirely) low-status social origins.[17]

Continental sources, as sparse as they are, perhaps enable us to offer a plausible reconstruction of important aspects of very early fifth-century British history. In so far as texts may inform us of later fifth- and sixth-century Britain, we must turn to sources from Britain during those centuries. As we shall see, these too offer some beams of light in the darkness, but are inadequate alone to build a detailed account of these centuries.

After the end: written sources from Britain 400-600

Apart from Gildas' reference to the appeal to Aëtius, Insular sources (that is, those from the British Isles) tell us nothing reliable regarding the formal end of Roman rule in Britain which we cannot find in other texts. The earliest substantial written sources from Britain are two texts written by St Patrick himself, although surviving (as do all these texts) only in much later copies.[18]

The first (the *Confessio*) describes his capture from Britain as a boy, his life in Ireland as a slave, his escape and return to Ireland as a Christian missionary. It was written to explain his actions when back in Ireland as a missionary to British clergy, who apparently found his work hard to understand. The response from Patrick may well imply that circumstances in Britain and Ireland were quite different from each other at the time he was writing, as these misunderstandings largely rest on difficulties in comprehending aspects of Irish society and economy. This may suggest that these areas were far from a common 'Celtic Sea' cultural zone at this date. The second text (the *Epistola* or 'letter'), was written to a British king (Coroticus) otherwise unknown, condemning him for carrying off St Patrick's converts as slaves, when as a Christian he should have known better. These texts do not carry their own internal dates, and the originals do not survive, but may belong to the fifth century, perhaps to the second half of that century.[19]

Patrick writes at length in Latin, refers to *grammatici* in Britain (scholars of secular higher education in Latin learning), and expects his readers to be well-educated in the Roman manner. Like his contemporary in Gaul, Sidonius Apollinaris, he is a third-generation Christian, well-acquainted with both the Late Roman Church hierarchy and with monasticism. As a boy he lived at a villa-estate (*villula*) near a 'small town' apparently close to a major town, with formal Roman-style administration in which his father had a role. That is, Patrick had grown up in exactly the sort of 'settlement pattern' archaeology tells us characterised the late fourth-century Romano-British landscape, but this is unlikely to be much before 450. When he returned home, after his escape from slavery, relatives attempted to persuade him to run the still-surviving estate. This is clear evidence that the basic rural fabric of Late Roman Britain survived well into the fifth century, alongside the emergence of a Christian society with bishops, priests, monks and nuns. Patrick tries to tell us in the *Confessio* exactly where his parental home was (*Bannaventa taberniae*), but the place-name is unknown to modern scholars. It was clearly an area with villas, 'small' and 'large' towns, and probably accessible directly from Ireland by sea. The West Country seems the most likely location, perhaps Somerset near the Severn estuary, but it is impossible to be sure.

A second group of writings come from a clergyman called Gildas. His main work, *De Excidio Britanniae*, is a condemnation of contemporary kings and church-people, although it is prefaced by a historical account and suffixed by supporting Biblical quotations. Gildas wrote in extremely good Latin, and in what is termed a 'rhetorical' style — not because it uses rhetoric (although it is very 'rhetorical' in the usual sense) but because it is part of the Roman educational tradition of *rhetorici* for those trained to the highest level of bureaucratic and legal technical Latin writing. 'De Excidio' is a carefully structured and precisely worded work, and this gives it both great value and many difficulties of interpretation. Gildas makes frequent use of metaphor and allusion to other events, he assumes much more knowledge on the part of the reader than we have today, and we know that he was extremely well read for a man of his time, quoting from many other Christian and Classical writers (without giving their names) and extensively from the Bible.[20]

It is uncertain exactly where Gildas wrote *De Excidio*. It was almost certainly composed in Western Britain, and geographical hints suggest that it was probably written in the West Country, possibly Dorset more specifically. Nor is it certain exactly when he wrote, although this was most likely in the sixth century, probably *c*.500-50, and perhaps *c*.525-50. But Gildas's *De Excidio* depicts an essentially Late Roman society, in which Latin literacy and extensive libraries of Latin texts, manuscript production, Roman terminology and symbolism, Roman higher education and law, and Roman-style bureaucratic government have all survived the formal 'end' of Roman Britain. It outlines a social structure in which kings rule at least in some places, but where there is an episcopal and

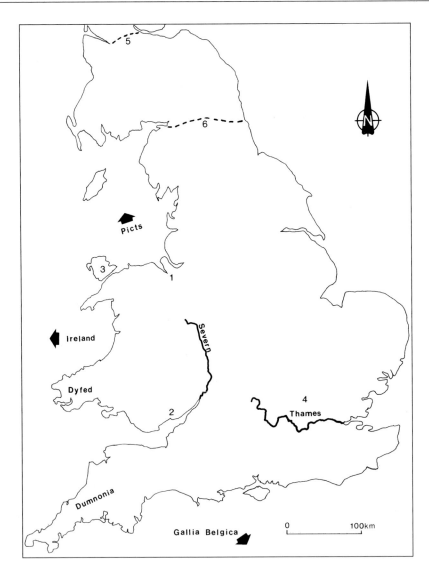

4   *Gildas's Britain: places mentioned, or possibly mentioned, in the text of* De Excidio:
   1 *Chester*
   2 *Caerleon*
   3 *Anglesey*
   4 *St Albans*
   5 *The Antonine Wall*
   6 *Hadrian's Wall*

monastic Church, apparently within the tribal political structure known to us from Roman Britain. There are towns but 'not as they once were', and also hilltop and coastal fortifications which sound as if they are what archaeologists today would call 'hill-forts'. Gildas' exact role in this society is not specified, although he hints that he is a deacon in the Church and that he is not a monk. David Dumville has argued that Gildas subsequently became abbot of a monastery, accounting for his later works.[21]

In *De Excidio*, Gildas describes the arrival in Britain of a Germanic population from outside the Empire, whom he calls 'Saxons'. These people came, he tells us, as mercenaries under Late Roman treaty terms: that is, as *foederati*. They at first defended Britain (or part of Britain) and then rebelled. These events all happened, Gildas believed, after the appeal of the Britons to the Continental Roman official Aëtius, who he calls — probably echoing a written source unknown to us — 'thrice consul', so dating the appeal to 446-54. This was brought about by a continuing concern to secure Britain, which sounds credible in view of the recurrent efforts to achieve this during the previous century. However, according to Gildas the 'Saxon' rebellion was extremely successful, and large parts of eastern Britain passed into 'Saxon' control, separating them from Gildas' own people. The Britons fought back, securing victories culminating in the battle of Mount Badon (*mons badonicus*), an unknown, but presumably hilltop, location. After this there was a generation of peace with the 'Saxons' up until Gildas' own time.[22]

The arrival of the 'Saxons' (*Adventus Saxonum*) and the subsequent calamity of their rebellion have occupied historians for centuries. The linkage of the battle of Mount Badon with (king) Arthur, in *Historia Brittonum* and *Annales Cambriae* (discussed below) — but not in Gildas' *De Excidio* — has also attracted an astonishing amount of historical and pseudo-historical work on this topic. Suffice it to say, almost no clarification whatsoever has been gained by this latter pursuit, and in the last few decades it has become fashionable for archaeologists and historians to express scepticism about Gildas' account of fifth-century British history altogether. There are certainly many problems in using *De Excidio* to write history, not least that Gildas does not provide dates, so that one has to estimate a relative chronology from his text. Nevertheless, it may be that he did have some reliable information about the circumstances he described, although it is uncertain exactly what his sources were.

Using Gildas' version of events it is possible to date the arrival of the 'Saxon' *foederati* he describes anywhere between the mid- and late fifth century, assuming we can date the appeal to Aëtius to 446-54. Unless one believes the *Gallic Chronicle*, this is our first direct evidence of 'Saxon' settlement in eastern Britain in any of our written sources. Previously, the 'Saxons' appear as raiders, along with the Irish and Picts, not as a people living within Britain. The rebellion was long after this, probably therefore an event of the late fifth century — one recent detailed estimate suggests the 490s. If so, eastern Britain remained under British political control for almost the entire fifth century.[23]

In addition to *De Excidio*, Gildas also wrote a number of lesser works, or at least these are attributed to him and are probably sixth-century western British products. The minor works of Gildas comprise a 'penitential' (a series of rules for monks decreeing the appropriate penance for particular sins and wrongdoing) and the 'Letters', literally a collection of brief extracts from letters by Gildas. These had been preserved because

Gildas was revered from the late sixth century onward as a 'Father of the Church', his writings of doctrinal merit. This status also may have produced a crucial piece of dating evidence, because his death was recorded in a potentially contemporary Irish annal at 570. Gildas says he was 44 when he wrote *De Excidio*, and by sixth-century standards this might suggest he was born after 500. As he tells us, the year of his birth was also the year of the battle of Mount Badon, ending the war between the rebelling *foederati* and Britons. Gildas' own society, with so many aspects of its Roman past still intact, would seem then to represent sixth-century western Britain.[24]

There are a number of other 'British Penitentials' of probable sixth-century date. Again, where they were written and exactly when and for whom remain unknown, but they and the penitential probably composed by Gildas give direct information concerning sixth-century Britain. For example, at least in the communities they regulate, food was plentiful and varied, so that even someone who was deprived of food as a punishment ate very well, and Late Roman weights and measures were in use. Again, this tends to bear out the impression of *De Excidio* and the *Confessio*, that much of the legal, social and cultural fabric of Late Roman Britain had survived through the fifth and well into the sixth centuries, at least in some localities.[25]

Apart from these important texts, the same impression is also conveyed by the only manuscript which may have been produced in Britain during these centuries. This is the *Vergilius Romanus*, an illuminated manuscript written in handwriting datable to the fifth or early sixth century and illustrated with 19 coloured pictures, some of which may contain details of contemporary life. The pictures are perhaps the best evidence for where the manuscript was produced, as they are very similar to the Late Roman art of southern Britain and (in particular) of what is today Dorset. This manuscript may, therefore, come from the same area, and at about the same time, as Gildas.[26]

The text in the manuscript is of very little help to us, as it is a copy of the works of Virgil and Ovid, Classical Latin poets of the early Roman imperial period. However, if it is British and belongs to this period, the mere existence of the manuscript and the evidence it provides for the transmission of Classical texts are, of course, important. The scenes depicted include some plainly meant as 'antiquarian' images of the 'Classical past', and may tell us about how that past was imagined in fifth- and sixth-century Britain. Although fascinating in this regard, by far the most interesting depict scenes possibly based on everyday elite life. These are used to illustrate the Virgilian narrative and one must be aware that artistic licence may account for some of the details. For example, the inclusion of a shepherd's hut of a form associated in Late Roman art with depictions of North Africa, clearly relates to the textual account of Aeneas' meeting with Dido, queen of Carthage. Although it is certainly intriguing that a fifth- or sixth-century British artist knew one 'should' depict North Africa in this way in the conventions of Roman art, this does not mean that such buildings really stood in Britain. Likewise, although the figures shown occasionally wear Phrygian caps, this relates to Late Roman artistic norms, not British realities.[27]

Even excising the aspects we can identify as part of Late Roman artistic tradition in general, and the ones that appear antiquarian (such as folio 44v), we are left with a substantial body of material with which to work. If fifth- or sixth-century Britons dressed and looked as depicted, and dined reclining on couches as the heroes are shown, then we have to envisage a much more 'Late Roman' look to this period than is usually imagined. Moreover, the art of the manuscript shows at least two different styles. In one, a very abstract version of Late Roman art is presented, in the other the style is more 'Classical' and naturalistic. This may imply either that the manuscript was produced while Romano-British artistic traditions were breaking down, or more likely that naturalistic and abstract art coexisted wherever this manuscript was illuminated.[28]

The very existence of the manuscript, if correctly attributed to Britain, is strong evidence too of the survival of this same 'Late Roman' culture we have seen in the writings of Gildas and Patrick, and in the penitentials. However, it also suggests that the artistic heritage of fourth-century Roman Britain may have been preserved, if only partially, in the fifth century, and that Roman-period styles of dress and manners, depicted in the illuminations, were at least known and probably followed at least in one place in fifth-century Britain. Clearly, if religious militancy required fifth-century Britons to reject aspects of the Late Roman past, these were not among them. Interestingly, Gildas knew Virgil's *Aeneid* very well, and from fourth-century Britain there are inscriptions and pictures showing a particular interest in Virgil and the *Aeneid*. So we may have a particularly British liking for this writer being preserved through to the sixth century. Recently, Heather James has pointed out that the use of 'of Latium' as an epithet on a sixth-century inscribed stone from Llandysilio in Wales, probably derives from Virgil's text.[29]

An important point which is implied by Gildas' quotations from other writers is that these survivals are only the 'tip of an iceberg' of what may well have once existed. Gildas had access to an extensive library in the sixth century, containing the major works of many Classical and Christian authors, and he knew of other writers learned in the Late Roman tradition. Thus, libraries such as that used by Gildas may have been more common than one might suppose, and Latin literacy more widespread than could be anticipated from these few examples. This is borne out by three main pieces of evidence.[30]

First, literacy in secular contexts is implied by the discovery of what may be writing styli at fifth- and sixth-century secular settlements such as Cadbury Congresbury and Dinas Powys, and a signet-ring gemstone (imported from the Byzantine Mediterranean) at Cefn Cwmwd settlement in north Wales. Literacy was not then an ecclesiastical preserve, and written texts were written on wax tablets and sealed with wax if the signet ring was used in the way it was intended.[31]

Second, the emergence of a distinctive script ('Insular half-uncial') within Britain during the fifth and sixth centuries attests the use of writing for informal purposes. Insular half-uncial derives from Late Roman cursive (that is, handwriting) script which was used for letters and minor communications rather than for books, inscriptions or official purposes. The emergence of Insular half-uncial attests, therefore, the vitality of everyday literacy in Britain (or part of it) during the fifth and sixth centuries. It is absent from the late fourth-century pagan curse-tablets, but found on the *Cathach of St Columba*, an ecclesiastical manuscript produced in Ireland at the end of the sixth century or beginning of the seventh century. Manuscript production, libraries of Christian and Classical works, and the use of handwriting for letters to communicate, all seem well-attested among the fifth- and sixth-century Britons.[32]

5 A Class-1 inscribed stone with metrical Latin inscription from Cynwyl Gaeo, Carmarthenshire

The third body of evidence demonstrates just how widespread such Latin literacy was in fifth- and sixth-century Britain. This comprises a large number of Latin inscriptions on stone ('inscribed stones') found widely distributed throughout western and north Britain. These inscriptions contain Roman-style and Christian personal names, use Roman capitals and half-uncial script, Roman-period terminology (such as *civis* and *magistratus*) and even, in a couple of cases, Latin poetry in Classical style. Thus, we can be sure that Latin literacy was very widespread in western and probably northern Britain in the fifth and sixth centuries, although its fate in the east of Britain was — as we shall see in the next chapter — very different.

The body of inscribed (that is 'epigraphic') evidence from the west and north represents the second most substantial body of 'written' evidence for fifth- and sixth-century Britain, after the texts already described. These (mostly western) British inscribed stones are referred to as Class-1 inscriptions, following a classification established in Wales by V.E. Nash-Williams in 1950. There is also a related series of uninscribed stone monuments ('cross-marked stones') bearing only crosses (which also occur on a few inscribed stones of Class-1) from broadly the same area, termed by Nash-Williams Class-2 stones. Further classes were defined by Nash-Williams in Wales, but post-date the seventh century and lie outside the scope of this book.[33]

Most Class-1 inscriptions probably belong to the fifth and sixth centuries, but are extremely hard to date more precisely. Attempts have been made to link inscriptions with historical figures (most of whom have turned out not to be reliably documented anyway), but almost never successfully. Only two such correlations can be accepted for the whole period 400-700: that for Catamanus king of Gwynedd (in north Wales) who died in the seventh century, and (less certainly) for Vortipor, a king mentioned by Gildas as ruling in Dyfed in south-west Wales. The style of the crosses and other symbols found on a few of the Class-1 stones and Class-2 stones are no more help, as most (if not all) of these were in use throughout the period at which these stones appear to have been erected.

Even the attribution of every one of these inscriptions to the fifth and sixth centuries cannot be accepted without discussion. A few Class-1 stones may be reliably assigned to the seventh to twelfth centuries, and more may date from just as late. Only one British inscription carries an 'internal date' — a stone from near Penmachno is dated 'in tempore iustini consularis' (that is Flavius Justinus, dated 540) — although Continental stones sometimes use this formula later than 540.

We cannot always even be sure that such inscriptions date from the period examined in this book. It is likely that most do, by general analogy with the similar series of inscriptions elsewhere in western Europe, but this further highlights the problem that the British inscriptions (unlike some of their Continental counterparts) contain no other intrinsically datable features or texts. Despite this, several archaeologists and linguists have felt able to offer very precise dates for these inscriptions. For example, the famous philologist Kenneth Jackson based much of his — now conventional — chronology for the early development of the Brittonic languages (partly ancestral to Welsh and Cornish) on his dating of these inscriptions. More recently Charles Thomas claimed that those stones with longer Latin ('extended Latinate') inscriptions might predate those with the formula 'X son of (*fili*) Y', but this is flawed by its reliance on a chronology based on epigraphic and 'historical' dating suffering from the problems already mentioned. Other archaeologists believe the stones are dated *by* Jackson's chronology for the languages used, but this is untrue: the Brittonic philology of this period relies largely on the dating of the stones, not vice versa![34]

Although any attempt to date these stones by detailed comparison with internally-dated Continental examples is fraught with problems, British Class-1 stones clearly share 'formulae' such as '*hic iacet*' (here lies) or '*in hoc tumulo*' (in this burial mound or tomb) with Continental inscriptions, perhaps — as Jeremy Knight has noted — particularly with inscriptions in Gaul dated 422-80. This supports the suggestion that the British examples belong to the fifth to seventh centuries, but as both dated and undated types occur together in France, Spain and Italy we cannot use comparison with a series of dated formulae to date British inscriptions more accurately.[35]

Nevertheless, the formulae and symbols on Class-1 stones demonstrate that fifth- and sixth-century Britain was not isolated from Continental Europe and that the British Class-1 stones belong to a wider tradition of Christian tombstones, found throughout the former Roman West. They attest ongoing contacts with at least Gaul, and probably the Mediterranean, throughout this period. For example, the ring-cross (a circle containing an equal armed cross joining with the circle) occurs in the Catacombs at Rome first in *c*.500, and in Britain on a datable monument (to Vortipor) by at latest *c*.550. The newest Christian symbolism from the Mediterranean was probably reaching sixth-century Britain within a generation.[36]

One approach which could give very approximate — but reliable — dates for Class-1 stones is the tendency for known sixth-century or later features to correlate with vertical inscriptions, especially those pocked rather than cut into the stone. In particular, 'half-uncial' occurs on these stones mostly on vertical inscriptions, and on pocked rather than cut inscriptions. This suggests that vertical pocked inscriptions may be later than horizontal cut ones, arguably with those which combine both characteristics forming a transitional phase.[37]

These monuments also contain rare, but important, references to occupation or title. Thus, we find doctor (*medicus*), a magistrate (*magistratus*), and priest (*presbyter*) referred to. Clusters of Class-1 inscriptions may, although need not, indicate religious establishments such as monasteries, and one from Aberdaron in Wales commemorates a monk buried with 'many of his brothers'. Most may be tombstones, and several stood by Roman roads in a way reminiscent of Roman-period tombstones or milestones, perhaps a further hint of their implicit *romanitas* ('Romanness').[38]

Thomas Charles-Edwards has pointed out that the spelling of Latin in these inscriptions implies it was a living language, actually spoken in western Britain during the fifth and sixth centuries. Recently, David Howlett has suggested that these inscriptions were composed using very strict rules, which he relates to the 'Biblical Style' of Latin composition that he argues characterised Late Roman Christian Latinity. Whether or not this was the case, the stones attest the use of Latin and Latin terminology across a broad area of western and northern Britain through the fifth and sixth centuries and beyond.[39]

Another, much smaller, group of inscriptions are those in ogam (also spelled 'ogham' and 'ogom'). This was a script developed in the fifth century in Ireland or western Britain from the Roman alphabet and influenced by Roman grammatical writings. It uses lines and dashes carved into stone (and also perhaps wood which has not survived) to convey brief messages, usually names, in the Irish language. Broadly linguistically datable, but not so closely as to assist us in dating Class-1 Latin texts, ogam inscriptions are found in two types. In Ireland, where many more exist, they are, in all but a single case, in ogam alone. In Britain they usually occur in bilingual texts with Latin inscribed in Roman capitals or in half-uncial script. Invariably, the Latin text gives more information, and is placed on the face of the stone, with ogam on its edge. A few monolingual ogams are known from Britain, and these might be earlier in date than the bilingual stones. A monolingual ogam stone from Silchester, Hampshire (an outlier in eastern Britain), was found in a pit containing material radiocarbon-dated to the fifth century, but this does not necessarily date the ogam inscription.[40]

Ogam inscriptions attest a living Irish language in western Britain, particularly in south-west Wales and what was later Breconshire. They also show that some of those commemorated felt it necessary, or desirable, to use two languages. Purely Latin Class-1 inscriptions sometimes also carry Irish, as well as in other cases British, Christian and 'Roman' names, confirming the existence of probably high-status people with Irish names in western Britain.[41]

It might be imagined that this shows a community entirely outside of the 'Roman' cultural world we have seen so far. However, before leaping to this conclusion the Latinate origin of ogam should be borne in mind, as should the probability that it is associated with the spread of Christianity in Ireland brought by missionaries from what was, or had been, Roman Britain.

The Class-1 inscriptions support the picture we have built up from the writings of Patrick, Gildas, the penitentials, and *Vergilius Romanus* of the cultural and political survival of the structure of fourth-century Britain across large parts of the west, and probably north, of the former Roman diocese. They also seem to attest widespread Christianity in sixth- if not fifth-century Britain. It is from the north that another, more problematical, source of written evidence comes: the extensive corpus of early Welsh poetry purporting to relate to the sixth and seventh centuries.

The two main groups of this material are a heroic poem (*Y Gododdin*), recounting a raid from Edinburgh (*Din Eidyn*) on Catterick (*Catraeth*), and *Canu Taliesin* (the song of Taliesin, a poet). The latter is a series of poems relating to the rulers of what is today the Lake District, in north-west England, at the end of the sixth century. These poems have been much discussed, and at first sight appear to offer much information about the north of Britain in the later sixth century. However, the situation is not so simple.[42]

Although widely believed to be credible sources until the later 1970s, work since then has tended to cast severe doubt on the historical reliability and utility of these poems. The debate over this material has recently been reinvigorated by the linguistic work of John Koch, who has argued that both bodies of poetry contain, amid later material and extensive reworking, original wording from the sixth and seventh centuries.

It must be stressed that this material is not well-dated and needs to be used with extreme care, and that it is also far from presenting any sort of narrative. Each of the collections of poetry represents short addresses to particular people about particular events or behaviour, rather than presenting the sort of continuous and structured poetry found, for example, in the (probably eighth-century) Anglo-Saxon heroic poem *Beowulf*.[43]

The world *Y Gododdin* and *Canu Taliesin* depicts is in many respects very different from that of Gildas and Patrick. The poetry emphasises personal bravery, generosity and loyalty as the key secular virtues. There is very little obvious survival of the social and cultural institutions of Roman Britain in this material. Like Patrick and Gildas, the poets assume that Christianity is the only religion among the Britons, and the warriors who they acclaim are praised too for their piety and benevolence toward the Church. This may be the reason, too, why some very 'un-warriorlike' qualities — shyness for example — are commended alongside those which we might expect from a 'heroic society', perhaps related to Christian modesty. Nor is the context of this poetry totally apart from Gildas' Britain: he mentions secular stories and possibly 'praise poetry' directed at kings. The rulers denounced in *De Excidio* might well have ascribed to the values of this poetry if his description of them is accurate.[44]

Date and context could explain these differences. If the poems date from the end of the sixth century at earliest, they would be at least one or two generations later than Gildas' *De Excidio*. Context is also crucial: *Y Gododdin* is court poetry from beyond the northern frontier of Roman Britain, and even *Canu Taliesin* relates to the very northern frontier of the Late Roman diocese and possibly beyond. Thus, physical distance, date and secular courtly context may all explain the differences between the societies evidenced by Gildas, Patrick and the northern British poetry, even if it belongs to the late sixth century.

Moving further down the scale of historical reliability we come to hagiography, that is accounts of saints' lives. Of a vast mass of saints' 'Lives' (*vitae*) purporting to relate to the so-called 'Age of the Saints' in western and northern Britain and Ireland in the mid- to late sixth century, only two may genuinely give information about the period before 600. The most reliable, the *Vita Columbae* (the Life of St Columba of Iona), was written by Adomnán of Iona in the 690s, based on both lost textual sources and oral traditions concerning the sixth-century saint at Iona itself. It is an invaluable source for the conversion of the northern Picts and the sixth-century history of western Scotland and its relations with Ireland.[45]

Far less reliable, and less certainly dated, is *Vita Prima Sancti Samsonis* (the first life of St Samson of Dol, in Brittany) written by a Breton hagiographer (writer of saints' lives) before the ninth century. Exactly when is unclear, but it might be as early as the seventh century to judge from hints contained within its text. *Vita Prima Sancti Samsonis* may have been based on local knowledge of the areas in Britain across which the saint travelled according to the text, and on oral traditions regarding him preserved in his monastery. We are told that St Samson traversed south-west Wales and south-west Britain during the mid-sixth century, and several details of his activities there are recorded. *Vita Prima Sancti Samsonis* could, in principle, be a valuable source for the mid- to late sixth century in western Britain.[46]

David Dumville has argued that one textual source of post-600 date may have bearing on the fifth- and sixth-century British Church. He has identified a colophon (a dedication-inscription) on a manuscript of the works of Pelagius, as dating the manuscript to the late seventh or eighth century and locating its production in Wales. The relevance of this to the period discussed in this book derives from the denunciation of Pelagius as heretic in the early fifth century, by the Continental Church based at Rome. This shows that Pelagius was considered still orthodox by the British Church, or else royal commission of such a manuscript would have been unthinkable.[47]

This does not suggest that the British Church harboured deviant religious beliefs from those that many modern Christians would see as mainstream. Pelagius' heresy was no more than a denial of the intrinsic badness of humanity and as a consequence a rejection of the necessity for the intercession of clergy between God and humanity, then being promoted by the Continental Western Church. Pelagianism may even have been particularly 'British': Pelagius, although active in the Mediterranean, was probably a Briton. The *Vita Germani* implies that his views were widespread in Britain in the 420s, and Gildas appears to have approved of Pelagian writings in the sixth century.

This may also imply that the British Church took a very conservative line on the theological controversies of its day in the early fifth century, a point also highlighted by the British practices disliked by Bede in the early eighth century. In particular, Bede disliked the custom of the Britons to celebrate the date of Easter at an 'old-fashioned' time and that British monks wore an 'old-fashioned' tonsure. In such respects the Britons had disregarded ecclesiastical changes after the start of the fifth century, but as we have seen this cannot have been due to isolation. Only deliberate conservatism can explain this. The implication is that the British Church in the fifth and sixth centuries was much more akin to the Church of the fourth century than to other contemporary Christians in the West, in theological terms and perhaps — as Bede tells us for the seventh century — in practice.[48]

These are all the British written sources for the history of fifth- and sixth-century Britain. Apart for a few brief runic inscriptions, there is nothing else whatsoever from eastern Britain. These show the use of runes (a Germanic symbolic script), of Germanic languages and occasionally the existence of Germanic paganism, in eastern Britain during the fifth and sixth centuries, but that is all. The most salient feature of the Insular sources for fifth- and sixth-century Britain is, therefore, that they are almost entirely 'British', in that they relate to the Britons, and just possibly the Irish. The Picts and 'Anglo-Saxons' left none of their own texts from this period, unless one counts the few runic scraps and a few ogams from Pictish sites.[49]

Inadmissible evidence

Some readers might be surprised to see well-known texts left off this list. The Anglo-Saxon Chronicle, *Historia Brittonum* (often erroneously called 'Nennius'), *Annales Cambriae*, the Llandaff charters and the genealogies (family trees) of the Welsh, Anglo-Saxon, Pictish and Scottish kings are frequently claimed as written evidence for the fifth and sixth centuries, but there are major problems with using any of them as sources for this period. Let us take each in turn.[50]

The Anglo-Saxon Chronicle was written to support the political aspirations of the Late Saxon kings of Wessex. Work on the anthropology of oral tradition (especially David Henige's studies) makes it extremely unlikely that memories can be transmitted without writing for more than 200 years with any accuracy. Any text of the ninth century is only as reliable a source for the fifth and sixth centuries as the written material upon which it was based and the accuracy with which it reproduces that material. As we have seen, there is no reason to believe that the fifth- and sixth-century 'Anglo-Saxons' wrote any substantial texts.[51]

If the Anglo-Saxon Chronicle used texts purporting to relate to the fifth and sixth centuries we do not know what these were — or whether we would find them credible were they to survive. Most likely, the only 'sources' used for these centuries were place-names, heroic poems, the writings of Bede, and genealogical materials. We shall come to the latter shortly, but let us say it would be unwise to place too much significance upon them. If poetic sources lay behind the Chronicle, the only hint of what they might have contained is in the existing text, and the suspicious occurrence of personal names plainly derived from place-names in the Chronicle's fifth- and sixth-century entries urges a sceptical view. It may be slightly more likely that entries after *c*.550 (perhaps that for the battle of *Searburh* and later) are trustworthy, as these could have been in living memory when the first post-conversion written texts were compiled in 'Anglo-Saxon' England, but even this is uncertain.[52]

Although there is nothing intrinsically impossible about all the events recorded in the Anglo-Saxon Chronicle for the fifth and sixth centuries, there is no reason to believe they occurred. We have, then, no positive reason to believe any of the fifth- and sixth-century entries and positive reasons to doubt at least several of them. In view of the propagandist purpose of the text we may, therefore, exclude it as a source for these centuries, at least prior to the mid-sixth century. Even if any of the later sixth-century entries are accurate records of people and battles, as could be the case, the significance of these is probably lost to us, and may have been lost to the compiler of the Chronicle.

Problems plague any attempt to use *Historia Brittonum*. This text was compiled in 829/30 for the kings of Gwynedd in north Wales. It may well have been written to bolster their own political position, and — in a series of brilliant studies — David Dumville has shown that it is a carefully-constructed piece of dynastic propaganda. Many of the more historically-interesting passages, such as that referring to the migration of Cunedda from north-east Scotland to north-west Wales, have been shown to have clear ninth-century political purposes, and cannot be taken at face value.[53]

In short, *Historia Brittonum* provides important evidence for the politics and culture of ninth-century Gwynedd, but not for the fifth or sixth centuries. Like the Anglo-Saxon Chronicle, it cannot be employed as a source for the period covered by this book, and perhaps not even for the early seventh century. Unfortunately, *Annales Cambriae*, the 'Welsh annals', are almost as likely to be flawed as *Historia Brittonum*, with which they bear some association. It is, as yet, unclear exactly when these annals became 'contemporary' (written during the same year as the event described), but this was probably not prior to 550, and perhaps not until much later. Various dates have been suggested: David Dumville has tentatively suggested the 570s and Kathleen Hughes proposed the late eighth century. *Annales Cambriae* are, therefore, more likely to contain material of sixth-century date than the Anglo-Saxon Chronicle, and might have been compiled when oral traditions about the fifth and sixth century still contained fact. If this is the case, what information regarding these centuries should be considered factual remains unclear.[54]

Sadly, even if this were the case, *Annales Cambriae* for the period 550-600 tell us almost nothing of use not also found in other sources. Hughes argued, convincingly in my view, that *Annales Cambriae* are related to (and probably derived in part from) the Irish annals, and as Richard Sharpe has pointed out, these need not have been contemporary prior to *c*.550. That is, *Annales Cambriae* provide little or no extra contemporary information about sixth-century Britain, in so far as can today be discerned.

At best we are faced with a mere half-century of unhelpful annal-keeping in western Britain and Ireland. More likely only retrospective British annals survive for the period 400-600 and these are derived from Irish sources written by annalists who need have known little or nothing of British events. Again useful as they seem at first sight, *Annales Cambriae* are not much help for this period.

The Llandaff Charters are even less likely to contain reliable material about the fifth and sixth centuries. These claim to be land-grants to the monastery at Llandaff in south-east Wales, allegedly dating from the mid-sixth to eleventh centuries. Suspicion might initially be aroused by the fact that they were collected and set out to support the claims to land of the bishop of Llandaff after the Norman conquest. When one examines the detail of the 'charters' it is obvious that they are riddled with inconsistencies, clear evidence of textual corruption, and dubious features such as pieces of narrative inserted in them, often of a hagiographical character.[55]

Wendy Davies has argued that these 'charters' retain genuine information from the mid-sixth century onwards. However, she herself admits the degree of questionable elements within them, and other leading historians of Britain in the fifth and sixth centuries, including David Dumville — perhaps the foremost in this field — discount them as unreliable for the sixth and seventh centuries at least. It is likely that there is some pre-Norman material contained within the Llandaff Charters, but whether any of this can be extracted usefully from its manipulation by the Norman propagandist, and relates to the seventh century or earlier, seems much more doubtful. New work is needed to establish, for example, whether the Llandaff material contains anything at all of pre-800 date apart from personal and place-names, and if so whether it can be used to write history.

Last — and probably least — we come to the genealogies. Again, David Dumville has taken the lead in analysing this material. Building on the important and meticulous studies by Molly Miller, Dumville has shown that the lists of kings preserved in various sources cannot be taken as historical rather than political statements. Once again, history has fallen foul of political rewriting, and genealogies have been emended and edited, with names cut out and, as likely as not, added in.[56]

The lists have no dates given in them, so the method of dating was to count generations (assuming a generation to be 30 years), but the work of Dumville and Miller has rendered such 'generation-counting' methodologically invalid. We cannot date genealogies unless they can be certainly related to other sources containing datable names — of which there are obviously very few. Similarly, none of the lists that survive were without question written in the period before 600. Only that for Dyfed, in south-west Wales, can be checked against a similar genealogy compiled outside Britain (in Ireland), although the possibility that one list copied the other, or the lists were compiled by the same people or for the same reason, cannot be discounted in that case too.

None of these sources will be used here, because none of them need refer to Britain during the fifth or sixth centuries. While, of course, new textual sources might be discovered, the amount of textual material directly relating to fifth- and sixth-century Britain appears to be far less today than, for example, seemed the case in 1975.

Later sources for fifth- and sixth-century Britain

It might be hoped that later writers would help supplement this meagre haul of source-material. One later writer whose works have long been central to the study of fifth- and sixth-century Britain is Bede, a self-consciously Anglo-Saxon monk who wrote at his monastery at Jarrow-Monkwearmouth in the early eighth century. Bede was a superb historian and has been rightly praised for his skills in collating and evaluating his material. He wrote a number of works, of which the *Historia Ecclesiastica* ('Ecclesiastical History') is both the most famous today and most often used as a source for Britain in the period 400-600.

Bede wrote over a century after 600, and in a monastic context which he may seldom have left. Thus, while one need not doubt his integrity or ability, there might well have been much about the fifth and sixth centuries which he either did not know, or was misinformed about by less critical reporters. It is doubtful if any reliable oral traditions could still have survived in Bede's own lifetime for events of the fifth century, and there is no evidence that the 'Anglo-Saxons' produced any text longer than a runic phrase prior to their conversion to Christianity in the late 590s onward. Bede is, therefore, extremely unlikely to have had any substantial written evidence for the fifth century unknown to us, and his account should be treated with extreme caution for the period before St Augustine's mission in general. We will see that he perhaps provides some interesting information about mid- or late sixth-century Britain, but his work comes into its own only after 597, when better sources were available.[57]

The Tribal Hidage is another source of post-600 date that might well assist us in reconstructing fifth- and sixth-century British history. This text probably dates from the late seventh century, and gives a taxation assessment for the territories owing tribute to an Anglo-Saxon king, probably the king of Mercia. While the text does not directly relate to the fifth and sixth centuries, it refers to many political units by name, and enables a rough political geography for late seventh-century Anglo-Saxon England to be constructed. It is possible, but not necessarily the case, that some of the political units mentioned could have originated in the sixth century. The text includes two especially interesting groups of territorial names. One bears the suffix -*saete* and seems to relate to areas politically taken over by the Anglo-Saxons in the seventh century rather than earlier. This might hint at areas still outside Anglo-Saxon rule in the sixth century. Another refers to extremely small 'folk territories' which have been argued to represent the sort of unit pre-dating the rise of large-scale kingdoms, believed to be prior to the seventh century.[58]

Place-names offer the only other assistance. In many parts of Britain place-names survive which arguably date from the fifth and sixth centuries. While this might seem a potentially invaluable source, the study of place-names, too, is beset with problems. First, it is not at all clear what the date of most place-names actually is. Many can be shown to predate the ninth or even seventh century, when Anglo-Saxon charters give the first detailed written descriptions of the English landscape. But how much earlier than 600 any are is debatable. For example, although place-name elements such as -*ham*, -*ton* and -*ing* were once argued to indicate settlements and communities of fifth- and sixth-century date, these names appear to be much later, perhaps indicating 'infilling' in the settlement-pattern. Moreover, place-names are more frequently changed and replaced than is often appreciated, so that their distribution has to be treated with great caution.[59]

In Wales, Cornwall and parts of northern England, as well as in Scotland, many 'Celtic' place-names exist. However, these remain relatively unstudied compared to the English counterparts and are only attested generally at a far later date. In particular, ecclesiastical place-names may indicate early church sites and burial grounds, as in Cornwall where the place-name element *lan* (Welsh *llan*) has been associated with an archaeologically-identifiable feature, raised curvilinear churchyards, arguably originating before 800.[60]

A particular type of place-name evidence, classically studied by E.G. Bowen, of greatest relevance in this case to the west and north, is that of church dedications and especially those dedicated to local saints. Church dedications may be thought less liable to modification in such ways as other types of place-name, given the persistence of local saints' cults through the medieval period. However, it would be unwise to suppose that all dedications which refer to saints of a particular period are contemporary with those saints. For example, it may be rash to assume that a dedication to St David, the patron saint of

Wales, who is claimed to have lived in south-west Wales in the sixth century AD, actually relates to churches in any way associated with that saint's lifetime. While dedications might be more 'stable' than other sorts of place-names, we must only use these with great care, allowing for possibilities of fashion, rededication and the honouring of distant saints by dedication at churches otherwise having no relation to them at all.[61]

Consequently, place-name and dedication evidence is only of much help as a supplementary support to arguments based on other grounds, given the problems of chronology and distribution connected with it. This is not to underestimate the considerable importance of place-name studies, but to acknowledge that place-names are not as straightforward a source as might at first be supposed.

The general picture from written sources

In summary then: there are very few reliable written sources for Britain in the period 400-600, and those that exist nearly all have severe limits and problems of interpretation associated with them. No contemporary source presents a true narrative history, nor was the primary purpose of any of the sources to convey general historical information. A large body of pseudo-historical material exists but this is valueless as a source for 400-600. Place-names and church dedications are of more help, but the value of such material is limited by chronological and other problems.

Despite its severe limitations this enables us to reconstruct the circumstances surrounding the formal end of Roman rule in Britain, albeit in the most skeletal detail. It also permits us to see the role that social upheaval and the introduction of Martinian monasticism might have played in this, and in the emergence of a post-Roman society in Britain. We can observe that society surviving into the fifth and sixth centuries, and retaining much of the cultural world of Late Roman Britain, was alongside a vibrant — but somewhat conservative — Christian life. That is, for all the limitations of our sources we can see the emergence and survival among the Britons of exactly the sort of Romano-Christian culture that characterised Late Antiquity in other parts of the former Roman world.

Textual evidence even gives us a few possible details, such as hints at the survival, in reduced form, of towns and villas into the fifth century, and the emergence of hill-fort settlements associated with kingship in western Britain. It shows accomplished Latinity and Roman-style education among at least some of the Britons, and allows us to observe the arrival of a pagan Germanic population, called by contemporaries 'Saxons' — perhaps as part of British policy — into eastern Britain. This population had been involved in warfare against the Britons and defeated, by the time of Gildas' birth. They were again fighting the Britons in the late sixth century and seventh century according to the north British poetry and Bede's narrative, but this time defeated them. This resulted in the replacement of British political dominance by that of Anglo-Saxon kingdoms, newly converted to Christianity in the seventh century following the initial mission of St Augustine to Kent in 597.

This evidence strongly implies that the 'Late Antique' model indeed fits Britain in the fifth and sixth centuries. It urges further investigation of that hypothesis, and heightens the potential held by placing Britain firmly in the world of Late Antiquity. The mass of pseudo-historical material deemed inadmissible here can be seen to have clouded the image of this period in previous studies, helping to promote a 'Celtic haze' over the British west, and myths of an ancestral 'pagan Anglo-Saxon England' in the fifth and sixth century east of the island.

We have also seen that the lack of available reliable sources means that a more detailed picture of fifth- and sixth-century Britain is unlikely to be produced using written evidence alone. Recourse to pseudo-historical materials is plainly not an acceptable option. Clearly, then, if we want to know more about what happened in the period 400-600 in Britain it is only through archaeology that we are likely to find out.

We may begin by examining what archaeology tells us about the fate of those aspects of Late Roman Britain which were shared by the whole diocese: the diocesan and provincial government, the military, the taxation system, and large-scale production. As we shall see, together this provides us with an 'archaeology of decolonization' for Roman Britain, which supplements rather than refutes the picture gained from written sources.

The archaeology of imperial withdrawal

The importation of fresh imperial coinage into Britain appears to have ceased after the reign of Constantine III, implying both a disconnection from the imperial payment of troops and the imperial taxation system. This hint that the Roman army was no longer being paid in new coin later than the first decade of the fifth century is borne out by excavated sequences of occupation from fort sites. No Roman fort in Britain undeniably shows occupation in the second quarter of the fifth century, and the pattern of disuse is not due to a lack of extensive modern excavation. Forts have been excavated using state-of-the-art methods on a large scale, but no occupation definitely later than 425 and earlier than 450 has been identified.[62]

Archaeology bears out the view that Britain became detached from the Roman Empire in the early fifth century, whatever claims to the island the Eastern Roman government may still have harboured, and no matter what sentiments lingered among some Britons. Archaeological evidence also supports the view that the Roman army and taxation system ceased to operate in Britain after *c*.410. This begs the question of how eastern Britain was defended after this date, if at all, given that texts refer to fifth-century 'barbarian' raids. The answer may come from archaeological material relating to Germanic migrants in fifth-century Britain.[63]

In 1986, H.W. Böhme — the leading expert on dating Germanic metalwork of the fourth and fifth centuries — argued that the earliest 'Anglo-Saxon' artefacts in England (such as supporting arm brooches and early cruciform brooches) date from the first quarter of the fifth century. Böhme observed that these are restricted to East Anglia, and associated with cremation burials in equally 'Germanic' urns. Chris Scull has suggested that this material should be dated slightly later, perhaps *c*.425-50, and this is consistent with Böhme's own later revision of the relevant Continental metalwork chronology.[64]

6   *The earliest fifth-century*
      'Anglo-Saxon'
      metalwork (filled circles)
      with 'quoit brooch style'
      objects and 'Late Roman
      fixed-plate belt sets'
      (open circles) in eastern
      Britain (after Hawkes,
      with additions)

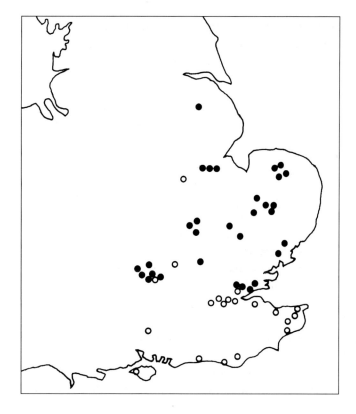

These burials are unlike any Romano-British cremations, but relate closely to those from 'free Germania'. They might well represent the graves of Germanic migrants and, unlike the earlier thin scatters of Germanic metalwork in Britain, represent a distinctive regional distribution.

Böhme noted that the restricted area containing these brooches is complemented by the find-spots of other types of metalwork (some found with inhumation burials), especially that in the 'quoit brooch style'. The latter have been seen as linked to Roman, as well as Germanic, art styles and might represent badges of rank worn by soldiers or officials employed by the Britons. This would account for the use of inhumation burial rather than cremation, as the former was the common Late Roman custom, but rarer in 'free Germania' than within the Roman Empire (**colour plate 4**).

There are also burials accompanied by weapons — atypical of Late Roman mortuary customs overall and unknown in fourth century Britain. Weapon-burials (*Waffengräber*) are commonly found in 'free Germania', and usually considered distinctively Germanic in Late Roman cemeteries in Gaul.

In 1986, Böhme dated these inhumations to the mid-fifth century, that is, slightly later than the cremations. Again this could be shifted slightly later in view of his subsequent Continental dating evidence, to *c*.450-75. This group, with mortuary customs including weapon burial, and Romano-Germanic metalwork and inhumation practices, could well represent in archaeological terms exactly the sort of fifth-century Germanic troops depicted by Gildas in his *De Excidio*.[65]

Bearing in mind the dates provided by archaeology, like those from Gildas's text, can only be approximate, it is salutary that both sources seem to coincide to suggest that by the mid- to late fifth century there were Germanic peoples settling in eastern Britain, and that at least some of these were working in a sub-Roman British context as soldiers. Both Gildas and archaeological evidence suggest that this situation was established *c.*450-75.[66]

The same evidence might elucidate the fate of the diocesan administration in Britain. Although both sets of boundaries are unable to be closely defined, two of these groups approximately define two of the late fourth-century British provinces, in so far as their areas are known. A third is arguably visible in another group of Late Roman (perhaps official) metalwork, without Germanic associations and mostly unassociated with weapon burials, currently the subject of a major project by Mark Corney. This — comprised largely of belt-fittings — focuses on Cirencester and Gloucester and appears to continue to the later fifth century also. Corney would specifically associate the distribution of this material with the province of Britannia Prima.[67]

That is, the three southern provinces of Late Roman Britain each may have a distinctive set of mid- to late fifth-century archaeological attributes that might well indicate either soldiers or a Germanic presence, or both. An obvious interpretation of at least two — and probably all — of these distributions is that we see a provincial level of defence when the diocesan defensive system has ceased to function. It seems possible, then, to argue that the provincial structure had survived, but the diocesan level of administration had collapsed by the mid-fifth century when these patterns began to be established. Their chronology also implies that, if so, the provincial structure survived until at least the late fifth century.

Further evidence for the survival of fourth-century provinces into the fifth century might be found by examining the provincial capitals: London, Lincoln, York and Cirencester. If the provinces survived, we should see some evidence that each of these places was still an administrative centre, or at least occupied by high-status inhabitants, into the fifth century.

Evidence from London is ambiguous. In the fourth century London had a defensive wall, at least part of which (within what is today the Tower of London) dates from the end of that century. A substantial area to the immediate north and south of the Roman bridge across the Thames remained occupied by substantial stone buildings to the end of the century also, and burial continued in the extramural cemeteries outside the walls.[68]

A broader area of 'dark earth' occupied the area inside the walls. This deposit began to form in the late second century and comprises a (often very thick) soil deposit containing Late Roman finds, bone, charcoal, slag and the reworked remains of wattle and daub. It is not a burning deposit, but might represent either desertion or — much more likely — the remains of mud-walled or timber-framed structures, associated with intensive occupation. This occupation would render the inhabited area of late fourth-century London larger than is often supposed, albeit with most of the population living in timber-framed structures or mud-huts. 'Dark earth' is a common feature of Late Roman urban archaeology in Britain, occurring at most major towns. If the interpretation of the deposit as representing intensive, but 'un-Roman', urban occupation holds true in London, then this has implications for late fourth century Romano-British urbanism as a whole.

The most remarkable, and perhaps most important, building known from late fourth-century London is a large basilican structure found at Colchester House, again near the Tower. This was constructed no earlier than the mid-fourth century, and probably later. It made extensive reuse of 'second-hand' building materials to create a very large aisled structure which closely parallels in plan the church of St Tecla at Milan. The latter was a major church constructed in 388 in the then capital of the western Roman Empire. The building in London may be interpreted as both a church, assuming that it emulates St Tecla and not vice versa, dating after 388. It seems very likely (although not certain) that this building was the cathedral of late fourth-century, or later, London.

If so, then several features of the building require comment here. The reuse of building materials for such a structure is remarkable in Britain. It is the only major public building where this occurs on a large scale in any Romano-British town, although it is found — less commonly in Britain than elsewhere — in the town walls of major centres, including London. The re-use of materials for a possible cathedral could, therefore, imply a date after the ready availability of new building materials. This is clearly not London's first fourth-century cathedral: there was already a bishop of London in the early fourth century, so another fourth-century cathedral must exist somewhere in or near the Roman city. This may allow a very 'late' Late Roman dating for the building indeed, analogous to that proposed for St Paul in the Bail, Lincoln (see below), perhaps even after 400.

Whatever the precise date of the structure, the combination of a church and late fourth-century walls recalls the pattern of urban regeneration noted by Bryan Ward-Perkins in Italy at the end of the Roman period. There, resources were typically diverted from the construction of public buildings in general to build walls and churches. Ward-Perkins takes this as evidence of urban vitality, and of the way that within a Late Antique context defence and Christianity had become the priorities for urban communities. In this way, then, London at the end of the fourth or in the early fifth century would be in these respects, at least, a typical Late Antique city.[69]

Evidence for fifth-century occupation in London is extremely difficult to recognise. This is principally because of broader problems of identifying fifth-century British artefacts, to which we shall return later, and the difficulties of urban rescue archaeology. Fifth-century occupation has been suggested at several sites, such as at St Peter's Hill, but no fifth-century British structures have been undeniably located. Burial appears to have continued in the extramural fourth-century eastern cemetery into the fifth century with no sign of declining numbers. Fifth-century Germanic material is more easily dated, and identifiably fifth-century Germanic pottery has been found within the City, at St Bride's church. This need not indicate 'Anglo-Saxon settlement' in London at this date, but it could indicate a Germanic component within the local population, or links between Britons in London and nearby Germanic settlers.[70]

The most convincing evidence for the continuing significance of London into the fifth century comes from outside the Roman city. A series of cemeteries containing the sort of artefacts associated with sub-Roman Germanic soldiers by Böhme has been found forming an approximate semi-circle around the south of London. These, partially surrounding an area roughly equivalent to twentieth-century 'Greater London', began in the mid- or late fifth century. This may well be an indication of its remaining hinterland to the south, and other such settlements, as at Mucking, Essex, appear to guard the mouth of the Thames. The distribution of these sites, and their proximity to Roman roads and other strategic locations in the fourth-century geography of the London area, suggests a defensive system specifically designed to protect London from both land and sea attack. It is hardly likely that a defensive system of this sort would have been afforded to protect empty walls, no matter how prestigious. When it was established — in the mid- to late fifth century — there was probably still something to defend in (or very near) Roman London, and an organising authority capable of positioning troops based there.[71]

Lincoln was also enclosed by walls in the late fourth century, containing areas of 'dark earth' like that found in London and substantial town houses of late fourth-century date. Once again, public buildings seem to have been disused before the end of the fourth century, again with the exception of a church. Built within the forum courtyard, this appears to be of very late fourth- or early fifth-century origin, as detailed stratigraphical and chronological analysis by Michael Jones and Kate Steane has shown. It subsequently developed to become a medieval and modern parish church, St Paul in the Bail. The location of St Paul in the Bail provides Lincoln with a candidate for its late fourth- or early fifth-century cathedral. But again, Lincoln had a bishop (and so probably a cathedral of some sort) in the early fourth century, like London. That is, we can see a similar array of features of late fourth- or early fifth-century date, albeit on a smaller scale, at Lincoln as we saw in London. As in London, a new cathedral was apparently built in the heart of the city at the very end of the fourth century or the very start of the fifth. However, in Lincoln the evidence of fifth-century continuity of use of this cathedral is somewhat stronger: St Paul in the Bail was apparently continuously used until its replacement by an early seventh-century 'Anglo-Saxon' building.[72]

Kevin Leahy has pointed out that Lincoln, like London, appears to be 'ringed' by fifth-century Germanic burials. Again, at least some of these are located at strategic nodes in the fourth-century geography of Lincoln's hinterland, suggesting their deliberate positioning to defend the city, although this conspicuously lacks much evidence of fifth- or sixth-century 'Anglo-Saxon' occupation. Again, the situation appears to resemble London closely.

At York too, the late fourth-century town was also enclosed by walls and contained areas of 'dark earth' alongside elaborate town houses in the later fourth century. Again, no secular public buildings are known to have been in use until the end of the fourth century, and the *principia* (headquarters building) of the fortress area of the town was re-used for 'industrial' purposes by that time. Once more, recognisably fifth-century finds are sparse within the town, although more indications of fifth-century or later occupation are known within some fourth-century buildings. No late fourth- or early fifth-century church is known from York, but the town was the seat of a fourth-century bishop, and the location of the medieval church of St Michael le Belfrey within the courtyard of the *principia* so closely parallels that of St Paul in the Bail in the forum at Lincoln as to suggest a similar situation. So, it is at least possible (and perhaps likely) that York — like Lincoln — shows the same pattern of late fourth- and fifth-century use as we saw at London. One difference is that York is not surrounded by 'positioned' cemeteries with Germanic metalwork, but fifth-century 'Anglo-Saxon' cremation cemeteries have been found immediately outside the walls, and these could represent military detachments defending it.[73]

The similarities between London, Lincoln and York in these respects are also, at least arguably, shared to some extent by Cirencester. Cirencester shows evidence of 'dark earth', late fourth- and early fifth-century town house construction and had Late Roman walls. It also seems to lack public buildings still in use in the late fourth century, and there is extensive evidence of activity in the town in the fifth century or later, including pottery and buildings. Cirencester too had a fourth-century bishop, but like York has produced no evidence for a possible late fourth- or fifth-century cathedral. Nevertheless, this may be no more than a chance of modern discovery, and much of the centre of the Roman town remains unexcavated. Although to the west of the distribution of Germanic metalwork dating to the fifth century, the belt equipment studied by Corney seems to concentrate in part on Cirencester, suggesting that it still had a political importance.[74]

That is, evidence from London, York, Cirencester and Lincoln suggests that the towns survived as places of importance and centres of political and (at least at Lincoln) perhaps ecclesiastical authority into the mid- to late fifth century. This combines with the evidence already outlined regarding the fifth-century defence of the provinces to support the view that the provincial structure of late fourth-century Britain survived until the late fifth century. This seems to coincide so precisely with what Gildas tells us, that perhaps we should credit his version of the collapse of this system: that it ended with the 'Saxon rebellion'. This was probably close to 500, perhaps in the 490s, and would mean that what had been Roman Britain remained under British rule for almost the whole fifth century.

These would be among the longest-lived Western provinces, but diocesan government had been overthrown in the first decade of the fifth century. This would explain why the borders of the provinces had become militarised, protected not only from coastal attack, but from other provinces. The imperial bureaucracy and the army had gone and Britain's new rulers may well have had exactly those priorities which we have found expressed in their capitals — Christianity and defence — priorities they shared with other (Late Antique) communities across Europe. But as the writings of Patrick and Gildas show, this new elite was not against all things 'Roman', while possibly recognising the Roman Empire (as in Gildas's *De Excidio*) as a 'foreign' former coloniser. More correctly, its culture was 'Romano-Christian' just like that of Continental Late Antique societies, and we have already seen from written evidence that this culture was to survive for the next two centuries — at least in some areas and in relation to some people.

Fashion victims: the end of mass production and the transformation of architecture

Texts passing critical evaluation in the first part of this chapter imply, therefore, that Britain was not — as generally assumed — the part of the West to most swiftly abandon all traces of Roman culture and organization. The 'British revolution' did not destroy the provincial structure, but apparently took it over, expelling only the diocesan authorities. When the emperor Honorius wrote to the *civitates* in 410, he may have communicated with the 'next layer down' in the administrative hierarchy to the provincial government in order to avoid acknowledging the legitimacy of the rebels.[75]

While the provincial administration may have been maintained, one aspect of the Late Romano-British economy collapsed. There is no evidence that large-scale manufacturing (and the province-wide distribution of products) known in the fourth century survived long into the fifth century. Although small-scale production and localised exchange of these products might have lasted for a century or more longer, the major 'industries' of Late Roman Britain had stopped large-scale production by the mid-fifth century at latest, and probably earlier.[76]

This sudden collapse may be rooted in the fourth-century economy, and is most clearly seen in relation to pottery production. By the end of the fourth century there were only a handful of major pottery producers, alongside an increasing amount of local products. The range of these mass-produced products also decreased substantially, so that very few forms of pottery remained in production by *c*.400, although these were still widely marketed. This might represent the success of particular products or producers, or a narrowing range of uses for pottery, perhaps in competition with wood, stone, leather, glass or metal containers. In the fifth century these products ceased to be marketed widely, and conventional interpretations claim production stopped totally thereafter.

The end of the monetary economy is often seen as the reason for this collapse. While plausible on general grounds, this depends upon assumptions about the final circulation of Late Roman currency in Britain. It is often asserted that Roman coinage (which ceased to be imported in substantial quantities by 402) ceased to circulate in Britain by 430. But this is really no more than guesswork. The latest Roman coins that entered Britain in large numbers may have been accompanied by already circulating coinage of earlier issues. Fourth-century coin hoards in Britain show coin circulating much later than its date of issue. For example, the latest 'Roman' coin hoard (the Patching hoard), which dates after 461, contains coins from 337. These were 124 years old when deposited. By this token, coins imported in 402 might have circulated in 526. This is not, of course, proof that this happened, only that it is not inconceivable.[77]

Roman coin remained in circulation in rural contexts in the Mediterranean — even in parts of Spain — into the twentieth century, and nineteenth-century Western travellers were amazed to see Roman small-change in use at North African oases. In the fifth to seventh centuries, when fresh coin was in short supply, earlier coin was used alongside later issues. Everywhere in the West, when no later issues were available, 'old' coin would have been the only currency. This was true in Gaul, Italy, North Africa and the Balkans.[78]

The argument that this did not occur in Britain rests upon very flimsy assumptions. Usually it is claimed that the absence of coins from either fifth- and sixth-century settlements or graves necessitates that no coin was in use. However, this is not an accurate representation of the settlement or burial record. Coins occur at fifth- and sixth-century settlements in western Britain, but only in small numbers. Many fourth-century settlements in the west of Britain produce no greater a number of coins, and coin-use might have taken on a restricted range of functions, for example for paying dues or taxes. A reduction in coin use had already taken place in parts of Britain before 400, so this is no surprise. Moreover, Germanic migrants in 'Anglo-Saxon' England need not be expected to employ coins even if they circulated in areas among the Britons, as the societies from which they came did not use coins in the fourth century. So the absence of Roman coins from 'Anglo-Saxon' graves, in which they are in fact found in small numbers, would again be unsurprising even if coins were used by their British neighbours.[79] It is, then, unclear from on-site evidence whether or not coin circulated in Britain after 430-40.

Patrick and Gildas both mention coins, in contexts that refer to contemporary society, and in Gildas's case he plainly knew the economic use of coins. If coin was not circulating we have to explain why coinage remained a meaningful concept in sixth-century Britain.

Two important coin hoards of fifth-century date — those from Hoxne and Patching — may help us understand the fate of coinage use in eastern Britain, where we might suppose it to have been the most short-lived. The Hoxne hoard dates from after 407 and contains coin of Constantine III. This had been clipped, a practice against imperial law, implying a post-imperial date. Cathy King and Catherine Johns have argued that clipping found on Roman coins in Britain may have taken place over decades, continuing until the 430s or '40s. So, the Hoxne hoard alone may suggest coinage use after the formal end of Roman Britain, and perhaps until the 440s.[80]

The Patching hoard includes Continental coins of the 460s. It confirms that as late as the late fifth century, fourth-century coin still had value and was being stored as wealth. This probably implies that continuously since the early fifth century, money was still valuable, even if it was being replaced by non-monetary exchange. Even on this evidence, then, coinage retained value and circulated until the 440s (at least) in East Anglia and probably 460s (at least) in Sussex. Other fifth-century coins have been found along the east coast, as at Chatham Lines, Kent. This might suggest that coinage retained its value until the 460s, even in eastern Britain. In the west, where British control persisted long beyond the 460s, coinage use might continue even longer.[81]

We can see, therefore, that the conventional picture of monetary collapse by the 430s is more problematical than generally supposed. Coinage-use may have been declining in the late fourth century, and this may have continued gradually into the fifth, with old coins remaining longer in circulation once supplies of new coinage ceased. It seems rather risky to claim that the — undated — disuse of currency brought about the — also undated — total collapse in Roman-style pottery production. The truth is, we do not know when either occurred, although the importation of large quantities of new coin and large-scale pottery production probably did not outlast the early fifth century. Coinage-use (to a declining extent) and localised pottery production might have lasted much longer, points that have chronological as well as other consequences.

Pottery produced in the fifth century could also have remained in use when pottery production ceased, and the later the collapse of production the later large quantities of pottery might be available 'while stocks lasted'. As some types of Romano-British pottery (such as the shell tempered wares) only became mass-produced after the 390s, this could plainly have been well into the fifth century. Nor is the end of production well-dated at kiln sites: at Harrold (the most widely-cited shell tempered ware kiln site) the excavator concluded that production continued into the fifth century, but could not ascertain for how long. As we shall see in the next chapter, there is evidence that pottery production continued at some Late Roman kiln sites well into the fifth century, if not later, but that distribution was very localised after the early fifth century.[82]

It is easy to explain why pottery ceased to be widely distributed at this time. The growing insecurity in Britain in the early fifth century is attested by Patrick, Gildas and the *Vita Germani*. This may have decreased the attractions of long-distance travel and raised transport costs, while the withdrawal of the army and the imperial administration may have limited previous markets for food, ceramics, metal goods and building. The increased impermeability of provincial boundaries resulting from separate government and military organization may also have limited potential markets, if these became military frontiers. Likewise, where the Roman army was the main market for food, specifically in the north, we would expect the same to be true for agricultural production, as appears to be the case. Lost markets and closed borders restricted distribution networks and with them the possibilities of large-scale production. But this did not eliminate local markets.[83]

If this argument holds true, artefacts used by mid- to late fifth-century Britons might well have been superficially the same as the latest Romano-British material culture currently identified. Partly this would be because old objects remained in use, partly because new artefacts may have been almost identical to those produced generations earlier, although now marketed more locally. We shall return to this point later in this book, but this should not lead us to assume that nothing had changed from the fourth century in the material culture of the fifth-century Britons.

A major factor in material culture change in the fifth century may be fashion and taste. In the Late Roman period we see forms and wares of equivalent function compete for the same markets and both gain and lose popularity. While regional and cost factors most likely played a role, an element of fashion is also visible, as in trends in burial customs and dress in fourth-century Britain. Fashion change might well explain the shift away from aspects of fourth-century Roman-style material culture in the late fourth and fifth centuries. Hilary Cool has noted that dress fashions and hairstyles were changing — changes she attributes to the impact of Christianity on dress fashions — and Carol van Driel-Murray has also detected change in fashions of footwear. People were apparently looking rather different from head to toe, but no less 'Roman', in the late fourth century and later than they had in the middle or earlier parts of the century. Such fashion changes might also affect material culture in ways which make innovations harder to detect.[84]

For example, we have records of wall-hangings and carpets from Late Antique contexts in France and the Mediterranean. If wall-hangings and carpets or patterned rugs became popular in the late fourth or early fifth century in Britain (and the manufacture of woven goods had been a fourth-century British speciality), this might explain why mosaics and wall-plaster ceased to be used. Any flooring and walling under the carpet or wall-hanging would suffice. These could have been just as beautifully decorated and coloured as mosaics and wall-plaster but they would not survive on the typical British site.[85]

Another important factor may have been the impact of Christianity on fashions in fifth-century Britain. Those features of Late Roman elite culture most associated with the pagan elite, or with temples and paganism, might well have been consciously rejected. On the basis of known fourth-century villa sites with pagan decoration, these could have included mosaic floors, painted wall-plaster, sculpture and other lavish interior decoration. If even Sidonius Apollinaris, a relatively moderate Gallic aristocrat, could claim that the absence of wall-painting in one's villa was creditable, one might imagine more stringent views among extremists. This could explain why, in fifth-century Britain, occupation at villas where it continues at all, often has an apparently 'low-status' appearance, deliberately disregarding decorative aspects of the Roman rooms.[86]

A simple combination of fashion and religious values may, then, explain aspects of Romano-British material culture as diverse as interior furnishing and hairpins, which all seem to disappear from the late fourth century onward. But Romano-British culture did not entirely disappear, and other parts of the fifth-century material culture of the Britons may have so closely resembled that of the late fourth century as to render it particularly hard to recognise archaeologically.

This would be the material correlate of the rural society described briefly by Patrick. He takes it for granted that villas and small-towns still existed, and local councils still met at larger towns to run their affairs in a Roman manner. What archaeologists used to call 'squatter occupation' at villas and in town-houses (in which the councils presumably met) could represent this final phase of use, by owners who rejected many of the values of the builders of the houses they occupied. The towns themselves, as we have seen, remained administrative and ecclesiastical centres, perhaps with newly-central churches. Times had changed, but society had not collapsed catastrophically before Gildas's 'Saxon rebellion'.

Conclusion

Standard views of the end of Roman Britain seem flawed and open to reinterpretation. Reliable written sources suggest that fifth- and sixth-century British society and culture retained far more of the Late Roman past than has usually been supposed, and did so within a political framework inherited from the fourth century. Although the diocesan administration may have been swept away in the first decade of the fifth century, the provincial structure may have survived until the end of the century. Archaeological evidence lends support to Patrick's picture of the survival of Romano-British rural society into the mid-fifth century, and to Gildas' account of the employment of Germanic troops in mid- to late fifth-century Britain. Their rebellion may have collapsed the provincial structure and permitted them to take over parts of eastern Britain. To examine the consequences of this, we must look again at the evidence for Britain in the later fifth and sixth centuries.

2 Eastern Britain in the later fifth and sixth centuries

The development of Germanic political control in Britain

To Gildas, the 'Saxons' were a heathen Germanic people who seized control of areas in the east of Britain, probably during the later fifth century. But not all people of Germanic descent in fifth-century Britain shared the same relationship with Late Romano-British society and culture. To the south of the Thames, and in the south Midlands, we have seen that the first generation of Germanic migrants may have adopted Romano-British burial practices, and that their leaders wore brooches and buckles at least partly of Late Roman character. It would be reasonable to suppose that these migrants had taken on other aspects of Late Romano-British culture that are less easily identified. North of this, cremation cemeteries, in East Anglia and Lincolnshire, were also established in the mid-fifth century, perhaps at a slightly earlier date. These represent a Germanic society relatively untouched by the way of life of their hosts, and where ongoing migration was to reinforce the Germanic character of cultural practices.[1]

While his work is of seminal importance, Böhme may have been mistaken when he assumed that the first of these cremations represent settlers outside the control of the British authorities. The juxtaposition of fifth-century cremation cemeteries and Romano-British settlements is striking throughout East Anglia, as at Caistor-by-Norwich and Spong Hill. An obvious interpretation is that these cemeteries were deliberately positioned at, or near, Roman towns because those foci still retained some sort of importance in the fifth century. If Germanic communities were granted land near to the places which they were intended to protect, then this pattern becomes explicable. This does not necessitate a substantial British population at such centres but may imply their lingering political importance, and perhaps an official presence, possibly in the manner of the fifth-century enclosure at Wighton.[2]

That is, in areas with cremations too, local defence in the mid- to late fifth century was in the hands of Germanic communities. When these ceased to obey the provincial authorities then the area (or parts of it) might well have slipped swiftly under Germanic control, with local people unwilling to live under such rule fleeing across the borders or across the seas to areas of safety. Some sectors of the British community may have been especially well-organised to facilitate flight. In particular, it is notable that East Anglia was one of the most visibly Christianised parts of Late Roman Britain, yet there is very little trace of Christianity in the zone during the late fifth and sixth centuries. Perhaps the Church, the best organised fifth-century institution on the Continent, was able to gather and move its 'flock' far more effectively than any other sector of the local population.[3]

Whereas the large cremation cemeteries may imply the immigration of whole structured communities into the area between the Wash and Chilterns, this was not necessarily true further south. More 'acculturated' Germanic migrants, perhaps outside structured migrant communities, might be represented by the mid-fifth-century inhumation cemeteries to the south of this zone. Individual soldiers, or small family-units, may more readily have intermarried with Britons, encouraging still greater cultural interaction. The term *Gewissae*, which perhaps means something like 'the reliable ones', was the tribal term for the 'Saxons' of the Upper Thames in the seventh century. The expression might relate to the protective role of Germanic troops in the fifth century, and graves in this area contain indications of this greater cultural compatibility, such as the use of Romano-British-style toilet articles. We shall return later in this chapter to the implications this was to have for the adoption of shared material culture and burial practices among Britons and Germanic communities, but the area affords an opportunity to see how cultural coexistence could work in a particular locality during the fifth century.[5]

The fifth-century material at and near the Roman small-town of Dorchester-on-Thames (the centre of the *Gewissae* according to Bede) illustrates the context in which this cultural synthesis occurred. Two convincing fifth-century buildings have been found in the town: a 'sunken-featured building' and a masonry house of Late Roman design. These occur close together on the same Roman street, while outside the walls were fifth-century burials, some probably British, other probably Germanic. In the cemetery at Queensford Farm, a fifth-century British burial ground continued in use while 'Anglo-Saxon' cemeteries were established in the surrounding area. That is, Britons and Germanic migrants apparently lived side by side, the former maintaining aspects of Romano-British culture well into the fifth century.[6]

Different subsequent histories might be explained in terms of different relative numbers of Germanic migrants, whether these migrated as structured communities, the ways in which they were accommodated into the local community and perhaps the different backgrounds from which they came. It could well be that those communities employed in East Anglia were less familiar with Roman culture before their introduction into Britain, and it would be logical to expect larger numbers of troops to be employed on the more endangered east coast. There, the relative proportion of Germanic to local inhabitants in what may have been a depopulated area may have been higher, even before flight and evacuation. This suggests that the two provinces concerned could have passed rapidly under Germanic control, as Gildas again says, removing the provincial governments and leaving separate locations occupied by different Germanic groups.

A related pattern can be seen in relation to rural settlement. We have seen that much of the rural infrastructure of Late Roman Britain was perhaps still functioning during the fifth century. It is intriguing, then, to find a close association between Late Roman villa sites and later fifth-century 'Anglo-Saxon' settlements and burials in both of the areas already discussed. But this is not evidence of continuous occupation: the villas can be shown to have been disused when the burials or structures were placed on their ruins. For example, at Meonstoke such a building cut the main aisled house and at Barton Court Farm, an 'Anglo-Saxon' settlement was constructed immediately adjacent to a small villa. A few burials were inserted into the site, but this was neither a large nor wealthy settlement, nor was it a cemetery. Most likely, it is a single farm-unit of late fifth- to sixth-century date.[8]

As at Barton Court Farm, the 'Anglo-Saxon' settlements which follow villas do not seem especially distinguished, nor do they share any particular affinities with the architecture or material culture of the villa population. Tamara Lewitt's interesting suggestion that these 'Anglo-Saxon' farms represent the villa community in a new guise seems hard to reconcile with the lack of apparent contact between the two periods of occupation. The relationship between the villas and later settlements seems 'butt-jointed' rather than a continuum, as David Brown put it. The villa-owners seem to have left the estate, in archaeological terms at least, immediately prior to the reuse of their home for timber buildings. In some cases the villas have artefacts suggesting use right up to the period of the 'Anglo-Saxon' takeover: such as a quoit brooch at Clatterford and a 'quoit brooch style' belt-plate at Meonstoke. The British population might literally have moved out immediately before the 'Anglo-Saxon' population moved in, and the apparently deliberate demolition of villa buildings at some of these sites suggests that the former residents may have left ahead of the new tenants.[9]

Flight or death seem the only possible ways of explaining the fate of these villas' final inhabitants, unless we evoke Lewitt's interpretation. There is no compelling evidence of bodies lying amid the ruins, nor usually of catastrophic final burning layers. Here we may see detailed evidence for the evacuation or flight of Britons, accounting for the large numbers of British refugees noted in north Gaul in the late fifth century, in northern Spain before the sixth century, and most of all in Brittany during the fifth century. These were sufficient to be counted in their thousands in Gaul outside Brittany, and to change the names of both Armorica (to Brittany) and part of north Spain (to Britoña) by the sixth century. At least some of these immigrants appear to have arrived on the Continent as organised communities with Christian leadership. One of these leaders was Riothamus who corresponded with Sidonius Apollinaris.[10]

Gildas said Christian Britons fled across the sea 'singing hymns' after the 'Saxon rebellion'. Once again, the most remarkable thing about the archaeology of fifth-century eastern Britain is, then, its similarity to his story. This is hardly surprising, as he was writing of events that occurred in his parents' generation, but the expectation among contemporary scholars is usually that Gildas 'got it wrong'.[11]

The late fifth century, therefore, left the Germanic population in control of large tracts of eastern Britain, some perhaps otherwise depopulated. In this zone we can see a distinctive late fifth- and sixth-century material culture, derived partly — but not wholly — from Germanic sources.

The nature of the evidence for later fifth- to late sixth-century eastern Britain

For most of the twentieth century, archaeologists and historians focused on the 'Anglo-Saxons' as the key to understanding later fifth- and sixth-century Britain. While archaeological traces of mid-fifth-century Germanic migrants are scarce, after the late fifth

7   *A gilded copper alloy square-headed brooch from Keminghall, Norfolk.* Reproduced with the kind permission of The British Museum

century the archaeological evidence for the 'Anglo-Saxons' becomes plentiful and highly visible. A large number of later fifth- to early seventh-century 'pagan Anglo-Saxon' graves have been identified, usually on the basis of old, poor quality, excavations or chance finds. Complete pots and jewellery from these burials have been collected and recorded for centuries, although only since the time of John Kemble in the late nineteenth century have they been studied in a systematic manner. In the twentieth century, the archaeological study of the artefacts from these cemeteries was pioneered by E.T. Leeds and J.N.L. Myres.[12]

Although many 'Anglo-Saxon' burials are known, therefore, a far smaller, but still substantial number, of these burials have been excavated according to stratigraphical principles and recorded and published in detail. An even smaller number of whole cemeteries have been extensively excavated in this way. Of hundreds of cremation cemeteries known from fifth- and sixth-century eastern Britain, very few (such as Spong Hill) have been anywhere near completely excavated, although a few others (such as Sancton) have been excavated on a large scale. Yet, many hundreds of 'Anglo-Saxon' cremation urns are known, some of which contained burnt or unburned 'grave-goods' in addition to cremated bone representing one or more humans, and sometimes also animals.[13]

So, there are a lot of data about 'Anglo-Saxon' burial practices in the later fifth to late sixth century, although these data differ widely in quality. One important result of archaeological activity devoted to 'Anglo-Saxon' graves has been to accumulate a substantial quantity of artefacts identifiable with general (that is 'parish level') or more detailed locations. Most commonly, dress-fittings or personal objects, pottery, metal or glass vessels, and weapons have been found. This important body of material will be discussed in more detail later in this chapter, but first it is necessary to consider the nature of the settlement evidence of the 'early Anglo-Saxons'.

Although 'Anglo-Saxon' settlements began to attract attention after E.T. Leeds excavated Sutton Courtenay in the 1920s, few of these sites were excavated (or even known about) prior to the 1960s. It was only with advances in methods in the 1950s and '60s that such sites were more readily identified in fieldwork and understood in

8 'Anglo-Saxon' beads from Howletts. Reproduced with the kind permission of The British Museum

excavation. They remain difficult to recognise without excavation even today, because domestic pottery of this period is difficult to recover from fieldwalking, as much of it is easily destroyed by weathering and ploughing.[14]

'Anglo-Saxon' settlement sites have, nonetheless, been discovered both through aerial photography and by chance, often in the course of gravel-extraction, as at the important site at Mucking in Essex. Even today, extensively-excavated 'Anglo-Saxon' settlements are much less common than is often supposed, and when Philip Rahtz wrote a classic review of 'Anglo-Saxon' settlement archaeology in 1977, most such sites were only partially excavated and there were few plans of whole settlements. Despite this, partial plans of many settlements are known today and many separate buildings are published, so some general observations about these sites and structures are possible.[15]

'Early Anglo-Saxon' structures divide into two types: sunken-featured buildings and surface-fast structures (sometimes called 'framed buildings', and less acceptably 'halls'). Sunken-featured buildings (SFBs) or *grubenhäuser* (singular: *grubenhaus*) were timber structures built above a normally rectilinear shallow pit. This pit appears to have been used as the floor in many such structures. However, at the extensively and well-excavated settlement at West Stow, the excavator (Stanley West) claimed that the pits were floored over with planks to form an underfloor space. No evidence for floor-timbers above such pits has been detected elsewhere, but activity at SFBs, often either hearths or rows of fallen clay annular loom-weights (from a vertical loom, post-holes for which have occasionally been found), has been recognised directly on the floor of the pit.[16]

This casts doubt on the interpretation offered at West Stow. The presence of animal skeletons and other debris beneath the apparent floor planking (such as the bones of two

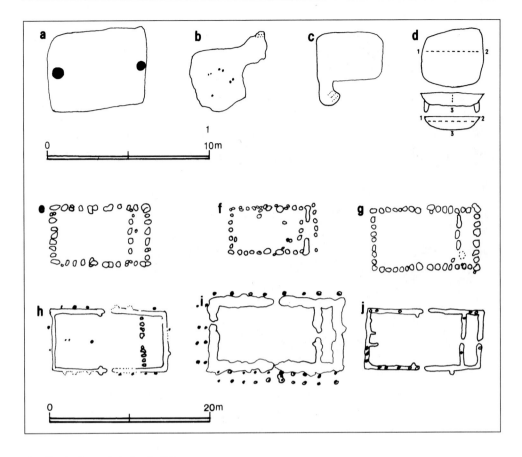

9 *'Anglo-Saxon' timber buildings.*
Top row: Sunken-Featured Buildings (SFBs):
a West Stow SFB 15; b Dorchester on Thames; c Sutton Courtenay XII; d Mucking GH
82, showing cross-sections 1-2 and 3.
Other rows: 'surface-fast' buildings, showing distinctive bipartite plan:
e Chalton A20; f Mucking house 3; g Mucking house 1; h Cowdrey's Down C8; i
Yeavering C3; j Chalton AZ1.
(After Zimmermann, Hamerow, Rahtz, James, Marshall and Millett and Dixon)

dogs beneath what was the 'floor' of SFB 16 at West Stow) suggests that the planks were at least secondary to the original form of the structure. One possibility is that the apparent remains of burnt floor planks, found in SFB 15, represent a fallen timber platform set at the level of rafters above the building. Such an interpretation cannot be countered by the evidence of hearths overlying the edge of the SFB pit found in buildings SFB 44 and 49, because this could represent later hearths built across a disused and filled pit, as Martin Welch has pointed out. It seems more likely that the simple 'tent-like' interpretation of SFBs proposed prior to the excavation at West Stow may need to be reinstated, although variations within the structural tradition represented by SFBs may be expected.[17]

Surface-fast buildings are easier to interpret in structural terms. These were clearly rectilinear timber structures with organic roofing, probably of thatch, and planking, earth or straw flooring. Rahtz suggested that these developed from post-built to wall-trench construction during the course of the 'Anglo-Saxon period'. Evidence from excavated settlements such as at West Stow, Mucking, Chalton, Bishopstone and Cowdrey's Down, would seem to bear this out (**colour plate 5**).[18]

Chronological problems exist at all of these settlements. At Chalton, the few datable finds suggest a seventh-century date, and the site may not pre-date 600 at all. At Cowdrey's Down radiocarbon dates are the clearest indication of the settlement-chronology. This might support a seventh-century date for the settlement, although the occupation may have begun in the later sixth century, and it is possible that a relative scarcity of SFBs relates to this. At Cowdrey's Down there are no SFBs and at Chalton there was only one, an unusually large example. However, SFBs are rarer on chalk subsoils (as at Cowdrey's Down and Chalton) than on gravel or sand, so this might simply be a result of geology constraining or enabling the construction of specific structural types.

At West Stow and Mucking SFBs cluster around surface-fast post-built structures, suggesting that they have an ancillary function to these. The combination of SFBs around a smaller number of post-built structures might be seen, therefore, as characteristically later fifth and sixth century, with the use of fenced compounds around buildings, as at Cowdery's Down and Chalton, a later sixth- and seventh-century characteristic. A few settlements apparently with only SFBs — such as Abbot's Worthy — may date to the fifth and sixth centuries, and the earliest phase of the Mucking settlement may have comprised only SFBs.[19]

Superficially, Mucking and West Stow are large settlements, but Stanley West and Helena Hamerow (who analysed, but did not excavate, Mucking) suggest that each site shows evidence of a shifting settlement pattern. Hamerow argues that gradual shifts within a settlement area characterised 'early Anglo-Saxon' settlements, and are paralleled elsewhere in Migration-period Europe. She interprets these sites as a few farms, moving their location over successive phases (perhaps generations) of occupation. West argued exactly this pattern for West Stow, observing that the number of such 'farm-units' grew, possibly due to population growth.[20]

This suggests a contrast with Romano-British and fifth- to sixth-century western British settlements, and with 'Anglo-Saxon' cemeteries, which usually stayed in the same locations for centuries. The most obvious explanation is that the social structure of these settlements was such that generational change necessitated new buildings, as new households were formed. This may suggest that these new settlement types were associated with a new type of non-British social organization, but as we have seen this would involve very small communities of people at each location, at most a few families. At West Stow the excavated cemetery hints that the settlement had a small population, perhaps at each phase no more than 50 or so, but one in which social ranking between individuals is also visible. As Chris Scull has pointed out, this may well suggest that each settlement contained a 'lineage' group, a kin-group such as a 'clan' or 'extended family' claiming common descent.[21]

One site which may be an exception to this pattern is at the limit of the area discussed in this chapter, in the Vale of Pickering, Yorkshire. Dominic Powlesland, the excavator, has argued that West Heslerton 'Anglo-Saxon' settlement shows a very different pattern. This shares structural similarities with sites further south, such as West Stow or Mucking, but Powlesland interprets the settlement as showing 'functional zoning', where different activities were confined to distinct areas of the site, rather than shifts over time. That is, what might appear to be chronological differences at other sites may, on the basis of Powlesland's excavation at West Heslerton, be considered mere functional differences within larger, but synchronous, sets of buildings.[22]

Powlesland's work is challenging and demands careful consideration. There is no reason to doubt the skill of his very large-scale excavation of the site, but both models of 'Anglo-Saxon' settlement form are incompatible, unless one argues for regional differences or interprets West Heslerton as an atypical site. Recent surveys and regional studies have produced no evidence to suggest a wide range of variation within 'Anglo-Saxon' settlements of the fifth and sixth centuries and it seems unlikely that regional variation explains this anomaly.

The most clearly functionally-distinct zone of West Heslerton was an area comprised wholly of SFBs, given over to craftwork. This specialised zone of the settlement may imply craftworkers employed by others within the community and indicate that surplus agricultural products to support those not involved in food-production were continually available. This, and possible hints of high-status artefacts, may imply that West Heslerton was an elite site. Although the structures show a great conformity, this need not be a counter-argument as status could have been displayed in ways or even 'disguised' by an illusion of equality.

The Romano-British background of the settlement supports the view that it was an atypical site. Late Roman occupation there included a pagan shrine and ancillary structures. This is the only known case of a Romano-British shrine being used as an 'Anglo-Saxon' settlement site, although others were used for burials, and pagan religious associations — or the role of the locality as a focal place — could have been used to legitimate an 'Anglo-Saxon' pagan elite resident at the site. One parallel — albeit later (from the late sixth century) and further north — may be at Yeavering. There, a British ritual focus became an 'Anglo-Saxon' pagan royal site mentioned in Bede's *Ecclesiastical History*, although this was north of Hadrian's Wall. The first 'Anglo-Saxon' phase at Yeavering was a much smaller site than West Heslerton, but had no more elaborate architecture. Later Yeavering acquired elaborate timber halls for which it is archaeologically famous. The analogy is only partial, but perhaps the British background gave each site special associations to the 'Anglo-Saxon' elite.

Perhaps the settlement did not shift location because it was not affected by the same generational patterns of household formation as 'normal' farming communities. The site could even have retained a religious function (as apparently did Yeavering), especially given the focal role of shrines in the Iron Age Germanic world, as at Gudme and Lundeborg. The main difficulty with this latter suggestion is that no obvious temple of fifth- or sixth-century date has been found at West Heslerton, but 'Anglo-Saxon' pagans there may have worshipped outdoors or at the Roman-period shrine.[23]

If West Heslerton was an elite site, this implies both an 'Anglo-Saxon' elite and that other similar sites existed in eastern Britain during the later fifth to mid-sixth centuries. But no other potentially elite settlements of this date have been found in eastern Britain: the so-called 'Anglo-Saxon palace-sites', such as Sprouston, Milfield, Yeavering, Cowage Farm (near Malmesbury) and Atcham appear to date from the later sixth to eighth centuries.[24]

One approach to recognising high-status 'Anglo-Saxon' settlements of this date has been to claim that all visible 'Anglo-Saxon' settlements are high status! Nicholas Higham has argued that virtually all the recognisably Germanic aspects of fifth- and sixth-century eastern Britain were associated with the ruling elite, so that the 'Anglo-Saxon' settlements and cemeteries mentioned above represent the burial places of leading families, rather than whole rural populations.[25]

SFBs have generally been considered characteristically 'Germanic', but surface-fast buildings have been likened to Romano-British structures by Philip Dixon. The degree to which these buildings might be interpreted as wholly British has been debated among the proponents of this approach. Dixon has proposed typological similarities with Dunston's Clump, an early Romano-British settlement, although others see 'Anglo-Saxon' structures as a combination of British and Germanic features. On this basis, Higham has suggested that the 'Anglo-Saxon' settlements were built by Britons for their 'Anglo-Saxon' lords, but occupied as elite sites by 'Anglo-Saxons'. The British affinities of the structures derive — in Higham's view — from the use of forced British labour to construct the houses of 'Anglo-Saxon' lords.[26]

This all depends upon how similar 'Anglo-Saxon' timber buildings and Romano-British timber buildings really are. As Dixon has observed, these structures show much greater similarities across eastern Britain than those seen in burial evidence — perhaps suggesting a common British background shared by all parts of the region. But specific similarities between British and 'Anglo-Saxon' buildings, not also shared by north-west Continental European buildings, are harder to detect. Dunston's Clump, the most frequently compared Romano-British site, was disused long before AD 400, and so may be irrelevant to the issue.[27]

Typical non-villa timber Late Roman buildings in eastern Britain are 'roundhouses' (curvilinear structures) and less commonly rectilinear buildings of entirely different plan to usual 'Anglo-Saxon' structures. Often these Romano-British settlements were enclosed by banks and ditches, while 'Anglo-Saxon' settlements are not. So the similarities may be much less than often claimed. On the basis of detailed comparisons with Continental buildings of this date, W.H. Zimmermann has pointed out that they offer possible analogies for 'Anglo-Saxon' buildings and there seems no reason to evoke British construction.[28]

However, some late fifth- and sixth-century settlements in eastern Britain might not be 'Anglo-Saxon' at all. For example, at Frilford, Oxfordshire, and Chalton, Hampshire, grass-tempered pottery — probably dating to the sixth century — was found at neighbouring Romano-British farm sites. At Bentley Green, Hampshire, the 'Anglo-Saxon' settlement sited 500m west of a Romano-British settlement has nothing distinctively Germanic. The fourth-century Romano-British settlement at Maydensole Farm, Kent, was followed by a large post-hole building. An SFB was associated with the

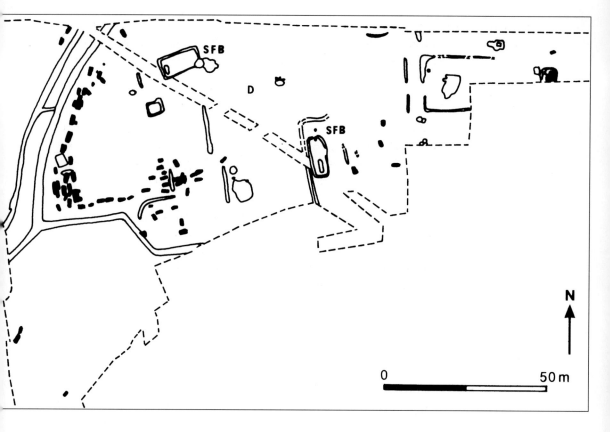

10 Late Roman Sunken-Featured Buildings at Alington Avenue, Dorset. Graves shown in black. (After Woodward)

fourth-century occupation, but there is nothing specifically 'Germanic' about the possible post-Roman building at this site too. These might well be the settlements of Britons living within areas which also had 'Anglo-Saxon' communities.[29]

As this shows, SFBs have been identified at Romano-British sites. Others include Monkton in Kent and Appleby Magna in the Midlands. This casts doubt on just how 'characteristically Germanic' they are, but these structures are also found widely in Germanic contexts on the Continent, so it does not mean that they, rather than surface-fast buildings, are British. Again, they cannot be specifically associated with Britons or 'Anglo-Saxons', nor can their presence indicate high social status, unless one adopts Higham's view that they are storage pits for food-renders paid by subservient Britons.[30]

The lack of apparent status variation visible between almost all 'Anglo-Saxon' settlements dating to the fifth and sixth centuries is not matched by a lack of variability in the apparent wealth and status of graves. In inhumation graves, 'grave-goods' are usually taken as an indication of status, and in cremation cemeteries it has been argued that a narrower range of status variation is visible, although Catherine Hills and Martin Carver have both argued that ranking on the basis of grave-goods included in urns is indicative of

67

11 Two copper-alloy cruciform brooches, a typical artefact of the 'Anglian' area, Lakenheath, Suffolk.
Reproduced with the kind permission of The British Museum

status. Julian Richards has proposed the fascinating interpretation that the shape of cremation urns may reflect social position, whether age, gender, kinship or social rank. Thus the apparent lack of status variation within cremation cemeteries may be illusory.[31]

Burial practice and artefacts have also played a central role in debates about the Germanic migration and the origin and composition of the migrants. Although Bede seems to have known nothing about the fifth or sixth centuries independently of his written sources, his picture of the ethnic or cultural divisions of this period has been extraordinarily influential in shaping modern interpretations. Bede tells us that the most important Germanic settlers were the 'Angles', 'Saxons' and the 'Jutes', each of these originating in a specific zone of the Continent and connected with a specific part of eastern Britain. In his depiction of the migration, the Angles settled in areas called East Anglia, Middle Anglia, Mercia, Lindsey and Northumbria by his time. The Saxons settled further south, in areas he knew as the East Saxon, West Saxon and South Saxon kingdoms. The Jutes occupied Kent and the Isle of Wight. Bede also appears to have heard that other peoples took part in the same migration, but does not assign particular areas to them in this way. It is interesting that other peoples (notably the Frisians — who may or may not be the same as the 'Saxons' in Bede) were also connected with sixth-century Britain by Procopius.[32]

The picture presented by Bede looks suspiciously as if it has been projected back from the seventh- and eighth-century political geography with which he was familiar. However, this picture also resembles that found if we look at the archaeological evidence for sixth-century Britain. Thus, although Bede's account is likely to derive from his knowledge of later circumstances, distribution-patterns of artefact types and cemeteries of the early to mid-sixth century have been claimed to show the same divisions.[33]

In the fifth century, cremation cemeteries were established throughout Bede's 'Anglian' area. In these, cremations were usually placed in pottery vessels ('cremation urns') which were buried in small pits to form cemeteries. The urns show close stylistic affinities, in form and decoration, with the cemeteries of the areas from which Bede believed the Angles migrated. As Catherine Hills has carefully demonstrated, these urns were filled using mortuary customs — such as the placing of miniature objects in the urn — identical to those of this area of northern Europe. It is hard to doubt that they were products of the same culture, and probably population. It may be valid to term this culture 'Anglian' (**colour plate 6**).[34]

In Bede's 'Saxon' zone too, there is a series of late fifth- and sixth-century inhumation burials with objects showing stylistic and formal affinities with the Continental area he ascribes to the 'Saxons'. While most of the cemeteries of the 'Saxon' area on the Continent contain cremation burials, as we have seen that the inhumation rite can be explained by contact with the British population during migration. Even the Jutish associations of Kent and the Isle of Wight have been argued to be borne out by archaeological evidence. Objects placed in inhumation burials there have been claimed to show affinities of the same sort with artefacts from Jutland, the 'ancestral homeland' of the Jutes in Bede's account.[35]

Bede is often said to be confirmed by archaeology in these respects, at least regarding the sixth century, but we should be wary of assuming that this evidence verifies his account. Region-names and associations might be more long-lived in popular memory than historical details, and groups later important in the kingdoms known to him might have over-emphasised their earlier roles. Archaeology appears to confirm this, in that we know from material evidence of connections — and probably cultural groups — which Bede omits from his account. For example, John Hines has shown that southern Scandinavians were important migrants in fifth- and sixth-century East Anglia, while — as Vera Evison first argued — Frankish connections seem to have been a lot more important (especially in Kent) than Bede tells us.[36]

So, even if later kingdom-names contained some hint of earlier cultural affinities (which is unclear from this evidence) Bede's account cannot be 'the whole story'. In particular, he shows himself to have been extremely hostile to the Britons, and appears to have excluded them from his version of events wherever possible.

Britons and Anglo-Saxons in late fifth- to late sixth-century eastern Britain

In the cremations not only Germanic artefacts, but Germanic burial customs, seem to have been widely in use. 'Anglo-Saxon' cremations sometimes occur in Roman-period cremation cemeteries (as at St John's Cricket Field and Girton in Cambridge), but fourth-century cremations are rare in those areas which have large numbers of 'Anglo-Saxon' cremation burials. Indeed the distribution of fourth-century cremations almost exactly excludes the area of fifth- and sixth-century 'Anglo-Saxon' cremation cemeteries! So the chances of the 'Anglo-Saxon' rite being a continuation of that of Late Roman Britain are low.[37]

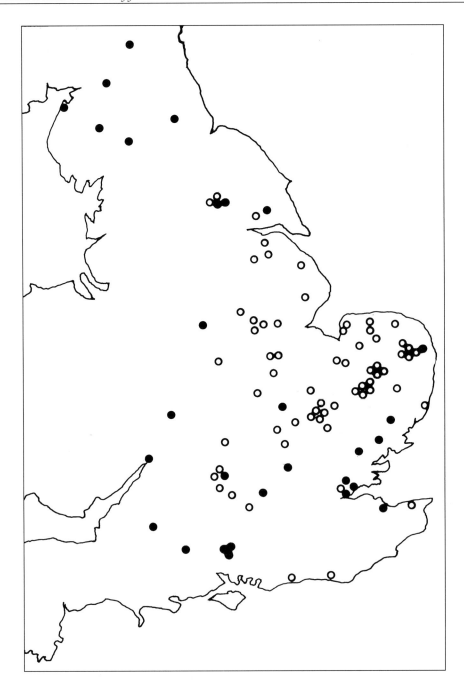

12 Late Roman cremations (filled circles) and 'Anglo-Saxon' cremations (open circles). (After White and O'Brien)

The earliest fifth-century inhumation burials containing Germanic-style weapons are probably those of Germanic migrants, not least because weapon-burial is unknown in Late Roman Britain. But later fifth-century and sixth-century 'Anglo-Saxon' inhumations are not obviously those of Germanic communities. 'Germanic' objects were sometimes deposited in graves, but Romano-British customs such as burial with a single brooch on the shoulder (to hold a cloak), burial with hobnail boots, and decapitation also occur. These might all represent continuities in burial rites from Roman Britain, and focusing on burials with grave-goods alone overlooks the large number of inhumations without 'grave-goods' or with few grave-goods. In particular, the relative rarity of the most distinctively 'Germanic' objects in late fifth- and sixth-century 'Anglo-Saxon' cemeteries is often ignored. For example, Härke has noted that only 47% of all males were buried with weapons, and few men were buried with anything else distinctively 'Germanic'.[38]

Although most women in 'Anglo-Saxon' cemeteries wore 'gender-specific' items, at any one time only a few women were buried dressed in full 'Anglo-Saxon' costume. Dividing the total burial population by an approximate 30 year generation and the duration of the cemetery's use, one can get far lower figures for the use of 'Anglo-Saxon' brooch-sets. For example, at Holywell Row, Suffolk, we see perhaps five women in each generation dressed this way and at Bergh Apton perhaps three, at Swaffham, Norfolk, possibly a single woman per generation wore an 'Anglo-Saxon' brooch set. These could represent a set for the senior female member of each of the households at a site such as West Stow, but no-one else, at each of these sites.[39]

Thus, in inhumation cemeteries a minority of people per generation were afforded the sort of burials that typify the 'early Anglo-Saxons' in the modern archaeological imagination. These burial rites could well be 'badges of rank' or identity — the interpretation for male 'weapon burials' proposed by Härke, who would link this rank to ethnicity.

Instead of thinking of all burials in late sixth-century eastern Britain as 'Anglo-Saxon cemeteries', it might be more valid to see at least four types of burial taking place, often within the same cemeteries:[40]

1 Cremation burial resembling that common in 'Germanic' north-west Continental Europe.

2 Inhumation burials with grave-goods, some of which are of 'Germanic' north-west Continental European types.

3 Inhumation burials with characteristics found in burials in fourth-century Britain, such as decapitation or 'crouched' burial posture, but rare in fifth- and sixth-century western Britain.

4 Inhumation burials similar to those in fifth- and sixth-century western Britain.

Cemeteries comprised only of cremations (type 1) or 'Anglo-Saxon' inhumations of type 2 are known. That at Queensford Farm contained both 'British' types (3 and 4), and all the other types occur in inhumation cemeteries otherwise of type 1 or type 2 burials. All of these types of burial could apparently coexist within a single cemetery and there is evidence, as at Leatherhead, where 'crouched' accompanied and unaccompanied inhumations occur in the same cemetery, that one burial rite could affect another.

Types 3 and 4 could be interpreted either as belonging to Britons living in 'Anglo-Saxon' contexts or 'Anglo-Saxons' who had adopted British customs. The fact that indigenous burial rites persisted suggests that the 'Anglo-Saxons' did not impose their own customs on the entire population by force. It is more likely that inhumation customs were a matter of personal or family choice, not collective expressions of group-affiliation applying to the 'burial population' of a cemetery as whole. For example, three 'British' penannular brooches were found at Morningthorpe 'Anglo-Saxon' cemetery, worn at the shoulder singly in British fashion.[41]

As we have seen in the previous chapter, accompanied inhumation burials are found throughout Europe in the later fifth and sixth centuries, and associated with a range of peoples — Goths, Franks and others. Inhumation was found in north Germany and Scandinavia, as well as the Roman Empire, during the Late Roman period and (as Edward James has argued) accompanied inhumation became apparently acceptable during the late fifth century to sub-Roman citizens in Gaul. The ethnic affiliation of type 2 burials (that is, 'Anglo-Saxon inhumation burials' of 'classic' form) seems therefore slight (**colour plate 7**).[42]

Rather, we should see accompanied type 2 inhumation burials as status indicators. Härke has shown that social rank was both signalled by weapons placed in inhumation graves, and that this rank was conferred by birth. Children too young to fight and those with medical reasons rendering them unable to fight would be unlikely to have used the weapons placed in their graves.[43]

Recent work by Sally Crawford has also discovered social position reflected in burial customs of the 'Anglo-Saxon' inhumation graves of children. Similarly, work by Ellen-Jane Pader noted the symbolic role of objects and their locations in these graves, again suggesting that the messages conveyed were not simply encoded in the selection of grave-goods for ethnic reasons.[44]

The use of grave-goods in inhumation graves can, then, be seen as a reflection of social position, especially gender (shown in choice of different grave-goods for males and females), age and social rank, and these may all have been related in a society based on the family. These customs were largely 'Germanic' in origin, but acceptable to Late Roman and sub-Roman provincials in Gaul. That is, 'accompanied' late fifth- and sixth-century inhumation cemeteries do not necessitate Germanic ethnic origins, but the use of a shared 'code' to convey social position.

If type 2 accompanied inhumation burials need not be those of Germanic settlers, or even those coerced into adopting aspects of Germanic culture, then their distribution does not necessarily tell us anything about the spread of 'Anglo-Saxon' domination or the spread of Germanic population. The usual view that plotting the distribution of such cemeteries by date gives us a detailed impression of the spread of 'Anglo-Saxon' control, if not of actual 'Anglo-Saxons', may be misleading. All it documents, from the later fifth century onwards, is the distribution of a burial custom conveying social position, ultimately of partly Germanic origin.

The use of objects with Germanic cultural connections shows that these people were *in contact* with Germanic culture, and this may be a more fruitful line of inquiry. However, finds from both western Britain and from Late Roman Continental Europe show that Germanic artefacts found in inhumation cemeteries do not mean that the people buried with them had adopted the complete portfolio of Germanic culture. Unless Germanic-style objects were used in a distinctively Germanic way, for example as fittings for traditional folk-costume (*Tracht*) as Hayo Vierck suggested, they may only imply contact with people producing these objects. The use of such artefacts to convey meaning within a burial code of Germanic origin suggests close contact with Germanic culture, but this is unsurprising: as we have already seen, many parts of the area where these cemeteries occur were probably under 'Anglo-Saxon' political control from the later fifth century onwards.[45]

From the sixth century onward, regional variations in dress-style are visible in terms of the disposition of objects in 'Anglo-Saxon' burials, broadly reflecting the 'Bedan' regions already mentioned. The one major exception to the 'Bedan' regions, in respect to dress styles, is Kent. In Kent, Frankish fashions appear to have had some influence on 'Anglo-Saxon' clothes, but this is hardly surprising given the ease of cross-Channel sea transport. The spread of these dress-styles could be an index of the formation of new collective identities, perhaps as the outcome of gradual trends in the adoption of 'Anglo-Saxon' culture from the fifth century onward. This might suggest that even in the 'obviously Anglo-Saxon' inhumation cemeteries, 'Anglo-Saxon' identities were only becoming dominant in the sixth century. Even then such clothes (and so potentially this process of identity-formation) remained restricted to only a minority of the population. Others in society still chose different burial customs (types 3 and 4), and presumably separate identities.[46]

Although cremation seems an entirely Germanic form of burial at this date, there is therefore a serious problem in 'Anglo-Saxon' archaeology: exactly where *was* the Germanic population in later fifth- and sixth-century Britain?

Where were the Anglo-Saxons in the later fifth and sixth centuries?

If we want to trace 'the Germanic origins of Anglo-Saxon England', we must return to the only burial rite which may be exclusively Germanic: cremation. 'Anglian' cremation practices governed the minutiae of burial ritual, the choice of urn and the mode of burial. That is, the details of getting this burial rite 'correct' seem to have mattered to those burying the dead in this fashion and they, therefore, probably shared beliefs and values with Continental peoples who used these burial customs. These were people acting in a wholly 'Germanic' manner for reasons which might well relate to wholly 'Germanic' rather than 'Romano-British' or 'Germano-British' beliefs.

Some cremation cemeteries were clearly very large, and their size implies that people from several settlements used them, if we assume that each settlement contained only a few farms. On this basis, cemeteries such as Loveden Hill or Sancton would have served people from a wide area. Both the transport of the dead to them in procession and the

13 An 'Anglo-Saxon' cremation urn from Lovedon, Lincolnshire, inscribed with runes.
Reproduced with the kind permission of The British Museum

cremation itself might well have been part of the burial ritual. Evidence for where cremation took place is sparse, and only two possible pyre sites at cemeteries are known in Britain, at Snape and Sancton, although this may be due to issues of preservation and the scale and quality of excavation.[47]

The method of cremation seems to have been that a clothed body was placed on the ground surface, facing upward. Grave-goods were positioned around the corpse and a pyre constructed over the whole. This was lit, and when the cremation had been achieved, the ashes were selectively recovered. Attention appears to have been paid to retrieving the skulls and upper body bones, although sometimes long bones were also recovered. Although a few un-urned cremations are known (as at Alton and Worthy Park), most ashes were then placed in a cremation urn.[48]

Several individuals are often found deposited in one urn, and the rite of opening the urn and depositing each individual's ashes frequently occurred at the cemetery as part of burial rites. This necessitates some way of identifying the correct urn: correlation between the contents and form of the urn shows that the choice was not random. The uncovering and reburial of urns, their marking by small mounds of soil — like miniature barrows? — or with piles of stone, may have been part of the ritual. Cremation burial was a complex process, probably lasting days.[49]

The use of shared burial sites between a large number of farms, probably those of separate extended families, suggests a sense of communal identity and supports the argument of shared cultural or religious identity. If funeral processions had to pass through land occupied by other families, then this too (less strongly) might suggest cooperation or assistance. There are hints of family burials clustering in cemeteries, and at Appledown and Alton small rectangular post-hole structures — like small houses — were constructed over cremations, with ashes in the post-holes, arguably implying the veneration of ancestors. Ancestral origins may, therefore, have been important in how this shared identity was imagined.[50]

Given the Germanic origins of the burial rites, of the material culture involved and — to judge from the runic messages occasionally placed on cremation urns — the language of these cremating people, the common beliefs and culture concerned might be termed 'Germanic'. Whether in the sixth century this Germanic identity was understood in Bede's terms as 'Anglian' must be uncertain, but this presents an almost wholly 'Germanic' image of shared belief and culture. These people were, it appears, 'real Anglo-Saxons', in the sense that their ancestors had traversed the North Sea in ships, and made their homes in eastern Britain.[51]

Mixed messages: Anglo-Saxon inhumation burial

'Anglo-Saxon' inhumation cemeteries are usually much smaller than cremation burial grounds. Many may represent burial grounds of specific settlements. For example, Phase 1 of the Buckland cemetery at Dover in Kent seems to have catered for a community of only 10 people. Such cemeteries may be family- or kin-cemeteries (a point supported by some skeletal data), and perhaps were more commonly adjacent to the settlements that they served than were cremation cemeteries.[52]

We have already seen a British component to 'Anglo-Saxon' inhumation burial customs and this may also be seen in artefactual terms. Among the most common forms of brooch found in inhumation cemeteries are those with 'circular' shapes, such as 'quoit' and 'disc' brooches. These seem to derive (at least partly) from Romano-British prototypes, although such 'circular' brooches were also common in north Germany and Scandinavia, and here again we may see aspects of material culture acceptable to both Britons and 'Anglo-Saxons' alike.[53]

That 'Anglo-Saxon' inhumation cemeteries represent a 'fusion' of British and Germanic customs could be taken to suggest that the families using these cemeteries were equally 'mixed' in culture. As the settlement evidence already outlined might relate to both British and Germanic antecedents, both settlements and cemeteries may have catered for people with a 'pick-and-mix' approach to cultural practice. But there is no indication that Germanic cultural practices were always dominant in this, and often the very cultural practices adopted were those employed by both fourth- and fifth-century Britons and found in north Germany and Scandinavia.

To give a well-researched illustration of this last point, the habit of burial at prehistoric ritual monuments was widely found in Late Romano-British and 'Anglo-Saxon' contexts, as the author, Howard Williams and Betty O'Brien have demonstrated. This custom was also found in 'free Germania' in the fifth and sixth centuries as Eva Thate has shown, and

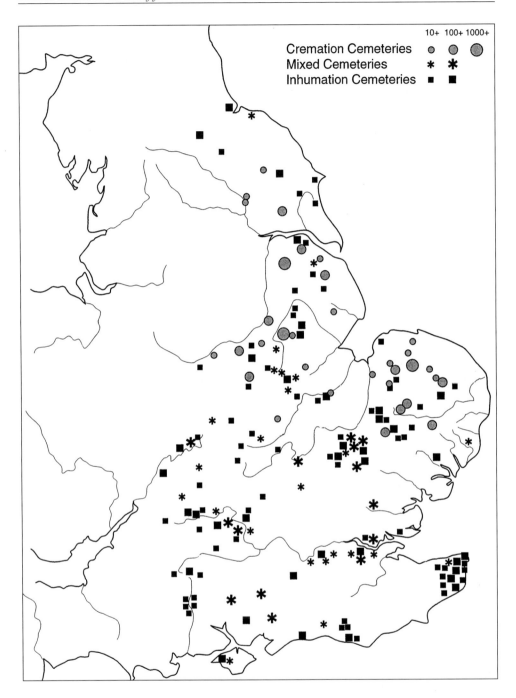

14 *Cremation in fifth- and sixth-century Britain.* Drawing by Howard Williams

15 *A quoit brooch and disc brooch, 'Anglo-Saxon' brooch-types arguably derivative of Late Roman metalwork.* Reproduced with the kind permission of The British Museum

was probably acceptable to both British and Germanic cultural communities in Britain. Interestingly, it is also found in Christian contexts in the fifth- and sixth-century west of Britain and may relate to superstitions about the landscape, not religious beliefs, at least in Britain.[54]

The men and women buried without grave-goods, or with few grave-goods, could well represent the most 'British' component of the same families. As grave-goods were not used by all Britons as status symbols, some of these could have been of senior rank, but have displayed this in other forms than costly burial. To give an example, a prone burial of an adult man at Collingbourne Ducis, accompanied by a single Romano-British brooch and an inlaid late fifth- or early sixth-century buckle at his waist, might represent a high-status Briton.[55]

If type 2 inhumations represent a 'fusion' of Germanic and British cultures, then we might expect them to be common in contexts where these cultures were able to mix most easily. These contexts may be where there are gaps in the distribution of cremation cemeteries in zones where cremation predominates, or on the periphery — especially the western periphery — of zones with predominantly cremation burials. This is exactly what we find: inhumation burials occur on the western periphery of the distribution of sixth-century 'Anglo-Saxon' burials and fill out the gaps in the distribution of cremation burials where cremation otherwise predominates.[56]

Where inhumation and cremation cemeteries occur closely together, inhumation cemeteries were frequently established later than most cremation cemeteries. This is found in Lincolnshire, East Anglia and Kent, and may suggest that the Germanic population used cremation on its arrival, and then mixed British-Germanic communities adopted elements of Germanic culture alongside British customs. Moreover, the proportion of inhumation burials in predominantly cremation cemeteries appears to rise over time. Perhaps this shows that what had been wholly Germanic communities started to adopt aspects of British culture.[57]

Purely cremation cemeteries occupy a much more restricted distribution than usually imagined. The western periphery of the distribution of 'early Anglo-Saxon cemeteries' contains inhumation cemeteries. 'Mixed cemeteries' (containing inhumations and cremations) seem to represent yet another band of gradation between predominately cremation cemeteries to unaccompanied inhumation cemeteries.

The only truly 'Anglo-Saxon' area — if we mean by this term 'inhabited by Germanic migrants and their descendants, with a largely Germanic culture and retaining a Germanic group identity' — may be the 'Anglian' area in which cremation predominated. The number of self-identifying 'Germanic' people might have declined as the proportion of cremation burials declines away from this area. Whether most of the people buried in inhumation graves considered themselves descended from Germanic migrants is another matter, although if the arguments proposed in the previous chapter are correct, they largely lived under 'Saxon' rule.

Paganism and Christianity in fifth- and sixth-century eastern Britain

The most surprising aspect of interpreting 'Anglo-Saxon' inhumation cemeteries in this way is that all the communities they represent need not have been wholly pagan. It is frequently assumed that accompanied burials are always pagan but this was certainly not true of every accompanied fifth- or sixth-century inhumation in Europe.[58]

Almost wherever one looks in the Late Antique world there is evidence for the use of 'grave-goods', in the sense of objects deposited in the tomb. As in 'Anglo-Saxon' cemeteries, some of these objects were worn as dress, some placed in the grave. Those placed in the grave may have been put there for symbolic reasons, for sentiment, because they belonged to the dead or were owed as dues. Continental European Christian elites were often buried with grave-goods in the fifth or sixth century; jewellery and glass vessels were even placed in graves in the Vatican.[59]

In the West, the Franks developed burial customs like those of the inhumation cemeteries of eastern Britain only *after* their conversion to Christianity (I am grateful to Professor Edward James for this point). Their leaders were buried in this manner close to, or under, the churches they founded.

That is, not only was there nothing specifically pagan to contemporaries about burial with objects, but in Frankia they may be associated with a society undergoing conversion, rather than an entirely pagan one. One could well 'read' the need to demonstrate status and kinship as expressions of social stress, accompanying important changes in other aspects of everyday life, such as religious belief. If so, the inhumation cemeteries in eastern Britain might be understood as part of a much more widely distributed rite, perhaps partly of Germanic origin. The parallel with Frankia may be more profound than the deposition of shared types of objects and the use of Frankish imports in graves. That Richard Hodges has suggested that accompanied inhumation was adopted by the Britons in emulation of the Franks suggests how alike these two traditions of accompanied burial appear.[60]

The mere use of grave-goods cannot, therefore, be taken as an indicator of pagan religious belief. However, this is exactly what is generally taken for granted about 'Anglo-Saxon' inhumation. But the best parallel is with a society (late fifth- and sixth-century Frankia) undergoing conversion to Christianity, not a completely pagan one. Of course, it does not make it likely that everyone buried in an 'Anglo-Saxon' inhumation cemetery was a Christian, but it is equally uncertain that they were all pagans. In the same way as accompanied inhumation cemeteries do not enable us to identify 'Germanic areas' in the way usually supposed, they do not allow us to identify fifth- and sixth-century pagans without additional analysis.

It seems much more likely that these cemeteries contain pagan Germanic migrants or their pagan descendants, pagan Britons and Christian Britons. They might indicate a situation in which challenges to perceived social status and kin-relations existed, and these were to be reinforced through burial practices displaying them. A possible reason might be the juxtaposition of different religious beliefs and forms of social organization. It also seems plausible that contacts between Britons and Germanic migrants or their descendants, particularly intermarriage, will have led to conversion of some of the latter to Christianity, as in other parts of the West. There, no extensive conversion to Germanic paganism took place, perhaps because this too was associated with specific group-identities or did not attempt to proselytise, and Christian 'Germanic' elites eventually took control. But in fifth-century Gaul, for instance, pagan Franks dwelt alongside Christian Gallo-Romans in the same communities.

Because Bede said that 'Anglo-Saxon England' before Augustine's arrival was wholly ruled by pagan kings, does not mean that there were no Christians among the fifth- and sixth-century Germanic population. Nor that these converts could not have comprised the ruling elite in some part(s) of the zone usually termed 'pagan Anglo-Saxon England'. Again, we do not know whether or not this was the case.

The truth is that only Bede tells us that no 'Anglo-Saxons' converted to Christianity prior to the Augustinian mission, with which he felt a strong affinity. Other evidence makes it abundantly clear that Bede wanted to suppress the history of any missionary activity he saw as hostile to the Papal Church. Even if eastern Britain had been teeming with British Christian missionaries, Bede would not have let us know. Bede's testimony is of no value as negative evidence concerning the 'Anglo-Saxons', and we might note that he is concerned only with the conversion of the 'Anglo-Saxon' *gens* (people), not with all the population of eastern Britain. One could read Bede to imply that the British population of eastern Britain might have been Christian.

The direct proof of the survival of Christianity in eastern Britain in the fifth and sixth centuries is likely to be as difficult to detect as is the Church in fourth-century Roman Britain. In the archaeology of Roman Britain we would generally take the following as possible evidence of Christian burial: a lack of grave-goods, the presence of Christian symbols on objects within the grave or tombstones, inscriptions with Christian content, and the existence of regular rows of east-west burials. The existence of church buildings or martyrial shrines more strongly indicate a Christian population.

A large minority of the graves in 'Anglo-Saxon' inhumation cemeteries have no, or very few, grave-goods. Such burials might be those of the very poor, but they might

16 'Bucket' from Long Wittenham showing Christian scenes. Reproduced with the kind permission of The British Museum

represent the part of the local population adhering strictly to Late Roman, perhaps Christian, burial practice. As the group of burials with 'Anglo-Saxon' brooch-sets or weapons would seem to be smaller in most cemeteries than is this group of graves, one could argue for the possibility that there was a larger number of Christians in these cemeteries than usually considered conceivable, even on this basis. Given that what may be pagan British burial customs, such as decapitation, are identifiable among the dead in these cemeteries, then the argument that those not afforded characteristically pagan burial practices of British or Germanic origin could be Christian might be strengthened. This need not necessitate a substantial Christian population in eastern Britain, but permits us to take the possibility seriously.[61]

A further (although hitherto neglected) point enhances this possibility. More specifically Christian objects have been found in 'Anglo-Saxon' inhumation burials in Britain than the total found in Roman-period and fifth- to sixth-century British and 'Early Christian' Irish burials combined! To give an example, there is no reason why the two burials with Christian objects at Long Wittenham should be seen as pagan. Martin Henig and Paul Booth have argued independently that one of these may be the grave of a local Christian.[62]

Nor is this material geographically limited. Like the Long Wittenham burial, a grave at Strood, near the Roman-period town of Rochester, contained an object with Christian symbols, and one of a group of east-west graves at Risely Horton Kirkby, Kent, contained an imported glass bowl with a Chi-Rho symbol. This is close to Darenth villa, where contemporary structures were built on and around the principal villa buildings. The 42 unaccompanied graves in the cemetery could represent a Christian population surviving from the villa estate. More ambiguous, but potentially Christian, are objects bearing cross-symbols, such as the bracelet from Chatham Lines grave XVII with 'Celtic' interlace and an equal-armed cross among the motifs incorporated in its design. Obviously a cross might merely be a decorative motif, but it could have carried Christian symbolism.

Of course, Christian objects might be owned or placed in graves by pagans, or the graves might be those of Franks. These are the standard interpretations of the examples above and could be correct. But they might also be Christian graves in 'Anglo-Saxon' England, well before Augustine's mission, and there are 'pagan Anglo-Saxon cemeteries' that look very Christian in general. At Saffron Walden, 200 graves contained few finds, except for an assemblage of seventh-century or later date in one woman's grave. This could be an earlier Christian cemetery, used in the seventh century for a 'Final Phase' burial, or a wholly seventh-century cemetery. Vera Evison has argued that some burials in the nearby Great Chesterford cemetery are also Christian, and further to the west graves at Beckford have already been identified as potentially Christian in the final report on that site.[63]

Roman coins were often pierced and worn around the neck by those buried in 'Anglo-Saxon' inhumation cemeteries. Roger White has noticed that these are not randomly selected, but there were clear preferences for particular types. Among them are coins with the Chi Rho symbol 'prominently displayed', as if to create necklaces bearing a central Christian symbol. Perhaps this too might suggest a Christian group in 'Anglo-Saxon' inhumation cemeteries.[64]

There are even possibly Christian burials from 'Anglo-Saxon' inhumation cemeteries in the area in which cremation was the principal 'Anglo-Saxon' burial rite. Eight graves from Little Wilbraham, Cambridgeshire, with only single annular brooches, worn in the Romano-British style, comprise 24 per cent of a small fifth- or sixth-century cemetery close to the findspot of a Christian lead tank of fourth-century date. If these areas were evacuated systematically under Church organization in the fifth century, then we would not expect to see substantial surviving Christian populations in them, but as at Lincoln, some Christians may have stayed behind as a minority of the local population.[65]

It is not possible to prove that there was a substantial Christian community in eastern Britain in the later fifth and sixth centuries, but we should not discount this possibility simply because Bede does not refer to it directly. Archaeological evidence hints that the number of Christians in fifth- and sixth-century eastern Britain may have been greatly underestimated. This could have led to false contrasts between 'pagan Anglo-Saxon England' and contemporary Continental societies.

Direct archaeological evidence for paganism in late fifth- and sixth-century eastern Britain is also thin, aside from the cremation burials already discussed. Decapitated burials, those with coins in the hand and those with hobnails might (although in all cases need not) be the graves of British pagans but Germanic paganism is elusive in inhumation graves. Discounting the presence of grave-goods and north-south orientation (none of which need be specifically pagan), there is nothing clearly pagan about almost all 'Anglo-Saxon' inhumation burials. This is further evidence that burial was not 'about' religion, but it hardly helps us find Germanic pagans in 'Anglo-Saxon' cemeteries.

Well-attested 'Anglo-Saxon' pagan shrines of this date are unknown. All the possible examples are either probably seventh century (as at Yeavering, Northumberland and Blacklow Hill, Warwickshire) or dubious. Most claimed cases are no more than structures of unknown function. Gullies, slots and posts among graves were identified at Sewerby, Lyminge, Portway, Alton, Alveston and other cemeteries that could be shrines. They might equally well be gravediggers' or cemetery custodians' huts or sheds, booths for mourners or funeral feasts, the equivalent of later 'lych gates' for supporting the coffin during burial rites, or funerary monuments. John Blair has identified a burnt rectilinear planked structure with a post surround at Friar's Oak, Sussex, as a shrine, but although perhaps the most convincing example, this too was not certainly for ritual use (**colour plate 8**).[66]

None of these features has any associated artefacts necessitating a pagan religious function. The one possible example of an artefact of this sort comes from Rendlesham, Suffolk. This was a fragment of embossed sheet metal analogous to those at pagan sites in Denmark, but might date from after 600 also. To be exact, at present there is — at least arguably — more direct evidence for Christian churches in eastern Britain during the later fifth and sixth centuries (at Lincoln, St Albans and possibly Canterbury) than there is for pagan temples.[67]

John Blair has argued that a class of rectilinear ditched and fenced enclosures might represent 'pagan Anglo-Saxon' shrines, but the dating evidence is slight. He divides possible sites into classes A-F and, of these, he observes that only E and F seem convincingly non-funerary and possibly 'Anglo-Saxon'. Blair dates classes E and F to the later sixth and seventh centuries, and — if they are 'Anglo-Saxon' pagan shrines — they may be more relevant to the collapse of Germanic paganism in eastern Britain than to its assumed fifth- and sixth-century heyday.[68]

Written and linguistic evidence demonstrates that Germanic paganism was widespread in 'early Anglo-Saxon England'. Bede thought that sixth-century 'Anglo-Saxons' had been pagan and mentions several aspects of this set of pagan beliefs. Bede tells us that 'Anglo-Saxon' paganism involved gods and goddesses, sacrifice, temples, altars, male priests and a pagan calendar. These are consistent with what we might guess from looking at Continental Germanic paganism of this period and the Roman historian Tacitus' description of the peoples of 'free Germania' centuries earlier — the *Germania*. The most detailed section of Bede's account of pagan practice is comprised of the answers sent by the Pope to questions regarding the appropriate response of missionaries to the situation they found in England. Of course, it might be asked whether the Pope in Italy really understood much about this Germanic paganism.[69]

We might add to this Sidonius' description of the 'Saxons' sacrificing captives and casting lots, and note that Gildas too considered 'Saxons' pagans. Anglo-Saxon language ('Old English') place-names mentioning pagan gods or shrines are not well dated and David Wilson has noted that their distribution is almost entirely within the area in which inhumation predominates. Although this is particularly true of the place-names referring to pagan deities, the pattern seems convincing for both groups in general. Wilson ascribes this to chance survival, but equally likely is that there was no need for Germanic pagans to assert their religious identity where Germanic paganism was dominant, that is, where cremation predominates as a sixth-century burial rite.[70]

In areas where a large number of Christians and British pagans coexisted with Germanic pagans, then it may have seemed important to stress identifying features, especially the names of deities. A similar pattern is seen in reverse in relation to the term *wealh* ('Briton') and related place-names implying a British community. These seem far more common in the most 'Germanic' areas according to the assessment here, rather than in the most British ones. While the place-name evidence may indicate the spread of Germanic paganism in pre-Viking Britain, it cannot be used as evidence of the wholly pagan religion of these areas, or even their domination by a pagan elite.[71]

Archaeologically, one might look for hints of pagan symbolism. The swastika symbol is often associated with Germanic paganism by contemporary scholars, although this also occurs widely in Romano-British contexts. Whether or not it has specifically Germanic associations, it is found both on cremation urns and as a brooch design in the fifth and sixth centuries, perhaps suggesting it carried symbolic significance. Perhaps the most elaborate example comes from Sancton, where an urn bears a frieze showing the swastika among a range of ten or more other motifs, four of which could possibly be taken as depictions of a settlement amid trees.[72]

Artefacts carrying the swastika motif have a distinctive distribution within the area in which cremation was predominant as a burial rite, as too does the use of animal symbolism on pottery. Catherine Hills has suggested that these animal motifs also carry symbolic, perhaps religious, significance and we have seen already that cremation urns may have been carriers of elaborate symbolic codes. The encoding of religious information is also implied by the runic symbols known on 'Anglo-Saxon' cremation urns, as at Spong Hill. Some runes themselves could symbolise pagan gods and the rune indicating the pagan god Tiw has been identified on urns at Spong Hill. Runes are also found on portable objects, such as brooches and swords but not on domestic pottery such as that at West Stow or Mucking.[73]

Julian Richards observed that, when viewed from above (as they would have been seen in the grave), cremation urns carry designs similar to those of some brooches. John Hines has noted that they resemble bracteates to an even greater extent in this way, a very important point because it links two types of material culture carrying associations with Germanic paganism.[74]

Bracteates are discs of gold or silver bearing (to us) abstract images perhaps ultimately derived from Roman imperial coins. They are found both in Scandinavia and in eastern Britain, mostly in the areas where cremation burials are common, and in Kent, where cremation was more common than elsewhere south of the Thames. Some of the examples found in Britain differ in iconography and method of manufacture from Scandinavian pieces, while others closely resemble them. Bracteates have been divided into four classes:[75]

A Imitating fourth- and fifth-century Roman or Byzantine coins.

B A combination of human figure with an animal head, often with runic letters.

C A human head above a quadruped animal, often with runic letters.

D A mythical animal, perhaps a dragon.

Gold bracteates of type D, most common in Kent, are also found in Jutland, the same area which Bede associated with Kent. Sonia Hawkes and Egil Bakka have shown that the Jutish connection implied by this material cannot be as early as the initial settlement depicted by Bede. The 'Anglian' bracteates, that is those of the area where cremation burial was commonest, are more frequently made of silver and also include Types A and C in addition to D. They vary more in design from the Continental finds than the Kentish pieces, possibly suggesting that the ideology represented by their symbolism (and by extension that of the cremation urns) underwent changes during transmission to England.

The precise meaning of bracteates is unclear, but they may tentatively be accepted as direct evidence for Germanic paganism in eastern Britain, including Kent. This is far from claiming that everyone who wore a bracteate was a Germanic pagan, but the existence of Germanic pagan communities in both Kent and the east Midlands is suggested by this material even aside from Bede's account.

Archaeology perhaps attests ritual offerings deposited in rivers and at water sources and a large quantity of ox skulls found at Harrow, where the place-name suggests a pagan shrine, could have been the remains of sacrifices. Possible sacrifices were associated with the probable temple at the 'Anglo-Saxon' palace at Yeavering, albeit seventh-century in date. Arguably earlier is the curious deposit containing a 'large number of human bones, the perfect head of a stag, antlers from several stags, some boars tusks' and other objects from a lost location called 'Benhill' in the Aylesbury area. This might be a ritual deposit, perhaps within the 'mixed cemetery' which Mike Farley associated with the nearby Walton settlement. 'Walton' may mean 'British-settlement', so the Germanic character of religious practice in the area is not certain.[76]

Other cases of what might be sacrificed animals placed in inhumation burials might equally be food deposits for the dead to 'take to the next life' (assuming Germanic pagans of this date believed in an afterlife, which we do not know they did) or the deposition of an animal associated with an individual's kin-group. The latter could explain the deposition of animal skulls at cemeteries, such as the ox skulls at Soham, Cambridgeshire, and a pig's head buried in the cemetery at Frilford. The separate burials of horses, as at West Heslerton, may represent sacrifices analogous to the horses associated with the burial of the Frankish pagan king Childeric at Tournai in 481/2.[77]

Cases of possible human sacrifice have been widely noted. At Sewerby a woman was seemingly thrown alive into the upper part of a wealthy female grave (grave 41/9). This practice was also found at Finglesham, but there the underlying burial is of a man. At Mitcham and Farthingdown a female was apparently abnormally buried between two male graves, possibly representing a similar custom, and other possible examples have been noted.[78]

Some 'ritual' may not have been connected with religion at all. The deposition of pottery sherds in graves has often been reported, as at Bergh Apton, Swaffham, Bishopstone and Wakerley. At the latter, about 50 per cent of graves contained pottery sherds. The practice could be seen as evidence of the ritual destruction of pottery over the grave as part of burial ritual and so possibly a part of pagan rites, but might equally be the result of funerary feasts.[79]

According to Bede there was a pagan priesthood, but evidence for this prior to the seventh century is extremely ambiguous. The only possible examples of priest's graves of fifth- and sixth-century date are those at which skeletons sexed 'male' have 'female' dress items such as brooch sets. These might be explained in terms of the reversal of sex-roles in death, or as expressions of past sexuality, but Tacitus mentions Germanic priests dressing as women in 'free Germania' during the first century AD. This could be what we see in such graves, but these are very rare and the sexing of skeletons is not so exact a matter as to render incorrect sexing impossible. Consequently, these burials are neither convincingly those of priests nor examples of 'cross-dressing'. Separate to these burials, David Leigh has suggested the possibility that 'masked' or 'dancing' figures (these are modern interpretations of less than naturalistic figures) found on Germanic-style metalwork might be 'shamans'. This could fit the ambiguous nature of the art on these objects, but it is uncertain that Germanic paganism employed shamanism at all.[80]

So, Germanic paganism did exist within fifth- and sixth-century Britain and was probably the religion of the vast majority, at least, of people buried in cremation cemeteries. However, its extent among the people buried in inhumation cemeteries may be far more uncertain. Some families buried in inhumation graves may have contained both pagans and Christians, the Christians not necessarily being only 'British' family members. Other families may have been wholly Germanic or British pagans, or Christians. But accompanied 'Anglo-Saxon' inhumation cemeteries cannot be termed 'pagan cemeteries' without other evidence of paganism than grave-goods or north-south burial.

Even in the areas where cremation was widespread, some local Britons appear to have maintained Christianity. British paganism also appears to have survived in eastern Britain, but there is no reason to believe that British pagans were any more acceptable in political or religious terms to Germanic migrant elites than were British Christians or Christianity, and we do not know how compatible British and Germanic pagan beliefs were during this period. There is no reason to suppose that Germanic elites imposed their own religion on whole populations, or that any conversion to paganism occurred.

That is, not all of 'pagan Anglo-Saxon England' was necessarily either pagan or mostly occupied by Germanic settlers and their kin. However, people buried with 'Germanic' ceramics and metalwork had to get these from somewhere.

Material concerns: production and exchange

Throughout eastern Britain most excavated settlements were involved in mixed farming, with sheep, cattle and pigs being kept in varying proportions from one site to another. Horses, at least occasionally for riding, were also raised and dogs were kept, although not necessarily as pets. There seems no clear distinction in agricultural terms between the area distinguished by mostly cremation burials and that where inhumation was commonest.[81]

The boundary between these areas is clearly seen in terms of manufactured goods such as pottery. Groups of stamped pottery, the Sancton-Baston group and Illington-Lackford group, are widely distributed in the zone where cremation was the main burial rite, but not beyond.[82]

Stamp dies are also known from other sites, as at Lackford, Little Eriswell and Illington. Pottery stamps have been exhaustively studied by Teresa Briscoe and her daughter Diana Briscoe. This shows clear distribution patterns for some stamps, suggesting their use across wide parts of the area in which cremation predominated as a burial rite. Alan Vince has demonstrated that at least some pottery was probably locally produced, and Andrew Russell's work suggests that pottery was made from many different clays. Local manufacture of some 'Anglo-Saxon' pottery seems likely, although the potter and his or her stamps travelled, giving rise to the distribution of motifs and the regularity in pottery shapes from one site to another.[83]

Vince has also convincingly shown that one type of domestic pottery, tempered with granite, was widely traded. This was domestic pottery, yet the trade network seems restricted largely to the area in which cremation was the most popular burial custom.[84]

Networks of circulation of specialists, shown by cremation urns, and of trade, shown by granite-tempered pottery, can both be detected, therefore, in the 'Anglian' area. This was the zone in which Germanic culture and cremation (and probably Germanic migrants and their kin) were dominant from the late fifth century. As John Hines has argued, these areas may also have been subject to continuing migration from across the North Sea throughout the fifth and sixth centuries. This may have increased the non-British character of local culture and brought new tastes in artefacts.[85]

Not all domestic pottery was traded, as Vince has demonstrated in his petrological analysis of pottery from Brixworth, and there is no equivalent evidence for trade in cremation urns — possibly due to clear distinctions between the types of pottery deemed suitable for domestic use and for cremation urns. In particular, Helena Hamerow has pointed out that urns with bosses (especially *Buckelurnen*) and arched designs (especially the *stehende Bögen* or 'standing arches') have mostly funerary functions, whereas stamped pottery of other types is found on settlement sites, as at Mucking and West Stow.[86]

The unstamped pottery found on settlement sites is not wholly specific to each individual settlement, but definable types exist. There are five main types: grass-tempered pottery, sand-tempered pottery, combed pottery, 'rusticated' or 'pinched' pottery, and the granite-tempered pottery already mentioned. These all seem to belong to the later fifth and sixth centuries in part, although grass-tempered pottery became more popular toward the latter part of this period and beyond.

Decoration on 'early Anglo-Saxon' domestic pottery is subject to chronological

17 Distribution of granitic-tempered pottery in eastern Britain. (After Vince)

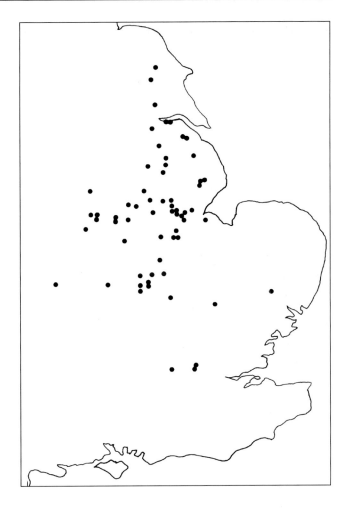

variation, and although this is poorly understood at present, a few variations may be broadly dated. For example, linear decoration appears to belong to the fifth century, whereas 'comb-point' decoration may post-date AD 600. Changes in the shape of 'Anglo-Saxon' domestic pottery are also visible. For example, Hamerow's work has confirmed the suggestion by J.N.L. Myres that 'carination' originates in the fifth century in this ceramic tradition, although faceted carinated bowls may not be a specifically early fifth-century form as he proposed. 'Biconical' forms also originated in the fifth century, while pottery rims tended to become shorter and more upright over the fifth to seventh centuries. Other 'early' features — perhaps also of the fifth and sixth centuries — are coarse-slipping (*Schlickung*), combing and pinched rustication.[87]

If 'Anglo-Saxon' domestic pottery shares similarities from one site to another, and some was produced for trade, this raises the problem of how far this material reflects cultural identity. Grass-tempering provides a case study of the problems of connecting 'Anglo-Saxon' pottery with cultural identity. There are areas in eastern Britain where this type of pottery is rare, as in Northamptonshire. At West Stow it formed only 2 per cent of the assemblage. Nor is it securely 'Germanic': grass-tempered pottery was widely used in parts of western Britain in fifth- and sixth-century contexts, as at Crickley Hill and Cadbury Congresbury.[88]

The same may be true of annular baked clay loom-weights, characteristic of 'early Anglo-Saxon' settlements, but also found in western British contexts far from known 'Germanic' material culture, as at Longbury Bank in west Wales. Likewise, sand-tempered pottery has also been identified in western British contexts, as at Gloucester. Thus, although some of this material may have Germanic associations, it is difficult to be certain how Germanic all 'early Anglo-Saxon' domestic pottery really is. If it was traded, its mere presence on site does not indicate a Germanic population there.[89]

No specialised manufacturing site for 'Anglo-Saxon' pottery of this date is securely known, although it is likely that manufacture of Illington-Lackford pottery took place at West Stow. There, unused clay was found surrounded by a ditch, and antler stamps bearing similar motifs to those found on pottery were discovered. The lack of production-sites for pottery compares well with the evidence for jewellery, most of which seems to have been made from recycled Roman-period metal. No fifth- or sixth-century 'Anglo-Saxon' jewellery-making site or furnace has been found, although crucibles — which might have been used in this way — have been found at Yeavering, Walton and Sutton Courtenay. A failed casting of a saucer brooch has been found in an SFB at Purwell Farm. There was also a brooch mould (for a Hines Group III square-headed brooch) in one of the SFBs at Mucking, and a seventh-century jeweller's grave is known from Tattershall Thorpe in East Anglia.[90]

The Germanic origins of many (although not all) types of 'early Anglo-Saxon' metalwork seem much more secure. The earliest types of Germanic metalwork found in eastern Britain are well-paralleled on Continental cemetery sites and can be dated by association with coin-dated graves there. Likewise sixth-century cruciform brooches, wrist clasps, annular brooches and square headed brooches all occur in northern Europe and Scandinavia, and in Britain mostly within the same zones as the predominantly cremation cemeteries and mixed cemeteries. Not all of these artefacts were common outside England, suggesting again that some transformation of identity had taken place in the course of migration. In particular, 'girdle hangers' ('inverted T'-shaped metal objects hung in pairs from the waistband or girdle, probably by mature women) are rare outside Britain.[91]

Karen Brush observed that 'Anglo-Saxon' brooches are not necessities for supporting the costumes with which they were associated. This implies a decorative or symbolic rather than simply functional interpretation for them. Vierck's suggestion that identity might be signalled through folk-costume (*Tracht*) could well hold true, but as we have seen this would apply to only a few women in any one settlement at any one time. Perhaps these costumes were representing the women involved as 'bearers of tradition', with equivalent males buried with weapons recalling the origins of Germanic political control.[92]

The representation of identity through dress may also help explain settlement evidence. Most settlements contain one or more SFBs. Weaving equipment — especially annular clay loom weights indicating presence of vertical looms — is found at SFBs more frequently than other hints of function. Alternative interpretations such as grain stores or homes seem less likely than a multi-function ancillary role including widespread use as weaving sheds. If they were used in this way, at least at times, then weaving would have occupied (at least at those times) much of the roofed space probably not directly used for human habitation at many 'Anglo-Saxon' settlements.

At Mucking it has been estimated that each 'hall' (surface-fast building) would have accommodated ten individuals at any time, assuming the population buried nearby resided on the site. These are not big structures, although extra space may have been available for sleeping in the rafters. If the living space is represented by surface-fast buildings, then more roofed ground-space was being devoted by each family to SFBs, at least some being used for cloth-production.[93]

This implies that the production of cloth at each settlement was important, and might well relate to the wearing of the costumes represented by grave finds. One possibility is that SFBs had specifically female associations, because of this connection with weaving and ancillary activities which were perhaps undertaken by women. The division between surface and subsurface buildings might have symbolised a male:female dichotomy and even perhaps the patriarchal domination of society. After all, the notion of symbolism, and of symbolic equivalence, was hardly alien to 'early Anglo-Saxon' society, as we have seen.[94]

Cloth production could have been used to symbolise identity through individual farms producing their own distinctive fabrics and designs. Alternatively, shared identities might be highlighted by designs associated with more extensive groups. Although largely invisible in archaeological sources, cloth-production could have been closely related to the manufacture of the metalwork fittings for folk-costumes symbolising distinctive identities in these communities. Or perhaps this is how people who did not wear such costumes indicated their identities.

An indication that settlements tried to maintain distinct social identities comes from burial evidence. Several scholars have observed that different cemeteries have subtle differences in what initially seem to be standardised burial rites. It might well be questioned whether such rites would have existed at all if these communities had buried the dead simply with an audience of the family-group. Even at the more 'private' inhumation burials, the funeral was a 'performance' for the wider community. That burial customs were altered to assert settlement-identities may suggest that neighbouring populations attended each other's funerals, and that local variations in metalwork decoration indicate identities displayed in both dress and burial.[95]

The brooch types found in the area in which inhumation predominated are not always wholly Germanic in origin. Both annular brooches and the so-called button brooches (small discs with stylized faces in their centres) seem to derive from Late Roman disc brooches. Saucer brooches, often seen as the characteristic 'Saxon' artefact, and related to brooches found in the Elbe-Weser region, may also relate to Roman symbols and designs. Tania Dickinson suggests that their design could reflect a desire to indicate legitimacy of rank in terms of both the Roman and Germanic past. If so, most of the 'Saxon' objects from south of the Thames may have had both Germanic and British origins, appropriate to the mixed culture suggested above for communities represented by accompanied inhumations.[96]

18 *Four cast Saucer brooches, gilded copper alloy.* Reproduced with the kind permission of
   The British Museum

Too many chiefs: 'Anglo-Saxon' kingship and social organization in the sixth century

No text tells us anything useful about social organization in early 'Anglo-Saxon' eastern
England, prior to the late sixth century. There are no indisputable palace sites, nor definite
royal burials, dating before *c*.550. The only settlement which might be an elite site is West
Heslerton, as we have seen, and even that provides no help in recognising the late fifth-
to late sixth-century 'Anglo-Saxon' elite.

Cremation cemeteries are often said to offer no evidence of social ranking, but that is
not strictly true. Mads Ravn has shown in a detailed analysis of the evidence from Spong
Hill that social rank may have been represented in cremations. There are urns containing
cremated horses, and bridles and weapons have been found. 'Expensive' artefacts (those
which took a long time or much skill to produce, or used rare materials) are found in some

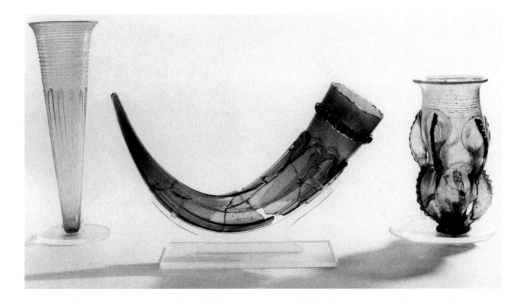

19 A luxury item in fifth- and sixth-century eastern Britain: 'Anglo-Saxon' glass vessels (from left: fluted vase from Kempston, Bedfordshire; drinking horn from Rainham, Essex; claw beaker from Castle Eden, Durham). Reproduced with the kind permission of The British Museum

cremations — Julian Richards suggests those with larger urns — but not in others. That is, social ranking can be discerned among the cremated dead. Additional evidence comes from cremations placed in metal bowls, often imported vessels, which might be taken to symbolise high rank given the exotic nature of the containers.[97]

It is possible that social ranking was shown more on the pyre than in the cremation urn. Evidence of burning shows that some 'grave-goods' in cremations accompanied the corpse on the cremation pyre. There is slight evidence that these might have been arrayed in the same way as the grave-goods in inhumation burials. In particular, glass droplets have been found on the upper bones, suggesting glass vessels placed near the head as in such burials. Perhaps it was believed that rank vanished when the cremated individual entered the collective world of the ancestors as the cremation smoke rose, but we have no way of telling.[98]

Alternatively, we can look at the minority of inhumation burials in cremation areas for evidence of local elites. While this might sound surprising, inhumations at Sutton Hoo, Wollaston, Snape and Lakenheath provide evidence of high-status items — again including horses at Sutton Hoo, Wollaston and Lakenheath, and horse burials have been found with 'warrior-burials' (that is graves with weapons) in inhumation cemeteries, as at Great Chesterford grave 142. The cost of maintaining a horse could have rendered it an elite symbol, or horse burial could have designated warrior status, although horses also seem to have held ritual significance to Germanic pagans as noted earlier (**colour plate 9**).[99]

At Spong Hill, a group of 'rich' inhumations were situated inside ring ditches near the periphery of the cremation cemetery. Such ring-ditches occur elsewhere in eastern Britain, although they are mostly found in inhumation cemeteries and cluster in Kent, as

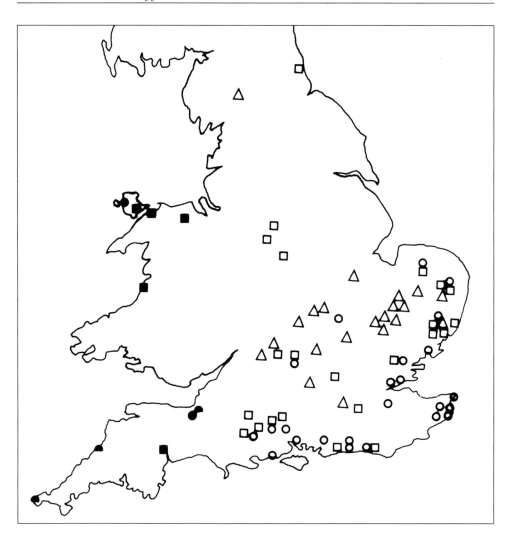

20 *Possible elite burials in fifth- and sixth-century Britain (excluding inscribed stones):*
   open circles = ditched enclosures around graves in 'Anglo-Saxon' cemeteries
   filled circles = ditched enclosures around graves in western British cemeteries
   open rectangles = 'chamber graves' in 'Anglo-Saxon' cemeteries
   filled rectangles = rectangular enclosures around burials in western British cemeteries
   triangles = horse burials in 'Anglo-Saxon' cemeteries
   filled semi-circles = 'mound burials' in western British cemeteries
   (Based on O'Brien with additions)

at Finglesham, and Broadstairs, at Appledown, Sussex, small ring ditches surrounded cremation urns, possibly in emulation of this practice. The lack of such features in other cremation cemeteries might well be a result of the extent of the excavated areas, or their location, so can be discounted as evidence of absence. The most likely role of these ditches is as a status marker for those buried inside, and the discovery of a cemetery of the late sixth to early seventh century including graves of this sort at Sutton Hoo may strengthen the case for an association with special social status.[100]

Grave 40 at Spong Hill was perhaps the focal burial of this group there. It comprised a ring ditch surrounding a single (probably male) burial in a wood chamber, accompanied by a spear, fifth-century sword and sixth-century shield boss. Four, probably female, graves accompanied by jewellery and pots were placed in the ring ditch and cut it at a right-angle. These could be interpreted as wives, family or slaves of the central male, although there is no direct evidence for this. A second ring ditch cut the first containing two, probably male, graves with a cremation placed in the surrounding ring ditch. Further ring ditches and inhumations followed. This could be an elite family group, over several generations, signalling its status by inhumation and enclosed burial.

The prospect of an 'inhuming' elite among a cremating population seems surprising if the basis of large cremation cemeteries was shared religious beliefs. It could be a result of religious variation between elites and the rest of the population, as William Filmer-Sankey suggested for variability in burial rite at Snape, but whether or not this is the case the local elite at this site apparently preferred inhumation to cremation. Perhaps Continental analogy may assist: throughout the West the Germanic elite emulated provincial Roman and imperial practices more extensively and at an earlier date than the mass of the population. The Spong Hill elite could be seen as more akin to the 'fusion' communities in the inhumation areas, with evidence for this being widespread coming from Wollaston, Lakenheath, Snape and — for the mid- to late sixth century — Sutton Hoo mound 3.[101]

A group of 'Anglo-Saxon' elite burials from sixth-century eastern Britain may, therefore, be recognised by unusual burial practices, such as those involving horse burial or the enclosure of the grave by a ring-ditch. Perhaps one might add to these 'chamber graves' (in which the wooden chamber contains the burial) and the earliest instances of 'Anglo-Saxon' barrow burial. More graves of this sort might remain undiscovered in partially excavated cemeteries, and at unexcavated sites. The sequence at Spong Hill suggests elite status was inherited and patriarchal, and this is what has been argued by Chris Scull more generally. Scull views the 'Anglo-Saxons' as organised into 'patriarchal patrilocal exogamous lineages', where women married 'out' of their male-centred kin. The emphasis on physical boundaries (such as ring ditches) perhaps suggests a degree of social exclusiveness.[102]

The construction of linear earthworks (such as the Cambridgeshire Dykes) in eastern Britain may also be evidence for this elite. These would necessitate a great amount of labour and, while this might have been a communal effort among peers, it is more likely the outcome of direction. The dykes represent another aspect of the fusion of British and Germanic culture — in 'free Germania' people did not construct such dykes, but they did in fifth- and sixth-century western Britain.[103]

The purpose of building such earthworks is too uncertain to assist defining this elite

21 Distribution of imported material in 'Anglo-Saxon' eastern Britain. (After Huggett)

much further, and although recently excavated, the Cambridgeshire Dykes remain enigmatic. They were apparently constructed in several phases in the fifth and sixth centuries, and may have had a ritual dimension, terminating at Roman-period temples and springs or wet areas associated with deposited weapons. A protective purpose seems to be their primary function, and ritual may be one aspect of this as perceived by their designers.

On these grounds it is probable that the Germanic peoples of eastern Britain had some form of inherited political leadership from the fifth century onward. Likewise, in the culturally-mixed inhumation cemeteries, a minority of burials stand out as unusual because of their grave-goods or the depth of the grave and some have curvilinear surrounds, especially those in Kent. This may imply an equivalent elite among the peoples using inhumation cemeteries.

These elites need not have controlled large territories, but may have been more analogous to the *ri* of Early Christian Ireland, with their largely judicial and military roles. Like Irish *ri*, they may have ruled only tiny political units, far smaller than the majority of seventh-century kingdoms. Traces of these are perhaps preserved in the smallest units in the late seventh-century Tribal Hidage.[104]

This elite may be responsible for the importation of exotica, such as amethyst and amber beads, ivory rings, cowrie shells, crystal balls and beads, and Frankish pottery and glass vessels. Byzantine copper alloy bowls ('Coptic Bowls') were also imported, and although there was no direct trade with the Byzantine world, more than 50 Byzantine coins reached eastern Britain. Scales for weighing coin — probably implying trade or taxation based on quantities of precious metals — are known from a number of sites in Kent and the Upper Thames Valley.[105]

Imported exotica in eastern Britain concentrate in Kent and the Thames estuary, although it is spread more thinly elsewhere, especially across a broad, roughly diagonal, band at the western fringe of the 'Anglo-Saxon' cemetery distribution. Local elites could have used items such as these to build up social relationships, and this might well be what we see here, with material being passed from chief to chief in multiple gift-exchanges, and distributed to followers for whom this was the only source of these materials. Such patterns of exchange would give those closest to the Continent a chance of acquiring the highest status. It would also link them more closely with Frankia, a link Frankish kings claimed rendered the rulers of Kent subservient to them.[106]

The first records of larger-scale control in 'Anglo-Saxon' England are from Kent in the later sixth century. Even Aethelbert was described as 'a king in Kent' not 'the king of Kent' at the time of his marriage to Bertha, the Christian Frankish princess whose external connections led to the Papal mission. Similarly, the 'king of the Angli' mentioned by Procopius, in his *Gothic War* (iv.20) could be more than a minor chief, as his daughter was betrothed to Radiger, prince of the Warnii, *c*.545-80. It may be salutary that Irminric, the only 'Anglo-Saxon' king mentioned by the late sixth-century Frankish historian Gregory of Tours had — according to Nicholas Brooks — a Frankish name.[107]

The origins of 'Anglo-Saxon' kingship in its seventh-century form along the east coast of eastern Britain, because of access to prestige exotica unavailable elsewhere, may also explain why Sutton Hoo mound 1, the clearest evidence for a pagan royal burial in

22 Ring from Snape. Reproduced with the kind permission of The British Museum

seventh-century 'Anglo-Saxon' England, contains so many Continental objects. New royal identities were still perhaps being manufactured by 'snatching' at symbols of diverse origins and meanings from Frankia, Scandinavia and Britain. The message being sent in mound 1 may evoke overseas contacts (the exotica), Scandinavian origins and migration (the helmet and ship), royal rank (epaulettes and sceptre), warrior status (spears, shield, sword) and wealth (the gold buckle, coins, silver plates and bowls, and perhaps cauldron). This type of royal symbolism had been developing for a while in East Anglia, as shown in the earlier ship burial at Snape, but the one known truly royal object there, as William Filmer-Sankey has shown, is an imported signet ring. Again, Continental connections and the emergence of large-scale kingship appear directly connected. Within a generation of Sutton Hoo mound 1, the kings of East Anglia were Christians like the Franks.[108]

The source of 'Anglo-Saxon' kingship in its seventh-century form in the west and north of 'Anglo-Saxon' England may have been through contacts with the Britons. The seventh-century kingdoms of Wessex, Mercia ('the border region') and Northumbria all formed in areas where British royal links are well-attested. Mercia was probably named after the 'borderland' between the two peoples, Northumbria formed out of two constituent kingdoms with British names — Bernicia and Deira — and the late sixth- and seventh-century kings of Wessex sometimes had British names. Perhaps due to emulation of their political organization, contact with the Britons appears to have led to larger scale kingship in these areas.

Hints that the 'Anglo-Saxon' communities bordering the British west may have learnt other cultural practices from the Britons have been identified at several sites. Simon Esmonde-Cleary has drawn attention to the possibility that a Late Roman cemetery at

Wasperton — at the western edge of the 'Anglo-Saxon' cemetery distribution in the late fifth and sixth centuries — remained in use to become an 'Anglo-Saxon' cemetery on the same site. Esmonde-Cleary argued that there was a transitional group of burials that exhibited a mixture of British and 'Anglo-Saxon' characteristics, although this group may not be as well-defined as it appeared when he wrote.[109]

Eastern Britain may have been divided into small chiefdoms, as one might term them, only a few of which developed to become the larger-scale kingdoms known to Bede. The scale of these may explain why they proved unable to gain control of the whole of Britain in the fifth and sixth centuries, unlike any of the other Germanic rulers in Europe. The growth of large kingdoms could, then, explain why a few kingdoms were able to expand rapidly after the later sixth century at the cost of the Britons. Ironically, these were the kingdoms that had formed through emulation of British — not Frankish — politics. The implication for eastern Britain is, that if political and military disorganization assisted in keeping Britons in the West free from 'Anglo-Saxon' rule, then one would expect parts of eastern Britain where the local population had organised themselves effectively to have stayed outside Germanic political control.

Thinking the unthinkable: British kingdoms in eastern Britain in the fifth and sixth centuries

Textual sources offer almost no help in recognising British territories in late fifth- and sixth-century 'Anglo-Saxon' eastern Britain. Gildas tells us he was 'cut off' from eastern Britain and Bede does not mention British rulers in the east, but then we would not expect him to. Archaeology, and just possibly place-name studies, offer the only reliable way of recognising such polities.

Many archaeologists discuss 'Anglo-Saxon England' as if the distribution of 'Anglo-Saxon' cemeteries was evenly spaced across eastern Britain by 550. In fact, there are very large 'holes' in the 'Anglo-Saxon' cemetery distribution. The most celebrated of these has been identified as a 'British enclave' around London and the Chilterns since Sir Mortimer Wheeler first suggested that this might be the case in the 1930s. But there are almost equally large 'gaps' in the Weald of Kent (where shaky assumptions about woodland cover are usually adduced to explain this), in north Hampshire and on the Wash for which such an interpretation is not generally proposed. Yet it is hard to discover any evidence that these territories were under 'Anglo-Saxon' control or culturally 'Anglo-Saxon' in the fifth and sixth centuries.[110]

We have seen that the inhumation cemeteries of the areas which surround these 'empty' areas do not represent homogeneously Germanic communities. Thus, the distinction between areas employing these rites and those which employed, one must assume, unaccompanied or 'invisible' burial traditions, cannot simply be a British-Germanic distinction. An alternative is to argue that these areas — or their rulers — were Christian, and this excluded the use of grave-goods, but this may not be a wholly satisfactory explanation, because we have seen that the belief that fifth- and sixth-century Christians could not place objects in the grave is misleading too.

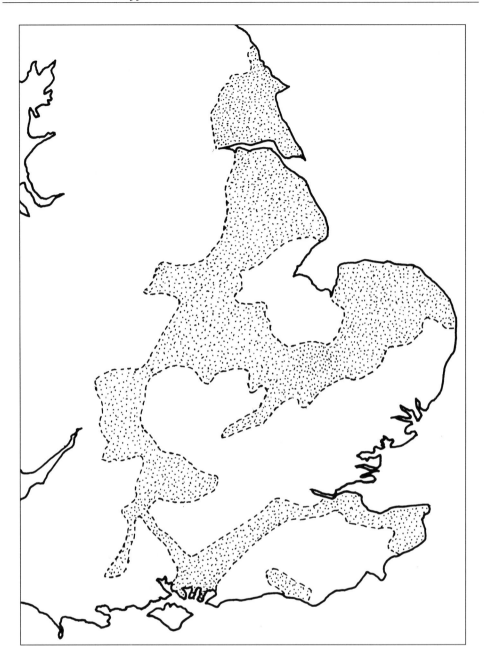

23 *Areas with few 'Anglo-Saxon' burials in late fifth- and sixth-century eastern Britain. Only in the stippled zones are 'Anglo-Saxon' burials commonly found. Did British rulers control the others, or were they more extensively Christianised than usually supposed?*

Nevertheless, the gaps suggest that extensive areas of eastern Britain were controlled by groups who did not follow either cremation or accompanied inhumation as their chosen burial practice. This is unlikely to imply 'Germanic' rule, unless the groups concerned had thoroughly adopted British culture. As this would effectively render them British anyway (for we have no reason to suppose that Britishness was racially-defined) it is likely that these areas remained in British political control so long as these 'gaps' are visible in the distribution of 'Anglo-Saxon' cemeteries and possibly after. That is, there were 'kingdom-sized' areas of eastern Britain under British political control throughout most of the period discussed here.

The archaeological evidence of late fifth- and sixth-century occupation within these zones shows differences from the areas in which many accompanied inhumation cemeteries or cremation cemeteries occur. In the 'enclave' around London and St Albans later fifth- and sixth-century activity has been detected at many Late Roman sites, but the City of London seems to be an exception.

Inside the Roman walls, in addition to possible fifth-century evidence, London has only a saucer brooch found at Lower Thames Street (in the rubble of a Late Roman townhouse, evidently still standing to this date) and a cruciform brooch at Tower Hill. Immediately outside the west of the City, sixth-century pottery and another saucer brooch have been found in the area of the seventh-century and later Anglo-Saxon trading settlement ('Lundenwic') which grew up in the area still called The Strand ('the beach'), on the north bank of the Thames. Perhaps the centre of settlement shifted westwards in the later fifth or sixth century, although the reason for this is unclear. It could represent the establishment of a new waterfront area for trade, a sub-Roman focus of interest outside the walls (for example a Christian church sited in an extramural cemetery as at Tours and, probably, St Albans), the survival of an extramural suburb or merely the foundation of an entirely new settlement adjacent to the deserted Roman walls.[111]

There is more later fifth- and sixth-century evidence from several sites in what is today the London urban area. Only one, at Harmondsworth, contains an object perhaps unlikely to be traded, an iron 'girdle hanger'. The artefacts and structures at Clapham, Upper Tulse Hill, Clerkenwell, Hammersmith, Brentford, Ham, Staines, and Kingston, demonstrate fifth- or sixth-century occupation, in several cases on or near Late Roman settlement sites. At Croydon, the latest material from the small-town includes early fifth-century pottery and the place-name derives from a Latin version (meaning 'saffron-valley') perhaps attesting the settlement's survival. Margaret Gelling has pointed out that outer London and north Surrey contain several place-names where a British origins seems credible, such as Penge and Caterham. To the west of the City, a fortified earthwork enclosure at Fulham may date from the fifth or sixth century, and opposite it across the Thames, a square headed brooch was found at the Romano-British settlement at Putney. Although some of these sites have 'Anglo-Saxon' pottery and brooches, these have not been found in distinctively 'Germanic' contexts and might have been traded.

At St Albans, Rosalind Niblett has collated much more evidence of late fifth- and sixth-century occupation at a string of sites in the town, and, at least arguably, at Park Street villa, King Harry Lane and St Albans Abbey outside the walls. Dating evidence for this occupation varies, at some sites fifth- and sixth-century local pottery, at one a sherd of imported

Mediterranean amphora of perhaps fifth-century date, and a few pieces of metalwork. Both Gildas and Bede imply that the shrine of St Alban, probably under the later Abbey, continued to function as a Christian centre through the period covered by this book.[112]

The evidence from Colchester is more ambiguous. There may have been post-400 activity at the disused temple on the site of Colchester Castle and two burials (one an infant) were found within the towns walls at East Hill House, ignoring the prohibition against intra-mural burial in Roman law. Two burials were also found within a large fourth-century barn building at Culver Street and another not far from East Hill House at Berry Field — perhaps indicating a larger intra-mural cemetery. SFBs have been found at Lion Walk and Culver Street, associated with what may be fifth-century 'Anglo-Saxon' pottery, and other fifth- and sixth-century finds have been identified from elsewhere within the Roman walls.[113]

At Rivenhall villa, Essex, although many aspects of the site require detailed reassessment, carinated 'Germanic' pottery was found on the floor of a fourth-century aisled building and the discovery of an annular brooch seems to confirm activity at or close to the site. That the majority of the approximately 275 sherds of 'Germanic' pottery came from the floor of this structure may well suggest it remained in use in the fifth century, and that its occupants were in contact with people producing this pottery. Unlike the examples mentioned earlier, Romano-British buildings remained in use rather than a nearby settlement being established following their abandonment. At Wickford, also in Essex, grass-tempered pottery was found at another villa site, although less certainly associated with occupation of the Late Roman structures.[114]

As we have seen, the few 'Anglo-Saxon' cemeteries in this 'enclave' are apparently strategically located in relation to the 'enclave' as a whole, suggesting that they too were military communities, at least originally. This may explain the location of Prittelwell, Orsett Cock, West Tilbury and Mucking at the mouth of the Thames, of the cemeteries of Croydon, Orpington and Beddington further south, each 'sealing' one of the Roman roads into London from the south. Sites such as Barling, Heybridge, North Shoebury and perhaps Bradwell, may suggest coastal defences, while Bulmer Tay could be located to guard a strategic river crossing. Obviously, 'Anglo-Saxon' settlements originating in this way may have been tolerated within a British-controlled territory if their inhabitants remained loyal to the British rulers.[115]

This area continued to lack other 'Anglo-Saxon' cemeteries well into the sixth century, implying that it retained its political unity until that time. As John Hines has recently pointed out, there seem grounds for suggesting that it was only in the late sixth century that this zone 'fell' to 'Anglo-Saxon' political control, although it must be stressed that the adoption of accompanied inhumation cannot alone be used to show Germanic rule.[116]

Another, perhaps less long-lived example, is the area around Chichester in Sussex. The east of Sussex contains fifth-century 'Anglo-Saxon' cemeteries, but the area around Chichester remained free of such burials into the sixth century, when the Mardens cemetery was established approximately 10 miles north of the town. 'Anglo-Saxon' burials are unknown from within Chichester, but a 'Late Roman' inhumation cemetery at Needlemakers outside the Eastgate post-dates coins of 364 and pottery identical to that associated with fifth-century 'sub-Roman' occupation at Chilgrove villa. At Chichester, this type of pottery appears to have replaced the final types of Alice Holt pottery, currently dated *c*.425. So, its presence here suggests that the cemetery dates from the second quarter of the fifth century at earliest. A coin of Valentinian III was found at St Pancras in Chichester, where a repaired sixth-century brooch has also been discovered. Hearths and wattle partitions were built over floors of Romano-British town houses (houses 1 and 2) within the walls and in the urban hinterland at Chilgrove 1 and 2 villa sites, where they were associated with the fifth-century pottery already mentioned, although Chilgrove 1 may have been given over to iron-working while the main occupation continued at Chilgrove 2.[117]

Interestingly, the Patching hoard comes from a site within sight of one of the earliest 'Anglo-Saxon' cemeteries in Sussex, at Highdown Hill, where there is also evidence of an 'Anglo-Saxon' settlement. The immediate area also contains a Late Roman villa and series of probably post-Roman barrow burials. A decapitated west-east male burial with a possibly 'Anglo-Saxon' knife was found in barrow 2, and in barrow 12 three west-east burials had their hands folded in their pelvis, in the way found in Western British cemeteries of the fifth to seventh centuries. If they are post-Roman in date they are more likely to belong to the local British population than Germanic migrants. Together this evidence might be taken to provide a context linking the Patching hoard with the British elite and its employment of Germanic soldiery, although it is also possible that these sites and finds are, of course, partly or wholly unrelated.

Another case of a British enclave centred on a former *civitas* capital may be at Silchester, Hampshire. The Roman town was occupied until the early fifth century at earliest, and archaeological deposits (notably pits with radiocarbon dates centring on the fifth-century), an ogam stone — the only example from eastern Britain — and objects of fifth- and sixth-century type suggest occupation beyond this date. Outside the town a wide area around is enclosed by the Silchester Dykes, linear earthworks which (unless pre-Roman) are likely to belong to the fifth and sixth centuries. No 'Anglo-Saxon' cemeteries have been found within the zone they encompass, and it is possible that here we have another example of British political authority being maintained through the fifth century and perhaps later.[118]

Occupation in Roman towns at sites within these 'gaps' in the 'Anglo-Saxon' cemetery distribution contrasts with the evidence from areas with 'Anglo-Saxon' cremation cemeteries, where no such evidence has been identified. At Caistor by Norwich, for example, the town was apparently disused before or shortly after the cremation cemetery outside its walls began in the fifth century. No evidence for post-Roman occupation has been found in Leicester, and material from Winchester comprises a few sherds of 'Anglo-Saxon' pottery and a triangular bone comb, although a Coptic cross pendant has been found which, if genuinely an ancient loss, would belong to this period.[119]

Canterbury is an exception to this rule, with evidence of 'Anglo-Saxon' occupation inside the walls. SFBs have been found on several sites within the town, and dated to the fifth and sixth centuries. The most informative sequence comes from Marlowe sites II and III, where the public baths were disused in the mid-fourth century and timber-framed buildings were constructed in the ruins.

Timber-framed buildings also almost blocked the street at some date after 388, and an adjacent portico was subdivided and refloored. A Visigothic coin of *c*.480 was also found at the Marlowe Theatre site, and a 'family-burial' (a man, woman, two children and two dogs) was found in a pit dug through a probable temple precinct in Stour Street. This denies both the exclusion of burial from within town walls and pagan norms, but is apparently a fifth-century British, not 'Anglo-Saxon', grave to judge from the accompanying artefacts. It is also difficult to imagine how, apart from violence or an accident, all could have died simultaneously, but someone buried them with respect.

As Dodie Brooks argued, evidence from Canterbury is insufficient to absolutely prove continuity of occupation, but unless Canterbury was still in British hands, the material from the city is anomalous. If the British authorities controlled their troops until the late fifth century there is time for the whole sequence, although the later SFBs might still present difficulties. This may not be another enclave following the 'Anglo-Saxon' control of the surrounding countryside, but show instead British occupation before and during the arrival of the Germanic community.

Even inside such 'enclaves' Britons may have gradually come to adopt 'Anglo-Saxon' material culture, as we see in that surrounding London and St Albans, while retaining political independence. A gradual switch from superficially Late Roman to 'Anglo-Saxon' material culture might have occurred in the fifth, and perhaps sixth, century. Pottery offers a clear example of this, and recent work has clarified ceramic developments that might enable this transition to be traced. In particular, work by Malcolm Lyne and Colin Wallace (to whom I am grateful for much unpublished information regarding this and permission to refer to here), has outlined the character of fifth-century pottery production.[120]

Lyne has shown that handmade wares become common after 370, and Alice Holt pottery increases its market-share in the area previously provided for by New Forest ware kilns. Across a large swathe of eastern Britain Overwey/Porchester D sandy-buff pottery and calcite gritted wares become widely distributed and form a major part of the latest 'Romano-British' assemblages. Both types were clearly produced into the fifth century, and although the end of production is undated, both occur alongside 'Anglo-Saxon' rusticated pottery of the mid- to late fifth century in an assemblage at Crown Office, Fareham Ditch. A copy in an 'Anglo-Saxon' fabric was found at Dorchester-upon-Thames, again presumably dating to the mid- or late fifth century. Other copies of Roman pottery forms in 'Anglo-Saxon' fabrics have been noted at Lovedon Hill, and a Romano-British tile from Farnham, Surrey, and an Oxfordshire ware vessel from Barrow Hills, Oxfordshire, both seem to carry 'Anglo-Saxon' pottery stamps. The latter could show no more than the survival of Roman pottery-stamps but they could imply the fifth-century production of Romano-British ceramics in contexts where 'Anglo-Saxon' pottery was also being manufactured.

Although detailed analysis by Colin Wallace has shown that most claimed cases of the simultaneous use of 'Anglo-Saxon' and Romano-British pottery are explicable in terms of the recycling, collecting and residuality of Romano-British pottery, probably from abandoned Romano-British sites, there are a few instances where this is not the only, or even the most probable, explanation. One of the clearest is at Beddingham villa in Sussex, where 'Anglo-Saxon' and Romano-British pottery are considered to have been in contemporary use both by the excavator and Wallace.

Other cases are open to varying interpretations, of which simultaneous use is one. The fill of an SFB at St Mary Cray contained both Romano-British pottery and 'Anglo-Saxon' carinated bowls and coarse slipped wares datable to the fifth century. Much of the Romano-British pottery was plainly residual from the ditch cut by the structure, but this was an early Romano-British feature, and one Oxfordshire ware bowl (dated conventionally 350-400+) was found with sharp fractures and in two large parts, comprising over half of the whole bowl. This was clearly not residual from the early Roman ditch, and Alice Holt pottery was also present in the deposit. The bowl might represent Romano-British pottery manufactured after 400 used alongside 'Anglo-Saxon' fifth-century pottery, but the late sherds may have been scavenged. At Foxton, fifth-century 'Anglo-Saxon' pottery was found associated with similarly preserved Romano-British pottery, at a Romano-British settlement with post-Roman features.[121]

Potentially the most direct demonstration of Romano-British pottery manufactured in the fifth century or beyond, is from Rookery Lane, outside Lincoln. There, the flue ashes of a kiln producing relatively conventional fourth-century coarsewares appear to have contained a complete, but misfired, 'Anglo-Saxon' pot. This was stamped and unlikely to date from before the sixth century, yet if correctly assigned to the flue it must provide a date for the manufacture of the last superficially fourth-century pottery at the site.[122]

The Britons in eastern England appear to have still been using, and probably producing, their own pottery into the fifth century and perhaps later. Of course, this production was on a much lesser (perhaps extremely small-) scale than fourth-century manufacture, and products might have been distributed only very locally to communities among whom pottery use had been declining for generations. Although it was used alongside 'Anglo-Saxon' products by Britons, this pottery is largely absent from 'Anglo-Saxon' cemeteries. In the past this has been thought to present a compelling argument against the production of Romano-British pottery at this date, but cultural values or accessibility might have excluded this material from cemeteries, just as not all types of 'Anglo-Saxon' domestic pottery were used for funerary purposes. If one wanted to signal a Germanic identity, would one have usually chosen a Romano-British burial urn?[123]

The simultaneous production and use by Britons of both 'Romano-British' and 'Anglo-Saxon' pottery might suggest that, following the collapse of large-scale production and distribution of Romano-British pottery in the early fifth century, greatly-reduced production continued locally. 'Anglo-Saxon' ceramics were first used alongside these products and then replaced them. This may be no more than another fashion-change, but it suggests that one aspect of cultural fusion during the fifth century was the replacement of distinctively British ceramics by what is today called 'Anglo-Saxon' pottery.

Conclusion

We can see that eastern Britain in the later fifth and sixth centuries was a patchwork of political units of different origins and sorts, not a homogenous 'pagan Anglo-Saxon' zone. Some were wholly British, some wholly Germanic, and probably more were mixed in origin. Likewise, culture and religion seems to have varied from place to place. In areas these too were entirely Germanic and pagan in character, in others wholly British and Christian, and in still more communities a mixture of these cultures and religions could have existed, although more likely side-by-side than in combination. The expansion of 'Anglo-Saxon' inhumation cemeteries suggests that through the sixth century culturally-mixed communities increased as more territories adopted a fusion of Germanic and British elements. Even Bede, always hostile to the Britons, possibly implies that Augustine's mission found Christian communities in the east of the island, and pagan Germanic elites. Whether or not there were Christian British (or even Germanic) elites left to welcome, or oppose, Augustine's mission is less uncertain. Bede does not tell us — but then he would not.

It will be immediately clear that this interpretation is far more similar to the situation found in Continental Europe — to the Late Antique world elsewhere — than conventional opinions permit. In fifth-century Gaul too we see a similar patchwork of assimilation and elite replacement, areas of cultural and religious transformation juxtaposed with zones of substantial survival and cultural conservatism. Somewhat similar burial customs, and replacement of Romano-Gallic by Germanic ceramics, are also evidenced, as is trade in exotica with neighbouring areas.

Differences in eastern Britain include that the 'Anglo-Saxon' elite did not mostly convert to Christianity before 600, large-scale 'Anglo-Saxon' kingship did not develop before the mid-sixth century and 'Anglo-Saxon' control encompassed a lot less than half of the former diocese before the end of the sixth century. These may be related, in that Christianity promoted large-scale kingship among the Germanic peoples, rendered Germanic elites more palatable to sub-Roman populations, and led to large-scale political units which could compete with Roman and sub-Roman resistance. When the 'Anglo-Saxons' of Kent and perhaps East Anglia adopted kingship on a larger scale this was probably through contact with Christian Franks organised in this way. Conversion of 'Anglo-Saxon' elites followed rapidly, also through Frankish channels, consolidating the emergence of the seventh-century kingdoms.

Unlike Gaul, aspects of Late Roman culture had already disappeared in eastern Britain before the Germanic migration. These include the villa system in its Late Roman form (although this did partially survive in a sub-Roman guise), and large-scale production. Urbanism had a more patchy fifth- and sixth-century history in eastern Britain than Gaul also, although some form of 'religious continuity' might be detected at least at St Albans and perhaps Lincoln.

Much of the east of Britain may have lacked in general the Romano-Christian culture typical of Late Antiquity, but differed less from the situation elsewhere in western Europe than often imagined. However, the zone containing 'Anglo-Saxon cemeteries' covers less than half of what had been Roman Britain, and far less than half of the island as a whole. Its population was probably only a minority of those living on the island after 400. It is time to look elsewhere in Britain for more straightforwardly Late Antique society.

3 Western Britain 400-600

To the west of the area in which 'Anglo-Saxon' cemeteries occur was the fourth-century province of Britannia Prima, comprising the whole of 'western Britain'. This area may conveniently be divided into two zones, which will be discussed in this and the following chapter. The zone examined in this chapter stretches from the Mersey to the south coast, and from south-east Wales and the rivers Parret (in Somerset) and the Avon (in Devon), to the western limit of the 'Anglo-Saxon' cemeteries discussed in the previous chapter. In the next chapter, the zone to the west of this area will be discussed, including Cornwall and the rest of modern Devon and Wales.

During the late fourth century the part of western Britain examined in this chapter had major towns, small-towns, villas and non-villa farms. In the fourth century the area shows much evidence of 'Roman' culture, such as Latinity and art, and strong evidence of Christianity, including some Christian villa-owners as at Hinton St Mary and Frampton villas. If a 'Late Antique' Romano-Christian culture existed anywhere in fifth- and sixth-century Britain we might expect to find it in this westernmost province of the Western Roman Empire.[1]

In order to explore this possibility it is convenient to begin by showing the survival of the Roman 'settlement hierarchy' through the fifth and sixth centuries, as this provides a clear context for the survival of other aspects of fourth-century Romano-British culture and the Christian community. We may begin with the top of that settlement hierarchy, the urban centres.

Towns

There is much evidence of fifth- and sixth-century activity from towns in western Britain. This comes both from 'large' and 'small' towns throughout the zone discussed in this chapter.

In Cirencester, fifth- and sixth-century evidence has been found in many parts of the former town. A town house (Insula VI.3) was not even built until the early fifth century at earliest and re-floored twice in places. Occupation into the fifth century at least seems assured. Other structures, such as Parsonage Field (Insula IV.1) and a house in Insula XIV.3, post-date late fourth-century coins, and could be of similar date. Other 'post-late fourth-century' activity spreads across the centre of the town. In Insula V (at V.6) a fourth-century shop was replaced by a possible timber-framed structure, standing on a compacted gravel spread, at a late fourth-century or later date. Rubbish pits were dug behind the structure. This too might belong to the fifth century, or even later, but no direct evidence enables us to resolve its dating more exactly. At Insula VI also, two timber-framed buildings and a post-built structure might attest humbler constructions at a similar date. The forum paving became heavily worn at a fifth-century or later date, and there are suggestions of road maintenance beyond 400. There is, therefore, evidence that would support the view that the town contained houses of various types, maintained roads and activity in the forum, in the fifth century if not later.[2]

Immediately beyond the Roman-period city wall the amphitheatre was turned into a fortified strong point, inside which post-hole buildings might be associated with grass-tempered pottery of the fifth to seventh centuries. The Bath Gate cemetery, located close to the amphitheatre, has groups of later graves that cut the fourth-century burials, and appears to continue after 400, as a *siliqua* of Honorius was found under the vertebrae of one skeleton.

Nine skeletons with 'Anglo-Saxon' grave-goods were found cutting the mosaics of a villa at The Barton, immediately near the town on Ermine Street, the Roman road leading north-west. A possible SFB was identified when the ring road was constructed in 1973, but was not excavated and so must remain questionable.

At Gloucester, 'dark earth' was found overlying parts of the centre of the town and an accompanied burial at Kingsholm may relate to Late Roman military presence. A coin of Valens was found beneath a mosaic in Southgate Street, and possibly fifth-century amphora sherds and a coin of *c*.440 suggest trade into that century. A Late Roman town house at Gloucester Castle was associated with 'sub-Roman' pottery, while elsewhere 'late' occupation occurs within other structures and a paved courtyard was constructed, in part above a street, after *c*.390, replacing a timber-framed building overlying the final Roman-style mortared stone house on its site. Public buildings were subdivided and a timber-framed building constructed in front of the forum, dated by radiocarbon to the late fourth or fifth century. Three pewter moulds found at Westgate Street in a destruction deposit dated to after 370 may be fourth-century or later in date.[3]

A possible Christian focus in Gloucester is at St Mary de Lode. At this site, a fourth-century town house (a 'house church'?) was used for burials and a timber structure in the fifth or sixth centuries, prior to its development into a medieval and modern church on the same site. This church is very close to St Oswald's priory, the great Late Saxon monastic complex in the north-west of the town, which also produced evidence of fourth-century burial and grass-tempered pottery. Biv, and more importantly what are said to be Bii, Mediterranean amphora sherds, are reported from St Oswald's, apparently attesting activity in the fifth or sixth century. Interestingly, both sites lie within a curvilinear medieval road line, which could continue the line of St Oswald's precinct and indicate a pre-existing enclosure, perhaps a monastic boundary of post-Roman date. To the west the old bank of the River Severn would complete the circuit.

Like Cirencester, Gloucester would seem to show evidence of houses, a public space and burials of fifth-century or later date. At Gloucester there is also evidence of what may be a contemporary church and of traded exotica from overseas.

Dorchester, Dorset, is another western British town with evidence of fifth- or sixth-century occupation. At Trinity Street, sherds of grass-tempered pottery are associated with the final phase of occupation of a Late Roman town house, and at Colliton Park a hearth within another Late Roman town house contained grass-tempered pottery. These two

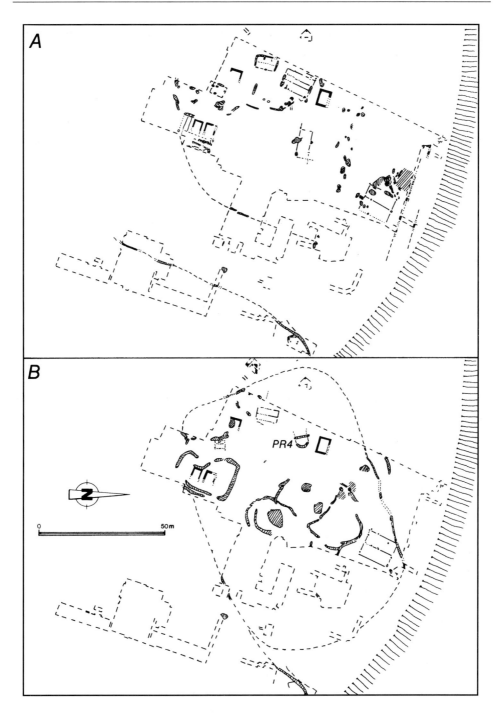

24 *Poundbury, the fifth- to sixth-century settlement. Phases VA and VB. The structures shown in thicker black and dotted lines are Roman-period mausolea sited with a fourth-century cemetery underlying the settlement. Shaded areas represent features dug into the contemporary surface. PR4 has been suggested as the apse of a possible church. (After Green)*

late-Roman buildings at least were in use in the immediately post-Roman centuries, apparently as dwellings. This might also be evidenced at Glynde Path road near Colliton Park and at the Library site, where rough paving, drystone structures and hearths provide evidence of occupation. At County Hall, a timber building was constructed in the fifth century or later, and at the Baths there was 'late' Black Burnished ware, to which we will return.[4]

Outside the town a series of settlements date from the fifth and sixth century. At St George's Road and Alington Avenue, these comprise timber post-built structures and SFBs, which were also present in the Romano-British period at the later site. At Poundbury a fifth-century settlement was established in a former Roman cemetery immediately outside the city wall, and adjacent to Poundbury hill-fort, which had been used for some sort of activity in the Roman period.

Two further sites, Maiden Castle Road and Fordington Bottom, outside Dorchester, may have been used in the fifth century, if the very coarse micaceous sandy grey granitic fabric of Black Burnished ware 1 (BB1) found there (in as yet unpublished but definitely fifth-century contexts at Dorchester) indeed post-dates the principal period of manufacture of that pottery. This latter point is made more likely by the apparently generally overlooked evidence from Ower.[5]

Ower is a fourth-century production centre on Poole Harbour. Well-excavated by Peter Woodward, it shows a detailed sequence of occupation directly connected with Black Burnished ware (BB1) pottery manufacture. The excavator interprets this as a specific seasonally-used manufacturing location ('primarily used for the manufacture of BB1 pottery, prior to firing'), not a farming settlement. The sequence began in the fourth century, and runs to a structure (909) associated with kiln bars and BB1 pottery. The latest datable finds are two Frankish glass beads of sixth-century type and it seems likely that activity was maintained into the sixth century. If so, this may have been BB1 manufacture, and the ability to obtain the beads implies wealth. If Ower remained in production — perhaps occasional and small-scale production — until the sixth century, finds of Black Burnished ware in fifth- and presumably sixth-century local contexts need not surprise us, although trade in this pottery beyond the *civitas* had entirely disappeared. Thus, the case for fifth-century (and perhaps sixth-century) BB1 is rather better than often appreciated, but this had become a local ware being made in small quantities.

Caerwent has two cemeteries of this date, at Vicarage Orchard just outside the town gate, and at St Tatheus church approximately in the centre of the town, which may imply a continuing extramural urban cemetery and a 'city-centre' church as we saw at Lincoln. Fifth- and sixth-century metalwork has been found in the town, and hints of post-Roman occupation have been identified in a comprehensive review of the evidence for fifth- and sixth-century Caerwent by Jeremy Knight.[6]

The most impressive evidence of fifth- and sixth-century occupation at a British town comes from Wroxeter. The whole town centre appears to have been remodelled in timber, according to 'Roman' architectural models and using Roman-period measurement, in the sixth century. Again occupation outside the town is attested. At Whitley Grange villa, the last firing of the villa baths has been dated to 410-510, and hearths and domestic refuse potentially of the same date have been found associated with the final occupation of the

25 Type G penannular brooch from the fifth- and sixth-century cemetery outside the Roman town at Caerwent. Copper alloy. Copyright National Museum of Wales

villa's rooms. After this phase the villa was replaced by timber-framed buildings, similar to those found at the Baths Basilica site in Wroxeter. At Whitley Grange, these included rubble from the baths, in use to 410 at the earliest. The villa may well be associated with the urban community and appears from its inception to have been only sporadically used, perhaps for hunting or recreation, rather than a farm (**colour plate 10**).[7]

At these towns, therefore, there is more evidence of continued occupation into the fifth and sixth centuries than often supposed. While this was not fourth-century urban life, it may have had some sort of 'focal' role for the surrounding area, given the cluster of sites around Dorchester and the relationship between Whitley Grange and Wroxeter. At Wroxeter, one or more Christian churches may have been situated in the town. At Dorchester and Gloucester, Christian foci may have developed outside the town, just beyond the walls, as we find in some Continental centres of the fifth- and sixth-century. This might imply that the walls still contained a secular community, which might also be one possible implication of the extramural cemetery at Vicarage Orchard Caerwent, although intra-mural burials at that site could equally be taken to suggest that a church was situated inside the walls.

The character of the structures which show fifth- and sixth-century occupation is consistent at Dorchester, Gloucester and Cirencester: these are fourth-century town houses and timber buildings constructed either by post-hole or timber-framed methods. This might indicate several households still located within the walls, and as Wroxeter shows such evidence may be the 'tip of the iceberg' of fifth- and sixth-century occupation. Large paved open areas which could date from this period have been found at Gloucester and Cirencester, arguably suggesting that some sort of market or fair could still have been held inside the town walls, and shops in the Baths Basilica complex at Wroxeter might imply commerce in the town.

26 Reconstruction of sixth-century (phase Z) Wroxeter. Copyright English Heritage

The picture seems one of the survival of residence at town houses, the survival of a fair or market and perhaps shops or stalls, and the maintenance or creation of Christian religious foci near to at least some of these towns. This sounds much more like the evidence of urban survival from Continental Europe, with its urban elite residences, religious complexes and continuing focal role, than is usually contemplated for Britain during this period. While the dating evidence is sometimes weak for specific towns, the pattern is convincingly consistent between them throughout this area, and archaeological evidence for contemporary Gallic towns is frequently no stronger, even when they have well-documented fifth- and sixth-century occupation.[8]

This pattern of urban 'semi-survival' is also found at the 'small' towns of western Britain. At Bourton-on-the-Water, a town house was refloored at a period when a stamped pot, either of sub-Roman British, or more likely sixth-century Frankish, manufacture could be lost at the site. Evidence of occupation comes from elsewhere in the town, in the form of an SFB associated with both Romano-British and grass-tempered pottery, while an 'Anglo-Saxon' inhumation cemetery was found nearby.[9]

At Bath, grass-tempered pottery has been found within the walled area (perhaps not strictly the Roman-period town), a timber-framed structure orientated east-west (a church?) was built above the main temple, and there were timber-framed buildings and undated, but late fourth-century or later, modifications elsewhere inside the walls. A penannular brooch from the main pool has been dated to the fourth century but could equally well be later in date. More interesting is a pewter vessel (probably continuing the Late Roman series of deposition of pewter bowls at the pool) decorated with an interlace cross that could well belong to a fifth- to sixth-century Christian context. As the evidence from Water Newton shows, the Christianisation of Late Roman ritual practice is not inconceivable in Britain and among the pewter finds at Bath this bowl was uniquely constructed of pieces of pewter soldered together, with sides curving inwards.[10]

Other evidence of non-pagan interest in the temple complex comes from the portico immediately adjacent to the reservoir to the north. This was repaved with limestone building stone taken from the temple complex. One block, placed upside down, depicts a relief of Diana's hound; another was part of the temple pediment. As Barry Cunliffe suggests, this implies 'some conscious process designed to remove the iconography of the pagan religion'. This could be later in date, but might just as well belong to a fifth- or sixth-century remodelling of the complex as a Christian religious focus, as at Uley (discussed below).[11]

Camerton, too, shows what is perhaps evidence for fifth- to sixth-century occupation, although this remains uncertain. Undated Late Roman or later structural modifications are recorded at buildings within the town, and outside the town a cemetery has been interpreted by Philip Rahtz as dating from the fifth to seventh centuries, and containing both British and 'Anglo-Saxon' burials, the latter probably post-dating the former.[12]

At Ilchester, sherds of imported Mediterranean amphora may have been found within the town, although more certainly 'Anglo-Saxon' metalwork (a square-headed brooch and disc brooches) is known from within the walls. It is unclear whether these date from before 550, and they could represent the spread of 'Anglo-Saxon' settlers into the area rather than a population occupying the town since the fourth century.

At Kingscote a spiral-headed pin and grass-tempered pottery were found at the fourth-century 'small town'. Grass-tempered pottery has also been found at Wycomb, and Shepton Mallet also seems to have timber-framed structures and burials from the fifth to sixth century.[13]

Thus, the majority of small towns in the West Country do show hints of fifth- and sixth-century activity analogous to that from the major towns. This pattern is also found further north in the area. At Droitwich and Middlewich salting was taking place in the fifth and sixth centuries just as in the fourth, albeit with technical innovations. In Droitwich a timber-framed structure appears to have replaced a 'villa' within the town, and although the community used 'Anglo-Saxon' pottery there is no reason to believe it was 'Anglo-Saxon' in character.[14]

Some sort of activity presumably also took place at Pennocrucium, as the seventh-century Tribal Hidage called the area around it the 'Pencersaete' after the town. At Ariconium, the town also gave its name to the zone around it in later centuries (Ercing). This could be taken to suggest that both not merely survived as places of activity but as foci for their hinterlands.[15]

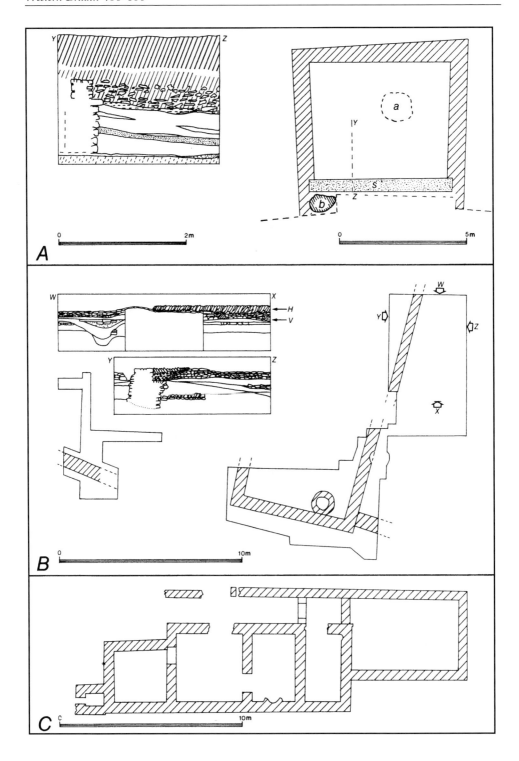

If so, over half of the known 'small towns' in this area show hints (albeit often no more) of survival into the fifth and sixth centuries. 'Small towns' in Late Roman Britain were closely connected with villas, which tend to cluster around them, and the survival of 'small towns' raises the question of whether any villas too survived after 400, and if so to what extent and in what numbers.

Rural settlement and villas

At non-villa, non-urban, secular Romano-British settlements, evidence for fifth-century occupation is elusive, but not unknown. This is probably because of the lack of large-scale excavation until recently at such sites, and the nature of the artefactual and structural evidence at these, even in the fourth century. However, the Late Roman farm at Catsgore was occupied after 400, although for how long is unclear, and on Salisbury Plain fifth- and sixth-century occupation has been identified by finds of grass-tempered pottery, and structural evidence, at Chisenbury Warren and Coombe Down, settlements associated with field systems used in the fourth century.[16]

In Somerset and Dorset, Roger Leech has shown that there is a close correlation between Late Roman and medieval settlement patterns. From this he argues that medieval settlements in this part of the West Country represent the successors of Romano-British counterparts.[17]

There is more evidence for occupation at villa sites. Villas were not evenly distributed across the zone discussed here in the fourth century. For example, a concentration of sites around Severnside contrasts with their absence from many parts of the West Midlands. Moreover, the West Country sites are far grander as a group than any of the West Midlands villas, such as Eaton-by-Tarporley.

At Barnsley Park, the final phase was characterised by the conversion of the site into a substantial platform, interpreted by the excavator as a place for fairs or gathering. Alternatively, the platform could have held a big timber-framed building, analogous to those at Wroxeter. Supporting evidence for post-400 use of Barnsley Park comes in the form of a ring-ornament, of the type widely found in Merovingian fifth- and sixth-

27 (opposite) Roman-period town houses with possible sixth-century occupation indicated by grass-tempered pottery at A and C, and a possible Frankish sherd at B.
A = Trinity Street, Dorchester (Dorset) (after Kirk)
B = Bourton-on-the-Water, 'Leadenhalls Villa' (after Donovan)
C = Colliton Park, Dorchester (Dorset) (after Drew and Collingwood-Selby)
H, Pitched stones with coin of Honorius in crevice
S, Secondary wall
V, Slabs sealing coin of Valentinian
W, X, Y, and Z mark section lines.
a: A heap of mortar, not of the final phase
b: A hearth associated with the possible organically-tempered pottery

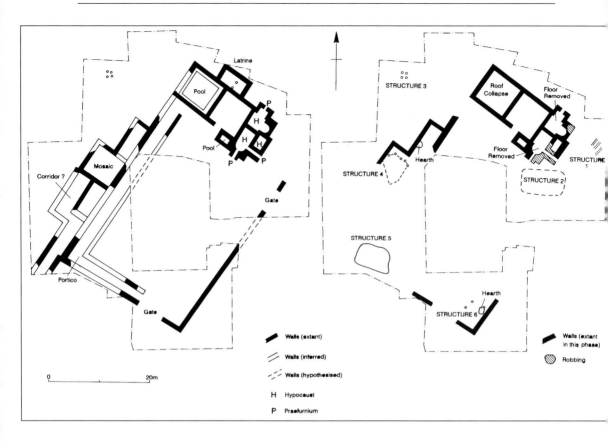

28 *Whitley Grange Romano-British villa. Left: late Roman phase, in use until at least the fifth century, right: immediately post-Roman, perhaps sixth-century, phase.* Reproduced with the kind permission of BUFAU

century graves on Continental Europe. Such ornaments only come from three other sites in Britain, all with well-attested late fifth- to seventh-century finds. Grass-tempered pottery was also found in the fields surrounding the villa, attesting activity at or near the complex in this period, but not from the villa itself.[18]

At Ham Hill villa imported Mediterranean amphora sherds and an 'Anglo-Saxon' shield boss have been found close to the fourth-century villa. These could represent occupation of the villa during the later fifth and sixth century or relate to the refortification of the multivallate hill-fort in which it stands.[19]

The evidence from Whitley Grange villa near Wroxeter has been mentioned above, but equally convincing is that from Frocester. There, the fourth-century villa was used into the fifth century before a fire destroyed part of the building. The front corridor of the main house was reoccupied, and at least two other timber structures built at the site. The post-fifth-century phase was associated with a large quantity of grass-tempered pottery, and an 'Anglo-Saxon' annular bead and part of a sixth-century glass beaker were found elsewhere on the site. The glass vessel may suggest that the settlement remained wealthy into the sixth century.[20]

Less clear-cut evidence comes from other sites. For example, a crucible of distinctive fifth- to seventh-century form was found at Llantwit Major villa, perhaps associated with a metalworking hearth formed from the disused furnace of the baths, and east-west burials cutting the demolition of three adjacent rooms (8, 9 and 10) on the other side of the main courtyard. At Cheddar villa there is a sherd of what may be a fifth-century amphora, and a ditch nearby may belong to the fifth or sixth century. None of this requires us to believe in fifth- and sixth-century occupation at either Llantwit or Cheddar, but it might suggest the possibility of such activity at both. This possibility could be strengthened by the existence of later monasteries at both sites, although not overlying the Late Roman villas.[21]

There are post-400 phases of modification at several villas in the West Country which cannot be dated with greater precision than *c*.400 or later. These are the western British equivalent of the 'squatter occupation' discussed in the previous chapter, and there argued to represent fifth-century occupation. For example, at Lufton, near Yeovil, the villa's floors (in rooms 2 and 3) were covered with a soil deposit containing artefacts and bone, a smithing hearth was found in room 2 and another, perhaps for cooking, in room 4. These features show that the whole of one end of the villa house was in use, but in a way unlike the fourth-century norm of villa occupation. This sort of occupation is found widely among western British villas. At Box, fires were repeatedly lit in the centre of one of the bathhouse rooms, at Low Ham the villa corridor was patched with roof slates and the baths repaired and patched with small stone slabs, and at Dewlish hearths associated with Honorian coinage overlay patterned tessellated floors.[22]

At Hucclecote (Gloucestershire) a worn Theodosian coin of 395 lay in the mortar bedding of a mosaic before the sort of occupation, including hearths overlying its latest floors, described above. If the last mosaics were laid in the late 390s or later, such activity presumably belongs at least to the fifth century. Elsewhere, timber-framed buildings may replace villas, and these could well have gone unrecognised during excavations before the 1960s at earliest. For instance, at Kings Weston, a platform containing re-used rubble from the villa overlaid the portico.

Such modifications relate to the broader trend for villas to end as small farms showing different cultural values to their fourth-century inhabitants. As we have seen, this could relate to the replacement of the villa proprietors by new landowners, but the possibility of refurbishment in a Roman manner after 400 should not be discounted without careful investigation. The technology of Roman building was still current in the West Country close to 400, and evidence from Wroxeter, Cirencester and Whithorn implies the construction and upkeep of mortared stone buildings during the fifth century and beyond. Given that the people living in villas still took steps to prop up roofs and patch floors it is possible that villa buildings might have been followed by new stone buildings if this technology still existed. Nor need all villas have passed out of use in the early fifth century, if families who were in some way free of the same dislike that led to the rebellion in 409 were permitted to continue to farm their estates.[23]

One example of a possible fifth-century mortared stone building at a villa site is at Wortley, Gloucestershire. There, an apsidally-ended structure with a sunken floor later than the fourth-century villa was infilled and modified using 'Roman-style' building methods, before being used for occupation. A 'Late Roman' buckle plate with a peacock design incised on it (probably a Christian symbol) found at the site in 1985 may imply fifth-century occupation at the villa.[24]

An explanation for the survival of some villas in western Britain in a more substantial form than small fifth-century farms (for example, Frocester and Wortley) may lie in their relationship to Christianity. The West Country is the one part of Britain with much evidence of Christian villa owners in the fourth century, the only convincing example of a Christian fourth-century villa community outside this area being at Lullingstone in Kent, where an association with diocesan government in London is perhaps possible.[25]

In Gaul, fifth-century villa owners frequently converted their homes into monasteries, or at least adopted ascetic forms of behaviour that are likely to have affected the interior of the villas in which they lived. Unfortunately, no direct evidence from the villas with the 'best' Late Roman Christian evidence is available, but a case can be made for the final occupation of Frocester villas being monastic, and at Chedworth, the nymphaeum of the villa was Christianised with incised Chi Rho designs of Late Roman form at a fourth-century or later date.[26]

Carolyn Heighway has pointed to an interesting group of sites in Gloucestershire, where fourth-century villas were used for medieval churches roughly following the alignment of the villa walls. At St Peter's church, Frocester, a villa became the focus for burials replaced in turn by a series of Christian churches from the Late Saxon to medieval periods. This is close to Frocester villa, already mentioned, where the combination of burials and domestic occupation of fifth- to sixth-century date has been found. Adult burial is extremely rare on settlement sites of 400-600 in western Britain and all known sites where it occurs could have been monastic. At King's Stanley, another Late Roman building was succeeded by a pre-twelfth-century church that retained the alignment of the villa walls. A similar case, close to the others at Woodchester (a palatial villa with the largest mosaic floor known from Roman Britain), shows a medieval church still following the alignment of the villa walls. The proximity of these sites and the fifth- and sixth-century activity at Frocester may strengthen the case that they represent religious reuse of villas in the immediately post-Roman period.[27]

At Llandough, burials of fifth- to eighth-century date have been found near a Late Roman villa and later monastery. Previous work had shown that burials radiocarbon-dated to the eighth century cut Late Roman villa structures, but the key evidence is from the 1990s excavation immediately north of the medieval church (and only 150m from the villa) where 858 burials were found with Romano-British pottery and coins, along with later fifth- or sixth-century Bii Mediterranean amphora sherds. The cemetery began while the villa was still occupied, and burials from this period contained fourth-century coins and hobnail boots, although radiocarbon dates range from the fifth to eleventh century. This might well be a monastery initially established in a Late Roman villa.[28]

The suggestion of the survival of some of the villas occupied after *c*.400 in the West Country as monasteries is supported by the relationship (noted by Susan Pearce) between Middle Saxon minster sites (rural communities of priests) and Roman villas. She argues that villas might have become monasteries in the fourth and fifth centuries and have survived as monastic sites through the sixth century to become 'Anglo-Saxon' minsters in the seventh. Burials of fifth- and sixth-century date have been found at some West Country villas, notably at Banwell, where the site was later a minster, but only at Llandough (which was not a later minster site) is there a convincing sequence from the villa to the sixth century, and then forward to later monastic use.[29]

Not all villas occupied after the early fifth century were necessarily monastic centres. It has already been mentioned that St Patrick attests in his *Confessio* that his family owned a fifth-century villa and, although this family was Christian at least since his grandfather's time, the estate was probably not Church property. Patrick's testimony is consistent with the view that Christian villa owners were at least occasionally in a position to retain their estates through the fifth century. When looking at a site such as Wortley or Whitley Grange we should be wary of assuming that fifth-century occupation means ecclesiastical use or ownership.[30]

How long villa occupation continued in western Britain seems less clear, and whether any non-monastic villas survived as long as any that were converted to monasteries remains problematical. However, the conventional picture of every villa being completely abandoned by or before the early fifth century is probably incorrect, although villa numbers had been declining through the later fourth century and most remaining villas were disused in the early fifth century. A more credible view is that a (perhaps small) minority of villas were still occupied during the fifth century, often as humbler farms, and this was sometimes — but perhaps only rarely — followed in western Britain by sixth-century monastic occupation at, or near, former villa sites.

Burials, temples and monasteries

Cemeteries of Late Roman form, but datable to the fifth and sixth centuries (David Petts's 'Central Rite'), are among the most extensively-studied aspects of the archaeology of the fifth- and sixth-century western Britain, where they are frequently termed 'sub-Roman cemeteries'. David Petts has pointed out that the burial practice characterising these cemeteries is already attested at sites such as Bletsoe and Ashton in the fourth century, but continues without apparent interruption in the area examined in this chapter through the fifth and sixth centuries into the seventh. This rite is characterised by east-west extended inhumation burials laid in approximate rows with grave-goods in few (probably less than 5 per cent) of the graves, wooden or stone slab-lined ('long-cist') coffins — if any — and little or no marking of gender, social position or status in observable burial practice. Unlike contemporary burials to the west of the river Parret (Petts's 'Western Rite') they lack internal foci and features such as burial surrounds. The impression given is of a homogeneous and unified community, and it is reasonable to suppose that this represents the Christian ideal of 'equality before God' rather than social egalitarianism. These graves are an ideal of burial practice in contrast to that of 'Anglo-Saxon' accompanied inhumations, with their emphasis on displaying rank.[31]

Many fifth- and sixth-century cemeteries of this type are located at fourth-century temples, as at Brean Down, Lamyatt Beacon, Maiden Castle, and Henley Wood. Others are on the same sites as Roman-period cemeteries, as at Caerwent and probably Barry

29 Long-cist burial at Henley Wood. Photo: E. Greenfield

30 Burials cutting the temenos ditch at Henley Wood Roman temple, so contravening pagan prohibition of burial at temple sites. Photo: E. Greenfield

Island. In other cases, including Portishead and Wint Hill, the cemetery was founded on the site without definite fourth-century burials, although the second of these was the findspot of a fourth-century glass bowl with Christian decoration. Another example that might be included in this list is the site at Bradley Hill, Somerset. There, a burial ground of 55 graves replaced part of a small complex of fourth-century mortared stone farm buildings. The buildings may have been occupied into the late fourth or fifth century, and yet one burial (F110) cuts the wall of building 3. Other buildings may, of course, have continued in use, although if this occurred the same arguments as used above regarding possible monastic occupation would apply to this site too.[32]

The geographical distribution of such cemeteries appears well-defined, although many more examples may await discovery and older poorly recorded finds often hint at burials of the sort, as at Evercreech, Saltford, Worth and Studland. 'Sub-Roman' cemeteries are distributed from what is today the Welsh border to the western limit of 'Anglo-Saxon' cemeteries, and attested at least as far north as Wroxeter, where a cemetery of this sort was established in the forum area. The absence of such burials further north in the zone discussed here is probably no more than due to archaeological discovery-patterns, as relatively little work likely to discover them has taken place in that area. The most southerly examples are probably in Dorset, at Swanage, if this indeed belongs even partly to the period before the seventh century, and undated burial grounds of similar appearance at Gillingham and Chickerill.[33]

These cemeteries may, therefore, represent the continuation of a Late Romano-British burial practice. Petts has pointed out the principal difference is in cemetery location, with burials located at sites previously considered prohibited, notably temples and within town walls. This may, as already observed, relate to the emergence of urban churches, as in towns elsewhere in what had been the Roman world, and the replacement of rural pagan foci with Christian centres.[34]

Petts has argued that the institutional context of the 'Central Rite' cemeteries is the survival of an episcopal Church on the Late Roman model in this area, presumably centred on the towns. This is entirely credible too, but raises the question of whether an archaeology exists for the bishops of western Britain. In this part of Britain we have few, if any, fifth- or sixth-century inscriptions to assist us in this. A lead pan at Shavington, Cheshire, bears an inscription to bishop Viventius. While this has been dated to the fourth century, a fifth- or sixth-century dating might also be plausible given the use of lead pans for salting at Upwich, radiocarbon-dated to the fifth to seventh century, and the existence of a lead coffin with a Latin inscription of fifth- or sixth-century date at Rhuddgaer, Wales.[35]

In archaeological terms we should look also to towns for bishops, given that bishops were probably located in the *civitas* capitals of late fourth-century Roman Britain. Obviously, the model of St Paul in the Bail immediately suggests that we search for such sites in the town centres, perhaps near the forum. The only intramural burials from towns in the area come from Wroxeter, where the burials in the forum mentioned above may date from this period, a burial with gold braid around its head at Worcester cathedral, and possibly in the centre of Caerwent.[36]

None of these burials must represent episcopal churches at the centre of Late Roman towns, but all could indicate such centres. These need not have been the only churches at Wroxeter, Worcester and Caerwent, and Steve Bassett has adduced textual evidence of late medieval date to imply that St Andrew's church in Wroxeter and St Helen's at Worcester were pre-Saxon ecclesiastical centres, and in his opinion the seats of bishops at this date. Whether or not this is the case, there seems sufficient evidence to support the possibility of urban-based bishops in fifth- and sixth-century western Britain, even if direct evidence for them is lacking.[37]

All pagan temples and shrines in this area seem to have passed out of use before 450. Burial within the religious precinct (the *temenos*) of pagan temples is critical evidence, because such adult burial seems to have been prohibited on religious grounds at fourth-century temples, although infant burials occur at some of them. John Casey has shown that there is no reason to extend religious activity at Lydney Park after 400, while at Brean Down, Henley Wood, Lamyatt Beacon, Nettleton and probably Maiden Castle, east-west burials replaced the Late Roman shrines, indicating the cessation of pagan worship at the sites. Uley temple was re-used for an enclosed settlement containing a probable church. Thus, the pagan religious sites which did survive until *c*.400 in this area characteristically end with Christianisation of their sites by burial or church-building. At Uley (and perhaps Bath) the pagan temple was converted to Christian religious use.[38]

The only cases where detailed evidence for the continuation of pagan religion after 409 is sufficient to merit discussion when looking at this zone, are at Pagans Hill, Maiden Castle and Cadbury Congresbury. At Pagans Hill the evidence for a continuation of pagan practices at the fourth-century temple site comprises an 'Anglo-Saxon' blue glass squat jar of seventh-century date deposited in a well or ritual shaft at the site. This has been argued by Philip Rahtz, the principal academic supporter of the concept of 'residual paganism' in western Britain, as hinting at continuing pagan votive deposition at the site after 400. However, the well might have been Christianised (by dedication to a saint?) by the time the vessel was deposited, or this could have been a pagan votive offering by a pagan 'Anglo-Saxon' in the seventh century with only the vaguest notion that the disused site was the 'local' pagan focus centuries earlier. It is not sufficient even as proof of post-fifth-century paganism at Pagan's Hill, let alone its continuous practice from the fourth century.[39]

The evidence from Maiden Castle is a timber curvilinear building immediately adjacent to a fourth-century temple within the hill-fort. Rahtz argued that the roundhouse was a fifth-century shrine post-dating the temple, as it contains pieces of a cult-statue and many coins. This is far from certain as both buildings could be contemporary, and no post-Roman material was discovered from these structures. A 'sub-Roman' cemetery, probably of fifth- to sixth-century date, appears to have succeeded the temple, and even if the curvilinear building represents 'pagan continuity' after 400, this apparently terminated within the fifth or sixth centuries. This — which is hardly definite and probably, at latest, early to mid-fifth-century — may be the most convincing evidence for post-Roman paganism anywhere in western Britain.

The opposite situation has been argued by Rahtz to represent fifth- and sixth-century paganism at Cadbury Congresbury. A roundhouse (structure II) with particularly *few* finds has been argued to be a pagan shrine because of its relative lack of finds, and because bone and copper alloy 'leaf-shaped' articles have been found associated with the structure. Whether such items need be specifically pagan is cast into doubt by the evidence from the Water Newton treasure, where leaves of this type are adorned with Christian symbols and associated with Christian inscriptions. Even if the 'leaves' at Cadbury Congresbury were taken to be pagan votive objects, the position of two of the leaves in the postholes of the structure suggests that they predate its construction and cannot be contemporary with the functioning of structure II. Two amphora handles were also found in the central entrance posthole of the building, but again the significance of these is uncertain. There is no evidence that broken amphorae were employed as ritual objects in Roman Britain or fifth- and sixth-century Ireland. Indeed, the desperation of the argument can be gauged by Rahtz's assertion that 'in a pagan context almost anything can acquire a votive character'! If so, specifically votive deposits are only identifiable by their context, which in this case is a curvilinear building with a central hearth, in a settlement site. The only really unusual thing about structure II is its relative lack of finds, perhaps implying an unusual function, but this does not make it a shrine. The most obvious interpretation is that it is a secular structure, with possible 'foundation deposits', which might be interpreted in a Christian, pagan, sentimental or 'superstitious' manner.[40]

Thus, there are no compelling archaeological grounds for accepting these as fifth- and sixth-century pagan shrines. The overall picture seems instead of an abrupt early fifth-

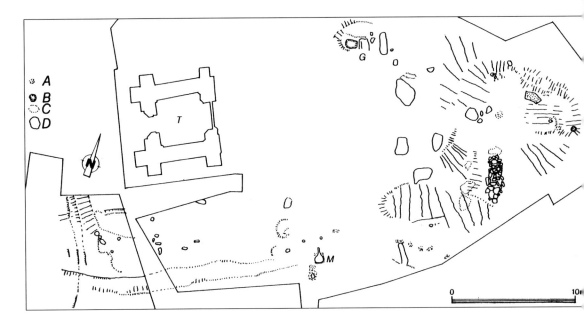

31 *The excavated sixth-century (?monastic) settlement on Glastonbury Tor (after Rahtz). The later
medieval church tower, still standing, is shown in outline (T).*

A = *Burnt rock*

B = *Postholes*

C = *Stony areas*

D = *Tor Burrs (natural features)*

G = *Graves*

M = *Possible metalworking hearths*

century termination of paganism in this zone of western Britain.

A fascinating counterpart of the end of Romano-British paganism in western Britain is
the emergence of a series of sites perhaps best interpreted as monasteries. These are
characterised by domestic occupation either associated with univallate and indefensible
enclosures or unenclosed. This is found at Nettleton, where the temple site shows
evidence of domestic activity associated with material of perhaps fifth-century date and a
Christian cemetery within a possible enclosure bank. At Uley the temple may have been
used as a church and there was domestic occupation inside an enclosure, although no
cemetery has been discovered.[41]

Glastonbury Tor may be another example of a sixth-century monastery. Occupation on
the Tor seems to have involved small post-hole buildings, probably rectilinear, associated
with a drystone bench or platform of unknown use, and metalworking associated with
imported Mediterranean amphorae and one sherd of grass-tempered pottery. A small
copper alloy depiction of a human head, perhaps from a vessel, staff-end or casket, was
also found on the Tor, probably associated with this phase.[42]

A monastic interpretation might even apply to some of the other sites already

32 Sixth-century grave-shaped cairn at Glastonbury Tor, a possible saint's shrine?
Photo: P.A. Rahtz

mentioned, such as Lamyatt Beacon and Brean Down, where there are hints of domestic and religious activity occurring together, and at several of the villa sites discussed earlier, as at Llandough. More problematical evidence comes from Poundbury, where the settlement might be interpreted either as a monastery or a low-status domestic site. In favour of a monastic interpretation is the presence of reused (perhaps Christian) mausolea, the construction of an apsidally-ended building that could be a church and the location of the settlement at a possibly Christian fourth-century cemetery. Against this is the lack of any compelling evidence of religious activity contemporary with the settlement.[43]

These possibly monastic sites represent, therefore, a new settlement type replacing the role of temples as religious foci in the fifth-century countryside. Like temples they might be seen as centres of pilgrimage and worship for more than their residents. This provides a possible explanation for the puzzling rectangular drystone feature at Glastonbury Tor. This could be a saint's tomb or shrine prominently placed within the monastic settlement. In so far as it has any additional attributes, the presence of charcoal and an iron ferrule of Roman or fifth- to sixth-century date within the structure would be explicable as representing the deposition of relics and perhaps the lighting of fires, torches or candles at the tomb or shrine. This might even explain the discovery of an iron lamp- or torch-holder at the site, a unique find from a British settlement of this date. One might guess that the trek up the Tor, hardly a leisurely walk even for the fit, might have been part of the pilgrimage experience for those visiting the tomb. Other localities in the area, possibly such as the Mount (where imported Mediterranean amphora has also been found), Chalice Well, or even the later abbey, could have contained associated foci, although not necessarily any occupation or non-natural features.[44]

A further example of the veneration of the relics at a monastic site in the West Country could be identifiable at Uley. The meticulous excavation at Uley discovered nine pieces of bone inlay, probably from a wooden box, all associated with the Phase 7 perimeter bank.

These consist of four squares with central ring and dot motifs, an undecorated square plate, a circular piece with a ring and dot motif, a triangular piece with geometric decoration, and a rectangular inlay with a well-defined equal-armed cross motif with splayed ends. The use of the triangular end recalling later reliquary boxes, and cross symbol, could allow these pieces to be interpreted as parts of a Christian reliquary, given the evidence for a religious dimension to the site.[45]

The findspot of the 'box' within the perimeter bank need not count against this, if we interpret this as an act of consecration of the perimeter. The presence of a folded metal vessel with Christian scenes incorporated in the Phase 6 demolition rubble of the modified temple has been interpreted as a pagan attempt to ritually 'kill' the Christian artefact, but could be interpreted in the same way if Christians were demolishing the temple. Similarly, the burial of the main cult statue head attributed to Phase 7 could well belong to this process of purification.

Other monastic settlements could be attested by less complete evidence elsewhere. At Much Wenlock, burials have been radiocarbon-dated to this period and there is a sherd of Germanic glass of the type found on sixth-century western British hill-fort sites. While these data need not imply a monastic occupation of fifth- to sixth-century date, they might be evidence of such activity.[46]

Monastic sites can be identified across the whole zone discussed in this chapter. That these sites vary in form need not surprise us: Gildas attests a diversity of monastic practice in his writings. One might see Glastonbury Tor as an example of an eremitical site (occupied by hermits), whereas Uley would be most plausibly interpreted as a coenobitic (communal) monastery. Moreover, if they are West Country writers, Gildas and Patrick both attest the existence of monastic values in this area from the fifth and sixth centuries, while in his reference to the battle of Chester (613 x 16) Bede refers to a large monastery at Bangor on Dee. Although the latter might, of course, have been established after 600, there is textual support for the existence of a vigorous, if not by Gildas' time numerous, monastic movement to supplement this archaeological evidence.[47]

We might, then, see the fifth century as a turning point for the character of religious foci in western Britain. Whereas as late as the mid-fourth century the principal rural religious foci throughout the region were pagan temples, by 500 this situation had ceased. There is no trace of organized paganism in western Britain after the early fifth century, and the main religious foci were now monastic sites and churches. The former might easily have taken over the role of the temples as places of pilgrimage, as well as for seasonal fairs, as we have seen. Monasteries may have acted as agricultural centres for estates, and the origins of those estates might be found in the social upheaval of the early fifth century, which may have freed large amounts of land from pagan owners, and in the donation of estates to the Church by their Christian owners. There are also traces of further patronage, in the presence of amphorae and imported glass at possible monastic sites. Whether or not this reconfiguration of rural religious centres would have been accompanied by a 'Christianisation' of time for country people, with pagan festivals replaced by Christian holy days, must be unclear, but remains a strong possibility.[48]

This, rather than the foundation of new settlements or the cessation of activity at Romano-British occupation sites, is the most dramatic change in settlement-form in western Britain in the fifth century. Yet it occurred alongside the survival of burial customs of Late Roman form and the continuing use of Roman-period urban and villa sites. Both survival and change can be seen in terms of artefactual evidence too. The most well-known aspect of this is the importation of Mediterranean pottery and glass, and the manufacture of post-Roman jewellery.

Imported artefacts and political identities

There are few obviously 'diagnostic' artefacts of fifth- and sixth-century date in this zone. Imported Mediterranean pottery has been found at several sites, and some of this material has already been mentioned in passing. It occurs at Glastonbury Tor (and the nearby — and enigmatic — Mount site, also in Glastonbury), at Dinas Powys, South Cadbury (also called 'Cadbury Castle') and Cadbury Congresbury hill-forts, Ham Hill, Llandough, and perhaps at Gloucester and Ilchester. Imported glass comes from Much Wenlock, South Cadbury, Dinas Powys and Cadbury Congresbury. At many sites imported artefacts are the crucial dating evidence for this period, and have attracted a great amount of archaeological interest since first being identified by Ralegh Radford and Mortimer Wheeler in the 1930s.[49]

The Mediterranean imported pottery divides into two main categories, and our understanding of these has been greatly clarified by the work of Ewan Campbell and Charles Thomas in Britain, and John Hayes, David Peacock and David Williams in the Mediterranean. First, there is a series of red-slipped finewares, manufactured in the eastern Mediterranean (Phocaean Red Slip Ware: abbreviated to PRSW) and in north Africa (African Red Slip Ware: ARSW). PRSW is a standard Byzantine tableware, produced in the Sardis area of western Anatolia, and very popular in parts of the eastern Mediterranean. This dates from the Roman period until the seventh century at least in the eastern Mediterranean, but British finds belong to a much narrower timespan, perhaps *c*.475-550. ARSW was produced in the Carthage region of North Africa, again through the Roman period until the seventh century and was another standard fine tableware. Western British finds seem to date from the early sixth century. The red-slipped wares were apparently perceived as finewares by Byzantines: for instance, similar pieces are known from the Great Palace of the Byzantine emperors at Constantinople.

The production of red-slipped finewares such as these was highly regionalised within the fifth- and sixth-century Mediterranean world, so that it is often possible to recognise the source of an assemblage partly by its composition. The British assemblage, assuming one can take it together, is notable for what it lacks as well as what it contains. If this material had come from Cyprus, one would have expected 'Cypriot Red Slip Ware', if from Egypt 'Egyptian Red Slip Ware', and so on — so the absence of these and similar local varieties suggests that it derives from a place where PRSW was found. ARSW is only found in large amounts in Britain at Tintagel in Cornwall and might be no more than a commodity picked up en route via Carthage, or less likely another North African port. This strongly suggests either Constantinople itself or Anatolia.

These finewares are accompanied in Britain by eastern Mediterranean amphorae, also

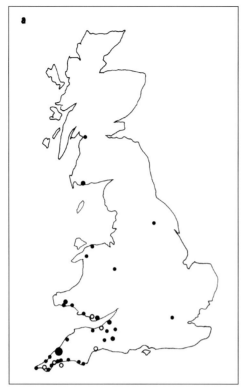

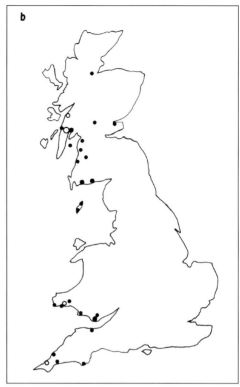

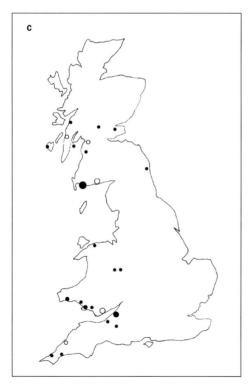

33 a Imported late fifth- and sixth-century
Mediterranean pottery (PRSW, ARSW,
and B-wares)
b Imported Frankish E-ware pottery
c Continental glass in western and northern
Britain

smallest black circle 1-4
smallest open circle 5-9
larger black circle 10-20
larger open circle 21-40
large black circle 60+
largest black circle 80+

(After Campbell, with additions)

manufactured within the Byzantine empire, and also extremely common in the Mediterranean itself. In Britain, but not usually elsewhere, these amphorae are called 'B-Ware' (the red-slipped wares are known collectively as 'A-Ware') after their initial classification at Tintagel, by Ralegh Radford in the 1930s-50s. B-Wares are divided into a number of categories (Bi, Bii, Biv, Bv and B misc.).

All the B-wares are broadly of buff colour and superficially similar to Roman amphora in overall appearance. Bi is easily identified by its external combed ribbing, and was probably produced in the Argolid region of Greece in the early fifth to late sixth centuries. Bii is also readily recognised by its external 'tegulated' surface of broad relief bands, and was produced in Anatolia, perhaps specifically Cilicia, in the mid-fifth to early seventh centuries. A variety of Bii fabrics are known (at least two from Britain), implying many individual producers. Biv is a darker red-brown colour and highly micaceous (one can see the mica inclusions 'sparkle' when they catch the light), and it was produced in the Sardis region of western Anatolia over several centuries from the early Roman period into the fifth and sixth centuries. Late versions of Biv are distinguished by having two handles, and two-handled forms belong to the mid-fifth to late sixth centuries.

Bv consist of a potentially more diverse category of North African amphorae, again mostly found in Britain at Tintagel. These were produced in a wide range of forms and over the Roman and Byzantine periods, but the British examples appear to belong to the same period as the other B-wares. More enigmatic are the wide range of wares in the 'B misc.' ('miscellaneous') category. These still require identification and sourcing, although they appear to be mostly or wholly Byzantine and of broadly the same period.[50]

The amphora support a Constantinopolitan or Anatolian origin for the British finds, but they also reinforce the unusual character of the Tintagel assemblage. This site will be discussed in the next chapter, as it lies outside our area, but it is worth noting that with the Tintagel finds aside this assemblage looks very eastern Mediterranean, and this material is not at all common outside the Mediterranean. Other than in Britain, PRSW, for example, occurs at only a few sites in western Spain and in France. Yet it is present at four sites in the West Country alone. One explanation for the finds on the western coasts of Spain and France is, therefore, that they were a 'by-product' of directional trade 'aimed' at western Britain. One wonders what the Byzantine interest was in the British west, a point to which we shall shortly return.[51]

First, the question of whether or not this material arrived directly from Byzantine ships needs to be resolved. This is made more problematical due to the existence of a small, but potentially important, category of stamped and rouletted shallow dishes, bowls and mortaria (D-Ware). This ware, termed 'Dérivées Paléochrétienne Grise' by French archaeologists, was produced in what is today western France (perhaps in the Bordeaux area and the Loire valley among other areas), and is also well-dated in their land of origin. The vessels are black-slipped wheel-made greyware bowls and belong to the sixth century. They occur only very rarely in Britain, and in western Britain only at Cadbury Congresbury and South Cadbury hill-forts.[52]

Germanic glass was imported into Britain and derives from Frankish sources. As Ewan Campbell's important work on this material has shown, this largely comprises conical drinking vessels, mostly pale or colourless and often decorated with opaque white bands

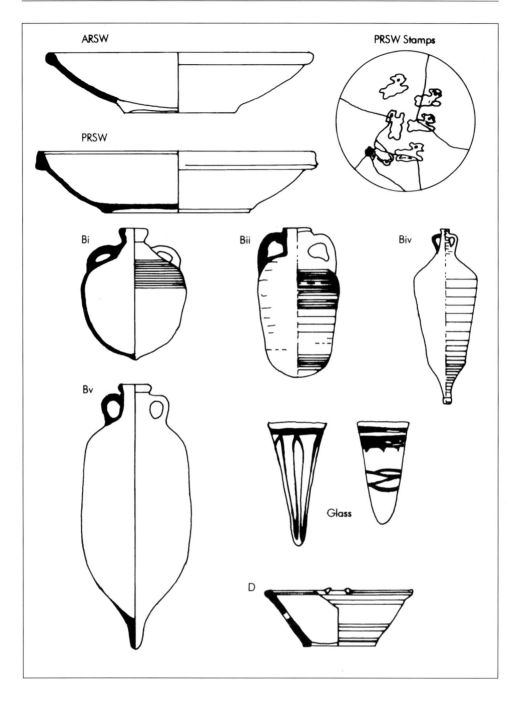

34 Fifth- and sixth-century imported Mediterranean and Frankish pottery and Continental glass found in Britain. These are representative of the forms of vessels found, although a wider range of forms are represented in Britain and no complete vessel of any of these types is known from Britain. (After Alcock, Thomas, Bowman, and Campbell. Not to scale)

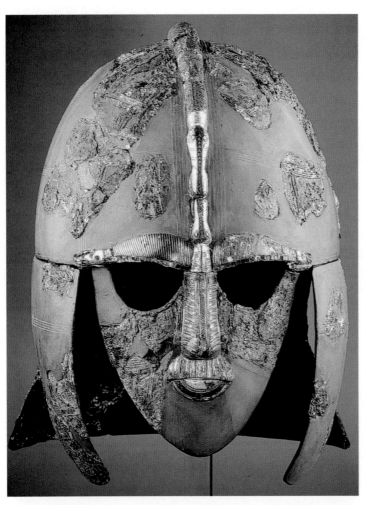

1 & 2
Symbols of 'Anglo-Saxon' kingship at the end of the period discussed in this book:
1 The 'Sutton Hoo helmet'
2 'Great Gold buckle'
— both from the seventh-century ship burial in Mound 1 at Sutton Hoo.
Reproduced with the kind permission of The British Museum

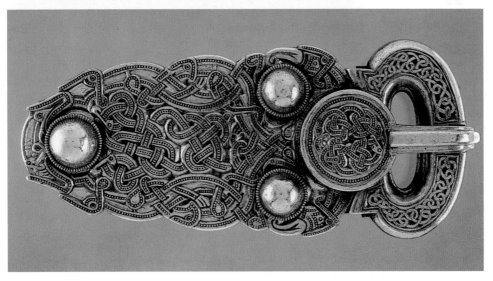

3 The walls of Burgh Castle 'Saxon shore fort', an example of Late Roman Britain's east coast defences

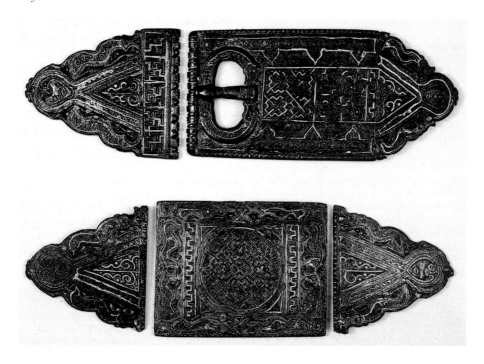

4 'Quoit-brooch style' buckle from Mucking. Reproduced with the kind permission of The British Museum

5   Reconstruction of an 'Anglo-Saxon' timber building at West Stow

6   'Anglo-Saxon' cremation urns at Spong Hill. Reproduced with the kind permission of the Norfolk Archaeological Unit. Photo: D. Wicks

7 *Reconstruction of an 'Anglo-Saxon' accompanied inhumation burial.* Reproduced with the kind permission of Hampshire County Council Museums Service

8 *Possible 'Anglo-Saxon' pagan shrine at Friar's Oak, Sussex.* Reproduced with the kind permission of Chris Butler.

9 Possible 'Anglo-Saxon' elite burial with horse at Lakenheath. Copyright: Suffolk County Council

10 Excavation of fifth-/sixth-century structures at Wroxeter. Reproduced with the kind permission of Philip Barker

11 The Tintagel 'Artognou' slate. English HeritagePhotographic Library

12 A fifth-/sixth-century structure reconstructed in situ *on an artificial terrace at Tintagel Head*

13 Class-1 inscribed stone at Southill, Cornwall

14 Reconstruction of a fifth-/sixth-century western British elite burial, with a Class-1 stone standing next to a Roman road. With the kind permission of Lady Fox and the National Museum of Wales

15 'Men Scryfa', a Class-1 inscribed stone in Cornwall, perhaps still in situ

16 Degannwy hill-fort, north Wales

17 Class-1 inscribed stone from Penmachno (the 'Carausius stone'), showing a Chi-Rho symbol, and referring to a cairn burial above which it once stood

18 Excavation of the settlement at Cefn Cwmwd. Reproduced with the kind permission of BUFAU: photo, Graham Norrie

cm

*19 Byzantine garnet intaglio (signet-ring gem) from Cefn Cwmwd, depicting a scorpion.*Reproduced with the kind permission of BUFAU

20 The fifth-/sixth-century settlement at Gateholm

21 *While intended to show a Romano-British 'small town', this reconstruction may resemble the interior of the larger fifth-/sixth-century settlements in western Britain, such as Gateholm.* Painting: Peter Froste

22 *Excavation of the fifth-/sixth-century hill-fort at Brawdy*

23 Class-1 inscribed stone from Brawdy, showing an 'Irish' personal name (Macutrenus) on a Latin-inscribed memorial

24 Class-1 inscribed stone from Lewannick, Cornwall, showing both Latin and ogam scripts

25 *Reconstruction of a hill-fort, probably resembling many fifth-/sixth-century elite settlements in western Britain, although few are known to have had so many ramparts.* Reproduced with the kind permission of Pembrokeshire Coast National Park Authority

26 *Long-cist burials at the Catstane cemetery near Edinburgh.* Copyright Royal Commission for Historical Monuments of Scotland

27 *Traprain Law hill-fort.* Copyright Royal Commission for Historical Monuments of Scotland

28 *A so-called 'Pictish silver chain' from Whitecleugh, Lanarkshire.* Photo: Trustees of the National Museums of Scotland

29 Excavation of a Pictish cellular structure at Buckquoy. Reproduced with the kind permission of Dr Anna Ritchie

30 Excavation of Pictish barrows at Redcastle. Reproduced with the kind permission of Aberdeenshire Archaeology Service

31 A Pictish Class-1 symbol stone from Burghead depicting a bull. Reproduced with the kind permission of The British Museum

32 Dunadd hill-fort. Reproduced with the kind permission of Kilmartin House Trust

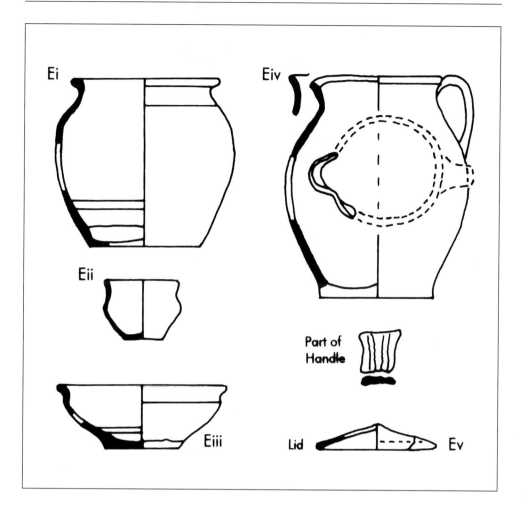

35 Imported E-ware pottery found in western Britain. (After Edwards and Alcock)

or vertical chevrons, although some deeply coloured red, blue, green and brown glass was also imported. Again, Bordeaux has been suggested as a source, but northern France seems ruled out, as is 'Anglo-Saxon England'. These glass imports may partly post-date the Mediterranean imports, although evidence from Whithorn in Scotland suggests some overlap, and in general the glass may be associated with E-ware.[53]

E-ware is a type of hard-fired coarse-gritted white or grey Frankish pottery comprising jugs, beakers, bowls and jars, belonging to the late sixth to late seventh century. While its origin remains unknown, work by Jonathan Wooding and, especially, Ewan Campbell has transformed the study of this material in recent years. For example, they have shown that E-ware was probably a 'fineware' in seventh-century Britain and Ireland but a 'coarseware' in Frankia, and that some at least was imported as containers for dye and perhaps other substances. Although the commonest of these imports in Britain overall, E-ware rarely occurs in the zone discussed in this chapter, being found at only Dinas Powys and the enigmatic nearby site of Lesser Garth cave.

There is also a round-bottomed vessel of squat globular form from Cadbury Congresbury (termed 'Gaulish ware' in the site report), which may be a western European import. It is dull buff in colour, with a gritty texture and pimply surface, containing quartz grains, blackened both inside and out. This is unlikely to be a Mediterranean product, and a Frankish ('Gaulish') or more likely Spanish source is likely. A single glass vessel of sixth-century Spanish form is also known, again from Tintagel, where it may support the view that trading ships picked up goods as they sailed towards Britain stopping in North Africa and Spain.[54]

It is interesting that D-ware could also come from the areas in which Byzantine ceramics have been found in western France. Perhaps this western material was also picked up by Byzantine ships en route from the Mediterranean.[55]

Another piece of evidence makes it plausible that Byzantine ships did reach Britain. These ships carried characteristic water jars, employing reused amphorae known from Byzantine shipwrecks but also found at Tintagel. They are unlikely to be objects of long-distance trade.[56]

The most probable interpretation for the fifth- and sixth-century imports, prior to E-ware and the shift to a Frankish-centred trading pattern as outlined by Wooding and Campbell, seems the direct and directional journeys from the eastern Mediterranean, most likely western Anatolia or Constantinople. Ann Bowman has calculated that such journeys would not have been economically profitable for Byzantine merchants, and a non-economic explanation may be the most likely. One has to explain why ships should sail to Britain from the heart of the Byzantine world in the late fifth or early sixth century.[57]

In the early sixth century the Byzantine government attempted to reconquer the former Roman Empire in the West. Invasions of North Africa, Sicily and Italy were accompanied by a diplomatic campaign to win 'hearts and minds' in western courts. Byzantine mercantile communities resident in the West played a key role in this, with traders acting as diplomats and agents for the Byzantine authorities. Such communities are attested in Gaul and Spain in written sources. We would not expect such sources to help us in Britain, but the imported Mediterranean pottery could be interpreted in this way, Byzantine merchants travelling between the Mediterranean and Britain for diplomatic reasons subsidised by the imperial authorities. This would explain the 'directionality', the Constantinopolitan character of the ceramics, and the apparent disregard for economic considerations. That is not to say that economic gain was no part of their activities: Lynette Olson observed that Mediterranean imports correlate closely in distributional terms with British metal sources unavailable in the Mediterranean, and tin was known as the 'British metal' to Byzantines. It would be a foolish merchant who, funded to engage in politics, failed to take advantage of the commercial opportunities while in Britain, and ingots may have been the most valuable commodity to bring 'home'.[58]

We may be able to identify at least one of the ports involved in this long-distance connection in the zone discussed in this chapter. The sand-dune site at Meols, Cheshire, was a coastal Romano-British settlement on the Wirral, with coins dating from the first to fourth centuries, set amid sand-dunes. Fifth- to sixth-century activity at Meols is only

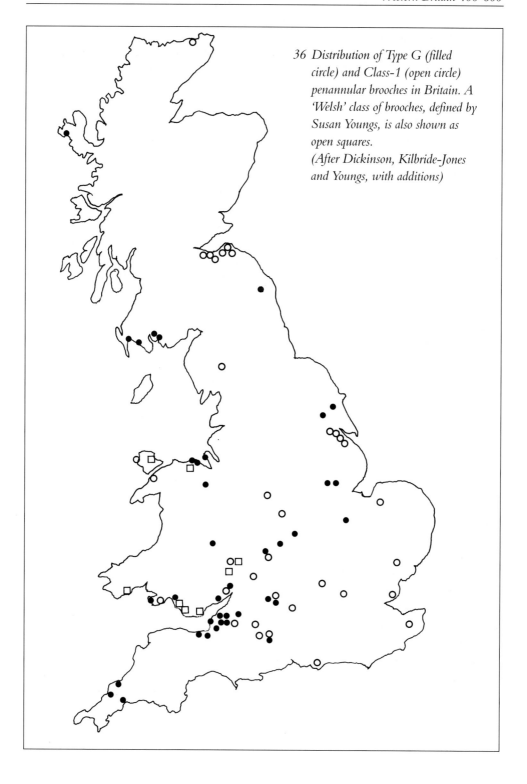

36 Distribution of Type G (filled circle) and Class-1 (open circle) penannular brooches in Britain. A 'Welsh' class of brooches, defined by Susan Youngs, is also shown as open squares.
(After Dickinson, Kilbride-Jones and Youngs, with additions)

visible through finds from pre-modern investigation, but material from the site includes a red pottery 'St Menas flask' from Egypt (the only find of its sort from a site in Britain), penannular brooches and metalwork of post-600 date.[59]

Although Meols does not appear to have high-status occupation, trade with the Mediterranean was probably directed at elite sites, and perhaps monasteries — although the latter may have received imports from members of the secular elite as gifts. This would explain the pottery and glass at Cadbury Congresbury, South Cadbury, Dinas Powys and Ham Hill hill-forts, all potentially elite settlements of this date. Another aspect of the hill-forts at Cadbury Congresbury and Dinas Powys is that they provide evidence of the patronage of jewellers by elites, in the forms of crucibles, hearths and other material, associated with jewellery-making.

Western British jewellery of this period includes a range of penannular brooch types, pins and hanging-bowls. These have been extensively studied, most recently by Tania Dickinson, James Graham-Campbell, Helen Geake, Ragnall O'Floinn and Susan Youngs. Penannular brooches are seldom found on excavated sites of 400-600 in western Britain but two Type G brooches (the most well-known type of this date) come from Cadbury Congresbury, and a lead die for manufacturing a Class 1 penannular brooch was found at Dinas Powys, where it apparently dates to the sixth century.[60]

Class 1 zoomorphic brooches probably date from the fifth to seventh centuries. The Class might begin in the fourth century, but as this is based on the Bath brooch, for which there is no associated dating evidence to securely assign it to before 400, it is uncertain whether any Class 1 brooches predate the fifth century.

Type G brooches are rare throughout the area and few examples of Class 1 zoomorphic brooches come from this zone, as at Bath, Calne, Dinas Powys and Oldbury hill-fort. These are also of this broad date and distributionally perhaps equally likely to have been manufactured in this area. Susan Youngs has argued that the long 'stick pins', of the type found at Wroxeter, belong to the late fourth to sixth century, but only four come from the area discussed in the present chapter, at Wroxeter (two examples), Cirencester and Caerleon.

In seminal, but as yet unpublished, work (which she has very generously allowed me to summarise here) Susan Youngs has advanced a radical new hypothesis based on detailed analysis of hanging bowls. These are copper alloy hemispherical bowls with decorative side discs (escutcheons) for suspension by a chain. Youngs has shown that, while frequently claimed as Irish or 'Anglo-Saxon' products (although the only moulds for their decorative escutcheons have been found at Seagray in Wiltshire and Craig Phadraig in Scotland) these may have been widely produced. She has demonstrated that the art and techniques of manufacture indicate a western British Romano-Christian milieu as their origin and identifies their supports as tripod stands of Roman form. Confusion has arisen in the past because most known examples are from early seventh-century 'Anglo-Saxon' graves, but these are secondary contexts which need tell us nothing of their origin or original role.[61]

Youngs notes that the bowls often carry Christian symbolism and the use of enamel suggests a high-status context. She dates hanging bowls to the mid-sixth to mid-seventh century, but an early sixth-century attribution may not be impossible in my opinion for

37 Hanging bowl from Winchester. Reproduced with the kind permission of The British Museum

some pieces, given the problems in dating this material. It is fair to say that Youngs' study revolutionises our understanding of these objects, and places them as crucial evidence for the Romano-Christian society of western Britain in the sixth and seventh century, perhaps particularly the later sixth century.

The total amount of 'diagnostic' British metalwork of this date is small, and it is hard to believe that these items were used by many fifth- and sixth-century western Britons. More likely is that these objects were prestige objects used for displaying status by the elite. As such, their presence at a site may indicate elite contacts, although we do not know if the brooches or pins carried other associations, of ethnicity, age, precise social position and gender.

If few Britons in this area were wearing these objects, and this comprises all the most diagnostic material, it raises the question of what material culture they were using. One possibility, of course, is that they were using the same material culture as the 'Anglo-Saxons' to their east. This too seems to be excluded by a lack of similar material, but 'Anglo-Saxon' metalwork has been found at Dinas Powys, Cadbury Congresbury, Worlebury hill-fort, Ham Hill, Ilchester, South Cadbury and Cirencester.[62]

For example, what may be the back plate of an 'Anglo-Saxon' brooch was found at Cadbury Congresbury, where there were also two drum-shaped 'Anglo-Saxon' glass beads, and an amber bead which might derive from contacts with the 'Anglo-Saxon' east of Britain. The small total amount of this material could be explained by the same elite use as postulated above, but this was clearly not the material culture of the western British community, or even the everyday material culture of the elite, unless current finds vastly under-represent the amount of this material in circulation. Nor did Byzantine or Frankish imports fill this apparent 'gap'. The only Frankish metal objects identified from this area are ring-ornaments from Margam and Barnsley Park and some possibly Frankish pieces of metalwork at Dinas Powys. The find of a Byzantine copper alloy censer at Glastonbury Abbey, the only Byzantine metalwork from western Britain, is somewhat suspect, and would be a liturgical item if genuinely from a sixth-century context at the site. Most likely the Britons were not supplementing their material culture with imported metalwork, nor manufacturing much of their own in diagnostically fifth- and sixth-century styles as these are usually imagined.

This problem is also seen in relation to ceramics. It is extremely unlikely that Mediterranean imports accounted for more than the pottery of the elite and perhaps some churchpeople in this area. Otherwise, there is only a handful of sherds of coarse handmade wares at Cadbury Congresbury ('miscellaneous tempered wares') and a small amount of grass-tempered pottery. This pottery has long been considered distinctively British, although it also occurs on 'Anglo-Saxon' settlements such as Mucking. In western Britain, grass-tempered pottery has been dated to the fifth century at Crickley Hill and to the sixth century at Cadbury Congresbury and Poundbury. Grass-tempered pottery is very rare in Dorset and south Somerset and it does not occur further north than Gloucestershire.[63]

The distribution in western Britain is, therefore, largely confined to the area of the fourth-century *civitas* of the Dobunni. This might be understood as suggesting that grass-tempered pottery was especially 'Dobunnic' in western Britain, alternatively it might have been 'Anglo-Saxon' and imported via Dobunnic territory, accounting for a greater amount in that Late Roman *civitas*. As grass-tempered pottery is anomalous in western Britain, in so far as it is the only seemingly indigenous post-Roman ceramic produced in any quantity, the second option might be favoured. This would imply that sites with grass-tempered pottery are unlikely to date from the fifth century as often imagined, instead they should be assigned at earliest to the sixth century.

While it seems possible to argue that these sites belong to the period after 500 this has major implications for the chronology of many sites in western Britain where this pottery has been recognised. It would imply that Romano-British town houses at Dorchester and Cirencester were still occupied in the sixth century and assign the post-Roman settlement at Crickley Hill and much of the activity at Frocester to the sixth century, leaving the 'squatter occupation', that is the modification of the villa in 'sub-Roman' fashion, as the fifth-century phase at Frocester.

The Britons in the West neither manufactured their own artefacts of characteristically post-Roman types, nor employed 'Anglo-Saxon' or imported pottery in sufficient quantities to offset this absence, except in specific areas and social environments. This is more than simply becoming 'aceramic' after centuries of using ceramics, which would be surprising. The majority of Britons either had nothing that survives for archaeologists to find, or we are 'missing something' about the already-known material from western Britain.

The most obvious remaining option is that superficially Romano-British material culture was still being used on a day-to-day basis in western Britain. If the Britons could be so conservative in other respects, such as burial practice, then why do we assume that fifth- and sixth-century artefacts should necessarily look different from fourth-century ones? It is quite possible to imagine that conscious effort might have been made to preserve the 'correct' form of artefacts over a period of a century or more, and that divergence from this might have had economic or social consequences unfavourable to manufacturers. Interestingly, Martin Carver has drawn attention to modern examples of exactly this trend, and to evidence of 'formal conservatism' over much longer timespans in first millennium AD Italy. It is untrue to say that no analogies exist for this sort of behaviour, even in first millennium AD western Europe.[64]

We could follow Hilary Cool's important suggestion that dress fashions and preferences for different coloured objects could reveal fifth- as opposed to fourth-century artefacts of identical form. She has noted, for example, that there is a tendency towards red pottery spindle whorls and counters made of reused ceramics (especially samian ware) in the very latest fourth-century deposits. Other types of artefacts which apparently came into fashion in the very late fourth or early fifth century include bone bracelets (perhaps copying ivory examples such as that at Barnsley Park, dated 375-80), opaque disc cylindrical beads and 'non-standard' beads of glass.[65]

Cool suggests that penannular brooches of types D and E also belong to the latest fourth or fifth century (one might then see the brooches discussed above as a continuation of this fashion), while black finger rings also appear popular in this 'terminal Roman' phase. She also draws attention to a decreasing number of iron tools and hairpins and an increasing number of knives and bracelets as exemplifying such assemblages. Her suggestion is that these characteristics prevailed as a distinct 'suite' of artefacts until replaced by something else, which was 'Anglo-Saxon' material culture in some areas of Britain, but which might not have been until the later sixth century in western Britain.

This hypothesis is based on detailed examination of actual finds assemblages from datable sites of the late fourth and early fifth century. Fashions beginning in the late fourth century might be imagined to continue into the fifth.[66]

Another approach would be to adopt Ian Burrow's suggestion concerning pottery curation and argue that Late Roman material culture was so plentiful in c.400 that it remained in circulation for centuries. Pottery is a poor example of this, being easily broken, but why assume that Romano-British jewellery or metal vessels were broken within a century? We only have to look around us to see jewellery more than a century old still used and valued, and this is in a twenty-first-century 'consumer society'.[67]

Returning to an even older suggestion, we might look at rivetted pottery and other 'mended' material culture that could have circulated until broken, but replacements were unavailable. This could explain why common objects in fourth-century Britain were restored in such dramatic ways. Plainly this approach has to be employed extremely carefully — one can imagine many reasons why pottery or other objects could be repaired, and not all repairs are likely to be of the same date — but it might draw attention to material common in the late fourth century repaired in possibly fifth-century or later contexts.

Let us explore all these options in relation to this part of western Britain in more detail.

Fifth- and sixth-century artefacts in black and white (and red)

The finds from Wroxeter, Uley, Dinas Powys and Cadbury Congresbury enable us to investigate all the above options. These sites were all outstandingly excavated in a meticulous fashion and have clearly-defined fifth- and sixth-century deposits, within which any distinctive group of fifth- and sixth-century artefacts may occur if it was present locally. First, it will be helpful to outline the main aspects of the fifth- and sixth-century occupation of each site.

The relevant excavation at the Roman town of Wroxeter took place on the basilica of the principal urban public baths (the 'Baths Basilica site'). The last reflooring of the bath's basilica was in Phase W, perhaps in the late fourth century. This was followed by the basilica's disuse in Phase X (probably between 410 and *c.*550). The site of the former basilica was given over to use as a builder's yard, and then dismantled in Phase Y and the site used as a market place (probably during the sixth century). The 'great rebuilding' of Phase Z saw the whole of the former basilica covered with substantial timber buildings (a minimum of 36 have been identified in the excavated area), some of two storeys, showing detailed knowledge of Late Roman architecture. The date of the rebuilding appears to have been between 500 and 580. The complex was probably used until the seventh century.[68]

At Uley, the fourth-century 'Romano-Celtic' temple was first drastically reduced in scale (in Phase 6b), with its *cella* (central ritual building) partially demolished. This may belong to the early fifth century, but was followed in Phase 7a by either a phase of disuse or swiftly by the construction of a basilican building, probably a Christian church

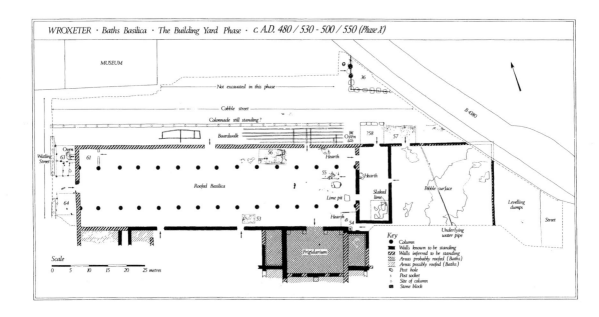

38 (above and opposite) Fifth- and sixth-century Wroxeter. Copyright English Heritage

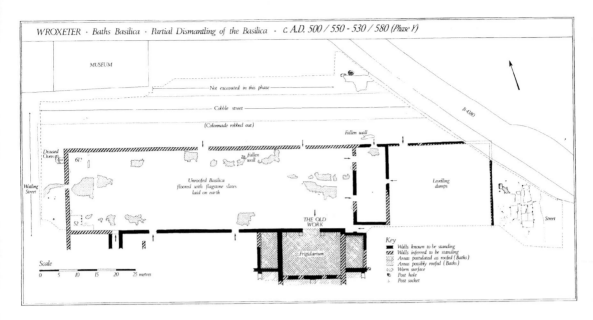

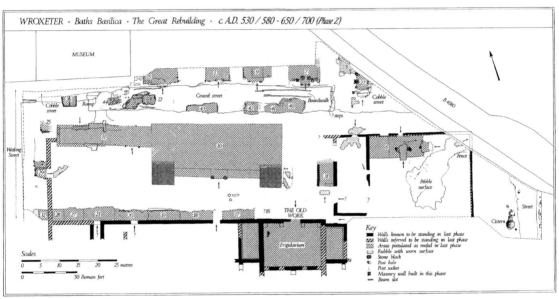

(structure XI). This may have occurred at some point during the fifth century, but need not have been long into that century. This structure was enclosed within a single, perhaps low, bank with at least two entrances. This complex included other structures, and was modified and the church replaced in stone in Phase 7bi, which has been dated by the excavators to the sixth century, but could well be later in date. The excavators see Phase 7bii as dating to the late sixth or seventh century, when this building and the re-planned complex were again modified. Finds from the temple preceding Phase 6 necessitate that the subsequent sequence dates from the fifth century or later, while the latest dated find is a piece of 'Anglo-Saxon' coloured window glass, likely to be of Middle Saxon date.[69]

Dinas Powys is a small multivallate inland promontory hill-fort near Cardiff in south-east Wales. Despite Late Bronze Age occupation on the hilltop, the hill-fort dates wholly from the post-Roman period, and was enclosed by four earthen banks, the exact dating of which is disputed. The interior contained two phases of buildings, all rectilinear. In the first internal phase there was only a single post-built structure (house IA); this was followed by two gullies defining buildings (house IB and house II). A single child burial, placed north-south in a crouched position, has been assigned to the post-Roman occupation, but might be Bronze Age, as the excavator has observed.[70]

The site produced a wide array of finds, including imported Mediterranean pottery, imported Frankish pottery, and glass. 'Anglo-Saxon' metalwork including shield ornaments, copper alloy vessel rims, lace tags, belt fittings and a strap end of a distinctively Kentish type, were found. Local artefacts included objects of stone and bone, and there is much evidence for metalworking, including a lead die, distinctive knobbed crucibles, slag, molten glass, hearths and scrap metal, some cut. The imported pottery includes PRSW, Bi, Bii and B misc. amphora, and D and E wares, confirming a late fifth- or early sixth- to seventh-century date. The hill-fort banks were probably built in at least two phases. The first was either univallate or more likely bivallate, and may date to the initial occupation, with the others added later, perhaps in the seventh century. Bank 1, belonging to this refurbishment, is the latest dated earthwork added to a hill-fort in western Britain, and overlies E ware dated to *c*.600.

Cadbury Congresbury is a multivallate contour hill-fort enclosed by earthen banks on a hilltop adjacent to a fifth- or sixth-century cemetery at Henley Wood. The site overlooks what is today moorland, and is within sight of the Bristol Channel. The sites at Worlebury and Brean Down, both arguably used at this date, were also visible from Cadbury Congresbury. Wenbreham villa, from which there is a possible Christian mosaic, showing a floriate cross, is roughly halfway between the site and the sea, along the river Yeo. Post-prehistoric occupation at Cadbury Congresbury may have begun in the fifth century (Phase 3.I), with at least two rectangular timber structures (structures I and VI), perhaps including a possible curvilinear building (structure III).[71]

The post-Roman inner hill-fort bank (the 'Diagonal Bank') was built in Phase 3II, perhaps assignable to the late fifth to early sixth century, when two curvilinear structures (structures II and III) dominated the excavated area, but a rectilinear structure V may have remained in use. During phases 3III-IV, in the sixth century, the inner bank was disused, but occupation continued in the form of new curvilinear and rectilinear structures (IV, VII and VIII) perhaps within a new perimeter bank (the 'Perimeter Bank'). Other features appear to include (ritual?) post-settings in small stony areas and areas of burning outside the main structures.

No later occupation occurred, and no substantial Roman activity is definitely known from the hilltop. So this would seem a good location at which to identify artefacts of fifth- and sixth-century date, especially as the site is well-dated by imported Mediterranean pottery of this date.

Having outlined the evidence for believing that each of these sites was a settlement of

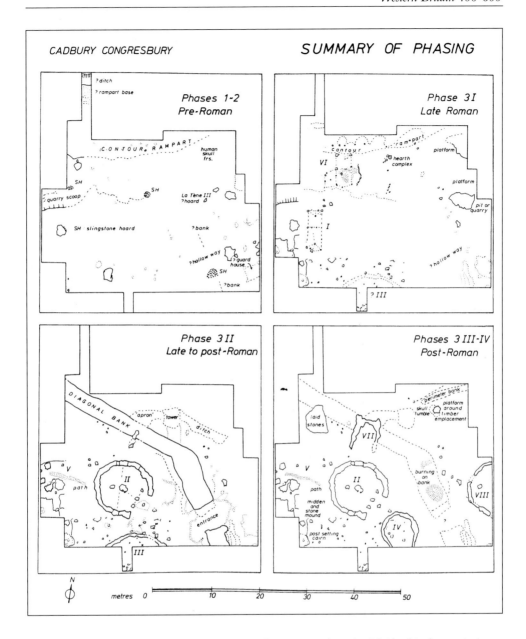

39 The main excavated area at Cadbury Congresbury. Reproduced with the kind permission of P.A. Rahtz

fifth- to sixth-century date, let us examine the associated artefacts from the point of view of identifying possible post-Roman finds among the superficially Romano-British material. It is convenient to begin with pottery, which 'conventional wisdom', established in the 1970s, has it was not in use after *c*.450 at latest.

The possibility of Romano-British pottery being in use contemporary with fifth- and sixth-century imported Mediterranean pottery at Cadbury Congresbury has been explored by both Philip Rahtz and Ian Burrow. However, their results are inconclusive, not ruling out simultaneous use, nor necessitating it. So we must look to the other two sites for a clearer indication of whether or not some Romano-British (or superficially Romano-British) pottery was in use during the fifth and sixth centuries.

At Uley, several types of pottery 'peak' in the fifth- and sixth-century phase. This is especially true of calcite gritted wares and Oxfordshire red-colour coated ware: 'black' and 'red' products. The use of calcite gritted pottery at this date is especially interesting as the ware only becomes common in the late fourth century elsewhere in the West Country, at Catsgore only *c*.400, and at Brean Down, where calcite gritted wares were predominantly associated with layers of *c*.390 and later. Paul Tyers has recently noted that these two wares come to play a major role in Romano-British pottery assemblages at the very end of visible Romano-British pottery production, with local imitations of east Midlands calcite gritted ware becoming widespread after an initial phase, in which east Midlands calcite gritted ware was widely distributed. On excavated evidence it would be possible to argue that the phase of imitation only began in the West Country after *c*.400, although earlier elsewhere. This would fit with Barry Cunliffe's 'long chronology' for the stratified pottery sequence from his excavation at Bath, which interprets this as continuing into the later fifth or early sixth century, and late in which calcite gritted ware imitations appear.[72]

Dinas Powys did not have Romano-British occupation, and all the pottery must have been brought to the site after 400. The assemblage suggests collection of Romano-British material from a site of first or second century date rather than comprising characteristically fourth-century material. Thus, the Romano-British finds from the site may be easily explained as equivalent to the Roman-period finds at West Stow, the products of scavenging from a nearby Roman-period settlement.

The Wroxeter sequence supports the view that 'Romano-British' pottery remained in use, if not production, until the mid-sixth century, with rivetted pieces surviving in small numbers until the end of that century. Despite the fact that Romano-British pottery appears to be 'residual' by the last phase of substantial use (Phase Z), the quantities of pottery being broken and discarded peak in Phase X (late fifth to mid-sixth century) rather than earlier, only declining during penultimate Phase Y (sixth century). This is not my own interpretation: according to the Wroxeter report 'pottery still seems to have been in use' in Phase X — in the late fifth to mid-sixth century — but in declining amounts. Even the shortest possible chronology would assign Phase X to the late fifth century, so demonstrating that these assemblages date from the period covered here.[73]

Mended and rivetted pots especially characterise Phase Y, dated by the report to the sixth century. This also occurred at Whitley Grange villa, and although 'pottery use seems to have *largely* ceased (my italics) by the mid-sixth century' rivetted pots were still circulating. In particular, distributional evidence might be taken to support the use of

Nene Valley and calcite gritted wares contemporary with timber framed buildings of fifth- and sixth-century date. Interestingly, again all this pottery is coloured black or red, and again Oxfordshire ware and calcite gritted ware were particularly favoured. The only possible fifth- or sixth-century import is one Palestinian amphora, which is also the only exception to this colour rule.[74]

This would seem to bear out the proposal that Romano-British pottery production continued later than is usually supposed, into the fifth century (that is, to Wroxeter Phase W), with supplies being used until the mid-sixth century in declining numbers. We have already seen that a possible producer of the fifth century was the BB1 manufacturing site at Ower, and fifth-century BB1 pottery has been recognised at Bath, Exeter, Dorchester and nearby. It need hardly be said that the salient feature of BB1 is its black colour. Even after the fresh supply of pottery ceased, small quantities of remaining pottery were employed with broken vessels mended with rivets.

This must highlight other sites where rivetted Romano-British coarse pottery has been found. For example, we might take the 'carefully mended' rivetted Romano-British coarse pottery found at Ely villa (Glamorganshire) as indicative of possible fifth- or sixth-century occupation. There, the fourth-century villa was remodelled at a late date by the addition of a smaller building (room 11) overlying the corridor of the main house, the hypocaust of room 4 of the main house filled in and an oven provided in adjacent room 5. Another structure (room 10) of similar size to structure 11 was added to the rear of the main house, across the fill of the ditch surrounding the fourth-century complex. This would render three smaller houses: one comprising rooms 4 and 5 (and perhaps the northern end of corridor room 6), one room 10 and perhaps parts of the villa house, and another the newly-built room 11. These buildings do not necessarily show impoverishment on the site, because room 11 had a mortar floor and plastered walls. This complex was enclosed within a bank and ditch which cut the second fourth-century building, while a burial was inserted adjacent to the villa structure and one ditch was cut further to the south-east, perhaps to enclose a broader court area.[75]

The evidence from Ely indicates the possibilities raised by reviewing instances of rivetted Late Roman pottery as a possible indicator of fifth- and sixth-century occupation. Returning to Wroxeter, Dinas Powys, Cadbury Congresbury and Uley, we may turn our attention to glass.

It might initially be supposed that, unlike pottery, glassware is unlikely to survive for centuries if subjected to regular use. All the olive-green glass at Wroxeter comes from Phases Y-Z including an unusually large number of sherds decorated with blue glass 'blobs', a feature found on fifth-century Continental glassware such as that from Ravenna, Italy. The glassware includes hemispherical cups and conical drinking vessels and the latter may relate to the survival of Late Roman customs of drinking. Kate Pretty noted that the pattern of deposition of glass at Wroxeter concurs with that of pottery, and the argument affecting the continued use of pottery can logically be extended to glassware.[76]

Glass cups were apparently used at Uley into the fifth and sixth century. At Dinas Powys all the Roman glass was again of the period before 300, and probably also scavenged, but at Cadbury Congresbury, 'fourth-century' glass was found in fifth- and sixth-century layers, in this case well-dated by imported ceramics. This helps makes sense of the imported material. If the fifth- and sixth-century norm in western Britain was to expect red or black eating bowls and conical glass drinking vessels, this might explain why red-slipped ware bowls, 'black' slipped D-ware bowls, and conical glass drinking vessels are the most visible imports apart from amphorae, presumably containing the sort of 'Roman' foodstuffs consumed in these. Eight Kempston-type 'Anglo-Saxon' cone beakers occur among the Cadbury Congresbury glass, suggesting that these could have been used as an alternative (replacement?) for 'Roman' conical glass drinking cups. This would imply either that Britons had some say in the products which they obtained from Byzantine and Frankish traders, or that these traders were sufficiently aware of the British 'market' as to cater for its specific tastes.

Knives are among the commonest finds on fifth- and sixth-century British settlements, and (writing?) styli surprisingly widespread. A large number of knives and styli were found in fifth- and sixth-century deposits at Wroxeter. A stylus was also found in Phase 7 deposits at Uley, as were two knives, and Dinas Powys produced 19 knives and a stylus. Twenty knives and what may be a stylus come from Cadbury Congresbury.

While it may be an overstatement to claim 'it seems that it is almost as if anything Roman was wearable in the fifth and sixth centuries', the material culture of fifth- and sixth-century Wroxeter seems to have been almost wholly 'Romano-British' in character. It is superficially indistinguishable from that of the late fourth century, except in the preferences for specific types of seemingly fourth-century artefacts. In addition to Cool's list, one can include shale armlets and glass hemispherical and conical drinking vessels, Oxfordshire ware and calcite gritted wares and perhaps iron writing styli.[77]

These artefacts have a certain consistency in functional terms and in colour choice. They are white, black and red and form a complementary set of eating utensils: pottery bowls, iron knives, bone spoons and glass drinking vessels. They also imply a particular style of (female?) dress, in which the arms are left free for bracelets and armlets. The bone combs found at Poundbury, Dinas Powys, and Cadbury Congresbury may suggest that long hair was kept tidy, although no longer pinned up. Here there may be a gender difference, in that bone combs are absent from Uley and Glastonbury Tor, although bone was preserved, but a (all male?) monastic interpretation is possible. The male figures in *Vergilius Romanus* have short hair and are clean-shaven, and the *Excerpta De Libris Romanorum et Francorum*, writing of the Britons of Brittany apparently perceived short hair as specifically British, or as it terms it 'Roman'. Perhaps armlets, bracelets and combs are female artefacts in this fifth- and sixth-century western British context.[78]

Artefactual evidence from Wroxeter, Uley and Cadbury Congresbury appears to bear out the impression from Patrick and Gildas regarding the culture of fifth- and sixth-century western Britain. The image gained recalls the illuminations in *Vergilius Romanus*, with a high standard of living on the Late Roman model being enjoyed by at least some members of society. This may be the artefactual counterpart of living in refurbished Roman-period buildings and timber-framed structures with Late Roman antecedents and using Late Roman forms of Christian burial practice.

Dinas Powys stands out as an exception in regard to the use of pottery and glass, and also has no trace of these colour preferences except in relation to imported ceramics. The site also has a high pin to bracelet ratio, which could indicate different dress styles, although there are about 20 combs. If one took the 'Anglo-Saxon' material at face value, one of the occupants would have been able to dress as an 'Anglo-Saxon' warrior, although there is no other evidence for 'Anglo-Saxon' occupation. This may suggest that Dinas Powys was used by people living outside of these norms, for cultural, religious or ethnic reasons.

Dinas Powys is possibly alone among the excavated hill-forts of the fifth to seventh century in western Britain in being on a site without Romano-British occupation (although this might be true of High Peak in Devon also), and if the first phase of the banks was univallate would be the only known univallate hill-fort. Inland promontory forts are not common in western Britain at this date, and most that were even arguably used are in areas with strong Irish associations further west. There are other hints of an Irish community at the site, in the large quantity of E-ware and the brooch die, which is best parallelled in Ireland. Jonathan Wooding has suggested that E-ware carried Irish associations in Britain (possibly because it reached Britain through a network of contacts centred on Ireland or the 'Irish' areas of western Scotland), and no site south of Scotland has as great a quantity of E-ware as Dinas Powys.[79]

Perhaps Dinas Powys is different because it is an Irish elite settlement in western Britain. Such a group might be raiders, high-status exiles or aristocrats related to or working for a British ruler. The latter might be most likely at Dinas Powys, because the settlement is not wholly Irish in character. Roundhouses characterise Irish settlements of this date, but the structures at Dinas Powys are rectilinear. The longevity of the site also implies some integration into the surrounding community, arguing against a raiding party or exiles. Irish warbands led by their own chiefs could have been used in a manner analogous to the employment of 'Anglo-Saxon' troops in eastern Britain, giving them land and provisions for defence, in the late fifth century. This would explain the anomalous character of the site, if interpreted as the residence of such an Irish leader, established in this way. Perhaps this explains the possible burial and peculiar name of Dinas Powys. This is the only burial at a hill-fort of this date in western Britain, and 'Dinas Powys' might mean 'fort of the pagans': an Irish ruler could still be a pagan in the late fifth century, although integration into British elite life implies they or their children may have been later converted. The place-name could have 'stuck', if only in an ironical manner, and the burial pre-dates conversion.

A topic upon which this material offers little help is the fate of coinage-use. At Uley it is impossible to differentiate between residual and still-used Roman coins. Only four Roman coins were found at Cadbury Congresbury and only one at Dinas Powys. At Wroxeter the chronological distribution of coinage is identical to that of pottery and glass. This could support the interpretation that coinage remained in use in the fifth and sixth centuries at the site. The impression that coins were used in some way during the fifth and sixth centuries at Wroxeter is reinforced by the finds associated with Phase Z. Although other 'Romano-British' material was becoming scare in Phase Z there are 33 Roman coins, and coins occur on 11/17 of the 'path' or 'floor' contexts. This is, of course, consistent with the use of coins in everyday life, and it may be salutary that not all such deposits, nor all deposits, at Wroxeter contain Roman coins. They are not, then, simply a ubiquitous product of redeposition.[80]

An objection to continuing coin use at Wroxeter is that large numbers of coins occur in the debris by open air hearths in the North Portico, and in the rubble platforms used as the bases for structures. Had coins been recoverable for use, then surely — it is suggested — these coins would have not been left lying about. However, we do not know what rules could have governed the recovery of coins in general or in this particular case. It might have been a prerogative of particular people, or some types of coin might have been more desirable than others, or the Wroxeter complex might have been 'private property' from which it was unwise even to 'steal' objects lying about in the soil. Moreover, every Roman town in Continental Europe and the Mediterranean must have continuously produced Roman coins when its soil was disturbed, yet 'old' coinage was widely used there in Late Antique and later contexts. So the objection 'you could just pick them up all over the place' does not hold water. Non-recovery does not preclude the fifth-century use of some coin, although it may suggest that this was not as indiscriminate as it might initially appear. Reusing selected old coins would render coinage-use precisely analogous to the trend affecting other artefacts.

Whatever medium of commerce was used, the rulers of western Britain never produced their own coins. However, it is too easily assumed that we know these rulers to have been kings.

Kings and governors

Modern historians and archaeologists have been unanimous in the view that western Britain was ruled by kings alone in the late fifth and sixth centuries. It might be supposed that Gildas tells us this, but that is not true.[81]

Gildas describes the sins of contemporary kings, naming five such rulers and implying the existence of a 'greater' king in Britain. It is possible to locate three of Gildas' 'targets': Constantine of Dumnonia, Vortipor of Dyfed and Maglocunus of Gwynedd. The order in which Gildas denounces these rulers implies that he is citing their names geographically, and this enables us to identify the probable location of the other kings named: Aurelius Caninus could be localised to south Wales and Cuneglasus to the north-east of Wales. Support for this comes from the identification of Bryn Euryn hill-fort as a site (*receptaculum ursi*), linked by Gildas to Cuneglasus.[82]

This pattern of localities resembles the Romano-British political geography of the western periphery of western Britain, reconstructible on Roman-period evidence. Cuneglasus is localised to the area of the Deceangli in Romano-British terms, while Aurelius Caninus would belong to the Silures, Maglocunus to the Ordovices, Constantine to the Dumnonii, and Vortipor to the Demetae. However, there is reason to believe that the Silures were split into two post-Roman polities, one in the west known later as 'Glywysing', one in the east called 'Gwent' — the 'territory of Venta' (*Venta Silurum*: Caerwent).[83]

If Aurelius Caninus is assigned to Glywysing rather than Gwent (and there is no reason to necessitate that he was ruler of Gwent), then there is no evidence in *De Excidio* of sixth-century kingship in that part of western Britain covered by this chapter. Nor does

Patrick or any other contemporary source inform us that there were kings in this area. Indeed, the only sources to mention British kings based in this region are the Llandaff charters, which we have seen are inadmissible, and the Anglo-Saxon Chronicle.

The Anglo-Saxon Chronicle refers to three 'kings' of Gloucester, Bath and Cirencester being killed at Dyrham (near Bath) in 577. There is a small univallate hill-fort, not dissimilar to Crickley Hill, at Dyrham, but this annal, written centuries after the event, has long been doubted. If it has any value at all, there is no reason to believe that the annalist would have understood any leadership role in battle other than kingship. So, it is possible to discount the annal for 577 as a reliable source for western British political organization, even if it records an actual battle.[84]

Only one other source exists which might enable us to discover British kings active in the area: archaeology. The main evidence comes from two sites, Cadbury Congresbury and South Cadbury. Written and archaeological evidence for the area examined in the next chapter and from north Britain connect hill-forts with kingship. So, it is worth examining the evidence for a kingly presence at these two sites.

South Cadbury is a large contour hill-fort, comparable in size to Tintagel in Cornwall. A small part of the site (approximately 5 per cent) was excavated by Leslie Alcock in the 1960s and early 1970s, in a classic campaign. Alcock showed that South Cadbury had been occupied in the late fifth and sixth centuries. A timber-laced rampart had been constructed around the whole perimeter of the inner bank of the impressive Iron Age multivallate contour hill-fort that preceded the Roman use of the site, perhaps for a temple. This post-Roman earthwork was pierced by at least one gate with a cobbled road running beneath a rectilinear wooden tower or gatehouse. Inside, few structures of this date were identifiable, although many undated post-holes were found. On a slightly raised area ('the summit') there was a large post-built rectangular building (19 x 10m) with an internal wall-trench (L1). This was near two parallel wall-trenches, indicating a far smaller structure (S1).[85]

These buildings and the rampart were associated with imported Mediterranean pottery of classes A and Bii and Biv, and class D Frankish pottery and imported Germanic glass, some similar to that from 'Anglo-Saxon' cemeteries. The pottery and glass show a notable concentration on the biggest structure, implying consumption of food and drink from high-quality tableware within it. 'Anglo-Saxon' metalwork (including a bronze ring or pendant, a button brooch and a bucket mount) was also found, in addition to a 'pin beater' similar to examples from sites in eastern Britain. A single low-tin bronze ingot implies metalworking. The only directly military artefact was a crossbow bolt, perhaps of fifth- or sixth-century date, attesting the use of this Roman type of weapon at the site. Although there was no evidence for large-scale occupation, this could well be a result of the zonation of occupation on the site, the limited sample size, plough-damage, and unrecognised roundhouses dating to the period of the imports which might lurk unnoticed among the excavated features.

The evidence suggests that South Cadbury was an important political or military centre of the fifth and sixth centuries, with elite occupants able to enjoy imported luxuries, and the same could be true of Cadbury Congresbury, where imported pottery and glass were also found. There, structures were more readily identified, although again a low percentage of the interior was excavated and evidence of internal zonation was identified. The precious metals among the finds and jewellery-making may both imply that this too was an elite residence, which like South Cadbury could have been a political or military centre.

Other hill-forts may have been in use during the fifth and sixth century. 'Anglo-Saxon' metalwork is claimed to have been dug up at Dolebury hill-fort and Late Roman or later material comes from Stokeleigh. The sites at Worlebury and Ham Hill have already been mentioned, and Brent Knoll has entrance features surviving as earthworks reminiscent of the unexcavated 'guardhouses' visible in the plan of the post-Roman inner bank at Cadbury Congresbury, as Ian Burrow noted. A possible refortification at Whitsbury Hill may be associated with grass-tempered pottery.[86]

A convincing site further south may be Hod Hill, where Late Roman metalwork and possibly fourth-century or later quarry pits connected with its rampart have been found inside the multivallate hill-fort and fifth-century 'Anglo-Saxon' metalwork has been identified by Bruce Eagles immediately outside it. 'Anglo-Saxon' spearheads have been found within both this hill-fort and the multivallate site at Badbury Castle.[87]

Two more sites in Dorset have been proposed as hill-forts of sixth-century date. Leslie Alcock has suggested that a group of four inscriptions sharing some similarities with the western British Class-1 series belong to the fifth or sixth centuries, and enable one to identify the massive earthen bank which precedes the Late Saxon burh at Wareham as such a site. However, as Alcock himself says, this is no more than speculation, and the stones and bank might well both post-date 700, let alone 600. David Hinton has suggested that Corfe castle may be the site of a hill-fort of this date. It is strategically sited above Poole harbour and has an undated pre-castle bank, but — while possible — use at this date remains unconfirmed.[88]

Another pair of hill-forts which might be assigned to this period are Maes Knoll and Stantonbury. Both sites are incorporated into the Wansdyke, a long linear earthwork of fifth-century or later date, but probably from earlier than the seventh century as it was assigned a pagan name by the 'Anglo-Saxons'. We shall return to the Wansdyke later, but here it is worth noting that a fifth- or sixth-century date for the feature is the most convincing.[89]

To the north of the Wansdyke there is no compelling evidence of similar hill-fort reoccupation. The only hill-fort site is at Crickley Hill, where rectilinear timber buildings inside a palisaded enclosure appear to be socially superior to a groups of scooped curvilinear huts, their floors containing the last types of Romano-British pottery found at neighbouring sites, built on the same hilltop. The structures, which on both sites were twice burnt to the ground, were associated with grass-tempered pottery, perhaps of sixth-century date, but no evidence of 'Anglo-Saxon' occupation has been published.

Crickley Hill seems different in several respects to the hill-forts south of the Wansdyke. It is a palisaded enclosure, not constructed of earthwork banks, and is much less defensible. It lacks imported pottery and glass and jewellery-making evidence. In these respects it reflects a broader trend. Although imports occur at Dinas Powys and at Cadbury Congresbury, no imported pottery has been found north of the Wansdyke in what may be seen as Dobunnic territory in Romano-British terms. One piece of Germanic glass from

Much Wenlock is the only imported glass from this area. While Type G penannular brooches are found in Somerset and Wales, none have been recognised in the Dobunnic area. This might imply a cultural division between the Durotrigan and Dobunnic elites and suggest that an absence of hill-forts in the Dobunnic area is conceivable.[90]

The hill-forts necessitate a control of labour and materials absent from Crickley Hill and other settlement evidence from the Dobunnic area. The construction of South Cadbury required large amounts of timber (20km at South Cadbury for the 12km length of earthwork defence) and hundreds of hours of hard physical work. This and the employment of metalworkers, who are unlikely to have fed themselves, necessitated substantial food supplies, indicating a surplus of food at sites where feasting seems widely attested. None of this is necessary at any site north of Wansdyke, and south of Wroxeter.[91]

Wansdyke would have absorbed even greater quantities of labour, and food. It also used up land, which presumably was owned by someone. Whereas the builders of Crickley Hill needed perhaps only the community represented by the scooped huts as labour, those of the hill-forts controlled substantial resources by much later standards, or for that matter by Roman military standards. As David Petts has pointed out, the control of these resources may have had a symbolic value, and this would have been visible by observing earthworks from a distance to those working in the surrounding fields or to passing metalworkers. Possibly the views from these hill-forts might be symbolic too of the domain of the elites within them.[92]

Crickley Hill may, therefore, be a different sort of site to those south of the Wansdyke or in Wales. A key to understanding the site may be the presence of a military buckle of fifth-century form. This could be an heirloom of a minor landowner, resident within the 'high-status' complex with a dependent population of estate-workers living in the scooped huts. Sites like this may have been common in the fifth and sixth centuries in the Dobunnic area but (especially if they lacked grass-tempered pottery) they would be extremely difficult to locate.[93]

This difference may reflect differing political organization. The 'Durotrigan' hill-forts could well represent royal centres, with a hill-fort based royal elite controlling a portfolio of resources, consuming imported goods and requiring status symbols such as fine metalwork. Clearly, there were few such sites, rather than many for minor local dignitaries. This would concur with the relative lack of evidence for urban survival south of the Wansdyke, except for the evidence from Dorchester, perhaps a special case being the Durotrigan *civitas*-capital.

The lack of hill-forts, of imports and prestige metal objects, along with the potential survival of urban elite residence, implied by the use of Romano-British town houses and seen at Wroxeter in Phase Z, may suggest that urban-based bureaucratic government continued among the Cornovii and Dobunni into the later fifth and sixth centuries. This might be what Gildas meant when he commented that Britain had *rectores* ('governors') as well as *reges* ('kings'), although he was perhaps writing in Durotrigan territory and living under royal government. In this context his reference to Maglocunus being 'almost' the greatest king is explicable simply in terms of tact or loyalty, since it may have been unwise to say another king was 'greater' than one's ruler![94]

We might, then, envisage two different forms of government in sixth-century western Britain: monarchy and bureaucracy. These forms of government would seem to have different archaeological 'signatures': urban survival and hill-fort occupation, neither of which are attested in 'Anglo-Saxon' eastern Britain. But a return to monarchy did not mean that the political units involved were post-Roman novelties, and of course monarchy has to have been a late fifth-century innovation if Britannia Prima was still being defended on a provincial level in the late fifth century as argued earlier. This accords exactly with the current chronology of hill-fort use in the Durotrigan area, where all the known sites begin use in the later fifth century. Just as one would expect, all cease in the late sixth or early seventh century as the area passed into 'Anglo-Saxon' political control.

Overall, it seems that provincial government, from Cirencester, was maintained until the late fifth century and the province then fragmented into *civitas*-based polities, which survived for another century or more. North of the Wansdyke these were governed by an urban bureaucracy, based at *civitas*-capitals, and south of this by hill-fort based kings.[95]

The collapse of provincial government may explain the devolution of authority to *civitas*-level but it cannot explain why kingship emerged. The two most likely sources for fifth- and sixth-century British kingship are tribal identities originating before the Roman period, or the Bible. The Old Testament mentions kings, such as King David and King Solomon, who might have been the source for British concept of kingship. Or notions of kingship preserved by tribal communities might have been the basis for fifth-century British kingship. As Petts has recently argued, the former seems more likely given the Christian concepts of kingship assumed by Gildas and the role of consecration referred to by him. However, John Koch has argued that legends about pre-Roman rulers were still circulating, and the political units that we see evidenced in the fifth and sixth centuries in this zone seem to have both originated in Late Roman *civitates* and revived aspects of pre-Roman tribal territorial boundaries.[96]

The apparent cultural division at the Wansdyke already outlined coincides closely with the limits of Iron Age Dobunnic/Durotrigan coin distributions. This may suggest that in the late fifth century, the Durotriges controlled their pre-Roman lands and the Dobunni ruled in what are now Somerset and Dorset. This could imply that the Late Roman *civitas* of the Belgae had collapsed, but it is uncertain whether this extended so far west. The survival of the names of both *civitates* may support this. The seventh-century name for the Durotrigan area in the Tribal Hidage was 'Durosaete', implying the survival of the prefix Duro-, either as a territorial or the town name of Dorchester. A sixth-century Class-1 inscription from Devon names the Dobunni, attesting Dobunnic political identity up to that time or immediately before.[97]

The area examined here would appear to contain five independent polities by *c*.500, all much larger and probably more efficiently organised than any of those in the 'Anglo-Saxon' communities of the east. The Cornovii, Dobunni, and Gwent possibly lived under bureaucratic rule. In this area, the sort of Romano-Christian society seen throughout Europe in Late Antiquity is well attested by archaeology. The Durotriges, and Glywysing to the west, eventually lived under royal government. We have already discussed Durotrigan hill-forts, but a hill-fort in Glywysing is known at Hen Gastell, where Bi and Bii amphora, Germanic glass, D-ware, E-ware, and beads, date a drystone multivallate fortification. Their elites occupied hill-forts but still maintained features of Late Antique Romano-Christian society. This is exactly what we would expect from Patrick and Gildas' writings, and the one possibly surviving fifth- or early sixth-century manuscript from Britain, the *Vergilius Romanus*, may have been a West Country product. That is, archaeology appears to provide evidence for the society depicted in the fifth century by Patrick and in the sixth by Gildas. This evokes a very different picture of fifth- and sixth-century Britain to that of the usual accounts of the end of Roman Britain, but one similar to Continental 'sub-Roman' societies.[98]

Christianity had become the conventional religion of the area from the fifth century onward. Monasteries of various types and episcopal government may both be recognised. Alongside these changes the settlement hierarchy may have survived, albeit somewhat modified. There is no hint of a dramatic decline in general wealth or of isolation, although cultural conservatism prevented innovations being adopted easily. The area was in contact with Gaul, the Byzantine world, and arguably Spain. The 'Anglo-Saxons' represented no military threat during this period, and the area was not politically dependent on 'Anglo-Saxon' kings or overkings, not least because none existed before the late sixth century. Our evidence suggests Irish raiding in the fifth century, but even this may have ceased during that century. The overall picture may be of peace and prosperity, even of a rich intellectual and cultural life.[99]

This does not look like 'societal collapse', instead it implies the emergence of a Late Antique society based on the same Romano-Christian culture as elsewhere in Europe. Next we shall see that the vitality of this culture led to its 'export' to areas which were, in fourth-century terms, somewhat peripheral.

4 The south-western peninsula and Wales during the late fifth and sixth centuries

Introduction

In this chapter, we shall see how the Romano-Christian culture of western Britain was exported to the western periphery of the province of Britannia Prima. This area had been far less integrated into ways of life shared with other parts of the Roman Empire in the fourth century and earlier. In the fifth century similarities with the area discussed in chapter 3 increased dramatically. This part of Britain actually became more 'Roman' after the formal Roman withdrawal than previously.

To demonstrate this, we may examine each of the western *civitates* and tribal areas of fourth-century Britannia Prima, and then compare this with the fifth- and sixth-century archaeology of the area. This may then be combined with the evidence afforded by the few relevant texts, to demonstrate that — like other parts of Britannia Prima — this zone was in the cultural mainstream of Late Antiquity. It will be convenient to begin in Dumnonia, the westernmost *civitas* of the Roman Empire, and arguably an area of Roman Britain in many ways dissimilar to most other parts of the Roman Empire.

Dumnonia

Dumnonia first appears geographically defined in Roman-period textual sources. Land's End was, to the geographer Ptolemy, 'the Dumnonian promontory' while Exeter was *Isca Dumnoniorum* — 'Isca of the Dumnonii', the *civitas* capital of this people. This makes it clear that the Dumnonian *civitas* stretched from Land's End to the Exe, encompassing that area which later became known as Devon, a name later derived from 'Dumnonia'. This political unit was long lived: it survived into the sixth and seventh centuries — as the testimony of Gildas and a seventh-century Anglo-Saxon monk, Aldhem, demonstrate. Dumnonia only ceased to exist in the face of Anglo-Saxon expansion in the tenth century, when the western part of this area — called 'Cornwall' by then — was finally taken under Anglo-Saxon rule. Its eastern zone — Devon — had passed into Anglo-Saxon control in the course of the seventh century, following the conquest of the West Country in the late sixth century.[1]

A hint that Dumnonian territory once stretched further to the east than Exeter is provided by the distribution of Late Iron Age Durotrigan coinage (the Dumnonii produced no coins of their own), and by the Anglo-Saxon Chronicle's reference to a seventh-century battle at the river Parret. The latter has been taken to suggest that the Dumnonii controlled territory as far east as the Parret and Dart — rivers which would form a topographical boundary along the east of the south-western peninsula. Recent studies have shown a possible correlation between native settlement-types and the *civitates* and peoples of western Roman Britain, so this is another possible means of ascertaining this frontier. The distinctive settlement type of the Romano-British period, the embanked hut-group — called in Cornwall a 'round' — does not appear to extend beyond the Dart and Parret, although of course new sites could be found. Hilary Cool observes that this boundary may also be visible in the distribution of Romano-British artefact types, supporting the view that it was a cultural — and so perhaps tribal — frontier.[2]

This encompasses all of the territory so far assigned to the Dumnonii by the sources already mentioned. Although attempts have often been made to extend later Dumnonia into Somerset or Dorset, there is no credible evidence which would support such a view. The eastern border of the Dumnonii is likely to have been no further east than the Parret and Dart, and conceivably even further west. The northern and southern boundaries of this area are not as problematical, apparently well-defined by the sea. Here, the main geographical problem is whether the island of Lundy and the Scilly Isles, perhaps then a single landmass, were within Dumnonian territory. There is no direct evidence either way, although later Lundy and Scilly were both to have inscribed stones of the 'Dumnonian group', and this may suggest that they were part of the same political unit in the sixth century if not earlier.[3]

If we can, in general terms, locate the land of the Dumnonii — that is 'Dumnonia' — chance may have also preserved the details of the Roman-period administrative geography of the western part of this area. Charles Henderson, and later Charles Thomas, William Picken and Oliver Padel, have shown that the 'Hundreds' of Cornwall — although first recorded in the ninth century in King Alfred the Great's will — might derive from Roman-period divisions in this area. The most convincing evidence for this lies in the name 'Kerrier' — 'the place of the *kers*' — which preserves the primitive Brittonic word *ker*: a term associated with many Cornish 'rounds', and which was obsolete — as were the rounds themselves — long before Alfred's time. *Ker* was probably replaced by *tref* (*tre-* in many place-names) in Cornwall as the standard term for 'settlement' in the seventh century.[4]

Another place-name, **lys* (the Cornish cognate of Welsh *llys*, or 'court') may be another relic of this political structure, although it is often assumed to belong to the post-Roman period. The archaeological sites which bear this name are themselves rounds or small univallate hill-forts, a type of site unlikely to have been used in the fifth and sixth centuries. Perhaps these are the local centres for the Romano-British administrative pattern reflected in the hundreds. Interesting too is the location of these **lys* sites, archaeological sites with evidence of high-status Romano-British occupation, and 'traditional royal places' of pre-Norman Cornish folklore (as identified by the leading expert on Cornish place-names, Oliver Padel) in relation to the later boundary lines of these hundreds. Such localities seem to be positioned either centrally within the hundreds, as at Trevelgue or Magor, or in the actual boundary line itself, as at Arrallas. Although none of this can be claimed to be certain, there seems some reason to believe that we can discern in this the administrative geography of the western part of the *civitas* of the Dumnonii in the Roman period. The administrative organization of the eastern part of the *civitas* is uncertain, although *civitas* government was apparently operating from Exeter until, perhaps, the early fifth century.[5]

Apart from Exeter, far to the east of the *civitas*, no Roman-period town is known from Dumnonia. Nor were any military sites in the *civitas* demonstrably operational as late as the fourth century. There were roads, and a few Latin inscribed milestones, but outside a narrow belt in south-east Devon, no villas with the exception of Magor, disused well before 350. To the east of Exeter, a pattern of villa estates flourished into the late fourth century. In the fourth century the situation may well have been analogous to that of Carmarthenshire in Wales, where Carmarthen itself supported villas in its hinterland, but otherwise this area, like Dumnonia, lay outside the 'villa landscape'. This is indicated too by the absence of Romano-Celtic temples — no certain example has been found in Dumnonia — and although inscribed altars have been located, religious practice might well have focused on curvilinear shrines and natural features, rather than full-scale Romano-Celtic temple sites such as those widespread in eastern parts of Late Roman Britannia Prima.[6]

The most striking thing about much of fourth-century Dumnonia is, therefore, how entirely without the characteristics we associate with Roman Britain it is. Romano-British pottery and glass from the major producers only reached Dumnonia, apart from the south of Devon, in small quantities. Most Romano-British ceramics were provided by local production such as the Gabbroic 'Romano-Cornish' wares apparently manufactured in the Lizard, and South Devon Ware. Many ceramic types are absent altogether or far less common than in other areas of fourth-century Britain. Interestingly for fifth-century developments, amphorae are seldom found at fourth-century Dumnonian sites — particularly west of south-east Devon.

The principal type of settlement was, as already mentioned, the embanked farm. Such sites seem to originate in the late Iron Age, and the latest constructed appear to date from the fourth century AD. All have an enclosure bank, often with an external ditch, and internal roundhouses. In the Roman-period, more oval house plans predominate but rectilinear buildings are almost unknown — unlike more eastern parts of Roman Britain — other than at villas. In this, too, fashions current in the broader Roman Empire hardly touched the majority of Dumnonia by AD 400.

In Dumnonia, the economy still closely resembled that of the late Iron Age at the end of the fourth century. One aspect of the economy was the existence of tin-mines, of which a number are known to have been open in the Roman-period from finds within the excavated shafts. Overall, although we do not have pollen data from this part of the fourth-century diocese, it is likely that Dumnonia remained predominantly agricultural in its economy, and rural in its settlement pattern.[7]

Elite continuity from the Iron Age to the fourth century appears probable in much of the *civitas*, then, and no intrusive elite element can be discerned. This forms the background to later developments, and casts them in a new light.

40 Tintagel Head, Cornwall

Dumnonia 400-600

The most striking thing about fifth- and sixth-century Dumnonia is not — as this background would lead one to expect — how different it was to the eastern parts of what had been Britannia Prima examined in the previous chapter. Instead, we see great similarities between the two areas appearing for the first time in the fifth century. The most famous Dumnonian fifth- and sixth-century site is Tintagel, a rocky eroded promontory on the north Cornish coast later used for a medieval castle. Excavations by C.A. Ralegh Radford, and more recently by Chris Morris, have elucidated the settlement that existed on Tintagel Head during the fifth to seventh centuries.[8]

Tintagel has over 100 rectilinear buildings (some on artificial terraces on the slopes), many or all of which appear to belong to a period in which imported Mediterranean pottery (PRSW, ARSW, Bi, Bii, Biv, Bv, B misc. and possibly other types only represented in Britain at Tintagel) from the Byzantine world — was widely available at the site. Frankish D-ware was also imported and glass, including vessel glass, from the Mediterranean, Frankia and Spain were found dating to the fifth and sixth centuries. What may be a Merovingian ring-ornament was also found at the Head.

Other finds include spindle whorls made from imported Mediterranean pottery, a rotary quern, crucible sherds, local pottery of fifth- to sixth-century date, slate discs and perforated slates, and carved slates — some of which, at least, may date from this period. One of the slates depicts a warrior with a sword and small circular shield, another a ship with a mast topped by a cross, yet another a stag. The most important carved slate bears two Latin inscriptions, one of these recording the construction of something for or by 'Artognou', after whom the slate is today named. Although this elicited much excitement when discovered, because Tintagel was associated in legend with King Arthur since the twelfth century at latest, there is no chance that this records the same name. However, the slate is very important as the only evidence for Latin literacy on a settlement site in Cornwall up to the sixth century and also could be as an attempt to emulate a Roman building dedication. Latin graffiti on imported Mediterranean sherds at Tintagel are often interpreted as being added in transit, as they are in Latin rather than the Greek spoken in the Byzantine East, but the possibility that they were placed on the sherds at Tintagel must be equally likely (**colour plate 11**).

There are also features cut into the rock surface that may relate to this period, including a carved 'footprint' on the plateau, and 'cup-marks' (hemispherical scoops) on a natural shelf beneath a rock overhang on the landward side of the Head. A rectilinear hollow by a natural rock 'jetty' above the only usable landing place on the Head (called the 'Iron Gate' after a later feature) has been claimed to date to this period also.

Tintagel Head is an impressive location, has a number of springs rising on it, commands excellent views across the sea as far as Lundy and overlooks a natural harbour (Tintagel Haven) to the north. The Head was defended by a major earthwork bank and ditch, beneath the later castle outer wall, cutting off the landward approach. A drystone wall, perhaps of this period, forms a small citadel above this bank, atop a rock boss later utilised for the castle Upper Ward.

Within the enclosed area there are traces of zoning — activities taking place in specific parts of the site. Since Radford's excavation in the 1930s the different complexes of buildings visible on the Head have been designated by letters (site A, B, C, D etc.) and this forms a convenient way of discussing zoning at the settlement. Sites B, C and F, contain buildings with slate-built benches along their sides, the tops of which have slots for wooden uprights, which may have been for storing imported materials. The top of the plateau contains a large and elaborate building, site A, which may have been one of the principal residential foci on the Head, and an enclosed complex in the centre of the plateau might well represent another such area, set apart from the buildings in general.

The greatest concentration of imported pottery comes from the area of the later medieval castle's Inner Ward, where a cliff-fall exposed evidence that the whole of this area of the castle sits on a huge artificial terrace. This is likely to be of fifth- or sixth-century date, and associated with a focal area of the settlement. Entry to the settlement would have to have been via this zone and perhaps this was a reception area for guests or a market area. This zoning continued on the landward side, as indicated by the discovery of terraces with apparently lower status functions in that area. While the interpretation of these zones remains debatable, and depends in part on the level of data available for them from excavation, we can see that this was an internally-structured community, probably with both high-status and low-status areas and at least one public space.

Tintagel parish church is on the cliff-top above the settlement. Here, excavations in the 1940s and 1990s revealed long-cist burials and a series of mounds, the interpretation of which is problematical. While the upper parts of at least some mounds appear to have been

41 Tintagel parish church: surrounding the medieval church on the cliff above Tintagel Head is a fifth- to sixth-century cemetery associated with mound graves, visible in front of the church

added in long after 600, long-cist burials beneath them appear to bear a consistent relationship with the mounds, suggesting that they are contemporary mound-burials. Other Dumnonian mound-burials are known, as probably at Cannington and Boslow, St Just. At the latter a Class-1 stone bearing a cross stands on an unexcavated mound, suggesting an association with the Latin-literate Christian elite. The Tintagel mounds may be burials of the community on the Head, and a link is further created by B-ware sherds and carved slates (here bearing crosses) at the church site. In the fifth and sixth centuries or later this cemetery was enclosed by a bank, and an undated granite monolith has also been found at the site.[9]

The scale of the defended settlement, the amount of Mediterranean pottery and hints of fine-metalworking, all suggest that Tintagel was an extremely important place in fifth- and sixth-century Dumnonia. While originally interpreted as a monastery, all current scholars agree that Tintagel is far more likely to have been a royal settlement, perhaps even the principal royal site of Dumnonia. The rock-cut 'footprint' and cup-marks have been compared by Charles Thomas to the features found at royal sites in Ireland, where the prospective king would place his foot in the footprint during the inauguration ceremony.

Although Tintagel was the site of a Romano-British settlement, and Romano-British pottery, Roman glass, a coin hoard and even perhaps cremations have been found on the Head, it is unclear what form this took. A Roman milestone has been found nearby, but there is no reason to suppose that the Head was a Roman military site.

155

More Roman-style rectilinear buildings and multi-room buildings are known from fifth- to sixth-century Tintagel than are known from western Dumnonia for the whole Roman period. At this time Tintagel had more 'Roman' sorts of pottery, the Byzantine and Frankish bowls, in use than are known from any Romano-British site in Cornwall also, and had a relatively large amount of glass too. On this basis Tintagel in the sixth century was more 'Roman-looking' than any site of the fourth century in Cornwall (**colour plate 12**).[10]

Similarly, Tintagel has more evidence of international trade, of contact with the Mediterranean and far more amphora sherds than from any fourth-century site in Dumnonia. It has the only evidence for Latin literacy on a settlement up to the sixth century in the west of Dumnonia, and strong evidence that its inhabitants were Christian — the fourth-century Roman imperial religion.

Tintagel was also more 'urban' than any settlement known from Romano-British Dumnonia west of Exeter. Sixth-century Tintagel had 'streets', zoned activities, what may be public space, manufacturing and trading functions, and a concentration of population of more than one social group. The settlement at Tintagel is similar in size and layout to some Romano-British small towns, and was much more similar to sites in the core area of fourth-century Britannia Prima than to any in Roman-British Dumnonia. It was, by almost any

42 Class-1 inscribed stone at Sourton, Devon mentioning a princeps — *possibly a ruler or abbot*

measure, very much a 'Late Antique' settlement.

Nor is Tintagel alone in presenting us with evidence of the adoption of 'Late Antique' Romano-Christian culture in fifth- and sixth-century Dumnonia. There are many Class-1 inscribed stones, of fifth- to seventh-century date, distributed widely across Devon and Cornwall. The most important — but possibly the most overlooked — point about these

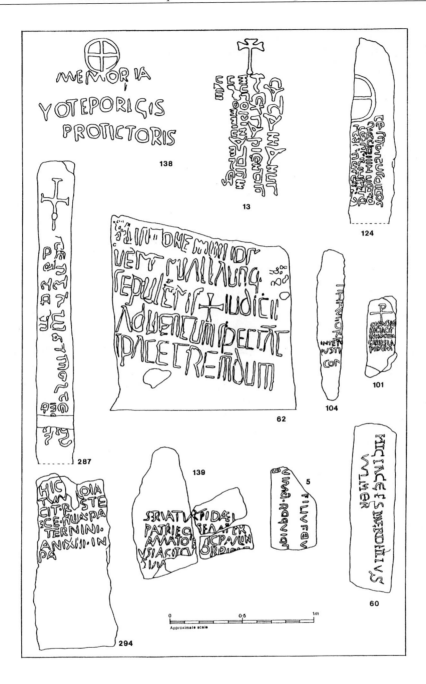

43 Inscriptions on Class-1 inscribed stones in Wales. Numbers are those assigned by V.E. Nash-Williams (whose drawings are the basis for this figure) 138, the 'Vortipor stone' from Castell Dwyran; 13, 'the Catamanus stone' from Llangadwaladr; 124, Llanlyr; 287, Towyn; 62, Llanleonfel; 101 and 104, Penmachno; 294, Llanerfyl; 139, Cynwyl Gaeo. The stones from 5, Heneglwlys and 60, Llangorse may date from as late as the twelfth century, showing the continuation or revival of the tradition of erecting such memorials even at that date

is that there is no evidence of inscriptions in fourth-century Dumnonia aside from a handful of milestones probably associated with the Roman army.

Yet Cornwall contains many Latin inscriptions approximately contemporary with the fifth- and sixth-century activity at Tintagel. This involved the erection of personal memorials, the use of Latin memorial formulae derived from Continental models and Christian symbols of Continental and Late Roman origin, the use of Roman terminology and evidence for Christianity. At Boslow, mentioned above, and at Carnsew (where the Class-1 inscription seems to have stood above a long-cist beneath a cairn), such memorials were erected over mound-burials. At Beacon Hill, Lundy, Class-1 stones were erected in a Christian long-cist cemetery in which there was a focal grave. Nothing similar has been found in fourth-century Dumnonia. Yet it resembles the Romano-Christian culture of Tintagel in general, and in particulars such as the evidence for Christianity, Latinity, contacts with Frankia and perhaps the Mediterranean, the emulation of Roman forms of material culture and the use of Romano-Christian burial practices (**colour plate 13**).[11]

The inscribed stones enable us to show that the culture represented by Tintagel was not specific to that one site. It was spread widely across Dumnonia, and the distribution of cemeteries of east-west unaccompanied graves, often using long-cists and containing infant burials, demonstrates that this new religion and culture was shared by more than the local elite, but on some level by all the people who were buried in this manner. These cemeteries are found in south Devon, as at Kenn near Exeter and in Cornwall, for example at Crantock, St Minver and Treharrock, and adjacent St Endellion. By far the most well-known is at Cannington near the Dumnonian border.[12]

Cannington appears to have begun in the Roman period, outside a multivallate contour hill-fort which was either occupied then or reoccupied in the fifth or sixth centuries. Between the cemetery and hill-fort was an extramural unenclosed settlement, also associated with Romano-British pottery. The cemetery was extensive, and 542 burials have been excavated, including both rock-cut and long-cist burials. The earliest focus was a ring ditch containing a young adult male under a stone platform or cairn at the periphery of the burial area (FT43), radiocarbon-dated to cal AD 210-440. A later focal grave was a low mound within the cemetery associated with a slab-built box and 0.36m high stone with indecipherable markings, approached by path (FT26). Below the mound was the grave of a young person (burial 409), radiocarbon-dated cal AD 620-1020. The re-use of stone from this in other radiocarbon-dated graves may suggest a seventh-century date. A child's grave dated cal AD 660-1050 contained an eighth-century penannular brooch and bead, but in general the burials contained no grave goods. The cemetery as a whole seems to date from the fourth to seventh century and probably later.

Thus, fifth- and sixth-century Dumnonia was more similar in cultural terms to the eastern part of what was earlier Britannia Prima than it had ever been in the Roman period. This is no trivial conclusion, and one which is analogous to post-Roman transformations in Ireland and in the inter-mural area of Scotland. In those areas, new material cultures formed in the fifth century as they were converted to Christianity. Characteristically, these material cultures involved the partial emulation of Roman technologies and tool types (**colour plate 14**)[13].

The spread of Romano-Christian practices from what had been western Roman

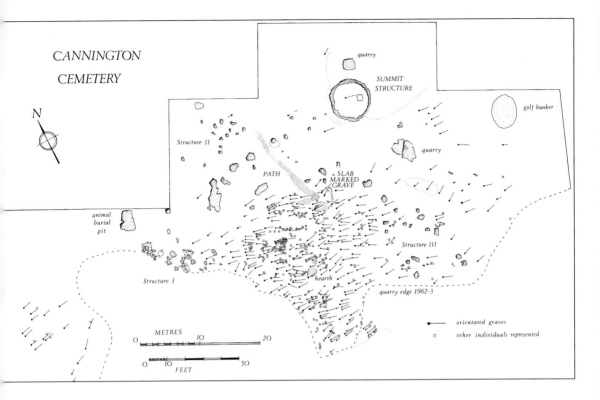

44 Plan of Cannington cemetery. Reproduced with the kind permission of P.A. Rahtz

Britain is the most likely source of such a transformation and the most likely agent for this is the Christian Church itself. The spread of Christianity in Dumnonia by seaborne missionaries might be implied by two sculptures, conceivably fifth-century, at the harbours of Hayle and Phillack, depicting the Constantinian form of the Chi-Rho, and the coastal distribution of long-cist cemeteries. Long-cist burials, in which the body is placed in a slab-built grave, are known from Late Roman Britain, and became widespread in Christian contexts in the fourth century and later more widely. Long-cists were used for centuries in Britain and Ireland (and are still occasionally used), but in western Britain at this date they may indicate contacts with what had been the east of Britannia Prima.[14]

In particular, as Romano-British technologies were transferred down to minor tools and agricultural implements, monasteries founded by people from (or in contact with) what had been Roman Britain were probably the sources of these innovations. There one might find the hardware of agricultural life in distant contexts, along with Christianity, Latin literacy and possibly wider contacts. Moreover, monasteries in sixth-century Dumnonia are evidenced by *Vita Prima Sancti Samsonis*, which refers to *Landocco* (probably at St Kew, where there is a Class-1 inscribed stone at the medieval church) and more reliably by Gildas, in his reference to Constantine of Dumnonia killing 'royal youths' dressed as an abbot. A Dumnonian monastery of this period may recently have been excavated, albeit on a small scale, at Carhampton, Somerset, by Nancy and Charlie

159

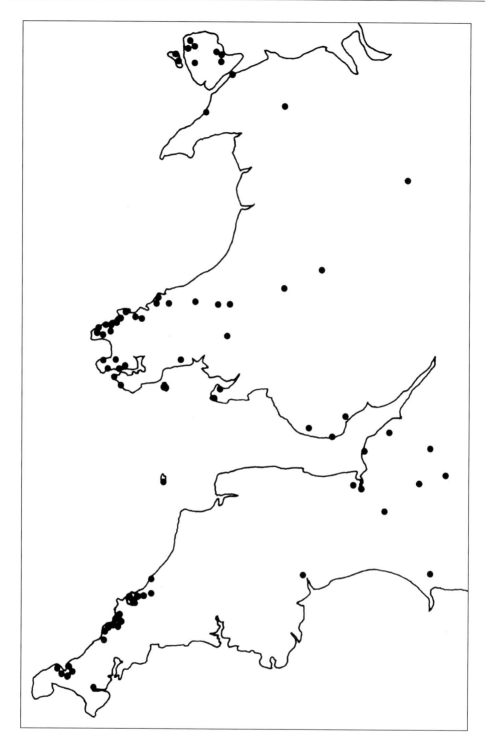

45 Long-cist cemeteries in fifth- and sixth-century western Britain. Each filled circle represents a cemetery containing at least one long-cist

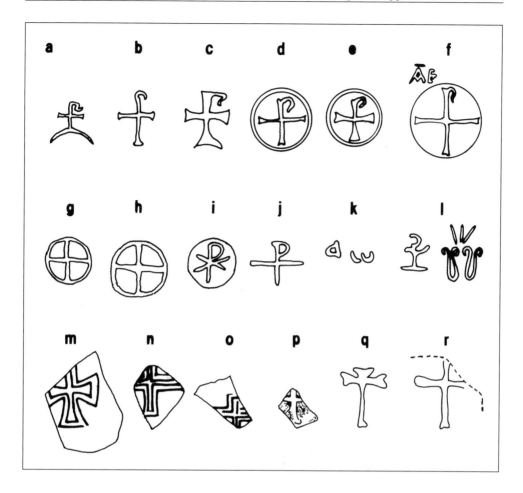

46 *Christian symbols on Class-1 inscribed stones (a-l and q-r) and imported Mediterranean pottery (m-p) in fifth- and sixth-century Britain:*
a Southill; b St Just; c St Endellion; d, e and f Kirkmadrine; g Lundy; h Castell Dwyran; i Phillack; j Penmachno; k Boskenna; l Sourton; m, n and o Tintagel; p South Cadbury; q Llangadwaladr; r Caldey Island. (After Thomas, Alcock, Nash-Williams, Okasha)

Hollinrake. Next to the medieval parish church they have found settlement, burial, and metalworking associated with B-ware and E-ware pottery. This was followed by a long sequence of Christian religious activity, some at least monastic.[15]

In Dumnonia this would be to envisage Christianisation from a part of western Britain where the monastic movement was arguably established by the fifth century and where the practices which accompanied religious conversion in Dumnonia were thriving. On the basis of the previous chapter two main areas seem most probable: either the West Country or south Wales.

Ann Preston-Jones made a case for the evangelisation of western Dumnonia from south-west Wales based on the similarity between churchyard form in Cornwall (of which she has made the most detailed and scholarly study) and churchyard form in Wales, and the use of inscribed stones, features common to both areas. This builds on Lynette Olson's important examination of the credible traces of pre-ninth-century monasticism in Cornwall, in which she suggested a Welsh origin for Cornish Christianity.[16]

In as yet unpublished work (which I am grateful for permission to refer to here) David Petts has effectively demolished the view that curvilinear burial grounds — even burial enclosures — characterised fifth- and sixth-century western British mortuary practice. Instead, he suggests open cemeteries were later replaced, in the seventh to ninth centuries, by those with clearly-defined boundaries.[17]

Nevertheless, inscribed stones are more common in Wales and Dumnonia than elsewhere, and the site with the greatest general similarity to Tintagel is perhaps Gateholm in south Wales. Although unexcavated apart from minor trenching, which produced Romano-British pottery and a ring-headed pin of the sixth to ninth century, Gateholm has evidence of many rectilinear structures similar to those at Tintagel, and at least one similar terraced area. The greatest problem with the Olson-Preston-Jones hypothesis is that most of the points made about the Dumnonii in the fourth century are equally true of south-west Wales: this is not an area likely to have 'exported' Romano-Christian culture in the fifth century.

It seems more likely that both south-west Wales and Dumnonia were evangelised from another area of western Britain, one that had a flourishing Romano-Christian culture and which had easy contact with both zones. This could be south-east Wales or it could be the West Country. Whichever option one chooses, this links the western periphery to the core of the former province of Britannia Prima in the fifth century and perhaps later.

Of course, another option is to imagine evangelisation from Gaul or, in view of all the imported pottery at Tintagel, the Byzantine East. Some evidence could be produced to support both possibilities. Dumnonian inscribed stones show some similarities with Christian tombstones in Gaul, but Frankish pottery occurs in tiny quantities at Tintagel and is absent elsewhere from fifth- and sixth-century Dumnonia so far as we are aware. This could not be said for Byzantine pottery, but there seem to be almost no discernible Byzantine features on Dumnonian inscribed stones whatsoever, and apart from pottery no other Byzantine artefacts have been found in Dumnonia, unless one counts the controversial coin finds.[18]

The latter have had a mixed reception among archaeologists and numismatists. Malcolm Todd argues that they represent genuine fifth- to seventh-century losses, but Michael Metcalf and George Boon considered them merely modern losses and this has become the standard interpretation. The coins at Exeter, accompanied by pre-Roman and Roman-period Mediterranean coinage, are probably best interpreted in this way, but most of the Dumnonian coins findspots seem harder to explain — they are from rural, remote, and sometimes now uninhabited locations, for example a coin of Anastasius I — a 40 nummi follis — from close to the entrance of Porthellick chambered tomb in the Scilly Isles. Unless they have been deliberately scattered to deceive archaeologists, or Devon and Cornwall had many coin collectors prior to World War II living in remote places, the coins are still puzzling. Until someone explains why so many Byzantine coins have been picked up in such improbable places for modern loss, it remains possible that some of these coins represent contemporary losses.[19]

With the exception of the pottery and possibly these coins, evidence of Byzantine contacts which might have brought about evangelisation is sparse. But there is a piece of evidence which hitherto appears to have escaped the notice of scholars investigating Mediterranean contacts with Britain in the fifth and sixth centuries. The 'Celtic saints' of Cornwall — mostly known through obscure dedications which otherwise occur only at a few British, Irish and Breton churches — have seldom been discussed in such a context. This is not surprising, as one might see these figures as obviously indigenous: their names might be said to show this. Medieval hagiography represents their early lives in Ireland or Britain, and their travels — for most were seafaring missionaries — within an Insular context. There is no reason to suppose that figures like St Samson or St Cadoc were Byzantines or Franks, but we may be able to see some hints among this corpus of dedications of contacts with the Byzantine east.[20]

Take for example, St Ia — Ia is unknown in an Insular context beyond West Cornwall. Later hagiographers plainly had no information about her and simply formulated a suitable Life. But St Ia is not 'otherwise unknown' as we are often told: she was martyred in Persia and the cult was prominent in early Byzantine Constantinople, when St Ia's church stood immediately outside the Golden Gate, the imperial ceremonial entrance to the Byzantine capital. If we want an even more Byzantine saint, there is St Stinian, whose cult is attested by a medieval chapel near St Davids in Wales. St Stinian is another saint about whom nothing appears to have been known in the Middle Ages, yet with a very interesting name. Stinian is the Welsh form of the name Justinian, a name notable as that of Justinian I, the Byzantine emperor in whose reign the imported pottery found in Britain seems to have largely arrived and who, incidentally, restored St Ia's church at Constantinople. Some of the most 'Celtic' sounding saints could also conceal Byzantine connections: St Madron — St Matrona in Latin — is often depicted as archetypally Insular and this might be so, but it is interesting that another of the prominent churches of Byzantine Constantinople was St Matrona. These are a few examples, and more names might be added to this list.[21]

It is possible, of course, that these dedications have nothing to do with Byzantine connections, and some or all may be later in date than the seventh century. Nevertheless, conceivably they contain hints of ecclesiastical links between Britain and Byzantium, specifically Constantinople perhaps, in the period of the imports. If so, they are our most direct evidence of Byzantine religious contacts with Dumnonia and the British West in general.

Nevertheless, while the 'Byzantine' and 'Gallic' options may not be out of the question, currently they seem a lot less likely than evangelization and attendant cultural change in Dumnonia from within Britain. The role of the upper Severn Valley, highlighted as a source for later Irish art and metalwork fashions in recent studies by Ragnall O'Floinn, may be important — and we have seen here evidence of a Romano-Christian culture in the fifth century and later. As David Dumville has suggested, perhaps we should even take the distribution of dedications to these 'Celtic' saints as indicating seafaring missionaries after all. If so, they were presumably coming from the zone discussed in the previous chapter.[22]

The secular elite of fifth- and sixth-century Dumnonia

Although the fifth and sixth centuries in the west of Britain have frequently (and unfairly) been caricatured as lacking data, we can in fact say quite a lot about the western British elite — even on archaeological grounds alone. Not only at Tintagel, but at other sites — at least High Peak, Chun, Killibury and probably both Trevelgue Head in Cornwall and Denbury in Devon (where 'Anglo-Saxon' metalwork has been discovered) — we can see the Romano-British Dumnonian custom of hill-fort use by elite groups continuing into the fifth and sixth centuries. These sites were enclosed by formidable earthen banks or drystone walls — the drystone defences at Chun stood over 5m high even in the post-medieval period — and plainly sited for defence. They fall into two categories: coastal promontory forts above harbours (suitable for seagoing ships) and highly-defensible multivallate inland hilltop enclosures. These are not simply a repetition of the range of pre-Roman and Roman-period hill-fort types in Dumnonia, but represent a clear selection from among these.[23]

The sites selected appear to have been chosen for defensibility and visual impressiveness, as well as access to the sea in the case of the coastal promontory forts. None of these forts were absolutely certainly built for the first time in the fifth century, but the coastal promontory fort at High Peak may have been on the grounds of radiocarbon dates and B-ware beneath one of its banks. At all, including High Peak, except for the multivallate contour hill-fort at Killibury (dated by B-ware, but where only a small area was excavated, and the unexcavated site at Denbury), there was fourth-century Romano-British pottery, and at Tintagel and Trevelgue there was evidence of Romano-British occupation. The social organization which they represent may have originated in the Roman-period rather than later, yet they survived as high-status settlements long enough to obtain imported Mediterranean pottery of the later fifth and sixth centuries. It would be unreasonable, then, to deny that the elite of fifth- and sixth-century Dumnonia derived at least in part from the elite of the Romano-British *civitas*.[24]

Only a few of these hill-forts have been identified. Even if we add to this all the possible sites which might be identified by combining the criteria of site-selection above with hints of fifth- and sixth-century use, such as the proximity of Class-1 inscribed stones, we are left with a smallish group of sites. This is barely enough to provide two hill-forts of each of the two categories mentioned for each hundred. These are unlikely to be just estate-centres, dotting the landscape, or even aristocratic farms. Instead, we may be seeing elite settlements associated with the ruling family of each of the hundred-level territories established in the Romano-British period. If Romano-British elites survived into the fifth and sixth centuries, as the on-site evidence might suggest, then these units might represent sub-territories within Dumnonia, with their own elites based at hill-forts. One possibility is to interpret these hill-forts as the political centres of sub-kingdoms represented by the hundreds, each sub-king owing allegiance in some way to a ruler of the whole of Dumnonia. We know such a ruler existed by the sixth century because in his *De Excidio* Gildas refers to Constantine *tyrannus* ('illegitimate ruler' — presumably Gildas' own opinion) of Dumnonia.

This ruler might also be king of one of the sub-kingdoms as well as the over-king of

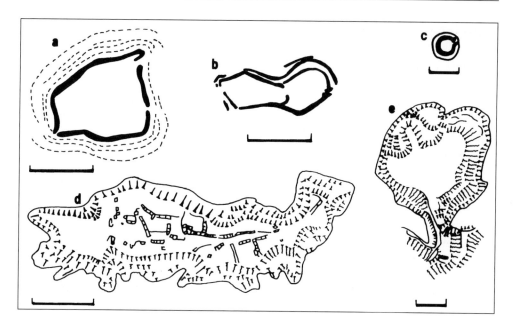

47 *Fifth- and sixth-century western British hill-forts. a South Cadbury (only fifth- to sixth-rampart shown in bold); b Cadbury Congresbury; c Chun; d Gateholm (structures shown in outline); e Tintagel (no structures shown, but defensive bank on mainland indicated). All scales 100m. (After Alcock, Fowler and Rahtz, Davies, Radford)*

the whole former civitas. In this context the location of Tintagel (among the largest and by far the most artefactually wealthy sites known from western Britain in this period) centrally along the coast of one later hundred (Trigg) may be relevant. It is better positioned for a ruler of both the modern counties of Devon and Cornwall than one holding sway mostly to its west, and could well have been one of Constantine of Dumnonia's sixth-century political centres.[25]

Even if Tintagel has 'over-kingly' connections, most of the Dumnonian hill-forts might well be the courts of local rulers, operating at the 'hundredal' (i.e. sub-kingdom) level. This level of the political hierarchy seems to have left an especially rich archaeological legacy throughout western Britain, because it may be largely associated with the Class-1 inscribed stones. The possibility that some of these stones commemorate ecclesiastics need not detract from this, because they could have been used for those of this rank who joined the Church, or for those in the Church who were equated with this social status. We know from fifth- to seventh-century Ireland that exactly this sort of equation in ranks existed.[26]

If Class-1 stones were primarily set up to commemorate this level in society, they constitute our most valuable source for it. They show that people on this social level, not only the top of the social hierarchy, participated in Romano-Christian culture and provide evidence of other, more secular, concerns. The names of the people commemorated appear to want to evoke associations with values of heroism, nobility, strength or fighting suggesting that they were born to their rank. That the commemorated were not a first generation elite (or did not want to be thought of as a first generation elite) may be also attested in the emphasis on genealogy exhibited by the inscriptions. They give at least one and sometimes two generations of patrilineage, which may suggest both inherited patrilineal status and a patriarchal society.[27]

Where their original locations are known, Dumnonian Class-1 stones are prominently sited and clearly meant to be seen. Some may well have stood beside trackways, and we shall see later that some of their Welsh counterparts stood beside Roman roads. The exact form of the inscriptions appears to legitimate social rank in many ways, by reference to religion, to the Roman past and, through Continental memorial formulae, to the foreign linkages open to the elite. They represent this elite as part of a broader group, connected to the Roman Continent, the Christian community and even (in their use of ogam) to the Christianised elite of contemporary Ireland. They carry another set of messages reinforcing the indigenous nature of the elite. This is seen in the Brittonic personal names — sometimes incorporating British titles such as *tigern* (king) — the use of Insular half-uncial script and of unshaped pillar stones for many inscriptions (**colour plate 15**).[28]

It must be stressed that the unworked form of the latter appears to be a matter of deliberate choice; inscribed stones which seem to be broadly contemporary were shaped. The visual reference could be to the pre-Iron Age standing stones which form a common part of the British landscape throughout the areas in which inscribed stones occur, or they may be intended to look like natural features. Many, although not all, inscribed stones closely resemble the prehistoric monuments in size and shape, yet this cannot be only a reflex of the availability of suitable stone. A much wider range of material is available in Dumnonia than was used for these inscriptions. It is unknown whether any Class-1 stones re-used prehistoric standing stones, but the possibility cannot be excluded in relation to every stone.

Interestingly, we have two pieces of evidence implying a Dumnonian or wider British interest in prehistoric standing stones. The first is the placing of Christian unenclosed cemeteries of fifth- to seventh-century date at the sites of standing stones in Wales, and perhaps at Tintagel in Cornwall. The second is the reference in *Vita Prima Sancti Samsonis* to the Christianisation of a standing stone by the saint, although this may relate to the Breton practice of Christianising standing stones or simply be an explanation of a local cross-marked stone. There is no suggestion that specifically pagan associations are being evoked in the use of stones similar to prehistoric standing stones for Class-1 inscriptions, but rather an indigenous — even 'timeless' — presence is being sought.[29]

The interpretation that fifth- to seventh-century and Roman-period burials at prehistoric monuments relate to the importance of ancestors, clan, or heroes has been suggested by the author, Jeremy Knight and Betty O'Brien. This evocation of ancestral legitimacy has already been seen in the context of the use of these monuments in eastern Britain, and here it is possible to discern it in the form of Class-1 stones. In effect, artificial 'ancestral monuments' were being created. These represented a physical presence for post-Roman Dumnonian elites across the landscape, a presence of political authority only previously encountered in Dumnonia in Roman milestones: monuments with which post-Roman inscribed stones also bear epigraphic similarities. These monuments could have, in a sense, made the presence of the ruler felt even when the ruler himself was absent, acting as a proxy for actual physical proximity.[30]

The Class-1 inscribed stones offer us then a glimpse of the political strategy and ideology of sub-kingship in post-Roman Dumnonia, and it may be possible to detect another aspect of fifth- and sixth-century local elites in Dumnonia. This is suggested by another class of sites, the so-called 'sand-dune sites' such as Bantham and Gwithian site GM1. Characteristically, 'sand-dune sites' are set amid coastal sand-dunes, hence the name, by small streams providing fresh drinking water. They have evidence of occupation, perhaps of a seasonal character, best attested at Bantham, and of trade — particularly imported pottery. The number of these sites may currently be underestimated. Other sites which might fall into this category include Phillack Towans (with imported pottery and an inscribed stone), the beach by the well-known St Enodoc church (having a Type G penannular brooch and a piece of Bi imported pottery) and perhaps Mothecombe, near Bantham (where B-ware was found in a small area of dark soil at the rear of the beach).[31]

Other shared characteristics of these sites seem to have escaped the notice of scholars. Most have evidence for burials potentially contemporary with the imported ceramics, yet separated from the settlement area. Several have what might well be a coastal fort located immediately above the beach, although apart from small-scale work at the fort at Gwithian (where a buckle of 'sub-Roman' form was discovered) none of these forts has been excavated. The possibility that this constituted a shared 'package' of features could hint at a smaller scale equivalent of the sort of control of external trade shown at Tintagel. This is unlikely to have been the same group who were trading through coastal promontory forts, unless this elite needed two levels of trading site. It is probable that these sites suggest a lower grade, beneath the sub-kingly level.[32]

It is possible to illustrate this with reference to the hundred of Penwith. The hundred has the sand-dune sites of Carnsew and Gwithian, and perhaps another at Gunwalloe, in addition to two or more hill-forts, including Chun and St Michael's Mount. Survey at the Mount has shown defensive banks similar to those around hill-forts and terraces, perhaps like those at Tintagel. On the Mount, work by the Cornish Archaeological Unit, and chance finds of B-ware amphora sherds by the author, provide evidence of Byzantine amphorae at the site, while native post-Roman pottery of approximately the same date was also found in recent work.[33]

Penwith had at least two hill-fort centres, one inland and one on the coast, to accommodate its sub-kings. But there were also at least two sand-dune sites possibly with associated forts. If the coastal and inland hill-forts are connected with the sub-kingdom's rulers this may enable us to recognise high-status sites below the sub-kingly grade. If so, participation in the same cultural values and adherence to the same political aspirations represented by Tintagel may have extended down to the level of the local aristocracy, below that of the sub-kings. Alternatively, we could disassociate the hill-forts and sub-kings and see every hill-fort as a sequentially used over-kingly centre, periodically visited by the over-king and maintained in his absence by small 'caretaker communities', perhaps with an official administrative role in the surrounding territory. Nevertheless, the former interpretation seems more likely, although both over-kings and sub-kings may have undertaken circuits to consume food-rents throughout their domains: it was easier to take the king to the food than the food to the king.[34]

Consequently, we see a society that is not only similar in cultural terms to that of what was eastern Britannia Prima, but which may offer hints of a definable strategy of political control shared on at least two levels of political leadership. There are hints of yet another level, taking this pattern down to the local level. According to this interpretation, major hill-forts positioned at harbours had inhabitants directly participating in 'directional' status-related trade with foreign, probably at least partly Byzantine, merchants. At lower-level local centres, as perhaps at Bantham, St Enodoc and Gwithian, aristocrats presided over seasonal coastal fair sites — if that is what the sand-dune sites represent — where both Insular and foreign goods were available. Sub-kings controlled territories equivalent to the later hundreds in Cornwall, multivallate hill-forts providing their inland strongholds and perhaps winter residences (given the inhospitable nature of coastal promontory forts in winter) and one of these — the ruler based at Tintagel — also held the over-kingship of Dumnonia.

This could imply a more sophisticated political organization within fifth- and sixth-century Dumnonia than warring tribal chiefs. However, the need for such extensive strategies of legitimation and control might equally suggest that this post-Roman kingship was not as firmly founded as those in control might have hoped. This brings us back to the wider picture of the relationship between the Romano-British *civitas* and the immediately post-Roman society and economy of Dumnonia.

Discontinuity or continuity in fifth- and sixth-century Dumnonia?

Tintagel was founded in the Roman period and remained in use until the seventh century. If Tintagel was the over-kingly centre of Dumnonia and the centre of the sub-kingdom indicated by the later hundred of Trigg, then it seems likely that the sub-kings of this area retained the over-kingship through that period. That is, the over-kingship did not pass from one to another of the sub-kingdoms through competition or rotate formally between them. The reason for legitimating royal control was not, therefore, the instability of Dumnonian kingship.

An intrusive character for Dumnonian over-kingship can also probably be discounted. With the possible exception of the use of ogam and Irish personal names on a few inscribed stones, the available evidence suggests that sixth-century Dumnonia represents the continuation of the Late Roman *civitas* in the form of a post-Roman kingdom. In fact, overwhelming evidence exists that almost every aspect of the fifth- and sixth-century archaeology of Dumnonia, especially in the west of the *civitas*, can be understood in terms of continuity from the Late Roman period, with the exception of the emergence of a Romano-Christian culture as already discussed, and a small high-status Irish presence.

The characteristic form of settlement of the immediately post-Roman period seems to have continued to be the embanked farm, as at Halligye, Trethurgy, Grambla and Hayes Farm II, Clyst Honiton. As no new 'rounds' can be demonstrated to have been constructed at this time, this probably represented continuous occupation of existing settlements. This was not impoverished survival: at Halligye the inhabitants had access to ARSW, those at Trethurgy to both imported Mediterranean pottery and Germanic glass.

Recent studies have shown Romano-Cornish Gabbroic pottery seemingly in use alongside imported Byzantine pots at Tintagel and Trethurgy, and Henrietta Quinnell has suggested that production was maintained into the fifth century if not later. The same could well be true for South Devon Ware, which also occurs at Tintagel, and Quinnell has also demonstrated that the Cornish stone bowls, a characteristic artefact of Roman-period Cornwall, continued to be produced into the same period. The tin-mines of Cornwall were plainly functioning at this date also. A possibly sixth-century tin ingot was discovered at Trethurgy, and a shipwreck found at Bigbury Bay, South Devon, dated to this period had a cargo of typologically Late Roman tin ingots. Evidence from the Blackdown iron pits and Burlescombe may attest continuity of iron production in Devon into the sixth century.[35]

More or less everything usually claimed to be manufactured in Romano-British Cornwall in 400 was apparently still in production (or might easily have been in production) in 500, and possibly throughout the century after. In effect, Romano-British ways of life survived through the fifth and sixth centuries in the very areas in which there is most evidence for an intrusive community. Apart from the evidence of the inscribed stones all other material once believed to show an Irish presence in fifth- and sixth-century Dumnonia is either questionable or likely to be far later than 600. The grass-marked pottery found in Cornwall may relate to northern Irish souterrain ware but dates after E-ware, and so to later than the seventh century. The Irish place-names of west Cornwall are undated, although perhaps pre-medieval, and problems of chronology and interpretation render Irish saints' names of little use in discerning fifth- to seventh-century Irish 'colonization'. The notion of a supporting archaeology for place-name evidence for the Irish population other than the inscribed stones must be discarded. This leaves us with very few confirmed Irish migrants in Cornwall and Devon in the fifth and sixth centuries: only those referred to on inscribed stones. The distribution of these stones is strongly suggestive of a route crossing Cornwall and Devon to the English Channel and on to the Continent. Perhaps the stones imply high-status Irish pilgrimage rather than settlement.[36]

Although Irish aristocrats might have been granted land in Dumnonia, and Irish ecclesiastics might have worked and been buried there, we have no reason to postulate an Irish colonization of any part of the former *civitas* of the Dumnonii. There is no reason to imagine that the origins of Dumnonian post-Roman kingship lay in an Irish political 'takeover'. It seems far more likely that we are observing the emergence or re-emergence of Dumnonian kingship itself, and this may be supported by the evidence for Romano-British occupation at the excavated hill-forts at Chun, Trevelgue and Tintagel. These sites may have been Late Roman secular elite sites, to judge from the quantity of Late Roman material found at some of them. Interestingly, the sand-dune sites, too, show hints of Romano-British occupation, ephemeral traces of which come from Gwithian, Bantham and more substantially from St Enodoc.

Perhaps, therefore, we can see Dumnonian kingship not as an entirely new post-Roman phenomenon, but a continuing tradition from the Roman period, potentially deriving from the pre-Roman Iron Age. This raises questions about the extent to which Romano-British Dumnonia was governed as a *civitas* at all, and the character of Late Roman rule in the west of Britain. It is possible that after the 380s, when coinage supply seems to have ended at Exeter (the *civitas* capital), the government and security of Dumnonia (or initially its west?) was 'devolved' to its hereditary rulers, or that this only occurred after the collapse of provincial authority in the late fifth century.[37]

This may not have been the only area in which pre-Roman kingship re-asserted itself in the Roman period, or where conversion by monastic missionaries in the fifth century resulted in a Romano-Christian culture. This may be observed also in north-west Wales, in sixth-century terms, Gwynedd.

Gwynedd

Late fourth-century north-west Wales had no towns, villas or (probably) Roman-style temples. The principal, and perhaps only, official presence by the late fourth century was at the Roman fort at Segontium, and an as yet poorly-understood series of signal stations (such as that on Holyhead Mountain) which might well have been dependent upon it. The mortared stone rectangular enclosure at Caer Gybi may also have been a Late Roman fort, but is less well-dated than often supposed. If so, it may have been a naval base. One other Roman fort, Caerhun, might have been in use at this time, but has not been the subject of recent excavation as has Segontium. It is, then, reasonable to assume that direct Roman administration of the area (in so far as this occurred at all by the last decades of the fourth century) was based at Segontium, and at least took place within a military context if not under military control.[38]

Local inhabitants presumably, therefore, paid taxes directly to the Roman military authorities at Segontium, and a cavalry unit based there could have enforced the tax collection throughout this area. Roman rule in late fourth-century north-west Wales cannot have been direct, at least in terms of the daily lives of the majority of the population and unlike Dumnonia, the British tribe in the area, the Ordovices, seem never to have been formally a Romano-British *civitas*. They had no *civitas* capital or Roman-style civilian government. As in the west of Dumnonia, local administration may have been left in the hands of local dignitaries.[39]

Hill-fort occupation which might indicate the residences of the local elite is attested in north-west Wales at Dinas Emrys and Bwrdd Arthur. These sites did not contain masonry buildings within their earthen or drystone enclosure banks, but buildings of timber or drystone. Most of these structures were of local curvilinear form, although rectilinear buildings were more common in fourth-century north Wales than in fourth-century Dumnonia. The high status of such sites is suggested by the presence of ornamental metalwork and glass vessels — otherwise absent or rare on sites in this area, apart from at Segontium.

Romano-British artefacts and rectilinear structures occur at the enclosed hut-groups and rectilinear embanked settlements of north Wales, such as at Bryn Eryr and the enclosed hut-groups of Graenog and Din Lligwy. These are usually interpreted as the centres of local agricultural estates, and seen as broadly the equivalent of Romano-British villas. This may be to overstate their social rank, not least because enclosed hut-groups are much more common in the north Welsh landscape than are villas in any part of England or Wales. The north-west Welsh enclosed sites might better be seen as the equivalent of the enclosed settlements of Dumnonia (including the Cornish 'rounds') and the 'small enclosures' of Romano-British south-west Wales. As such, they would appear to be the typical prosperous farms of the region, with their relatively rich finds indicating the production of a substantial agricultural surplus and an ability to trade this for manufactured goods from more eastern parts of Roman Britain. This might, in turn, imply the existence of a rank of well-to-do farmers throughout north-west Wales in the fourth century, and the presence of coins at many of these sites could suggest their involvement in the Roman taxation system.[40]

A lower class of farmers is indicated by the existence of unenclosed hut-groups — exemplified by the excavated site at Ty Mawr on Anglesey — in which pottery and other manufactured goods are far rarer and there are no displays of status in architecture. These sites were plainly involved in farming, as botanical remains and artefacts attest, and fields still survive as part of some such complexes. These might well represent a low grade of landowners, or the tenants of the occupants of the enclosed hut-groups. Again, Roman coinage occurs at such sites, and this might imply that even they were integrated into the Roman taxation system. Perhaps they paid taxes in coin and kind to their landowners, who paid taxes in turn to state officials or to local magnates.

Aside from sites which fit into these categories, there are no other fourth-century settlement sites known from north-west Wales. In order to trace the end of this social and economic system one can conveniently begin, as when examining Dumnonia, by examining what became of this settlement hierarchy in the fifth century. Here, too, the pattern of settlement seems remarkably similar in the fifth and sixth centuries to that we have seen in the fourth century, although some changes took place.

The Roman fort at Segontium seems to have been disused in the early fifth century. Extensive excavations in the 1970s and '80s produced no evidence of mid- to late fifth-century occupation. Thus, as one might expect, the official function of the fort at Segontium does not seem to have outlasted the official withdrawal of Roman rule. This does not mean that Segontium was completely abandoned: artefacts of a later date have been found in the fort, and a few traces of structures post-dating the early fifth century have been found within the enclosure. It has even been suggested that a medieval church — just outside the fort entrance — began as a Roman-period church for the garrison. None of this amounts to evidence of later fifth- or sixth-century occupation. No artefacts undeniably belonging to the period *c*.450-600 have been found within the enclosure, nor is there any stratigraphical or other evidence which would imply that the excavated post-Roman structures at Segontium are more likely to date from this period rather than later. There is no reason to credit any fifth- or sixth-century occupation at Segontium, let alone the maintenance of its official function into this period.[41]

The implication is that administration of this area in its fourth-century form ceased in the early fifth century at latest. The withdrawal of the garrison at Segontium may have seen political authority pass to another part of society. The most obvious candidates, on the basis of what we have seen in Dumnonia, is the local civilian elite, and especially the hereditary rulers of the Ordovices.

Far better evidence exists for the survival of local hill-fort based elites than for military

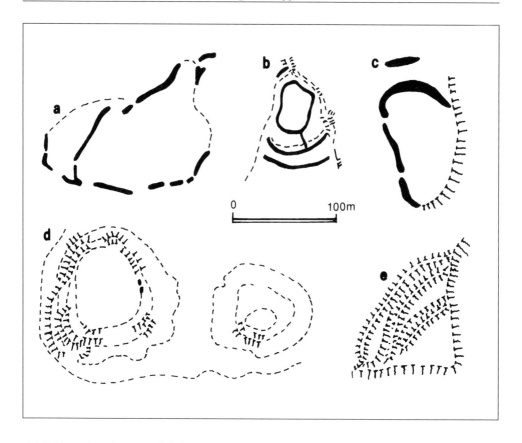

48 *Fifth- and sixth-century hill-forts in Wales: a Dinas Emrys; b Dinas Powys (earliest bank shown as broken line); c Coygan Camp; d Degannwy; e Brawdy. All scales 100m. (After Alcock except for Brawdy)*

sites. The hill-forts at Degannwy and Dinas Emrys both have imported Mediterranean B-ware pottery of late fifth- to sixth-century date (Bii at Degannwy and two-handled Biv at Dinas Emrys), and there is a unique D-ware roundel bearing a Chi-Rho symbol at Dinas Emrys. While the nature of the Romano-British activity at the craggy hilltop of Degannwy seems unclear at present, the fourth-century material at the drystone-built site at Dinas Emrys points to a high-status — probably secular — occupation, and this pre-dated the construction of the inner hill-fort bank. Both hill-forts are defensibly and visibly sited, Degannwy above the mouth of the Conway estuary, and Dinas Emrys dominating Nant Gwynant, one of the major Snowdonian valleys. Both were also used for castles of the later medieval Welsh kings, a point which may hint at other such sites where these castles are on earlier hill-fort sites. At other hill-fort sites in north-west Wales, evidence is much more ambiguous: excavations have been too small-scale, or were conducted too long ago (and too poorly by our standards), to ascertain for certain whether or not there was fifth- to seventh-century occupation at hill-fort sites occupied in the fourth century (**colour plate 16**).[42]

172

As in Dumnonia there are several other hill-forts which may well have been used in this period, and others which might have been. Again, these fall into the same two groups: inland multivallate hill-forts in strongly defensible locations, and coastal promontory forts above harbours. For example, at Dinas Dinorwic, where the place-name means 'the fort of the Ordovices' (implying re-use of an earlier Ordovician hill-fort centre), Late Roman pottery has been found, and at Twyn-y-Parc, near the later palace of the kings of Gwynedd at Aberffraw, where there may also have been a Roman fort. A particular group of such hill-forts, built with drystone banks, contains an inner 'citadel' enclosure and outer 'wards'. This includes sites with Late Roman pottery and rectilinear buildings of Late Roman or later date, as a Tre'r Ceiri and Carn Fadrun, and also the hill-fort at Bryn Euryn — probably Gildas' *'receptaculum ursi'* and the fortress of king Cuneglasus in the sixth century.

The evidence from enclosed hut-groups also attests the occupation of some of these sites into the fifth and sixth centuries. We need not expect all these settlements to continue into the fifth century or later, as they had been coming into use and being abandoned throughout the Roman period. The evidence of post-fourth-century occupation at them frequently consists of features post-dating late fourth-century pottery or coins, but which cannot be exactly dated as they were excavated before methods of 'absolute' dating (radiocarbon dating, luminescence etc) were used.

More certain evidence is available from a handful of sites, for example, from Graenog (where radiocarbon dating attests that the fourth-century settlement continued in use into and perhaps beyond the sixth century) and from Pant-y-Saer, where a sixth- or seventh-century tinned copper alloy penannular brooch may be associated with two 'late' rectilinear buildings. Finds from the fourth-century enclosed hut group at Porth Dafarch include a possibly fifth-century Type F penannular brooch and rivetted Romano-British pottery, and its site was used for a dug-grave and long-cist cemetery. One of the graves that cut a Romano-British hut contained a Roman carnelian intaglio, Samian ware and other Romano-British finds. Plainly, such material was still available, and probably still in use. This highlights the existence of Late Roman rivetted pottery in one of the final hearths at Din Lligwy as also possibly fifth- or sixth-century.[43]

The absence of imported Mediterranean pottery and glass from such sites may suggest that they remained middle-rank sites in the fifth and sixth centuries, given that finds include brooches and the Byzantine intaglio at Cefn Cwmwd. The settlement at Glyn, Anglesey, may be analogous, at least in social rank, to these enclosures. This is a D-shaped enclosure dated both by finds (including a knobbed crucible, 'Anglo-Saxon' bucket mounts, a polychrome glass bead, a bird-headed brooch of the seventh century and bone comb fragments) and by radiocarbon dates indicating occupation and metalworking of the fifth to eighth century. Roman glass, Roman coins (among them a clipped siliqua of the early fifth century) and Romano-British pottery suggest that the site began in the Roman period.[44]

The continuation of occupation into the fifth and sixth centuries may also be seen at the unenclosed hut-groups. Here we have only one site that provides clear-cut evidence: the multi-period settlement at Ty Mawr. There, the fourth-century site remained in occupation into at least the sixth century and rectilinear structures were first built at the

49a Penannular brooch from a Romano-British enclosed hut-group at Pant-y-Saer, Anglesey. Tin-coated copper alloy. Copyright National Museum of Wales

site at this time, associated with a continuation of agricultural activities. No imported material or metalwork was found at the site, and this could imply that it remained of low status into this period. Pollen analysis suggests that agricultural continuity — and even agricultural expansion — characterised north-west Wales in this period.[45]

On the basis of well- and extensively-excavated sites, fourth-century settlements of all the three main types continued in use throughout the fifth and sixth centuries. There is no hint that these sites were occupied by 'intrusive' population groups who replaced their original inhabitants, nor of dramatic cultural change in terms of the range of artefacts in use — in these areas only a small amount of mass-produced pottery and glass had ever been used. The same argument as employed in relation to Dumnonia applies here: the only evidence for an Irish presence is a few ogam stones (fewer in north Wales than Cornwall or Devon) and poorly dated place-names, which may post-date 600. We appear to be seeing the continuation of a Romano-British society into the fifth and later centuries, with at most small-scale Irish aristocratic settlement. The explanations as offered for many of the Dumnonian ogam stones, the granting of land to Irish elites in return for military service or to Irish ecclesiastics, may explain the Irish connections in this area too (**colour plate 17**).

The one widespread change in this area in the fifth century is also the same as that found in Dumnonia. This is the emergence of a distinctive and identifiable archaeology of religion and burial, associated with participation in a Romano-Christian culture. Like many parts of north and west Roman Britain, the fourth-century inhabitants of north-west Wales appear to have practised religious and burial customs which have proved

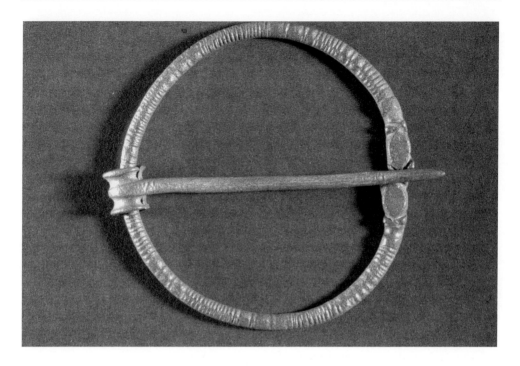

49b Class 1 zoomorphic penannular brooch from Porth Dafarch, Anglesey. Reproduced with the kind permission of The British Museum

almost impossible for archaeologists to identify. No temple or shrine of fourth-century date has been securely identified in north-west Wales, and no definite burials or tombstones of this date are known from the area.

In the fifth century this situation changes drastically: cemeteries and evidence of (Christian) religious belief become the most visible aspects of the archaeology of fifth- and sixth-century north-west Wales. The appearance of Class-1 inscribed stones, some bearing Christian symbols or memorial formulae analogous to those found in Dumnonia, represents both the Christianisation of the local elite and their adoption of Latin literacy, and other aspects of Roman culture (such as burial beside Roman roads attested at Bedd Porius at Penmachno), through contact with the Christian Church.[46]

Extensively-excavated cemeteries of probable fifth- to seventh-century date, comprised of east-west inhumations organised into rough lines, are known from Landegai, and Holyhead, Capel Eithin and Arfryn on Anglesey. All these cemeteries show evidence of having been focused on a structure with possible religious associations.

At Holyhead the cemetery consisted of long-cists focused on a Bronze Age barrow with a possible structure built on its centre. The ditch of the barrow had been infilled, apart from a causeway leading to the structure. The cemetery of dug-graves at Landegai was associated with a series of prehistoric ritual monuments, and one grave was enclosed within an east-west rectilinear timber building, perhaps a mausoleum or chapel. At Capel

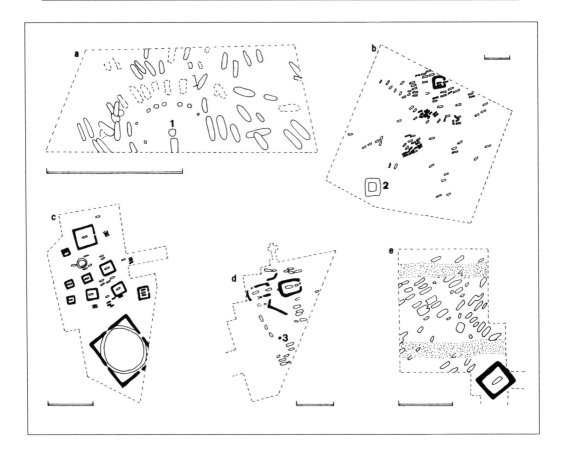

50 Early Christian cemeteries in Wales. a, Arfryn, Bodedern; b, Capel Eithin; c, Tandderwen; d, Plas Gogerddan; e, Llandegai. Rectangular enclosures around graves shown in black. Neolithic cursus monument shown in stipple on Llandegai and Bronze Age barrows on Tandderwen shown in outline. 1 = timber structure, 2 = Roman-period structure, 3 = standing stone. All scales are 10m. (After James, White, Murphy, Brassil)

Eithin the cemetery of both dug-graves and long-cists focused on what may be a Roman-period signal station, perhaps used at this date for some other purpose — such as a mausoleum or chapel. A structure or fenced enclosure contained two long-cists, one with post-holes by the head of the grave and centrally aligned. At Afryn the central feature was a curvilinear post-built surround around a pebble floor containing a post- or stone-setting (an inscribed stone re-used in one of the graves might conceivably have come from this). Other less well-excavated, or much less complete, cemeteries are known from elsewhere in north-west Wales which may be partly or wholly of this date.[47]

Nothing like these cemeteries is known from the area in the fourth century, and they represent a distinctive post-fourth-century development. The use of prehistoric ritual monuments for these sites recalls both Romano-British custom and fifth- and sixth-century burials elsewhere in western Britain. The reason for this sudden change in the visibility of religion and burial may, therefore, be the adoption of Christianity by the local inhabitants of the area, not just the elite.[48]

At this date, too, we see evidence of monastic communities and Christian clergy in north-west Wales. Monasteries are arguably implied by clusters of these stones at later church sites and — far less probably — by inscriptions where one name alone is cited. The Class-1 stone at Llantrisant commemorating 'the blessed Saturninus and his holy wife' may attest a cleric, and demonstrate that some clergy at least were married. That at Llangian mentions a doctor (*medicus*) who may well have been part of a monastic community and who called himself 'son of Martin'. One monastery where this date is identified more directly in north-west Wales is at Aberdaron, where the inscription itself may well refer to a (male) monastic community, as mentioned in chapter 1. As in Dumnonia, it may well have been the monastic movement that evangelised the area in the fifth century, and in Gildas' *De Excidio* even the king of Gwynedd, Maglocunus, had spent some time as a monk (presumably in this kingdom) before returning to secular life.[49]

As in Dumnonia, we might see the fifth century as a period in which religious conversion reconfigured elite identities. Evidence also exists to support the view that these religious and cultural changes affected more than just courts. The Byzantine gemstone from a signet ring found at the enclosed hut-group at Cefn Cwmwd, on Anglesey, where occupation associated with the gemstone is dated by a penannular brooch of the fifth to sixth century, suggests the adoption of aspects of this culture in a non-courtly secular context. This may suggest that the middle rank of north-west Welsh society participated in the same Romano-Christian culture as their rulers (**colour plates 18 & 19**).

In Wales, as in Cornwall, it may be possible to recognise specifics of the political geography within which these changes took place. The Welsh *cantrefi* (*cantref* is Welsh for 'hundred') are first attested in the *Historia Brittonum*, written in 829/30 in Gwynedd, and at least a dozen of the fifth- to seventh-century inscribed stones in north-west Wales lie at or near later *cantref* boundaries. Most of the remainder are in the geographical centre of these units — as if located near to administrative or religious centres conveniently located within them.[50]

This may be seen at Pen Llystyn, where a Class-1 stone near the centre of the *cantref* stood close to a disused early Roman fort. The fort was re-employed — probably during the same period as the stone — for a palisaded enclosure. A site which might be similar was discovered by geophysical survey at Llanfor, Merioneth. This comprises a polygonal enclosure immediately outside, but in an uncertain chronological relationship to, a Roman temporary camp. The polygonal enclosure may date to the Roman period, but could be another enclosed site of the type found at Pen Llystyn. A rectilinear enclosure containing a post-built rectilinear structure approximately 250m to the north has been interpreted as an enclosed settlement of post-Roman but pre-medieval date.[51]

Interestingly, in Welsh, the name for these hundred-sized territories may be preserved in the later term *alltud* (stranger) and the name 'Tudor' (as in Henry Tudor, the king of England). The relevant term is *tud*, the direct cognate of the Irish *túath*, possibly the political equivalent of these territories. In Ireland the *túath* was ruled by the *rí*, or (minor) king. In Welsh the cognate term is preserved in *breyr* (literally 'land-king'), the later expression for a noble, and 'Tudor', meaning literally '*rí* of the *tud*'. Gildas may hint at the terminology of kings ruling the tribal over-kingdoms in the sixth century when he denounces the western British kings as *tyranni* (illegitimate rulers), arguably punning the known Welsh term *tigern*, meaning 'lord' or 'king'. This term also occurs in early Welsh poetry for major kings, and has an associated word *teyrnas* meaning kingdom. So we may not only be able to detect this hierarchical structuring of royal government, but actually recover its contemporary terminology.[52]

Sub-kings in north-west Wales may have participated in the same Romano-Christian culture, and ruled equivalent-sized territories, as Dumnonian sub-kings. The archaeology of north-west Wales in the fifth and sixth centuries can also be seen as a continuation of the fourth-century settlement pattern, with the exception of the one site fully integrated into Roman imperial administration (Segontium) and the addition of newly-visible religious and burial practices, attendant upon the Christianisation of the area. This encompasses all the known sites of this date in north-west Wales, and resembles so closely the situation in Dumnonia that both areas might be seen as experiencing similar cultural and religious changes in the fifth century, and having a similar political, social, religious and economic organization.

Competing for the kingdom

There is also evidence for the continuation of the Roman-period tribal unit of north-west Wales, the Ordovices, into the fifth century and probably later. The name Ordovices is preserved, as *Ordous*, as the political affiliation of a man named Corbalengus commemorated on a Class-1 inscribed stone at Penbryn in Cardiganshire. This was sited at, and possibly on, a cairn containing a cremation, in the south of what is believed to have been Ordovician territory in Roman Britain. By the end of the sixth century a new name for this polity had been coined, *Venedotia* (or Gwynedd). This name — as *Venedos* — occurs on an inscribed stone at Penmachno. The origins of *Venedos* remain obscure (it may be compared to the Iron Age name *Venetii*, related to the Brittonic name for the Menai strait, or — less plausibly — be of Irish derivation), but it seems to refer to the same political unit in the sixth and later centuries.

Exactly when this change occurred, and why, is also unclear. It may relate to a shift of political focus from the south of the Ordovican area (where *Cantref Orddwy*: 'cantref of the Ordovices' was located) to Anglesey. The island of Anglesey was probably linked with Maglocunus, king of Gwynedd, by Gildas in *De Excidio*, when he calls him the 'dragon (probably 'military leader') of the island' (probably Anglesey) and was the burial place of Catamanus king of Gwynedd in the seventh century. This may suggest that, unlike Dumnonian over-kingship, the rulership of the Ordovican kingdom/Gwynedd passed from one line of sub-kings to another in the fifth or early sixth century.[53]

The limits of both the Roman-period Ordovices and of sixth-century Gwynedd are much more unclear than those of Dumnonia. They may well be indicated, at least generally, by the distribution of Class-1 inscribed stones, which form four distinct regional groups in Wales. One of these centres is in north-west Wales and is bordered by

51 Class-1 inscriptions in Wales in relation both to the later medieval boundaries of Gwynedd and Brycheiniog and to three major rivers. (Based on Nash-Williams and Lloyd)

the river Dee and Dyfi: rivers which formed boundaries of ninth-century Gwynedd. However, Penbryn lies to the south of the Dyfi and within the distribution which might be associated with the kingdom of Dyfed (see below). If Penbryn lay within Ordovican territory, some fluctuation in its borders must have taken place through the period examined here. If the Deceangli existed in the fifth century then the Dee cannot have formed their eastern boundary at that date. Archaeological evidence might be taken to imply that the boundaries of the Ordovices fluctuated through the fifth and sixth centuries.

Textual evidence implies that this instability in Ordovican borders is unlikely to have been only due to the loss of territory to other political units. Gildas remarks that Maglocunus' kingdom was 'greater than almost any other', suggesting that Gwynedd was at least one of the militarily strongest of those kingdoms located in what had been Britannia Prima. The same impression is given by later writers also. Bede refers to the early seventh-century Venedotian king Cadwallon, who defeated the leading 'Anglo-Saxon' kingdom of his time, Northumbria.

This evidence, taken together, suggests that the Ordovices did survive as a political unit into the fifth and sixth centuries. At some — perhaps early sixth-century — point they abandoned the name Ordovices in favour of the name Gwynedd. It suggests that their borders fluctuated through these centuries, but that north-west Wales remained under their control throughout, including at least later Carnarvonshire and Anglesey.

One apparently conflicting piece of evidence needs to be addressed. The ninth-century *Historia Brittonum* presents us with an alternative story of dynastic formation in north-west Wales. It says that Cunedda came from the territory of the Votadinii in north-east Scotland and drove the Irish out of north-west Wales. As we have seen, *Historia Brittonum* is a propagandist work for the ninth-century kings of Gwynedd, who had northern connections. The 'Cunedda' story has long appealed to modern scholars, and has even been supported by literary and place-name specialists in recent years, despite the compelling historical arguments against it.[54]

Migration myths

The only archaeological support for the Votadinian origin of the kings of Gwynedd which requires special attention may be afforded by Tandderwen. This site, in north-east Wales rather than the area covered in this section, comprises earthen rectilinear mounds surrounded by ditches, each containing one or more east-west inhumation burials without grave goods. Square barrow cemeteries are otherwise known only in this period in Scotland and in the Iron Age of south-east Yorkshire. The Tandderwen cemeteries cannot be taken as evidence of fifth-century Votadinii in north Wales for two reasons. They are radiocarbon-dated to no earlier than the seventh century, and probably either the late seventh or eighth century, and the Votadinii did not even use square barrows so far as can be determined! Cemeteries of long-cist graves characterise Votadinian burial practice in this period, and the only known mound-burials from what may be their territory are undetched curvilinear cairns.[55]

Square barrows, therefore, could not demonstrate a Votadinian presence in north Wales. Rather, they would be more credibly seen in the context of the same legitimising pseudo-history that produced the *Historia Brittonum*. This would see them as involved in the manufacture of a past complete with symbols (the barrow cemetery) and stories (the textual material), which we can only partially see today. When *Historia Brittonum* was written, Tandderwen was in Gwynedd, but in the fifth and sixth centuries it may not have been. Another possibility is that the Tandderwen cemetery is what it appears: a Pictish aristocratic cemetery in north Wales. This might be explained by the service of warriors in the courts of north Wales, just as one might explain at least some of the ogam stones. In any case, Tandderwen is not evidence for the veracity of the Cunedda story.

The kingdom of Gwynedd can, then, be most readily explained as the post-Roman continuation of the Ordovices, with dynastic replacement bringing about a change of polity-name and a shift of political control from Merioneth to Anglesey in the sixth century. Like Dumnonia, the elite governing his polity appears to have been converted to Christianity in the fifth century, probably as part of the same missionary endeavour and bringing with its the same collection of practices and symbols.

We may be able to trace this fifth-century evangelisation more widely throughout society than just among royal families and their courts. The development of substantial cemeteries of east-west unaccompanied graves, associated with what might well be Christian religious foci, implies that this was not merely a matter of elite conversion. At least a large number of the local population, and possibly the whole population, appear to have abandoned their generations-old burial practices and adopted this new, Romano-Christian rite.

As in Dumnonia too, burials of this sort of prehistoric ritual monuments might be taken to imply that ancestry — perhaps the descent of kin-groups — was as important to the mass of the population as to the elite who indicated patrilineage on their inscribed stones. This population was, it seems, still living in the same settlements as their fourth-century Romano-British ancestors, and probably still paying their taxes to local magnates as perhaps had previous generations within the Roman Empire. For them, like their Dumnonian counterparts, the Romano-British period had not ended in almost any meaningful respect and their integration in the broader Continental cultural community — by this time one that was Romano-Christian in character — had only increased, both in their own lifestyle and in the political displays of their rulers.

Fifth-century evangelisation led to the adoption of a Romano-Christian culture, in a general context of widespread political, social and economic survival across a wide zone of western Britain. This can also be observed in north-east Wales, this time among the Deceangli.

The forgotten kingdom: Tegeingl

In the fourth century, the territory of the Deceangli was probably a *civitas*, as inscriptions on Roman-period lead 'pigs' (ingots) produced in their territory imply. Where their *civitas* capital lay is uncertain, perhaps at Prestatyn or Ffrith. These were Roman administrative sites, probably connected with mineral extraction, and Deceanglian territory contained no towns or villas. Social and economic structure may well have resembled that of the Ordovices, and late fourth-century elite hill-fort settlement is known from the core of Deceanglian territory. At Dinorben there was a large multivallate contour hill-fort with evidence of wealthy fourth-century occupants involved in agriculture. As in Ordovican territory, there is evidence of enclosed farms of fourth-century date, in this case mostly timber-built and within earthen embanked enclosures, and unenclosed sites may also have existed. Lead shipped out of the *civitas* in ingot form is the main evidence of local industry, and Roman military presence may well have been confined to securing this resource.[56]

No Romano-Celtic temple is known for certain from the area. One possible site, Llys Awel, has produced votive objects of Romano-British date, but otherwise the lack of distinctive pagan religious practices and cemeteries resembles that of the north-west of Wales and Dumnonia. Evidence for Christianity in the fourth century is limited to a belt-buckle (Hawkes Type IB) from Pen y Corddyn hill-fort, showing Christian symbols, although this could be fifth-century in date.[57]

Nothing at Ffrith or Prestatyn need post-date the fifth century, although late fourth-century coins and calcite gritted wares have been found at Ffrith. There is no reliable evidence for the fifth-century fate of Romano-British enclosed or unenclosed settlements in Deceanglian territory, except for the hill-forts. Three hill-forts are known, from what was probably the Deceanglian polity, to show fifth- or sixth-century use. These are Bryn Euryn, mentioned above, Caergwrle — where a single mutilated hill-fort bank partially survives around a late medieval castle — and Dinorben itself. The evidence from all these sites does little more than demonstrate their fifth- and sixth-century use, and probably occupation.[58]

At Dinorben, finds include sixth-century 'Anglo-Saxon' metalwork, an 'Irish' slotted-and-pointed metal object (use unknown), rivetted fourth-century pottery, a possible Germanic glass bead, and stone ingot moulds which may date from this period. Bone in the outer ditch-fill gave a radiocarbon date centring on this period. There are plenty of post-holes and even bank phases which might belong to the fifth and sixth centuries at the hill-fort, but excavation undertaken ahead of quarrying, and largely early in the twentieth century, leaves their attribution to particular phases of use often uncertain. Later excavations (in the 1970s) at Dinorben are unpublished.

The hill-fort bank excavated at Caergwrle is radiocarbon-dated to the late third to fifth centuries, and a crudely carved spindle-whorl copying an 'Anglo-Saxon' coin design of much later date was found earlier at the site. At Bryn Euryn, excavation has shown the hill-fort to be of drystone-banked construction but has produced no datable artefacts. As mentioned above, the site may well be that mentioned by Gildas, and stands above a medieval manor house named Dineirth (the fort of the bear), which might represent a Welsh version of Gildas' expression 'receptaculum ursi' ('the refuge-fort of the bear').

One cannot say a lot more than that these sites probably represent the sort of hill-fort occupation we have already seen further west. If so, they may be the seats of elites of the fifth and sixth centuries. There are also a few inscribed stones of the type already discussed in relation to Dumnonia and north-west Wales. These attest the same pattern of the fifth-century elite adoption of a Romano-Christian culture, presumably through the same means, and this is supported by a few cemeteries, as at Ruthin (where this cuts Romano-British occupation) and Pentrefoelas, where a long-cist cemetery may have been associated with the Class-1 stone found face-down in one of the cists.[59]

We lack any non-hill-fort settlement archaeology from this area whatsoever, except for a small double-embanked enclosed settlement at New Pieces, immediately below the disused hill-fort at the Breiddin. This site was occupied in the fifth and sixth centuries, and has produced finds of imported pottery and Germanic glass, suggesting high-status activity. It may represent the sort of sub-kingly level represented by the Class-1 inscriptions elsewhere, but until the 1990s excavations are published it will be difficult to say more.

In all, the evidence from Deceanglian territory is much weaker than that from Gwynedd or Dumnonia. It merely hints that the same pattern of survival and religious change may well have occurred in this area also. Like the Ordovices and Dumnonii, the name Deceangli survived, to be preserved in the *cantref* name *Tegeingl*, in medieval Wales. The boundaries of the Deceangli in the Roman-period are obscure, and they remain so in the fifth and sixth centuries — perhaps with one exception. Wat's Dyke, once thought an 'Anglo-Saxon' construction related to Offa's Dyke, has recently been radiocarbon-dated to the fifth century. It runs along the eastern boundary of what, on the basis of the lead ingots and the later *cantref* name, one might believe to be Deceanglian territory. While the Deceangli do not seem to have constructed this barrier (its ditch faces west) it may define the limit of their territory where this bounded the Cornovii. To the west if, as is probable, Gildas' Cuneglasus was a king of the Deceangli and his fortress was at Bryn Euryn, then his domain encompassed the northern estuary of the Conway. This provides a clearly-defined north-east Welsh area, which encompasses the lead ingot distribution and the later *Tegeingl*.[60]

Nevertheless, that the 'Venedotian' inscribed stone distribution stretches across the Conway to encompass those in Deceanglian territory could hint at political expansion. We do not know that Wat's Dyke was constructed against the Deceangli: it might equally have been a check to an Ordovican advance across north Wales. That the Deceangli did eventually succumb to their western neighbour is suggested by its disappearance from political history (beyond a *cantref* level) before the ninth century. In 829/30, from the Conway to the Dee lay in the kingdom of Gwynedd, as *Historia Brittonum* shows.

This last point indicates that Deceanglian territory did not become the later kingdom of Powys, known in the seventh century and later. Powys probably included Bangor-on-Dee and Chester in its seventh-century territory. By the ninth century its also included Llangollen, where a stone cross, the 'Pillar of Elise', carries the Powysian royal genealogy in a long inscription. So Powys would seem to be east of the Dee, and the kingdom may well be the Cornovian *civitas* in its sixth-century or later form. The only piece of evidence which might militate against this is provided by a ninth-century entry in *Annales Cambriae*, which tells us that Degannwy was burnt at the time of the Viking attack on Powys. But it does not actually say that Degannwy was in Powys at the time.[61]

Tegeingl may well represent the name of the fifth- and sixth-century Deceanglian kingdom, reduced to a minor role by conquest at some time after Gildas' Cuneglasus. Perhaps the reason why Dinorben was later called 'the fort of the Ordovices' is a propagandist attempt to claim that this territory had always rightfully been part of what was, at this date, Gwynedd. The survival of the name *Cantref Orddwy* shows that the Venedotian kings did not eradicate traces of the former territorial name, and we know later kings of Gwynedd pursued propagandist programmes.

Although the evidence is slight compared to other areas, the fifth- and sixth-century political, cultural and social history of the Deceangli may be seen as analogous to the kingdoms already discussed. This is perhaps the least well-understood of any of these western British kingdoms. Much more evidence exists for the next polity, the kingdom of Dyfed.

Dyfed

Fourth-century south-west Wales was within the *civitas* of the Demetae, centred on Carmarthen, the most westerly Roman town. As in Dumnonia, a small number of villas surrounded the *civitas* capital, but away from this enclosed farms predominated. These had taken on a distinctive appearance by the fourth century, with timber or drystone rectilinear structures replacing the curvilinear buildings typical of early Roman south-west Wales, as at Walesend. Such farms are often associated with Romano-British pottery, but also sometimes imported amphorae and glassware, as at Dan y Coed.[62]

Other aspects of the settlement pattern and material culture also resemble those of Dumnonia, albeit with distinctive local aspects. Unenclosed settlements, of which the most fully understood is the coastal site at Stackpole Warren, and hill-forts, as at Coygan Camp, may represent the two ends of a settlement hierarchy in which such enclosed farms typified the middle grade. Rectilinear structures are found at the hill-forts and Roman-British manufactured goods occur on all of these sites. In general, a similar social and economic system to that seen in Dumnonia may also be evidenced in this area and again we have no sure evidence of late fourth-century Roman military bases, rural 'Romano-Celtic' temples, fourth-century rural cemeteries or fourth-century Christianity.

As in Dumnonia, much of this settlement hierarchy seems to survive into the immediately post-Roman period. An exception is the *civitas* capital: there is no convincing evidence for occupation in Carmarthen from the early fifth to seventh century. A large ditch cutting Roman-period features may hint at some later activity, although does not prove occupation. Llanteulyddog church, inside the city walls, was one of the bishop's seats in Dyfed in the Middle Ages. This may suggest that a bishopric persisted in the former *civitas* capital into the fifth century and later, especially as this church overlies a Roman cemetery. The fate of the villas surrounding Carmarthen is as yet poorly understood. Only at Cwmbrwyn is there a hint of later use — a cross slab seems to have been sited within the enclosure at some post-Roman date.

Hill-fort sites show considerable evidence of occupation after this date. Imported Mediterranean pottery, metalwork and crucible sherds from the small multivallate (then coastal?) promontory fort at Coygan Camp probably date from the fifth and sixth centuries, and a Class-1 inscribed stone was found in Llandawke church nearby. At Carew, a large multivallate inland promontory hill-fort predating the medieval castle has much fourth-century pottery and a few sherds of late sixth- or seventh-century E-ware. The

Carew cross, a later pre-Norman freestanding stone cross, comes from next to the site. The multivallate inland promontory fort at Castell Henllys may also have been re-used at this date — finds include an annular loom-weight and a ditch near its entrance cuts deposits associated with the fourth-century farmstead established outside the enclosure. Less certain are the cases of Porth y Rhaw, where one radiocarbon date (cal AD 475-515) suggests fifth- or sixth-century occupation in a coastal promontory fort with Romano-British artefacts, and Tenby castle. Tenby castle is probably mentioned as a hill-fort in the early Welsh poem *Edmic Dinbych*, but this poem is not exactly dated and the place mentioned is not clearly specified; it is simply a probably small (*bych*) coastal hill-fort with the same name as later Tenby. No artefacts of this date come from the castle, but an undated rock-cut 'chair' facing St Catherine's island just offshore might possibly be compared to the 'inaugural' features at Tintagel. The site at Gateholm is even more comparable to Tintagel. Like Tintagel, it is a rocky headland (now eroded into an island) covered in the remains of rectilinear structures, arguably of fifth- to sixth-century date (**colour plates 20 & 21**).[63]

More detailed evidence come from Brawdy, where extensive excavation showed that the univallate Iron Age inland promontory hill-fort was massively refortified, probably in the fifth century or later, to become a multivallate fortress. This contained a timber-aisled building of Romano-British form and other post-built timber structures. These are associated with unusual 'Romano-British' local pottery, considered by Peter Webster to date from the fifth century and represent 'sub-Roman' ceramics attesting 'terminal Romano-British' occupation. This phase was long enough in duration to involve rebuilding, but in a second period of use the site was remodelled to contain timber-framed buildings, probably associated with a bellows protector of sixth- or seventh-century form, and with knobbed crucible sherds of probably sixth- or seventh-century date. Other finds may belong to this period, and the occupation deposits include a range of stone artefacts, which cannot be closely dated, but including notched slates analogous to examples found at Tintagel. In the vicinity of the medieval church at Brawdy, at least one inscribed stone was located at a cemetery of dug graves (one filled with non-local limestone used in the first post-Roman phase of the hill-fort occupation), with an apsidal timber-framed east-west structure similar to those found in the hill-fort (**colour plates 22 & 23**).

Just as in Dumnonia, therefore, the local Romano-British elite seem to have remained in control in the fifth and sixth centuries, based on hill-forts which had — in many cases — been their fourth-century centres. Continuity of occupation is also found at the enclosed farms. While there is no known fifth- or sixth-century activity at Walesend, there is at both Drim, where a curvilinear timber hut may be associated with a copper alloy penannular brooch of fifth- or sixth-century type and a radiocarbon date centring on the seventh century, and Dan y Coed, where the evidence derives from a radiocarbon date for deposits underlying the final timber-framed rectilinear building at the site. No evidence tells us whether or not unenclosed settlements of fourth-century date survived into the fifth and sixth centuries.[64]

This enables us to adopt the same sort of interpretation for fifth- and sixth-century south-west Wales as we have for fifth- and sixth-century Dumnonia and Gwynedd. Again, all that seems to have been 'lost' in the fifth century was the apparatus of Roman imperial

52 Class-1 inscribed stone from Caldey Island, the site of a sixth-century monastery

government, in this case in the form of the *civitas* capital and perhaps the few villas around it. These similarities are borne out if we look at the evidence for religious change in fifth-century south-west Wales. Exactly as we saw before in other areas, this is shown in terms of the appearance of organised unaccompanied inhumation cemeteries of both dug graves and long-cists (as at Llanychlwydog church), and inscribed stones with Latin texts.[65]

These cemeteries have been found both at medieval churches and those unused in later generations. A series of medieval churches in south-west Wales are surrounded by undated crop-marks suggesting enclosures pre-dating the medieval church buildings. One of these, at Llangian, is the find-spot of an inscribed stone, and excavation of the churchyard boundary provided a radiocarbon date of cal AD 430-670, and a stick-pin and bead of similar date come from the site. As in other parts of western Britain, clusters of inscribed stones may indicate potential monasteries (as Heather James has suggested for four stones at Llandysillio), and the *Vita Prima Sancti Samsonis* tells of a monastery at Caldey Island, where E-ware and long-cist graves have been found. At Penally church nearby, a cross-marked stone might suggest that this important pre-Norman foundation was also established in this period.

On the coast there may be evidence of a series of sand-dune sites, as at Castlemartin Burrows (with spiral-headed pins), Linney Burrows (with E-ware, spiral-headed and other pins, a blue glass bead necklace, and bone comb of this date) and possibly

53 *Type G*
penannular
brooch from the
fifth- to sixth-
century site at
Longbury
Bank,
Pembrokeshire.
Copper alloy
with white
metal surface.
Copyright
National
Museum of
Wales

Goodwick Sands (with a Type G penannular brooch, analogous to those in Dumnonia and presumably part of the same system of trading contacts). This may suggest that the coasts of the Severn estuary were lined with such trading sites, while Bantham and Mothecombe shows that this extended along the south coast also. We seem then to be seeing a widespread and long-lived trading network encompassing much or all of the western British coasts, operating at this date and perhaps earlier.[66]

Perhaps, but not necessarily, related is the enigmatic riverside site at Longbury Bank. This is on a low hilltop near a later medieval manor house, inland from Tenby. Although only one possible structure (a small curvilinear hut terraced into the hillslope) has been located, the site has produced a wide range of fifth- to seventh-century finds, including PRSW and Bii and Biv imported Mediterranean pottery and E- and D-ware imported Frankish pottery, a Type G penannular brooch, Germanic glass, and metalworking debris. Erosion and plough-damage may account for the lack of structural evidence, even for the absence of any enclosure. If this is not a small elite site (perhaps the palisaded home of a sub-king) then it may be a seasonal trading place comparable to sand-dune sites on the coast. Alternatively, it might be a religious site, as an incised cross was found on the rockface of a cave in the hillside beneath, although this is undated and may be much later.[67]

The parallels between Dumnonia and Dyfed may extend even further, in the survival of 'Demetae' (later Dyfed) as the name of the post-Roman kingdom and evidence of sub-kingdoms, attested here by later *cantrefi* as in north-west Wales. In Dyfed, additional evidence about the sub-kingdoms may derive from a passage on the 'Seven Bishop Houses of Dyfed' in the 'Laws of Hwyel Dda'. Although this records a later medieval situation (the laws, despite their attribution to a ninth-century king, date from the thirteenth century in their present form), this may have preserved an earlier form of ecclesiastical organisation, in which each *cantref* had its own bishop. Thomas Charles-Edwards has pointed out that this implies that, like the Irish *tuatha* compared with the *cantrefi* above, each of the *cantrefi* of Dyfed may have had separate ecclesiastical organization. This is most likely to have been established when they were to some extent separately governed, that is when they were sub-kingdoms rather than administrative districts.[68]

Evidence from all of the areas discussed in this chapter presents a similar picture of continuity in social and economic terms from Roman Britain, with profound religious and cultural change throughout the area achieved through evangelisation in the fifth century onward. This might in turn suggest that the origins of post-Roman kingship in the area discussed in this chapter are also explicable in shared terms, by the resurgence of tribal kingship in a post-Roman context.

More migration myths

If, in Gwynedd, the story of Cunedda's migration and the expulsion of the Irish at first appeared to contradict this picture there, then in Dyfed almost the opposite is true. A ninth-century Irish text, 'The Expulsion of the Deisi', tells of the colonisation of Dyfed by an Irish dynasty, and initially there appears to be a lot of corroborating evidence for this. There are many ogam stones, showing both people with Irish names buried in Dyfed and the existence of spoken Irish, attested by spelling. There is even ogam on the tombstone of Vortipor, the Demetian king named by Gildas, found at Castell Dwyran in Carmarthenshire. There are many Irish place-names (such as *meidir*, found in north Dyfed) and dedications of churches to Irish saints, such as Bridget. In addition, a peculiarity of local Christian religious practice in Dyfed was the placing of burials in disused hill-forts and enclosed farms, as at Meidrim and Egwlys Cymyn, a custom only otherwise attested in Ireland and Scotland. On the face of it, then, the Irish origins of fifth- and sixth-century Dyfed seem secure, but is this evidence all that it seems?[69]

One's suspicions might first be aroused by Gildas' description of Vortipor. If Dyfed had been invaded by the Irish within his lifetime, Gildas might be expected to have mentioned this, as it would have fitted well with his theme of the punishment of the Britons for their failings. Instead he addresses Vortipor as if he, too, is a Briton, and praises his father. Nor does ogam on Vortipor's tombstone make him an Irishman. Vortipor also had a Latin inscription on his memorial stone and we might immediately ask: is this a Briton who wished to be seen as related to Irish culture, or an Irishman who wanted to be seen as part of British culture? Perhaps this is someone who is both 'Irish' and British simultaneously. We have no reason to assume that the only fifth- or sixth-century Demetian king about whom we know more than his name was Irish.

The ogam and linguistic evidence only supports Irish colonization on the assumption that the boundary between the Irish-speaking and Brittonic-speaking areas up to the fifth century was at the Irish Sea. In other words, any indication of Irish language in south-west

Wales, Scotland or Cornwall suggests migrants from across the sea. This is usually assumed to be well-established, but no earlier evidence than these stones necessitates such a view. The few place-names known from western Roman Britain demonstrate that places were named by Brittonic speakers, but this need not mean no one spoke any other language in the same areas. Although the boundary between Welsh and Irish lay at the Irish Sea in later centuries, we should not rule out the possibility that it lay further east in the fifth and sixth centuries. Perhaps ogam was used in Dyfed because, unlike other areas where ogam is far less common, at least some people spoke Irish from the Roman period onward. This could explain why Demetian ogams are usually bilingual, in Latin and Irish, whereas those in Ireland are monolingual and suggest that only the north of Dyfed was Irish speaking (**colour plate 24**).[70]

54 Ogam inscription at Bridell, Pembrokeshire, the cross could well also be of fifth- or sixth-century date

Nor is the practice of burial in disused enclosures convincing evidence. The most carefully-excavated site, Bayvil (where both dug- and long-cist burials cut an Iron Age enclosed farm), seems to begin in the seventh century, and none of the other sites are well-dated. None are likely to be as early as the postulated migration in the fifth century. This may suggest the adoption of an Irish cultural practice, even of Irish ecclesiastics, but it is not evidence of Irish colonization.[71]

This raises the possibility that the dynasty, and perhaps the broader British populace, of Dyfed actively cultivated an Irish identity, because of their linguistic affinities or out of simple proximity, in the fifth to seventh centuries. Gildas might have been oblivious to this either because he accepted that the Britons of Dyfed held an affinity with Ireland as obvious, or because he held the adoption of such an identity in contempt. If the latter, we might expect him to have referred to this as one of Vortipor's failings, so the former is perhaps more likely. The cultivation of a shared Irish identity may well have resulted in the adoption of Irish cultural practices, but it need not have involved dynastic colonisation any more than the north British identity cultivated by the second dynasty of Gwynedd in *Historia Brittonum* need have involved actual colonisation from what is today south-east Scotland.

In the most sophisticated recent analysis, by Damian McManus, it has been argued that ogam originated in south-west Wales rather than southern Ireland. If so, rather than seeing ogam as an indication of Irish cultural contacts in Dyfed we might see ogam in Ireland as an indication of the significance of contacts with this part of Britain. Perhaps this was an aspect of the evangelisation of Ireland from Britain, not of colonisation. This also raises the question of whether the people attested by ogam in Dumnonia came from Dyfed or Ireland: perhaps all the Irish evidence in Cornwall and Devon is really Demetian evidence.[72]

Although this does not exclude a fourth-century Irish immigration to Dyfed, as envisaged by Leslie Alcock, such an interpretation is unnecessary. Instead, it is possible that Demetians spoke Irish in the Romano-British period, only adopting Welsh at a later point. Reinterpreted in this way, Dyfed fits readily with the pattern we have already seen, and the distinctive character of the kingdom may be explained in other terms.[73]

Defining Dyfed

The distribution of Class-1 stones, including the ogam stones, seems to suggest the territory of the fifth- and sixth-century Demetian polity. This encompasses both Carmarthen and Castell Dwyran and stretches from St Davids to the river Tywi, on which lay the hill-fort-like citadel of the later medieval kings of Dyfed at Dinefwr castle, the name of which may imply a hill-fort at the site before the castle. If so, then Demetian territory in the sixth century may well have been similar to the fourth-century *civitas*. Perhaps significantly, its central area may have been the *cantrefi* of *Penbro* and *Gwarthaf*, just south-west of Carmarthen, where Castell Dwyran, Tenby, Longbury Bank, Penally, Coygan and Carew are all located.[74]

There are, nonetheless, hints of territorial tussles with Gwynedd to the north. The Penbryn stone lies within the Demetian cluster of inscribed stones. If this cluster represents the general extent of Demetian territory in the period, then part of that territory was — at the date of that stone — within Ordovican territory. The eighth-century and later kingdom of Ceredigion (the area involved) may have been a disputed border region in the fifth and sixth centuries, accounting for this.

A site which may support this interpretation is Plas Gogerddan. The fifth- to seventh-century cemetery at Plas Gogerddan contains dug graves and is sited at a barrow cemetery of Bronze Age date, but also includes rectangular enclosed burials very similar to those found in north-west Wales. Although the absence of such structures from Dyfed might be a mere accident of discovery, it could provide supporting evidence for this hypothesis if they represent the burial of local dignitaries with northern Welsh associations. Such a background explains why Ceredigion was later able to break away (presumably from

Dyfed) as a separate kingdom. Formation by 'splintering' from Dyfed also explains the smallest of the western British kingdoms: Brycheiniog.[75]

Brycheiniog

There is no known Romano-British predecessor for Brycheiniog; its territorial name includes an Irish personal name ('the kingdom of Brychan') and it is archaeologically represented by a cluster of ogam stones. However, almost nothing else is known about the kingdom in the fifth and sixth centuries. The territory was on the edge of three Romano-British polities — the Demetae, Ordovices and Silures — and had no Romano-British towns or temples. There are several Roman military sites, such as Brecon Gaer, in the area and a network of roads based on them was used for siting several of the fifth- and sixth-century ogam stones.[76]

The kings of Brycheiniog constructed a crannog (artificial island) in Llangorse lake which may have been designed to signal 'Irish' identity, but this was not until the ninth century, when *Historia Brittonum* shows us that dynasties were reinterpreting the past to serve their own ends. This provides no evidence that Brycheiniog was an Irish kingdom, although the possibility that Brycheiniog was the creation of 'Irish' adventurers — perhaps from Dyfed — seizing a marginal upland area of little interest to the surrounding polities seems plausible enough.[77]

However, the lack of additional evidence for fifth- and sixth-century cultural change may be due to a general lack of evidence for that period. We do not know whether or not Brycheiniog, too, fitted the pattern recognisable throughout the rest of the far west of Britain.

Conclusion

Throughout western Britain the fifth century appears, then, to have been characterised by overall settlement continuity and, so far as can be ascertained at present, the continuity of local social and economic practices, accompanied by the growth of kingdoms based on Romano-British political identities (**colour plate 25**).

The principal changes in the fifth century were religious and cultural. Although there is little evidence of Christianity in any part of this area in AD 400, to judge from the cemetery evidence and inscribed stones, or from Gildas' testimony, the entire population of the region was Christian by the sixth century. There is no evidence to the contrary.

The fifth and sixth centuries saw the adoption of Romano-Christian culture throughout the zone. Christian religious institutions, especially monasteries, were founded throughout the region. Where these religious changes originated seems best explained by looking toward the parts of western Britain which had been relatively Christianised in the fourth century, yet which lay to the west of the 'Anglo-Saxon' zone, and the rise of a monastic movement might give a context for the spread of Christianity to the west.

191

That such a transformation could occur attests the vitality of the Romano-Christian culture of the area discussed in the previous chapter. As we shall see in the next chapter, these characteristics are also found north of Hadrian's Wall, beyond the limits of Roman Britain.

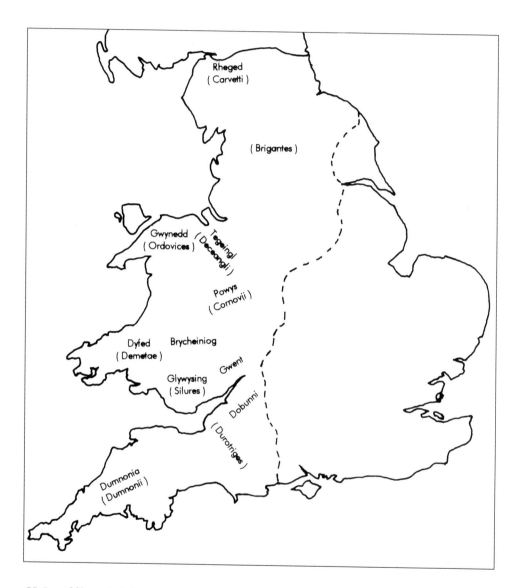

55 Late fifth- and sixth-century British political units known from texts and inscriptions, with names of Late Roman civitates and the tribal area of the Ordovices shown in brackets. The broken line indicates the western limit of early to mid-sixth-century 'Anglo-Saxon' cemeteries. The Durotriges and Brigantes may well have survived as political units into the sixth century

5 North Britain 400-600

In most of North Britain we can see the same pattern as identified in the last chapter: a Romano-Christian culture centred on the former Roman diocese spread by evangelisation from the fifth century onward — in this case to the north of Hadrian's Wall. However, we can also see the northern limit of this new cultural area, beyond which different practices prevailed. In order to identify these similarities, we may begin by looking at the area from the Mersey to the Wall. This exposes both these similarities and some remarkable differences from western Britain.

From the Mersey to Hadrian's Wall

This area was occupied in the fourth century by two *civitates*: the Brigantes and Carvetii. In the late fourth century both were based on towns (York and Carlisle) and had 'small-towns', such as Catterick in Yorkshire. In Brigantian territory there was a thin scatter of villas, fewer than in the south, and most farms in both areas were hut-groups of curvilinear structures. Unlike the west there are no hill-forts occupied in the Late Roman period, although these have been found immediately north of Hadrian's Wall. The latter point may suggest that the absence of such sites is genuine, especially as intensive fieldwork has taken place on both sides of the Roman Wall. Instead, there is much evidence of Roman military activity up to and after the end of the fourth century. This is represented in the *Notitia Dignitatum* as the Command of the *Dux Britanniarum*, with its headquarters at York.[1]

If early Welsh poetry and Bede's account of seventh-century North Britain are to be believed, the area was wholly or largely outside the zone of 'Anglo-Saxon' political control until after *c*.550. 'Anglo-Saxon' artefacts are sparse and almost all known 'early Anglo-Saxon burials' are inhumations, although Rosemary Cramp suggested that this was because the Germanic population adopted wholesale the burial practices of their British neighbours. The majority of the 'Anglo-Saxon' burials in this zone look so 'British' that one might doubt that they are in any respect 'Germanic': a lot have nothing more 'Anglo-Saxon' about them than a single knife, or the deposition of unworn 'Anglo-Saxon' artefacts in the grave.[2]

There are a few exceptions between the Derwent and the Tyne. At York cremation burials are located immediately outside the Roman walls at The Mount, within a Romano-British cemetery, and there was a 'mixed' cemetery at Norton-on-Tees, in which some people wore 'Anglian' costume. Cremation may indicate an 'actual' Germanic population as early as the fifth century, but it does not tell us whether or not this remained within an 'Anglo-Saxon' or British political context after the late fifth century.[3]

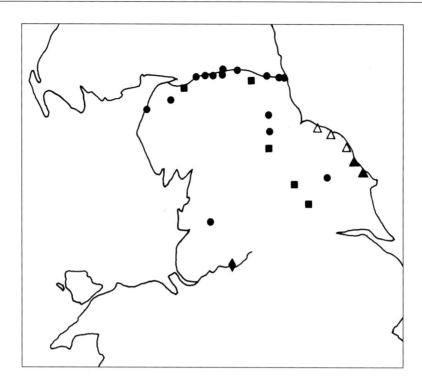

56 *Possible fifth- and sixth-century activity at Roman forts and towns in northern Britain. Sites*
   with fifth- or sixth-century evidence:
   filled circles = forts of the Late Roman command of the Dux Britanniarum
   filled squares = towns
   filled triangles = signal stations
   diamond = fort not in command of the Dux Britanniarum
   open triangles = signal stations without possible fifth- and sixth-century evidence.
   The line across north Britain along which several sites are situated is Hadrian's Wall

There are strong grounds for believing that Britons continued to control this area in the later fifth and sixth centuries. Although the Roman forts of Wales show no evidence of late fifth- and sixth-century occupation, the most remarkable aspect of this zone is that most of the known fifth- and sixth-century evidence from the Mersey to the Wall is at Roman fort sites. This is not a random selection of forts: all those with hints of activity at this date, with one possible exception, are known or likely to have been within the command of the *Dux Britanniarum*.[3]

Many of these sites are on Hadrian's Wall. At Vindolanda, an earthen bank was piled over the Late Roman fort wall, and an apsidal-ended structure (a church?) constructed in the courtyard of the headquarters building. A fifth- or sixth-century British penannular brooch was found at the south gate, and a Class-1 inscribed stone outside the fort. Birdoswald has also produced evidence of a similar bank overlying the fort wall, of late modifications to its gate, of internal structures and, perhaps, a church. At Housesteads, yet another 'late' bank seals the fort wall, again there is a possible church with an adjacent long-cist burial. At Chesters, stick-pins and undated burials were found within the Roman fort bathhouse immediately outside the fort, possibly indicating a British community living inside.

The Roman fort at South Shields has a complex sequence of fifth-century or later activity. This included refortification, burial immediately outside the fort and structural modifications within it. As Paul Bidwell has pointed out, all this is unlikely to represent continuity of occupation, as two burials cut the courtyard of the headquarters buildings, probably in the first three decades of the fifth century. At Benwell fort an 'Anglo-Saxon' brooch might hint at activity, as may sixth-century 'Anglo-Saxon' pottery at Wallsend, and Piercebridge was also apparently refortified at a fifth- or sixth-century date. 'Anglo-Saxon' artefacts were found both from this site and Binchester, where structures may show evidence of immediately post-Roman re-use.[4]

Although the material from these sites is somewhat scrappy, most were excavated prior to the development of current field methods. Moreover, the structural evidence discovered in recent excavations at Birdoswald would have been missed in earlier excavations. The remarkable thing is that any was found at all: it is absent from well-excavated forts elsewhere in west and north Britain.

A series of four, perhaps five, Class-1 inscriptions support an interpretation of British occupation at northern forts. In addition to the stone from Vindolanda, there are possible Class-1 stones from Brougham, Old Carlisle and Maryport, with a more doubtful example from Castlesteads. Inscriptions of this sort might have been set up at or near disused forts, but could be situated close to settlements, as would seem to be verified at Vindolanda. Class-1 stones do not appear to occur elsewhere north of the Mersey south of Hadrian's Wall, but are found north of the line of the Wall.[5]

This pattern is consolidated by evidence from the small-towns most closely connected with the fourth-century defence of the North. At Malton there are hints of fifth- and sixth-century activity within the town, and a ditch cut the main street as at South Shields. At Corbridge, immediately south of the Wall, 'Anglo-Saxon' objects and at least one burial have been found, accompanying other suggestions of post-Roman occupation within Roman structures, and at Catterick a complex sequence of occupation ranges from the fifth century onward. This comprises timber-framed and sunken-featured buildings, 'Anglo-Saxon' metalwork, and 'Anglo-Saxon' burials of the sixth century. There can be little doubt that Catterick was occupied during this period, and it may be the *Catraeth* of *Y Gododdin*. Evidence from Carlisle is extremely problematical, but occupation at Blackfriars Street and on the site of the medieval Cathedral may continue beyond 400, and at 66-8 Scotch Street a coin of Valentinian II was sealed in the ducts of the hypocaust in a town house, demonstrating fifth-century occupation.[6]

Further south three sites show similar re-use. At Manchester, SFBs were found immediately outside the fort, although these could belong to the Roman period. At the fourth-century fort at Ribchester, 'Anglo-Saxon' artefacts of uncertain provenance have been identified. Lastly, but more convincingly, a 'sub-Roman' ditch (to use the excavator's term) cuts the Late Roman signal station at Filey, on the Yorkshire coast, rendering it a fortified strongpoint at a date which is unlikely to be before *c*.400 given the evidence for use of the signal station. A hint of contemporary activity at Goldsborough signal station may be provided by a piece of what could be the distinctive bronze binding for an 'Anglo-Saxon' bucket.[7]

The similarities between the evidence from these fort sites prompts comparison between them. South Shields and Malton have similar defensive works, and the banks heaped over fort walls at Vindolanda, Birdoswald and Housesteads are the only instances in Britain of this form of defence definitely known. 'Anglo-Saxon' artefacts, otherwise extremely rare in this area, have been found at all of these sites except for Housesteads, Malton and Vindolanda. Most of all, these sites are the only cases in Britain of the well-attested defence of Roman military bases at this date, and it seems too much of a coincidence to attribute to chance that almost all these sites were part of the Roman command of the *Dux Brittaniarum* in the late fourth century.[8]

This could mean one of two things: the continued occupation of forts of the *Dux Brittaniarum* into the late fifth and sixth century by the families of their former garrisons, or their systematic re-occupation at that date. The evidence to resolve this is ambiguous at the majority of these sites. The earliest datable post-450 artefacts from the forts are at earliest late fifth-century; the latest might be late sixth-century. Likewise, the recognisable objects seem either to be high-status British artefacts (such as Class-1 stones or the penannular brooch from Vindolanda) or 'Anglo-Saxon'. This might be a reflection of the 'visibility' of such material in the archaeological record, but it implies that at least some of the people living in these former forts were elite Britons and had contact with the 'Anglo-Saxons', apparently at the time far to the south from Hadrian's Wall. Artefactually, it might be possible to support a view that these sites were in use throughout the late fifth and sixth centuries, but the finds do not enable us to tell whether sites went in and out of use during that period, as Tony Wilmott has pointed out. Stratigraphically, the evidence seems contradictory.[9]

At South Shields there appears clear evidence of disuse and reoccupation, while continuity of occupation has been claimed at Birdoswald, on the basis of which Wilmott suggested that the Wall area fragmented into minor warring chiefdoms competing against each other. Fragmentation could have permitted the fortification of nearby centres, sequentially acquiring 'elite' attributes such as Class-1 tombstones. The lack of refortified hill-forts in the zone south of the Wall suggests that this area did not contain a network of fortified settlements apart from the forts. Indeed, the only potentially contemporary settlements known in this area are undefended, as will be outlined shortly. If the Britons of the north maintained a patchwork of warring local lords, then one wonders where their other settlements are, given that British elite sites have been hard rather than impossible to find further south and local elites plainly had access to recognisable material.[10]

Moreover, this hypothesis cannot explain the refortification of Filey. This was an isolated tower, probably periodically used in the fourth century by the Roman army. It was not a farming community and the possibility that it simply continued as such into the post-Roman period can effectively be ruled out. Unless a beachhead for marauding Vikings or 'Anglo-Saxons', when the digging of the ditch might be thought unnecessary at a standing signal station within an already walled defensive enclosure during such brief use, it is extremely difficult to see what other use than as an observation or signalling post this site might have fulfilled.

Another piece of evidence suggests that continuity of agricultural communities was not a characteristic of this area. Although it cannot be used to comment on any particular site, the pattern of pollen data strongly implies general agricultural discontinuity in the area under consideration in the fifth and sixth centuries. Although short periods of continued farming on the Late Roman model might be hidden within the broad sweep of this pattern, it is extremely unlikely that general agricultural continuity characterised the area, except just possibly in the zone surrounding Carlisle.

If continuity of occupation is attested at Birdoswald then it was probably the exception rather than the rule. This might be because Birdoswald was an unusual site locally — geophysical survey has shown that a 'small town' grew up around the fort in the Roman period and perhaps the site is more correctly seen in the context of other small towns than forts. Nevertheless, it is also worth reviewing what the evidence for continuity at that fort actually is. From this it will be seen that continuity of occupation is only one possible interpretation of the excavated sequence. It must be pointed out that Birdoswald is an exemplary excavation and outstanding publication by its excavator, Tony Wilmott, makes re-evaluation much easier. Indeed, the ability to re-evaluate excavated data is frequently cited as the hallmark of good excavation, and reinterpretation of continuity at the site does not detract from its importance for our understanding of post-Roman occupation on Hadrian's Wall.[11]

The critical evidence is from the fourth-century fort's granaries. In 'Period 5' of the sequence of occupation at the site the underfloor channels of one granary (building 197) were infilled and the building used for occupation. Coins provide a *terminus post quem* of 347 for this infilling. Dark soil deposits formed over the resulting floor, which eventually subsided and began to break up. It seems reasonable to argue that it saw heavy use before or while these deposits formed. A layer of 'black, friable clay silt containing small pebbles' then formed over this soil deposit, creating a second layer on the floor. This was overlaid on the south side by a layer of reused roofing slate. More layers of dark soil accumulated over this. At the western end of the building two curvilinear areas of flat stones probably represent hearths; a compact deposit of reused roofing slates and flat stones overlay this deposit and this was covered by a layer of rubble and soil. The excavator considers that this represented the final collapse of this structure.

The floor of adjacent building 198 was not infilled as was that of 197, and its floor was robbed. The roof collapsed in or after AD 350. It was subsequently used as a dump, finds from which include a fifth-century (Type D7) penannular brooch and coins giving a *terminus post quem* of 367, and (among much else) Late Roman pins, pottery (especially Huntcliff ware) of late fourth-century date, a Roman-style earring, blue and green beads of Late Roman type, re-used red ceramic spindle whorls and counters, knives, armlets and a catapult bolt head. Glass included cups, bowls, jars and jugs and joining sherds of an early Roman flask.

While some similarities exist between this assemblage and that found on immediately post-Roman sites (notably the knives and red reused pottery spindle whorls and counters), some notable differences occur. For example, a high ratio of pins to armlets of 5:4 does not accord with the expectations of the obsolescence of hairpins proposed by Hilary Cool. The inclusion of an earring (and another found by the hearth) argues strongly against a later fifth- or sixth-century date, because no settlement of this date has produced strong evidence that earrings were still worn by Britons. The only earring at any later fifth- or sixth-century western British site is at Cannington cemetery, and could as easily be Roman rather than post-Roman in date. The catapult bolt head would also be unique at this time, and yet shows no evidence of re-smelting or modification.

A date at the transition from a Late Roman to sub-Roman 'suite' of artefacts appears plausible, following the argument proposed by Cool and amplified in chapter 3. This may be an assemblage of the first half of the fifth century, perhaps even the first quarter of that century — part-way between the assemblages known from standard late fourth-century settlements and those from the late fifth- and sixth-century sites discussed in previous chapters.[12]

Remains of roof collapse were found in the adjacent alley between buildings 197 and 198. However, roof collapse deposits were followed by attempts to rebuild buttressing and roof repair for 198, perhaps retaining the western part of the structure while the remainder was disused. This too ended with roof collapse. In Period 6 two phases of timber post-built buildings were constructed over 198 and its adjacent road, reusing the existing stone walls in places. The excavator allows that this whole sequence could pre-date AD 450, although it might extend far longer into the fifth to seventh centuries.

There were fewer finds associated with Period 6, which is perhaps because no midden analogous to that in building 198 was discovered. The finds recorded are interesting for their anachronism and difference to Period 5. The Period 6 finds include an atypical wheel brooch of unusual form and possibly second-century date, an A2 penannular brooch also of early Roman date, a fragment of a gold earring, few if any beads, no tools, perhaps glass bottle and cup fragments, and tweezers. The pin to armlet ratio was 0:4. This is an assemblage which would not be out of place at a fifth- or sixth-century site, but which is unlikely to be simply comprised of residual rubbish from Period 5. In particular, a much more restricted range of glass was found in Period 6 than 5, and whole categories of finds are unrepresented. The use of old brooches could be taken to suggest scavenging or the use of heirlooms, after normal supply ceased, again recalling later fifth- and sixth-century sites.

The disparities in the finds assemblage suggest that Periods 5 and 6 consist of use by different people or for different purposes. In particular, apart from an earring fragment (which might have been retrieved for its precious metal) there is no trace of material continuing in use from one period to the next. If material was so scarce as to lead to scavenging, it is hard to believe that, if continuity occurred, none of the material from Period 5 would have been still used in Period 6. This may bring the assumption of continuous development into question.

One possibility which appears to be unconsidered is that the junction between Period 5 and 6 represents the end of the Roman fort and the subsequent re-use after a period of desertion. In this alternative interpretation the infilling and occupation inside building 197 occurred wholly in the last part of the fort's Roman military use, say AD 350-400. This would permit building 198 to be buttressed and collapse by the 350s. It was then used as an adjacent rubbish tip for the occupied 197. The rubbish found in 198 would then be contemporary with occupation from at outside limits 350-450: as the excavator says 'the latest deposits in Building 197 contained a group of material very similar in composition to the Building 198 dumping'. The collapse of 197 represents then end of that phase and the end of Roman military community here prior to the mid-fifth century.

In a period between the final use of building 197 and the termination of dumping, and Period 6, the whole area was disused. It was cleared and consolidated for Period 6, building 199, with new floors laid over the dumped deposits. This demonstrates occupation at two distinct phases, using two distinct 'architectures': that of Period 5 re-used the granaries, but Period 6 disregarded them and consisted of post-built construction. This is not the only conceivable 'reading' of the stratigraphy of Birdoswald, but this 'short chronology' is at least equally credible to the 'long chronology' proposed by the excavator.

That is, there is no compelling reason to argue for continuity of occupation rather than re-use, even from the Birdoswald sequence. There are reasons (notably the redefence of Filey and the pollen data) to adopt the reoccupation hypothesis, but this hypothesis depends upon there being a potential organizing authority capable of systematically re-occupying forts, almost all belonging to a single Late Roman command. The string of sites along the road to York strongly implies that we should look there for such an authority.

The view that York was the pre-eminent Brigantan centre of the fifth and sixth centuries is hardly problematical, as it was a major political and religious centre both in the fourth and seventh centuries. There is evidence for activity within the walls in the fifth century as we saw in chapter 1. At the Minster, Martin Carver has shown that Derek Phillips' meticulous excavations beneath the medieval buildings could suggest fifth- and sixth-century occupation within the fortress, and sherds of Biv and Bii amphora has been identified among the pottery from the Roman town. 'Sub-Roman' pottery is reported from several sites at York, and bone combs from Wellington Row, York, include a triangular type usually dated to the fifth century. It is, therefore, at least a credible argument that an important settlement of this date lay within the walls of York.[13]

The refortification of the Wall forts and maintenance of a road linking them with York seems to most simply explain the distribution of the Roman forts and towns occupied in fifth- and sixth-century north Britain. This suggests that a shared military organisation in this area, based at York, survived or more likely was revived in the fifth and sixth centuries. The re-use almost only of sites of the same Late Roman command may suggest that this was an attempt to revive that command. The cluster of both Roman-period evidence for the Carvetii and Class-1 inscriptions in this zone at the west of the Wall might imply the survival of the Carvetian *civitas*, and this may conceivably be implied too by the Welsh poetry attributed to Taliesin. This recounts the activities of the British rulers Urien and his son Owain, kings of a territory called 'Rheged'. Rheged seems to encompass places within the Carvetiian *civitas* and may well be the Carvetii, employing a different tribal name.[14]

It seems likely that any organising authority based at York and holding sway on Hadrian's Wall and among both the Brigantes and Carvetii was above the level of the former *civitates*. Either the provincial structure survived later here than further south, perhaps into the sixth century, only to collapse before the late sixth-century situation of warfare between the Britons and 'Anglo-Saxons' depicted in the poetry and by Bede, or this represents Brigantian over-kingship in the north. It is hard to believe that an 'alliance of equals' between the two former *civitates* would have resulted in the Carvetii entrusting their security to a defensive system based in Brigantian territory. If each province arguably attended to its own defence in the fifth century, this could have been longer-lived in the north, arguably undisturbed by the 'Saxon' rebellion. This might explain a pattern of brief desertion in the early fifth century (as Roman forces left), followed by disregard for Roman military norms but reoccupation and refortification along 'sub-Roman' lines.

Alternatively, if we took Gildas's comment that Maglocunus was 'almost' the greatest king of Britain in his kingdom literally, then this could be evidence for the 'royal' option, Gildas being mindful of an over-king of the Brigantes ruling a larger and militarily stronger kingdom than that of Gwynedd. If so, large-scale kingship rather than fragmentation into many warring principalities should be envisaged in the north.

The lack of minor kings in this area is also perhaps to be inferred from the absence of many aspects of fifth- and sixth-century elite material culture found further south. At least outside York, imported pottery and glass is unknown. Inscribed stones again occur only at sites connected with this system, or that may have been linked to it. Hill-fort occupation is, as we have seen, absent and so is any other evidence of local elite occupation or burial. This might well imply that there were no minor hill-fort based rulers, with local administration in the hands of those integrated into the broader system already outlined, whether designated 'sub-kings' or 'military officials'.[15]

Whatever option we choose, and perhaps Brigantian over-kingship is the most likely, evidence permits us to envisage a very large and militarily strong British territory in the north. Such a political unit may well explain the lack of fifth- to late sixth-century 'Anglo-Saxon' settlement or burial — except when connected (at least arguably) with the system — in this whole area, despite the wealth of evidence for 'Anglo-Saxon' communities immediately to the south and east of York.

The location of churches in secular settlement sites of this date is another characteristic unknown in western Britain. In the areas discussed in the preceding two chapters, Christian religious structures and burial and occupation were apparently kept separate except at monastic sites. In this zone, possible churches were sited inside settlements, and this is also seen at undefended 'Romano-British' rural settlements, notably at Cow Green and Glencoynadale. The existence of these churches not only attests the survival of the settlements into this period but also to the Christianisation of the area around Hadrian's Wall and in what is now Cumbria.[16]

Thus, it seems likely that at least the ruling elite of the area were Christian, and the existence of a cluster of *eccles* placenames (a Brittonic loan-word meaning church or Christian community) in Lancashire seems to demonstrate that this area too was extensively Christianised prior to the 'Anglo-Saxon' political take-over of this zone. Extensive Christianisation in the fourth and fifth centuries might best explain these patterns, and Bede appears to have believed that Elmet, a British kingdom or sub-kingdom of the seventh century and perhaps earlier, near Leeds, contained many Christian religious sites also. A particularly problematical site in regard to fifth- and sixth-century British Christianity in this area is that of Bede's later monastery at Jarrow-Monkwearmouth.[17]

The earliest cemetery at Jarrow consisted of flexed east-west burials, one with a bead possibly of the fifth or sixth centuries. This could well be a British Christian cemetery predating the 'Anglo-Saxon' monastery and another pre-'Anglo-Saxon' cemetery has been found at Monkwearmouth. At Monkwearmouth, a west-east cemetery containing both male and female burials included a square stone platform overlying the burials of an adult male and two children. Again, a British Christian context seems best to fit this, and the juxtaposition of these cemeteries might suggest a monastic community at Jarrow with an associated lay community at Monkwearmouth preceding the 'Anglo-Saxon' monastic complexes at both sites.

The area from the Mersey to the Wall may, then, have shared a common Late Roman Christian culture with western Britain. It also seems to have been defended along sub-Roman lines, by a governing elite based at Roman-period political and military centres, possibly even with some form of provincial political organization. The only visible pagans in the fifth century in the zone examined here appear to be those buried according to 'Anglo-Saxon' customs. As we have seen, there are few such burials, and the lack of distinctive 'Anglo-Saxon' settlements may suggest that the populations buried in this way were living in less obviously 'Anglo-Saxon' accommodation than their counterparts further south.[18]

Deirdre O'Sullivan has drawn attention to an anomalous group of burials in the upper Eden valley at Kirkby Stephen, Warcop and perhaps Asby, Orton and Crosby Garret. A more dubious example has been found Brigg Flatt. All are barrow burials, probably all secondary internments in pre-existing mounds, they have rich grave-goods dating to the sixth century, and are situated within a few miles of each other. This appears to suggest high-status 'Anglo-Saxons' (perhaps pagans) in the core of the kingdom of Rheged. There are very few such burials, no more than six and probably fewer, and their proximity may imply that they could represent a particular group. This might be a family in the service of a British court, or the burials might all post-date the late sixth-century conquest of the area by the 'Anglo-Saxon' kingdom of Northumbria. Perhaps the latter is most likely, but they might be seen as analogous to the isolated cluster of burials in the Upper Tweed valley argued below to represent an 'Anglo-Saxon' group settled within a British kingdom. Whether the barrow at Castle Eden, where an 'Anglo-Saxon' blue glass vessel was placed above the face of the skeleton, is part of this group or a contemporary British burial is unclear.[19]

In this context the site at Fremington, Cumbria, might be thought to provide evidence of a fifth- or sixth-century 'Anglo-Saxon' community far to the west. However, this does not appear likely. At Fremington, a group of SFBs have been found 500m from Brougham Roman fort, and perhaps still within the occupied area of its extramural fourth-century civilian settlement. Finds from the settlement include repaired samian ware pottery, Black Burnished ware, Romano-British mortaria and a sherd of Huntcliff ware, but the SFBs appear to be post-Roman. Spindle whorls made from re-used Romano-British pot, annular- and bun-shaped loomweights, iron knives of post-Roman form and a possible comb. This might imply occupation of fifth- or sixth-century date, with later activity.[20]

The most problematical feature of the site is the homogenous handmade undecorated pottery that typified the ceramic assemblage. This is unparalleled locally, although it is similar to 'souterrain ware', found in Ireland and dating from the seventh to twelfth century. 'souterrain ware' has been found in Britain only at Iona, as we shall see below, but was apparently manufactured there as well as in Ireland. A related series of pots, 'grass-marked ware', was produced in Cornwall at approximately the same time.[21]

Fremington-style pottery is unknown at other sites, apart from a single sherd at Dacre. The Fremington pottery could date from as early as the seventh century, but is more likely to belong to later activity at the site — perhaps related to Irish or Hiberno-Norse contacts. Taken as a whole, Fremington-style pottery and grass-marked pottery could represent varieties of souterrain ware, arguably the result of Viking Age interaction around the Irish Sea. Indeed, Viking Age contacts would explain the Fremington SFBs.

Fremington may have been occupied during the fifth and sixth centuries, but the evidence for this is comprised of an annular loomweight and mended Roman-period ceramics, rather than pottery dating from this period. It may also be relevant that Brougham is one of the sites with a Class-1 tombstone.

As we have seen elsewhere, the vitality of the culture and religious life of the Britons may be suggested by their ability to 'export' their culture and religious beliefs beyond their borders. This is clearly seen in the North too, between Hadrian's Wall and the line of the long-disused Antonine Wall (roughly between Edinburgh and Glasgow) further north.

The Gododdin/Votadinii

Between Hadrian's Wall and the Antonine Wall lay territories occupied by British kingdoms in the fourth century. These had not been within Roman Britain for centuries, and may never have been fully integrated into the social and economic system of the Roman state. To the east, from Hadrian's Wall to the Antonine Wall and possibly beyond, were the Votadinii, the survival of whose name and polity are confirmed by the heroic poem *Y Gododdin*.

As already mentioned, *Y Gododdin* depicts their gallant defeat at *Catraeth* (probably Catterick in Yorkshire) in the final decades of the sixth century. According to *Y Gododdin* (the name means 'the Votadinii') groups of warriors, some from other parts of Britain, fought a pagan, or partly pagan, enemy force (including the Deiran 'Anglo-Saxons') at a fortified place at or near *Catraeth*. This resulted in their near annihilation after inflicting heavy casualties on the enemy.

The most instructive part of the poem is its description of the warriors — each has a few lines of praise — and the elaborate process of preparing for the raid. The context of these preparations is a fortress called *Din Eidyn*, which is almost certainly Edinburgh. The poem does not directly state that it was a hill-fort, but the prefix *din* might imply this.

Two possible sites for *Din Eidyn* exist: Edinburgh Castle and Arthur's Seat, a hill-fort above the city. Edinburgh Castle seems the most likely of the two, and excavations showed that its site was occupied in the fourth century and later, although the only diagnostic artefact of fifth- or sixth-century date is a bone comb. Excavations at Arthur's Seat have failed to find any traces of occupation of this date, although this may mean little given the difficulty of detecting such use.[22]

As with most parts of fifth- and sixth-century Britain, there is evidence that may relate to religious belief and practice. Of the few Class-1 inscriptions north of Hadrian's Wall, most are in what is usually agreed to have been Votadinian territory in the Roman period.

The Christian religious context of the inscriptions to 'Neitano sacerdos' ('Nathan the priest' — an appropriate name for a court clergyman) on a boulder at Peebles, and possibly 'locus sancti Nicholai episcopi' ('the holy place (shrine?) of Nicholas the bishop') appears clearcut. Another pillar stone at Over Kirkhope, Selkirkshire, depicts a praying figure with outstretched arms in the Late Antique attitude of prayer ('*orans*'). Not all inscribed stones in this kingdom necessarily commemorate churchpeople: the Class-1 stone at Yarrowkirk, Selkirkshire, reads 'Here is the *memoria* ('special tomb') of the very famous princes Nudus and Dumnogenus. In the tomb here lie two sons of Liberalis'.[23]

The fifth- and sixth-century cemeteries of this area also show similar connections. The most famous of these, the 'Catstane' cemetery near Edinburgh, is comprised of long-cist unaccompanied east-west burials organised into approximate rows. This rite was widely followed in this part of southern Scotland, and perhaps both indicates the extent of Votadinian territory and the activities of southern missionaries. The names and formula on a Class-1 tombstone found at this cemetery ('the Catstane' itself) — 'In this tomb lies Vetta daughter of Victricius' — derive from the same Romano-Christian tradition found further south, and like some Cornish and Welsh Class-1 stones this (and the Class-1 inscription at Manor Parish) sat atop a cairn. That the Catstane mentions a woman, like some stones immediately south of Hadrian's Wall, could also be significant. David Petts has pointed out that only *c*.5 per cent of Class-1 inscriptions refer to women. So it is possible to see these inscriptions as sharing common features with links to the south of Hadrian's Wall (**colour plate 26**).[24]

Such 'long-cist' cemeteries are found widely distributed throughout what was probably Votadinian territory. An unusual aspect of these long-cist cemeteries are 'built-graves' containing drystone construction. These have been found throughout the area in which long-cists occur, including the Catstane, Burnhouse West Lothian and Lochend near Dunbar. They attest a commonality of burial customs among those using long-cist cemeteries beyond the shared rite of communal long-cist burial in organised east-west lines. Another burial custom shared among long-cist cemeteries, but infrequently occurring, is 'log-burial'. This employs a hollowed log as the coffin, as at Thornybank, Midlothian, long-cist cemetery near Dalkeith.[25]

That is, these long-cist cemeteries may be grouped together for several reasons, and they collectively relate to burial customs that we have seen in Christian contexts south of Hadrian's Wall, although unsurprisingly also include some features derived from the local cultural background. Nevertheless, not all long-cist cemeteries are identical. For example, the long-cist at Camp Hill, Trohoughton, and Castle Dykes, Berwickshire, were in disused hill-forts and minor variations in orientation occur, as at Parkburn long-cist cemetery where groups of differently aligned burials were found together. These form zones within the cemetery that may be cultural or chronological, and there are clusters and 'strings' of burials and drystone walls perhaps indicating the 'official' separation of areas. To give an example, at Old Haaks Crail, Fife, and at Hanley, Gogar Burn, by Edinburgh, burials were in three distinct clusters.

The distribution of long-cist cemeteries may indicate the spread of the Romano-Christian culture we have seen south of Hadrian's Wall far to its north. But this did not entirely replace all aspects of existing culture. The densest distribution of long-cist

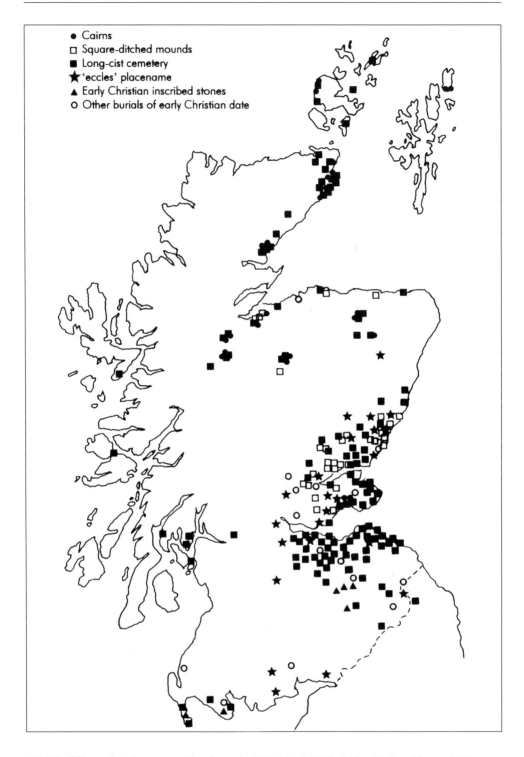

57 The fifth- and sixth-century Church north of Hadrian's Wall. (After E. Proudfoot and M. Carver)

cemeteries between the Walls coincides with that of so-called 'Pictish' silver chains. These are a group of heavy silver chains of unknown, but possibly decorative, function. Of the 12 which are known, two have 'Pictish symbols' on a broad silver ring which may have been the means of fastening them. Usually called 'Pictish', no other evidence for a link with the Picts exists apart from the symbols, and nine occur in Votadinian territory. Isabel Henderson suggested that those in Votadinian territory came south as booty, but equally the three to the north might be outliers. These chains might be more strongly termed 'Votadinian' on distributional grounds, and the find of one such chain at the great Votadinian hill-fort at Traprain Law strengthens this suggestion (**colour plates 27 & 28**).[26]

There is often a tendency to doubt whether there was fifth- or sixth-century occupation at Traprain Law, but finds include the 'Pictish silver chain' and two spearheads, a javelin head and a knife all of fifth- and sixth-century types. The structures include one that may be a church (there is also a long-cist containing a child burial from the site), and there are several other artefacts perhaps assignable to the fifth and sixth century. A summit enclosure and the 'Cruden Wall' could be defences of this period.[27]

Traprain Law has, then, no fewer finds and no less evidence of elite use than most fifth- and sixth-century hill-forts in Wales and Cornwall. This may well have been a major centre of the Votadinii in and after the fourth century, and in this context one should note that the famous Traprain Hoard of silver ware (containing 150 objects) could have been buried long after its postulated late fourth-century date of manufacture, for example in the face of Northumbrian advance into the Votadinian lands. It could well give us an indication of the 'tableware' of a British ruler of the fifth and sixth century, lost to us at other sites.

If it is hard to view Traprain Law as other than an elite settlement, then the silver chains may represent Votadinian elite insignia. The most obvious uses are as a dress accoutrement, but their heavy weight may imply they should be worn on the neck or shoulder not stitched onto cloth. This may be what is intended when *Y Gododdin* refers to Votadinian warriors wearing torcs, otherwise unknown in Britain beyond the Roman period. Perhaps it is indicating that they fought bearing the distinctive insignia of the Votadinian elite, whether or not they actually did.[28]

Unlike the area immediately to the south of Hadrian's Wall, there were defensible hill-forts and double- or triple-palisaded enclosures. At The Dod, a multivallate hill-fort contained rectilinear timber-framed buildings with rubble platforms post-dating Romano-British material and including a possible church. British coastal promontory forts may have been taken over in the late sixth or seventh century by the Northumbrian kings at Bamburgh and Dunbar.[29]

The place-name Dunbar means 'stack fort' and seems to refer to a British fortress on the site. Excavation at Dunbar castle (on the mainland part of the later castle) has borne this out. The site began as a trivallate promontory fort, containing roundhouses clustered around cobbled yards. This was followed by series of water tanks, one with a sluice gate and perhaps used for tanning. A possibly unfinished refurbishment of the defences may have followed this. These phases are not certainly dated, and the earliest identified post-Roman structures are SFBs assigned to the late sixth century. Long-cists have been found to the north of Lauderdale House, nearby.[30]

The triple-palisaded enclosure at Hogbridge, Peebleshire, might belong to this period, as may double-palisaded enclosures at Yeavering and Sprouston. At Philiphaugh, on the north bank of Ettrick Water near Selkirk, a well-organised inhumation cemetery within a polygonal enclosure was found close to a ditched enclosure and rectilinear buildings at the eastern border of the Votadinian zone, but whether or not this dates from the fifth and sixth centuries or is a Northumbrian site is unclear.[31]

An oft-quoted site which is unlikely to be fifth- or sixth-century at all might perhaps be disposed of at this point. Doon Hill is a small polygonal palisaded enclosure, containing two rectilinear timber buildings, one built on top of the other. There are cremations from within the enclosure, another rectilinear building, and inhumation burials immediately outside. Hall A, the first of these superimposed buildings, has a very unusual plan (its end-walls are triangular) and is often claimed as fifth- or sixth-century. Excavation at Balbridie showed that a structure with this exceptional plan was Neolithic and, as Ian Smith argued, the Doon Hill structure may be of this date also.[32]

Elite settlements of the fifth- and sixth-century Votadinii were thoroughly 'local', comprising hill-forts and palisaded sites, some of which had long been of local importance. As we have seen this was not — as might appear at first sight — a mere 'Iron Age' anachronism, but part of a synthesis of new and long-standing cultural practices and Christian religion.

We cannot supplement this picture of high-status settlements with lower status settlements, because few relevant sites have been excavated on a sufficient scale and in a manner which would provide evidence for use or disuse in this period. There are hints that Romano-British settlements of the fourth century remained in use during the fifth and sixth century. One site with direct dating evidence is at Crook Cleugh, Morebattle, Roxburghshire, where one of a pair of curvilinear drystone enclosures, both surrounding a single roundhouse, could be associated with a copper alloy annular brooch of 'Anglo-Saxon' form and possibly sixth-century date found in the open yard outside it.[33]

It has recently been suggested that some 'Anglo-Saxon' burials may be discernible in the area also. Notably, a female burial lying prone in a boulder-lined grave at Blackness has a *kolbenarmringe* armlet accompanying it, and Hound Point, Dalmeny, West Lothian, comprises one isolated long cist with 11 Anglo-Saxon beads dating to the sixth or possibly seventh century. Whether these represent Germanic women married into British families, or pagans or both or neither is uncertain.

There are archaeological hints of 'Anglo-Saxon' settlement in the Votadinian area. At Thirlings, post-and trench-built rectilinear buildings with enclosures were radiocarbon-dated to the sixth and seventh century and a cluster of 'Anglo-Saxon' burials has been identified in the Tweed Valley. Assuming that these people were ethnically Germanic at all, and the burials predate the late sixth-century Northumbrian advance into the area, they could well be settlers permitted land within the British polity rather than invaders. Otherwise it is hard to see how a numerically far smaller group of people, not all of them apparently warriors, could have taken and held these valley-bottom sites. It would be simple for even a small cavalry force of the sort described in *Y Gododdin* to overwhelm them rapidly, in dispersed and unfortified settlements.[34]

The only evidence of fortifications in this area at an 'Anglo-Saxon' settlement arguably contemporary with this comes from Yeavering. There, a British political centre implied by the palisaded enclosure may have been taken over by the 'Anglo-Saxons'. But the 'Anglo-Saxon' settlement was during the late sixth century merely a series of timber halls outside the enclosure – this does not suggest an expectation of attack. A similar sequence could be postulated for Sprouston and Milfield, but 'Anglo-Saxon' occupation at all may post-date the late sixth century, and this earlier settlement in the Tweed Valley was probably with Votadinian consent if it involved a Germanic group.[35]

The overall picture provided by archaeology is of political control by a local elite and the continuation of the Votadinian kingdom into the late sixth century. This was accompanied both by Christian evangelisation from the fifth century onward, and cultural survival, producing a local version of the Romano-Christian culture we have seen elsewhere. The impression gained, therefore, is of a situation like that we have seen in the western periphery of Britannia Prima. If so, we would expect this to the west of the zone between the two walls too.

The Novantae and Selgovae

The Novantae and Selgovae inhabited the south-west of the area between the two Roman walls. The religious history of the Novantae in the fifth and sixth centuries seems clearcut. Like the Votadinii this period saw the comprehensive Christianisation of the area in which this polity must have been situated, and this may well also have been the result of monastic-led evangelisation from south of Hadrian's Wall. Probably the first, and certainly most celebrated, monastery in the area was at Whithorn. This is associated with St Ninian, who Bede tells us led a Christian mission in the fifth century. This is not implausible, but nothing reliable is known about Ninian.[36]

Whithorn was the site of later monasteries and churches, and the surroundings of these have been the scene of large-scale excavation. This produced a wealth of evidence for fifth- and sixth-century occupation and burial at the site, and there is possible evidence of Roman-period occupation although this remains uncertain. Fifth-century occupation (including sub-rectangular buildings and paths) and burial was associated with evidence of ploughing. A mortared stone structure (evidenced by lime mortar) was built or refurbished by a second phase of this period at latest, and possibly before. Such a building would have been exceptional in local terms even in the fourth century, let alone the fifth when such structures were apparently very rare in Britain.

The use of mortared stone is not the only aspect of the fifth-century settlement that implies contacts south of Hadrian's Wall. Two watermill millstones demonstrate that at least one watermill of Roman-type was in use at the site. Again, this technology must have come from south of Hadrian's Wall if it was from anywhere in Britain, and interestingly this same technology appears to have been 'exported' to Ireland in the fifth to seventh centuries, probably via the Christian church. The millstones at Whithorn might come from Cumbria or the Solway coast, so conceivably might also have been imported.[37]

At Whithorn, a stylus attests literacy and a Latin Class-1 stone (the 'Latinus stone') was found adjacent to the later church, although not in excavation. Latin literacy, and the erection of personal memorials of Romano-Christian type are both attested at the site, the first time either Latin literacy or the erection of personal inscribed stone memorials are attested in this area other than from of a Roman military context.

There is yet another link with the pattern observed among the Votadinii: many long-cist graves, organised in rough rows, were found at Whithorn. Although dug-graves also occurred, these are a feature of more southerly long-cist cemeteries too, and need not distract from the similarities between Whithorn and the sites of south-east Scotland. Interestingly, and again in a way analogous to what we saw in the western periphery of Britannia Prima, in Period 1.2 burial partly focused on a timber shrine centred on a standing stone.

Whithorn attests the emergence of a fifth-century Romano-Christian culture among the Novantae, exactly as we saw further east among the Votadinii. We can assume that this community was in touch with the wider Late Antique world: Mediterranean and Germanic glass, imported Mediterranean pottery (of types ARSW, Bi, ii, iv, v, and B misc.) and Frankish D- and E-ware were found associated with this occupation, among a wide-range of more local material, including copper alloy pins and strap ends, metalworking debris (including crucible and mould fragments), evidence of antler-working and ironwork including knives.

Whithorn is, therefore, almost the perfect site to illustrate the 'post-Roman' adoption of a Romano-Christian culture through contact with the Britons south of Hadrian's Wall. But it was not an isolated cultural 'island': a number of subsidiary sites in the surrounding countryside may be connected with Whithorn. Anglian inscriptions at St Ninian's Cave, on the beach at Physgill, show its continuing use as a place of prayer and pilgrimage after Northumbrian rule, and Class-1 inscriptions attest its earlier use. At nearby Kirkmadrine, Class-1 stones tell us that 'here lies the holy bishops Ides, Viventius and Mavorius' and 'here lies . . . Florentius', and are decorated with Chi Rho symbols. These are the only other Class-1 inscriptions from this area, although carvings of horses and stags on a rock-face at Eggerness cave (south of Kirkmadrine church) might be interpreted as Christian rather than pagan symbols: the stag in particular is a rare but well-attested Christian symbol in Late Antiquity.[38]

Other than at Whithorn, most possible fifth- and sixth-century cemeteries in this area have dug graves, as at Ardwall Isle, where these focused on what was perhaps a small slab-built shrine in the earliest phase, but there are other hints of missionary activity from south of Hadrian's Wall. The area had no Roman-period stone buildings outside Roman official contexts, but at Hoddom a rectangular stone structure of the fifth and sixth centuries reused worked stone from Birrens Roman fort. This structure obviously had a specialised non-domestic function as it included a large sub-rectangular clay-lined pit with a clay-lined drain containing charcoal and lime, and was radiocarbon-dated to the fourth to sixth centuries. A rectangular post-built building to the south, with a hearth, may be contemporary with this structure. The most likely interpretation of the stone structure is that it is a church with a baptistery, perhaps that of a small monastery given the adjacent domestic building. The site was monastic in the seventh century and later.[39]

The evidence, therefore, suggests that — like the Votadinii — the Novantae were evangelised from south of Hadrian's Wall, probably at least partly by monks. The result of this was not religious conversion alone, but the adoption of a Romano-Christian culture. Like the Votadinii, the Novantae too had hill-forts. The best excavated example is the Mote of Mark, a promontory fort overlooking the Urr estuary, located on top of a defensible hilltop. The finds include B-ware, D-ware and E-ware, and Germanic glass, but the defences were only built after *c*.550 and post-date the arrival of E-ware on the site.[40]

Other hill-forts are known from this area that may have been from the fifth and sixth centuries, as at Tynron Doon. This was a multivallate hill-fort with hut circles and stepped drystone ramparts with external ditches, on a conspicuous summit. A date is provided by a piece of gold bracteate, far to the north and west of the usual distribution of these items, and presumably out of its usual cultural context. Another hill-fort perhaps occupied at this date has been identified at Castle Haven, Kirkcudbright, a D-shaped drystone built fort with an outer walled D-shaped enclosure, perhaps added later, around three sides. The walls of the main fort contain steps giving access to the wall walk. Finds include a penannular brooch, spiral finger rings and glass beads, perhaps of the sixth to ninth centuries. Another site, Trusty's Hill, is often claimed to be a further hill-fort of this date because a Pictish symbol is carved into rock. This is much further south than the usual distribution of such symbols, and the carving has a number of unusual aspects of its design that suggest it may be a modern fake.[41]

Although there are no definite examples of low-status settlements of the fifth or sixth century from the area, other site-types are known. For example, there is what appears to be a sand-dune site, like those we saw in western Britain, at Luce Sands, Galloway, and crannog occupation is attested at Dowlaton, Wigtownshire.[42]

Despite problems with some categories of evidence, the same overall pattern as recognised in the Votadinian zone again seems securely identifiable here too. This leaves one major territory in the west of the area between the Walls, for which we have evidence: Strathclyde.

Strathclyde/the Damnonii

Perhaps the most politically and militarily important British kingdom north of Hadrian's Wall, and definitely the longest-lived, was Strathclyde ('the valley of the Clyde'). This appears to coincide with a Roman-period political unit, the Damnonii, located approximately in the Clyde Valley and arguably also the adjacent coastlands. Somewhat different evidence suggests that this area, too, was Christianised from south of Hadrian's Wall in the fourth or fifth century, and Allan Wilson has shown in a series of fascinating studies that more aspects of a 'Romano-British' culture were being adopted in this area than hitherto supposed, perhaps even within the Roman-period itself.[43]

Caution is required, as Wilson realises, in ascribing all 'Roman-period artefacts' to the period before the fifth century. To give an example, samian ware is present in this area at settlements without Roman-period use, as at Buiston (Buston) and Lochlee crannogs. Other 'Romano-British' artefacts are those which have been seen to have been connected with fifth- or sixth-century activity in western Britain, such as bone spoons from Ashgrove Loch, Cleaves Cove and, again, Lochlee. At Lochspouts there was a cruciform jet pendant that is 'Late Roman' in style but may — as Wilson suggests — be of fifth- or sixth-century date. Much, perhaps even most, of the apparent evidence for the use of 'Romano-British' material in this area might relate to the fifth or sixth centuries rather than earlier, a point which might well prompt re-evaluation of other sites between the Walls.

Again, here — as at Whithorn and in Ireland — 'Roman' technology was adopted at a post-Roman date. Iron tools of the fifth and sixth centuries from this area show a Roman technological background in their design and other aspects of material culture. Once again, contacts south of Hadrian's Wall brought about cultural change in the fifth and sixth century, although so little is known of the cemetery archaeology or burial practices of the area that here the role of evangelisation in spreading this is not directly evidenced.

Other comparisons between this area and those already discussed also exist, such as the use of hill-forts as political centres, and crannog-use. The political centre of Strathclyde is the only British hill-fort frequently referred to in pre-Viking Irish written sources from the seventh century onward. This was Dumbarton Rock, then called *Alt Clut*, situated on the north bank of the Clyde. The Rock is a twin-summit craggy hill occupied by a fortress of sixth- to ninth-century date and later a medieval castle at the highest navigable point on the river, prior to the construction of the Industrial period canal. Excavation by Leslie Alcock revealed a timber-laced rubble rampart and finds of sixth-century date, including B-ware amphora sherds and imported Germanic glass.[44]

At Dundonald castle, a sequence of timber roundhouses were enclosed within a timber-laced rampart radiocarbon-dated to the fourth or fifth century, and dating for the occupation is also provided by E-ware pottery. Evidence for hill-fort use elsewhere in the area is less certain. The most convincing site is at Castle Hill, Dalry, Ayrshire, dated by a sixth-century spearhead, Germanic glass and a copper alloy penannular brooch.[45]

By far the most famous crannog in this area — and arguably in Britain — is at Buiston (or Buston). Buiston crannog lies in a shallow lake 12km from the coast, and access to the crannog was probably only by boat. Two log boats have been found associated with the crannog, which was apparently first built in the fourth century, and developed for at least the next 300 years. Its form shows both continuity and changes: its focus was always a large roundhouse with a surrounding wooden walkway on a platform within a perimeter defence. The perimeter changed form through the centuries: mortised palisades were a seventh-century development, and first the crannog was enclosed by a simple palisade of roundwood stakes. Likewise, the scale of the central roundhouse increased as time progressed: the first excavated was 7m in diameter (dated dendrochronologically to 585-94); this was replaced in 609 by a 8m diameter roundhouse. Similarities between these houses may be recognised, for instance each roundhouse had a central stone-built hearth.[46]

Buiston was associated with a number of unusual finds, attesting its external links and the adoption of 'Romano-British' culture by its inhabitants. For example, two crossbow bolts and a crossbow nut attest a military technology unknown in Britain before 400 outside Romano-British contexts. Other finds, such as double-edged bone combs, metalworking artefacts, a copper alloy annular brooch, a copy of a seventh-century 'Anglo-Saxon' coin, and what could be a carved saddle, attest elite occupation and its associated activities. As Leslie Alcock has observed, the size of the central house compares with the principal buildings of contemporary high-status settlements elsewhere, and massive amounts of timber were involved in its construction.

Crannogs — like hill-forts — seem to have secular elite associations. Finds provide further evidence of the spread of cultural practices in the fifth and sixth centuries associated with fourth-century Roman Britain rather than the local fourth-century cultural milieux. As in the Novantian area, low-status sites of this date have proved elusive, although a single sand-dune site at Stevenston Sands, Ayrshire, hints at the extension of the distribution of this site type up the western coast of what is today southern Scotland. It must be possible that a trading network based on these sites encompassed the whole west coast of Britain.

All of the zone between the Walls seems to have undergone the same process of fifth-century Conversion and the spread of Romano-Christian culture found in Cornwall, Devon and Wales. Again, these derived from neighbouring areas within what was Roman Britain in the fourth century, and again a certain commonality to this culture can be observed. The range of activities affected from tableware through tools to spindle whorls and dress fashions suggests that this was a far from superficial procedure. It seems absurd to claim that all the aspects of life affected were controlled by the Church or dominated by the elite in a direct way, so that these changes must represent the conscious choices of local people beyond a small governing group.

The Romano-Christian culture of the core areas of western Britain was exported into these areas, in a context of the maintenance of elites and political centres. This not only attests the fifth century as a time of profound change in these areas, but again demonstrates the vitality and attractiveness to contemporaries of this culture. It also means that the resulting cultural area was far larger than sixth-century 'Anglo-Saxon England' — this, not pagan Germanic culture, was the most widespread way of life in Britain *c.*450-600.

North of the British zone between the Walls were two non-British peoples: the Picts and Scots. The former had been in the area from the third century at latest, but the Scots claimed later to have migrated from Ireland (Latin *Scotti* means 'Irish') in the fifth century. As we shall see, whether or not this was the case is debatable, but these peoples maintained political identities which remained distinct from each other and the Britons for many centuries, until the unification of Scotland in the ninth century by Kenneth MacAlpin. These peoples, as we shall see, enable us to recognise the limits of Late Antique Romano-Christian culture in northern Europe. Unlike the Britons of the area between the Walls, who as we have seen were ruled by hill-fort based kings, neither the Picts nor Scots may have had large-scale kingship before the second half of the sixth century.[47]

The Picts

The fifth- and sixth-century Picts are a 'proto-historic' people, in that little is known about them from texts and nothing from their own writings. The only potentially useful written texts produced by the Picts themselves are king-lists of late date and extremely dubious historical truth, written in Latin. Among Roman writers, the Picts mostly figure as sea-

and land-raiders of fourth-century Roman Britain, as we saw in the first chapter.[48]

Even the name 'Pict' is not Pictish, at least in the form it is preserved. *Picti* was given to this people by Roman writers. First attested in AD 297, it is widely believed to refer to their habit of tattooing or painting their bodies, but this is uncertain. An alternative might be a derivation relating to the widespread Pictish placename *Pit-* (parcel of land), rendering a name '*Petti*' meaning something like 'people who call their territory *★pett-*'. This would be analogous to those known for other groups from the Roman-period and pre-Roman Iron Age. Obviously, a belief that 'primitive' people in places like Britain painted themselves could have helped the transformation from *Petti* to *Picti* via *depicti* (painted) in latin.[49]

Patrick, in the fifth century, and Gildas, in the sixth, still knew of people (probably, but not necessarily, the *same* people as Late Roman Continental writers called Picts) by this name. Patrick encountered them as slave traders who wanted to buy his converts in Ireland. Gildas also saw them as raiders of Late Roman Britain, operating as far south as Hadrian's Wall long before his own time, but his information about the north seems to have been flawed. Notably, he regarded the Picts as *transmarini* — an 'overseas' people. Later, Bede knew of Picts and Pictish kings from the seventh century, but tells us nothing beyond information in Gildas and Patrick which must relate reliably to the Picts of the fifth or sixth centuries. Of the information he does give, two points stand out: that Pictish royal lines were matrilineal and that the southern and northern Picts were divided by the Mounth mountain range.

Textually, the Pictish area cannot be established reliably until the second half of the seventh century. Place-name evidence may enable us to broadly locate 'Pictland' before this time, although the borders of the Pictish area and its internal divisions remain uncertain and only six place-name elements have been identified as Pictish. *Pett-* is by far the most widespread (there are 300 instances) but others are *carden* (thicket), *pert* (wood), *lanerc* (clearing) *caer* (fort), *pren* (tree) and *aber* (mouth). These names encompass most of eastern Scotland north of the Firth and south of Inverness, with outliers beyond. The Picts may also have held Orkney and other islands by the late sixth century, as Adomnan mentions a Pictish sub-king (*subregulus*) there. If so, how much earlier is uncertain on textual grounds. It is clear that the maritime capabilities of all the peoples of the north would have rendered the islands readily accessible. Orkney in particular might have been central rather than peripheral to the Picts, as art historian Isabel Henderson has pointed out in regard to later centuries.[50]

However, there is nothing to suggest that the Picts were other than a 'normal' Iron Age population, living an agricultural lifestyle which resembled in many respects that of Iron Age Britain. Archaeological evidence gives a clear picture of such agricultural communities in terms of settlements. It is perhaps worth noting that two types of structure sometimes claimed as Pictish buildings are irrelevant to the fifth and sixth centuries: wheelhouses (radially-divided drystone roundhouses), which were not constructed after the early centuries AD, and 'Pitcarmick' type rectilinear stone-based houses, which excavation suggests are seventh- to eleventh-century in date.[51]

Pictish houses of the fifth and sixth centuries are either cellular structures, as at Carlungie, Angus; Buckquoy, Orkney; Pool, Sanday; the Udal, North Uist; Jarlshof,

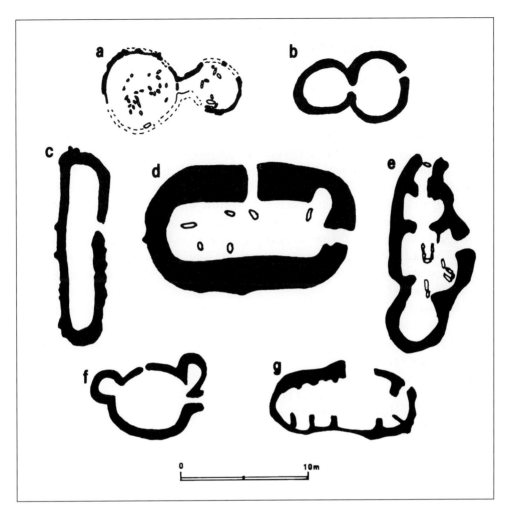

58 Pictish (and possibly Pictish) structures. a Pool; b Carlungie; c Pitcarmick; d Wag of Forse; e Buckquoy; f Udal; g Howe. (After Hunter, Ralston, Armit, Alcock)

Shetland and Traig Bostadh, Uig, or sub-rectilinear buildings, as at Howe, Wag of Forse, Caithness, and Skaill, Deerness, Orkney. As this list suggests, it appears that cellular buildings were by far the most widespread Pictish house-form of the fifth and sixth centuries (**colour plate 29**).[52]

None of the known Pictish settlements of the fifth and sixth centuries are more than small hamlets. Nor does evidence suggest these buildings were as 'exotic' as their shapes could to us imply. Cellular buildings dated to the first century AD were discovered at Cnip, Lewis. The development of such settlements can be traced archaeologically, as at Loch na Berie in the Hebrides, where there was a long stratified sequence from a Roman Iron Age roundhouse through to a Pictish cellular house. This demonstrates the long lineage of cellular structures in the Pictish area.

There are hints of development in this cellular architecture both before and after the period discussed here. For example, the possibility that formalised 'figure of eight' buildings date from the later pre-Viking period has been suggested and it is possible there is some connection with the Irish 'figure of eight' buildings (such as those found waterlogged at Deer Parks Farm in northern Ireland). Whether or not this connection is valid, the longevity of the style is well-attested. Old Scatness, Jarlshof, for instance, shows the continuation of such a structure at a time at which Viking artefacts were available. The cellular building tradition originates, then, in the local Roman Iron Age, if not before, and continues until the Viking Age.

These settlements probably form part of a very long continuous cultural tradition throughout most of the first millennium AD, albeit with outside contacts. It may be mistaken to assume that this was the only Pictish architectural type: sunken-floored curvilinear houses found at Easter Kinnear, Fife, may be first millennium AD, as may the sunken-featured buildings at Macrins, Colonsay. At Bornish (South Uist) what may be a fifth- or sixth-century curvilinear building, associated with metalworking, was followed by cellular structure.

It appears likely that a range of structures were in use among the Picts in the fifth and sixth centuries, but that cellular structures were the most common, at least in the islands. These structures seem to be the homes of the majority of the population rather than an elite, and connected with an agricultural economy.

Burial and religion among the Picts

The northern Picts appear to have been at least partly pagan until the later sixth-century mission of the Irish monk St Columba, the founder of the famous monastery of Iona. Some Picts had plainly been converted earlier, as Patrick derides 'apostate Picts' in the fifth century (that is, Picts who had been Christian but renounced their Faith) for buying his converts as slaves.[53]

Pictish paganism is extremely hard to reconstruct, although a site with possible evidence for this at Hermisgarth, Sanday (dated to the fourth or early fifth century), comprises inhumation burials beneath cairns and pyres which might have been used for cremation. It is also possible that the painted pebbles found, for example, at Jarslhof and Keiss, Caithness, had a ritual significance, but this is uncertain and rests on little more than their lack of an obvious function.[54]

Pictish burial practices are far easier to identify than pagan Pictish religion. Pictish burials have been found at many sites, for example at Sandwick, Unst, Shetland; Dairy Park, Dunrobin, Sutherland; Birsay and Westness, Rousay, Orkney. These provide evidence of both cist-burials and cairns. One definable type of north Pictish burial is the low curvilinear or rectilinear cairn, edged by stones, above a mound of sand, beneath which a long-cist has been placed. Pictish 'square barrows' of this sort were sometimes organised into cemeteries, and can be associated with round barrows, as at Garbeg. It has been suggested that the curvilinear form of cairn found at Birsay Red Craig, Ackergill and Garbeg may be earlier than the rectilinear, as at Sandwick or Dunrobin, although both

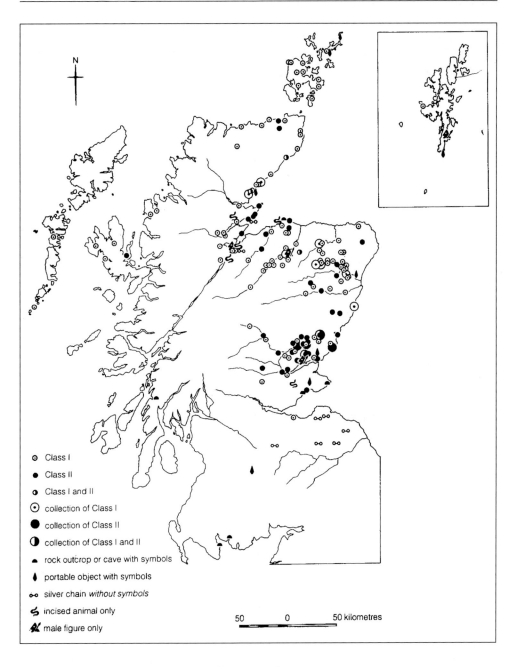

59 Pictish sculpture and associated artwork. Copyright S. Foster

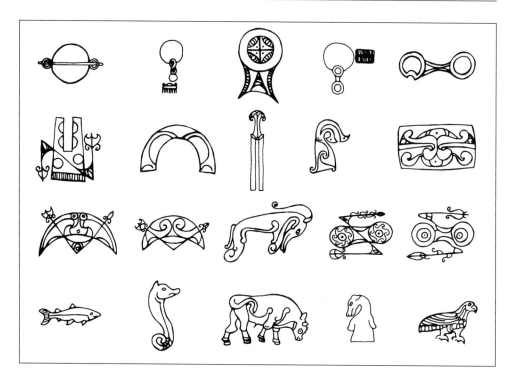

60 Pictish symbols. (After Ritchie)

types employ long-cists covered by a heap of findless sand (**colour plate 30**).[55]

Like Pictish architectural traditions, these forms of burial may have a long local 'ancestry'. At Boysack Mills, Angus, one was associated with a ring-headed pin of the first or second century AD; and Ackergill, a round-cairn in a cemetery including square-barrows of this type, was associated with a chain of the second century AD. However, they continued into the period under investigation here, as at Lundin Links, Fife — the most southerly example – radiocarbon-dated to the fifth to seventh century.

There seems to be a relationship between these Pictish cairns and the famous 'Pictish symbol stones' that form the Picts' most visible surviving memorial. For example, a square barrow stands close to the Collesie stone, and at Easterton of Roseisle a short-cist (perhaps enclosing a cremation) incorporated a Pictish symbol stone, as did an undated burial post-dating Oxtro broch on Orkney.[56]

It might be imagined that the Pictish symbol stones would provide the clearest evidence for the fifth- and sixth-century Picts, but this is far from true. Pictish symbol stones are extremely hard to interpret, or even date. These are usually divided into two principal classes: Class 1 comprises those in which symbols were pocked onto unshaped slabs. They show no distinctive Christian symbols and employ half-human/half-animal forms that might (but need not) represent figures from pagan Pictish mythology, although they also often carry extremely realistic drawings of fauna.

These are usually supposed to date largely from the fifth and sixth centuries, although they have been argued to begin earlier and continue later. Over 200 examples are known, and new stones are still discovered from time to time. There are six sites where Pictish symbols like those on Pictish Class 1 stones are carved on the surface of natural rockfaces, and other examples of such symbols occur on portable objects.

Views as to what Pictish symbols meant abound. Anthony Jackson, an anthropologist, suggested they represent marriage alliances, others that they assert land-rights or political groupings. Perhaps the most convincing interpretation is Ross Samson's suggestion that the frequent occurrence of paired symbols relates to the bipartite personal names favoured in virtually every known non-Latin language of the period. Such names, like 'Athelstan' (noble-stone) or 'Cuneglasus' (green- or black-hound) could be represented by animal symbols and more abstract designs, standing for each element of the name.[57]

That they contain some definable message seems implied by several patterns visible in the occurrence of the symbols. Only a few of approximately 40 Pictish symbols so far identified occur often, and the commonest are some of the most apparently abstract (of course they may not have seemed so to contemporaries): the 'crescent', the 'double disc' and the — exotically-named — 'swimming elephant'. The crescent is frequently overlaid by the 'V-rod' symbol, and the 'double disc' by the 'Z-rod' symbol. Crescent and double disc symbols tend to be elaborate and in general designs are paired (permitting Samson's argument), apart from the animals.

It has been suggested that a design frequently found on Pictish Class 1 symbols stones, the 'comb and mirror' (found near the bottom of around 20 per cent of the stones), is indicative of 'women', usually interpreted as meaning that the stone was either for or set up by the wife of the man commemorated by the stone. Although this argument is based on several dubious preconceptions, there was a long-cist burial of a woman with a stone bearing this symbol at Dairy Park, Dunrobin, and at Hilton of Cadboll a mirror and comb is placed alongside one of the small number of female depictions. So, perhaps the argument can be based on something other than preconception. Moreover, there is no doubt that women were afforded elaborate burial in Pictland as well as further south: at Kilpheder, South Uist, a Pictish square cairn contained the burial of a woman of about 40 years old, in a stone-lined inhumation grave. This burial also hints that Pictish cairns were not constructed immediately after internment, as the burial had been disturbed between the decay of the body and cairn construction.

Although the significance of the Class 1 symbols remains extremely unclear, the function of the free-standing slabs bearing them has been clarified by recent evidence. At least some, perhaps most, appear to be burial markers, as at Watenan, Caithness. This does not require us to assign all Pictish symbols a funerary meaning, because the symbols are on portable objects and in domestic contexts. For example, at Gurness in Orkney, a six-room Pictish house had a stone with three Pictish symbols placed in the wall. Likewise, at Old Scatness a multi-cellular structure shows Pictish symbols on a hearth stone and on a pebble in the hearth, probably not visible when the hearth was in use. A crescent-shaped copper alloy plaque from Monifieth Laws, Angus (of unknown function), bears Pictish symbols on both sides.[58]

Another pattern suggesting that these stones commemorate important individuals may be the tendency for Pictish Class 1 symbol stones associated with cemeteries to occur near the centre of the cemetery, as at Blackford, Perthshire; Collessie, Fife; and Edderton, Easter Ross. If these stones represent monuments built for the local elite, this elite must have been very numerous, or a wide social category represented. The existence of cemeteries of cairns could imply dynastic or kin-group cemeteries, lower status individuals being buried without markers of this type and might again imply many aristocratic or royal kin-groups. This may imply lots of minor dignitaries — perhaps like the Irish *ri* or the minor chiefs of late fifth- and sixth-century 'Anglo-Saxon' England rather than kings ruling larger tribal polities, as among the Britons.

An association with the local elite may be implied by the depiction of Pictish symbols on items made of silver. The most famous example is from the Norries Law hoard, found at the base of a cairn over (probably prehistoric) cremations, in Fife. Although this hoard dates from the seventh century, and not strictly from the period under discussion here, it contains Late Roman artefacts suggesting its accumulation over some centuries. Its special interest in this case lies in the use of Pictish symbols incised on two silver plaques decorated with red enamel.[59]

Exactly what the Norries Law hoard represents is unclear. It might be the private wealth of a Pictish chief or kin-group, the collective wealth of a political or ethnic unit, or a votive deposit. A similar point can be made about the most famous Pictish 'centre': Burghead. This is a coastal promontory fort, possibly constructed in the fourth century AD, although dating seems insecure. In the interior, which is now mostly built-over, there is an elaborately rock-cut well surrounded by a walkway, but this is undated. Most remarkably, 25-30 Pictish symbol stones — all depicting naturalistic bulls — were found here. This could, as Leslie Alcock suggests, represent the workshop of a symbol stone-carver, specialising in bulls, but it is at least as likely that these carvings were associated with a ritual centre. There are suggestions that Burghead was a ritual centre at an earlier date: a 'Celtic' stone head carved with drooping moustache is said to be from the well (**colour plate 31**).[60]

This interpretation may be strengthened, although is certainly not necessitated, by the proximity of another possible Pictish ritual site. At Sculptor's Cave, Covesea — 5km away from Burghhead — there are 15 or more Pictish symbols on the cave walls, and counterfeit fourth-century Roman coins, samian ware pottery and copper alloy toilet items and pins were found inside the cave.[61] This and another cave, at East Wemys, might have held pagan ritual associations, before later Christianisation. These caves have Pictish symbols, crosses and inscriptions, not all of which are necessarily either pre-modern or of similar date. A tendency for carvings to be more abstract as one goes further into the caves is visible, the naturalistic figures closer to the cave entrance. Perhaps a ritual passage is literally the intention.

Other clusters of Pictish Class 1 symbol stones could imply pagan religious centres. An enclosure visible in a cropmark at Barflat surrounded a group of Pictish stones, one bearing an imposing human figure carrying an axe. North of the Mounth, Pictish Class 1 symbol stones cluster near prehistoric ritual monuments, in particular stone circles and Neolithic henges. While this could merely represent the Pictish version of the British custom of burial close to disused prehistoric monuments, occasionally, for example at Edderton, Brandsbutt and Ardlair, symbols were even added to standing stones and at

Gaulcross, Banffshire, a Pictish silver hoard was placed in the stone circle.[62]

This connection between 'Pictish symbols', pagan beliefs and the local elite may suggest that this elite legitimised its status through religion, or acted as patron of religious rituals or that it was religious in character. Pictish symbol stones, although not necessarily having pagan associations themselves, may then enable us to identify possible pagan Pictish ritual sites north of the Mounth. However, in a second phase these symbol stones themselves became very visibly Christianised.

There are over 60 Class 2 stones, distinguished by displaying Christian symbols and employing relief carving and dressed blocks. Their designs differ in several respects from those of Class 1 to include depictions of aristocratic life and occupations (such as smith's tools at Dunfallandy, Pitlochry and Abernethy) and were not, so far as is known, tombstones. They probably post-date 600, and offer rich evidence for later aristocratic pursuits such as riding, war, hunting and so on for the period immediately following that discussed here. They may well have been associated with the Christian Pictish elite of the seventh century and perhaps later, and an inscription on the Dupplin Cross in Perthshire close to the Pictish royal site at Forteviot arguably links it with royalty. That Pictish symbol stones became so thoroughly Christianised in the seventh century brings us back to the question of the Conversion of the Picts in the fifth and sixth centuries.[63]

All the most probable evidence for fifth- and sixth-century Pictish paganism comes from north of the Mounth, the northern Picts according to Bede. While the Columban mission clearly intended the evangelisation of the northern Picts in the sixth century, the Conversion of their more southerly counterparts seems to have been undertaken much earlier by missionaries from the Romano-Christian British communities to the south. The key evidence for this is the distribution of long-cist cemeteries in Pictland, a link which once again prompts us to look south towards the Britons.

The excavated site at Hallow Hill, Fife, provides a clear example of this. There the long-cist cemetery was associated with dug-graves, both of sixth- to ninth-century date. The cemetery was partly well-organised and partly more loosely-structured, but a possible focal burial was found. The name of the complex, *Eglesnamin*, too arguably survived in later texts — showing the adoption of the Brittonic term *egles* (church) into the local vocabulary.[64]

An additional piece of evidence at Hallowhill supports the view that it may have originated as a mission site. Beneath later graves are the remains of timber structures, apparently a large east-west posthole building (a church?) and at least two possible structures defined by gullies suggesting rectilinear or sub-rectilinear plans. There were also traces of ploughing across the site, as at Whithorn, and a cobbled roadway.

The existence of the *egles* place-name (one of many examples in this part of Scotland) supports the view that these sites represent Christian cemeteries. Their similarities with the Votadinian long-cist cemeteries in many details of burial practice imply that they derive from a British cultural background — a point further strengthened by the discovery of a Chi Rho stone at Skeith, Fife. This is not to say long-cist burials are unknown in the area prior to these cemeteries, but the careful organisation of lines of east-west accompanied long-cists in large cemeteries with these features marks a new departure in burial practices.

Long-cist cemeteries of this sort are widely distributed in the southern part of the area in which Pictish symbol stones are found. Likewise, the distribution of *egles/eccles* as a place-name element, derived from British usage, suggests that the same arguments may be applied to this whole area. That is, we can see a wide zone, what we might term (following Bede's later usage) that of the 'southern Picts', as having been converted to Christianity as early as the sixth or even perhaps fifth century. This would explain why even Patrick had 'apostate Picts' to criticise. It is hard to imagine that these missionaries had come from anywhere but the Votadinian lands further south. If so, the Mounth may be the northern limit of the evangelisation achieved by British missionaries before 600.

Kings and forts

Interaction between Britons and Picts may have had political consequences too. Where we have found British kings controlling tribal kingdoms in fifth- and sixth-century Britain, we have also seen hill-forts with evidence of elite secular occupation. It is often supposed that all of the 'Celtic' peoples of Britain had royal fortresses on hills or coastal promontories during the fifth and sixth centuries, but a brief survey of the relevant sites shows how little evidence exists for Pictish royal strongholds before the late sixth century.

Craig Phadraig, Inverness, is a bivallate hilltop fort with E-ware and a hanging bowl mould, both arguably dating to the seventh century. A multivallate hill-fort at Clatchard Craig, near Newburg, Fife, also has E-ware and although it employed timber-lacing and re-used Roman stonework in its banks, these need not indicate a pre-seventh-century date. In fact, radiocarbon dating suggests banks 1 and 3 date from the sixth to seventh centuries, while bank 2 is eighth-century. A seventh-century and later date is also indicated by metalworking evidence. This included moulds of eighth-century type paralleled at St Ninian's Isle in its famous metalwork hoard of that date. None of the dating evidence requires a pre-seventh-century date for the fortress, and the fact that brooch moulds occur only here, and in a probably eighth-century layer at Birsay in Orkney, may suggest that specialist metalworkers were not necessarily being patronised by Pictish hill-fort elites much — if at all — prior to 600.[65]

The hill-fort site at Dundurn is one of a series of so-called 'nuclear forts' in Scotland, in which a higher central drystone-built citadel area stands above looping outworks. Occupation began in the later sixth or seventh century as a hilltop palisaded enclosure, and although later provided with outworks using material taken from a Roman military site 15km distant, this is clearly not a fifth- to mid-sixth-century hill-fort of the type found further south.

A promontory fort on the north coast at Green Castle, with a timber-framed rampart and metalworking evidence reminiscent of earlier forts among the Britons, is radiocarbon-dated to the eighth century, and the hill-fort at Urquart castle is perhaps later. A promontory fort at Dundarg, if it belongs in any phase to the post-Roman Iron Age but pre-medieval period, need be no earlier than these sites.

There are only three possible fifth- to mid-sixth-century hill-forts from the Pictish area. The promontory fort at Cullykhan, Castle Point, Troup, may date from the fourth century, but it is uncertain whether any activity continued into the fifth and sixth

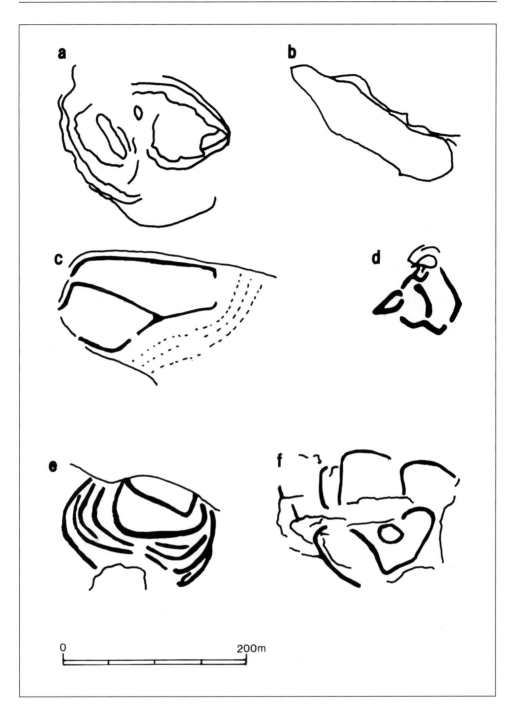

61 Hill-forts in north Britain. a Dumbarton (lines represent natural rock crags); b Bamburgh Castle (lines represent summit area below later castle); c Burghead; d Dunadd; e Clatchard Craig; f Dundurn. (After Alcock)

centuries. Another promontory site, Burghead, had four impressive timber-laced ramparts, paralleled at Dundurn. Radiocarbon dates for these are confused: the banks might belong to the fourth to sixth century, but might equally well be later in date. Even if the site was used before 600, this may have been as a pagan cult centre.

Leslie Alcock interprets yet another fortified promontory known as Bowduns, to the north of Castle Haven, as a hill-fort contemporary with a pagan cult-focus at Dunicaer, close to Dunnottar. A low bank around the coastal stack at Dunicaer was probably once faced with Pictish symbols stones. But while the 'ritual complex' on Dunicaer promontory is evidenced, the possible hill-fort lacks any direct dating material.

The possibility that Burghead originated as a promontory-sited pagan religious site could also enable us to interpret the evidence from Cullkyhan and Dunicaer. It may be that these sites are not fortresses but promontory-sited religious sites, as also found among the contemporary Slavs — although one assumes part of a different pagan religion. It would be possible to speculate about pagan beliefs about high places or the 'liminality' of the coast explaining a coastal promontory location. All three sites are north of the area with long-cist cemeteries, and two have clusters of Class-1 symbol stones as their main artefacts of this date. Slight evidence that some brochs (Iron Age drystone towers) were reused (for instance, a leaf-shaped spearhead in Upper Scalloway broch has been claimed to be fifth- or sixth-century) might relate to no more than settlement around a disused broch, presenting no problems for the argument.[66]

The cessation of use at pagan ritual foci is easy to explain in the context of conversion to Christianity. Subsequent re-emergence of some of the same places as fortified elite sites in the late sixth century among the Picts might represent the emulation of British culture. If there was a strong link between paganism and the Pictish chiefly class, then perhaps what we see is the transformation of one type of site into another, accompanying alterations in the character of kingship or in its legitimation. There is other evidence of Pictish elite links with the Scots also: ogam inscriptions have been found on artefacts in Pictland (so-called 'chattel inscriptions'), as at North Uist.[67]

Kathryn Forsyth has shown that Pictish ogam, once believed illegible, is in fact able to be read, containing texts in Irish and Pictish. Ogam texts from Pool, Sandy and Birsay have been dated to the sixth or seventh centuries. Ogam might, in Pictland, be connected with St Columba's mission to the Picts north of the Mounth. As Columba is said to have met a Pictish king, Brudei, at his fort, adjacent to Loch Ness, it may be that hill-forts and kingship based on British prototypes were adopted into Pictish culture earlier than the Columban mission, or perhaps Columba met the king at a ritual site associated with his religious authority in a pagan society.

The Dalriadan Scots

Bede wrote that the kingdom of Dalriada, in western Scotland, derived from Irish immigration and Dalriadan kings represented themselves as 'Irish' from the seventh century onward. There *was* a kingdom of Dalriada ('Irish Dalriada') in sixth-century northern Ireland, from which the Scottish Dalriada appears to have become independent in the late sixth century according to Adomnan. This may only mean a kingdom spanning the Irish Sea before this, and although the Dalriadan Scots seem to have spoken Irish (Gaelic), there is no convincing evidence to suggest that they migrated from Ireland. As in Dyfed, at least the elites in both areas might have spoken Irish since the first millennium BC for all we know. It is at least as likely that the story of migration could have been invented, like the story of a Trojan migration to Britain, to explain the origins of this people at a later date.[68]

Archaeology offers no support to the hypothesis of Scottish migration. Apart from at the monastery of Iona, there is no 'Irish' pottery to help. Many aspects of material culture, such as the forms of bone combs, were shared between north Britain and Ireland in the fifth and sixth centuries, probably having derived from earlier British precedents. Other than ogam inscriptions, few 'Irish' artefacts have been recognised in Scotland. As Leslie Alcock has said, if migration occurred 'the Scots came without luggage'. He and Anna Ritchie employ detailed knowledge of the material culture of fifth- to seventh-century sites throughout Scotland to argue that no distinctively Scottish artefacts may be discerned. There is, literally, nothing to support the 'Irish migration' theory of Scottish origins.[69]

Some Irish place-names (such as *Sliabh* 'mountain') attest the existence of an Irish-speaking community in western Scotland, focused on Argyll. The spread of E-ware on the west coast coincides well with the conceivable limits of Dalriada, as Ewan Campbell notes, if we assess the latter from seventh-century and later sources. E-ware itself may have been employed as part of seventh-century political legitimation, and while it may well hint at communities which made a claim to Irishness at that time, it tells us nothing for sure about the fifth and sixth centuries. Beyond Dalriada finds of E-ware may relate to the adoption of Dalriadan culture by the Picts more than the distribution of Irish immigrants or their descendants.[70]

In the area identifiable as seventh-century Dalriada in this way, the commonest type of settlements were small drystone walled enclosures known today as 'duns' (although *dun* had a far wider range of meanings in the Celtic languages of the fifth to seventh centuries than this). Examples of such 'duns' are found at Killdalloig dun (dated by E-ware) and Kildonan, a Kintyre dun with D-shaped walls.[71]

While duns are often supposed to be a long-lived settlement type, Leslie Alcock argued that few duns belong to the Iron Age, and that Romano-British material associated with duns might have been brought to the sites after 400. Many sites show occupation after this date, as at Ardifuir in Argyll, where the dun may be dated by E-ware, but some pre-date 400. It is not always clear that duns were isolated enclosures, as at Ardanstur dun on Loch Melford, where building platforms surround the enclosure. Sometimes it is unclear whether the dun or a later structure is associated with fifth- and sixth-century use, as at Dun Cruier, Barra, where a curvilinear structure post-dates the dun.

By far the most famous site to have 'begun life' as a dun is Dunadd. Dunadd is the archetypal 'nuclear fort' and is one of several Dalriadan hill-forts mentioned in the Annals of Ulster in relation to seventh-century battles. The site has produced a wide range of seventh-century finds, including much E-ware and evidence for fine metalworking. Some of the metalwork was probably for distribution to royal dependants: Margaret Nieke and Holly Duncan noted that a brooch mould at Dunadd fits a brooch from Kildonan dun.

One E-ware vessel at Dunadd shows traces of a pigment (Dyer's Madder) that may also have been imported, and Ewan Campbell demonstrated that cross-marked querns at Iona (discussed below) and Dunadd show links between them. The site also has features probably connected with the inauguration of the later Dalriadan kings: 'footprints' and a 'bowl' carved in the natural stone surface, and bears an ogam inscription cut onto the rock surface. Interestingly, another 'footprint' stone is known from close to another Dalriadan hill-fort mentioned in the Irish annals for the seventh century, at St Columba's chapel near Dunaverty (**colour plate 32**).[72]

Although Dunadd was an extremely important seventh-century site, the first phase is just an oval hilltop dun, arguably of the sixth century. That a simple dun could grow into a major site of this sort implies that these were the homes of individuals or kindreds that formed the basis of seventh-century royalty in Scotland. In the seventh century these elites were associated with hill-forts such as Dunaverty, Dunollie (a promontory fort above Oban harbour associated with E-ware) and Tarbat. This does not necessarily tell us anything about such groups or settlements in the sixth, let alone fifth, century.

Another site possibly connected with Dunadd was the crannog at Loch Glashan, Argyll. Only 8km from Dunadd, finds include well-preserved leather and wood (including a leather jerkin with short sleeves and shoe finds), a penannular brooch with an amber setting, perhaps manufactured at Dunadd, and E-ware. Whether or not Loch Glashan was occupied prior to the establishment of Dunadd as a nuclear fort is uncertain. Again, it could well be associated with seventh-century Dalriadan kingship, but it was not the only Dalriadan crannog of this date; for example, another crannog site was found at Loch an Dughail, Argyll. None of this necessarily provides any evidence for tribal kingship or hill-forts in the sixth century or earlier among the Scots.[73]

Dunadd and Loch Glashan were certainly important — probably royal — sites of the seventh century, but they do not help us to discern the nature of government or elite culture in fifth- or sixth-century Dalriada. That is, we have no direct evidence for any large-scale kingship among the fifth- and sixth-century Scots: they might well have had the Irish *ri* system, with very localised minor rulers resident at duns rather than the hill-forts later used by Dalriadan monarchs.

It might be hoped that religious sites would indicate larger-scale patronage by Dalriadan kings in the fifth and sixth century, but this too is not a fruitful line of enquiry. The great island monastic centre at Iona was certainly the premier monastery in Dalriada after 600, and was founded in the sixth century, by St Columba, whose missionary work in Scotland has already been mentioned. The monastery was not on a virgin site: Finbar McCormick has shown that the D-shaped monastic *vallum* (enclosure bank) encompasses Iron Age earthen banks, and this may well have influenced the form of the later monastic site.[74]

Iona was described in the late seventh century by Columba's biographer, Adomnan, and his description may retain aspects of the appearance of Iona in Columba's time. We should be aware that he was writing, albeit in a potentially informed way and at the same place, a century later, and changes could well have occurred. Adomnan's description of Iona depicts it as enclosed within a bank with a church (seemingly only one, unlike some Irish monasteries of the pre-Viking period) entered through a porch, and cemetery. There was a communal building, the 'great house', and apparently separate sleeping rooms for the monks, although Aidan MacDonald has suggested a single dormitory building might have contained these rooms. There may have been private quarters for senior clergy, and a guest house. These structures may have stood around a courtyard area, which was perhaps cobbled or laid with stone slabs. There were agricultural buildings such as barns and a kiln, but these probably lay outside the enclosure. Within the enclosure a single-sex structured communal life was practised under a written rule, and involving regular worship.

A rock outcrop, 'Torr an Aba', is close to the centre of the enclosed space. This is of especial interest as it shows traces of terracing and a structure stood on it. Although dating is uncertain, Adomnan refers to a building connected with St Columba in an elevated location, and McCormick has suggested it is possible that the outcrop is that mentioned. Elsewhere inside the earthworks no known structure is certainly as early as Columba's time.

Finds might give a little more indication of Columba's monastery. 'souterrain ware' at Iona has been shown by Ewan Campbell, using petrological analysis, to have been both imported and manufactured locally: it is almost the only definably 'Irish' material even from this 'Irish' site. Evidence from a waterlogged ditch-fill excavated at Relig Odhrain may belong to the late sixth or seventh century, and alder lathe-turned bowls in the fill copy E-ware shapes. Details of leather shoes, probably made at Iona, found in these fills suggest Roman styles and a horizontal watermill was a feature of the later monastery. So it could be argued that Iona shows the sort of evidence we saw at Whithorn, with a monastery introducing Romano-Christian culture, in this case in an Irish context.

Although it is possible to gain a picture of Iona in Adomnan's time, its original late sixth-century form seems less well-defined. Place-names such as *Cil-* and *Kil-* (derived from Latin *cella* 'monastic cell'), *annat* (abandoned church), *disert* (hermitage), *cladh* and *relig* (burial-place), and *teampull* (church), may indicate other Dalriadan Christian religious sites, but are not well-dated. Several sites that may be monastic centres of this date are known, but few have been extensively excavated and shown to originate prior to 600. Buildings and enclosures at Cill-an-Suidhe, Cladh a' Bhearnig, Ardnadam, Ceann a'Mhara, Eileach an Naoimh and Sgor nam Ban-Naomha may be small hermitages but, while at least some probably existed by the eighth century at latest, the foundation date of all these enclosures remains unclear.[75]

None of these sites tell us much about the patronage of Dalriadan kings before the late sixth century at earliest, nor even how 'Irish' they were. A distinctive Dalriadan culture is arguably visible in the seventh century and later, but there is no more evidence of elaborate hill-forts or large-scale kingship among the Dalriadans prior to the late sixth century than among the Picts. Fifth- or sixth-century Dalriadan rulers may have been akin to Irish *rí* and controlled only the same limited resources.

Not all fifth- and sixth-century duns need be royal, or even aristocratic, settlements, but the growth of nuclear forts around the core of earlier duns may indicate where the heads of fifth- and sixth-century Dalriadan lineages lived. These became major political centres for larger-scale kingship, as this developed from small-scale Irish-style polities during the sixth century.

This might also explain an otherwise surprising juxtaposition of the Dalriadan heartland with the principal centre of Strathclyde. The absence of warfare between the two is remarkable if they did not coexist according to a treaty, or by the dominance of Strathclyde with its virtually impregnable citadel. Peaceful relations between the Dalriadans and Strathclyde might be implied by the ecclesiastical site at Kingarth on Bute, close to the likely border. This could be an example of the border location of religious sites as a means of limiting conflict, noted by Harold Mytum in Ireland. The Irish annals present Kingarth as a seventh-century episcopal site, but it is unclear when the complex began. D-shaped lignite bracelets, ingot moulds, and a handled crucible could date before or after 600. If Dalriada was politically disunited and militarily weak in the fifth and sixth centuries, this could also explain the lack of imports of fifth- and sixth-century date north of Dumbarton, except for the single sherd of ARSW at Iona.[76]

Lineages might have kept alive Irish language and cultural identity in Dalriada and encouraged links with Ireland and the similarly fragmented Pictish polities rather than the Britons. The echoes of this from the political system may be visible in later centuries when Dalriada was divided into kindreds associated with particular territories: Cenel Loairne, Cenel Comgall, Cenel n Gabrain and Cenel n Oengusa. Unlike the northern Picts, the Dalriadan Scots and their rulers were Christians in the sixth century, as is shown by Columba's reaction to them and their relations with Ireland.[77]

The rise of centralised kingship may explain the expansionism of Dalriada in the seventh century, just as we saw the rise of 'Anglo-Saxon' kingship accounting for expansionism. This could also explain the expansion of Dalriada against the Picts not the closer — but militarily stronger — Britons, and it might also hint at the origins of this political transformation. Perhaps the Scots, like the western 'Anglo-Saxons', learnt the concept of tribal kingship from Britons or from churchpeople at ease with British culture and its Biblical models of rulership.

Conclusion

The British spread Romano-Christian culture far to the north, and the effect of this on the progress of Christianity in southern Pictland may have been underestimated in the past. This culture was introduced to the area between the two Walls in the fifth century, and beyond in the fifth and sixth centuries. To the north a culture largely untouched by this existed, whereas to the west a distinctive Irish culture developed, and this eventually affected that of the Pictish elite along with Christianity brought to the area north of the Mounth. Before the mid-sixth century neither Picts nor Scots may have had tribal kingship or hill-fort royal centres, instead employing much smaller-scale political organization, but these characteristics too were eventually adopted from the Britons, perhaps before the conversion of the Picts north of the Mounth. The importance of British Romano-Christian culture in northern Britain may then be attested in both British and non-British areas.

6 Conclusion: Britain in Late Antiquity

The imagined differences between what happened in Britain and Continental developments are largely, although not wholly, illusory. The archaeology of eastern Britain appears far more similar to that of the western barbarian kingdoms than usually supposed, although paganism lasted longer in parts of eastern Britain and large-scale kingship was only relatively slowly established. But the east of Britain saw the same patterns of fusion between Germanic and Roman provincial ways of life as witnessed elsewhere and even the organised Christian Church, based on its urban bishops, may have outlasted the early fifth century. The other really striking differences — such as the failure of 'Anglo-Saxon' rulers to gain control of the whole of former Roman Britain, the lack of a single 'Anglo-Saxon' kingdom before 600, and the relative longevity of Roman-period political units in Britain — are all related.

The reason that even in AD 600 most of what had been the Roman diocese was under British rule is probably that British polities were the most highly-organized and militarily strongest units in the island. According to this interpretation, Britain had the latest functioning Roman military command and last independent provinces in the West. It was by far the most successful 'sub-Roman' society in transmitting its religion and culture to neighbouring peoples.

British polities in west and north Britain (where we know most about them) were in almost every other respect typical of the wider Late Antique world. They had a shared Romano-Christian culture, preserved Roman-period styles of dress and symbolism, and maintained an intellectual life based on both Classical and Christian scholarship. Latin poetry was still composed and higher education establishments on the Roman model survived. Architectural styles reflected this also, as Roman-period buildings were modified and retained and new structures based on Roman architectural models built, albeit largely in timber. Latin language was widely understood by the secular elite, and letter-writing was maintained as a means of communication. Roman-period technologies, notably water-milling, were maintained and developed, and although some technologies seem to have been lost or disused after the fifth century, others were innovated.

This culture was spread by monastic contacts and evangelisation throughout the periphery of what in the fourth century was Roman Britain. This created a very large zone, from Brittany to the Mounth, and from Galway to parts of eastern Britain, in which this culture was synthesised with local customs, to form a common (although regionalised) culture. Often in the past characterised as 'Celtic civilization', what these people had in common was not a shared 'Celtic' ethnicity, nor a common language, nor even a shared experience of living in Roman Britain, but contacts with the British Church.

To the north of this zone, the Picts and Irish of Dalriada maintained ways of life based on longstanding local cultures, although the former and then the latter — perhaps through contacts with Ireland — were eventually drawn into this British-centred cultural world. Nevertheless, like the 'Anglo-Saxons', neither people was in a position before the mid-sixth century to challenge British military and political dominance.

Seen in this way, all of the usual assumptions about the end of Roman Britain that were outlined in the introduction may be seen to be doubtful. There was no clear east-west cultural divide, but in the east there was a patchwork of British and Germanic, Christian and pagan communities. Germanic and British groups, or Britons and Picts, were not very similar in cultural, political or technological terms. Nor was migration a predominant feature of most of the period. Only one (two-way) migration seems to have occurred, the Germanic migration into eastern Britain and emigration in response. Most aspects of Romano-British culture did not cease entirely by 400, or even 450, but gradually wound down over centuries. Christianity was not expunged from eastern Britain by Germanic peoples. Even urbanism did not collapse so wholly or completely as frequently believed, although the nature of occupation in towns did alter in the fifth and sixth centuries, probably as part of a longer-term transformation also witnessed on the Continent. In short, Britain was not an exception to wider trends of political, cultural and religious change, and although aspects of such trends were less pronounced in Britain than elsewhere, others were more strongly represented than in other western European societies.

Most importantly perhaps in this context, fifth- and sixth-century Britain was not dominated by 'Anglo-Saxon' culture: instead it was British Romano-Christian culture that was most widespread and that acquired most new adherents before 600. But this was also a period of profound change. This change can also be examined in terms of generation and memory. Anthropologists and historians frequently consider that the average generation in pre-modern societies is about 30 years. That is, the period 300-600 would encompass approximately 11 generations. Of these, the first would be born *c*.300, the second *c*.330, the third *c*.360, the fourth *c*.390, the fifth *c*.420 (that of Patrick?), the sixth *c*.450, the seventh *c*.480, the eighth *c*.510 (that of Gildas?), the ninth *c*.540, the tenth *c*.570 and the eleventh *c*.600. Obviously, these can only be approximations, but may suggest generational divisions.

Assuming that a lifespan of more than 60 was rare, then most people would have had access to eyewitness accounts of events less than 55 years earlier, allowing for the early childhood of the observer. At most, such accounts would extend 115 years into the past, that is three generations previously. But for most people the threshold of living memory would be much more recent. A person living in AD 300 might gain an eyewitness account of events of 185 at earliest. By 410, eyewitness testimony would 'cut off' around 295, with almost no memory of a Roman Empire without Christianity as its state religion. In 500, Britons would have been unable to hear these accounts of Roman Britain prior to 385. Pre-Saxon eastern Britain would have been beyond most people's recollection by the early seventh century.

This can again only be a very rough guide, of course, and makes no allowance for stories transmitted through generations. Such stories may be long-lived; even in the twenty-first century, stories of family history centuries earlier may be recalled and passed to new generations. Assuming this to be more common in a kin-based and localized community, then it is vital to allow for these stories in considering the role of memory in the fifth and sixth centuries. We saw in the first chapter that, without textual recording, facts are likely to be distorted beyond around 200 years of transmission. That is, an event 200 years in the past would be unlikely to be recalled accurately, as a broad generalization. This suggests that in AD 300 the construction of Hadrian's Wall might have been part of living story. In 400, the mid-Roman crisis could have been remembered with some accuracy, and by 500 Constantine I would be approximately the threshold of storytelling.

This raises an interesting point. The principal witnesses to fifth- and sixth-century Britain seem to bear some relationship to these limits of memory. For Patrick his family history extended two generations; that is just as we might imagine. For Gildas, details become vague before the 440s, just as one might expect from this approximation if he lived during the mid-sixth century. This may give us some encouragement to examine what these thresholds of memory and generational shifts may mean in terms of fifth- and sixth-century British political and cultural history.

In Britain, the end of the period examined here came in the last generation of the sixth century and after. Then, changes are visible in both the political organization and material culture of the Britons and 'Anglo-Saxons'. The 'Anglo-Saxon' kingdoms appear to emerge, and material culture exhibits more evidence of commonality across eastern Britain. This may well indicate the growth of a shared sense of 'Anglo-Saxon-ness', and possibly the consolidation of Germanic dialects into a single 'Anglo-Saxon' ('Old English') language. Among the Britons no trace of Late Roman administration and law seems visible after 600, and the kingdoms surviving 'Anglo-Saxon' political expansion (Strathclyde, Gwynedd, Dyfed, Glywysing, Gwent and Dumnonia) were ruled by tribal over-kings. This may be because the main victims of that political takeover were polities within the former core of Britannia Prima (the Durotriges, Cornovii and Dobunni particularly) and those of the British north. So, most remaining British kingdoms had been encompassed within Romano-Christian culture only as a result of fifth-century evangelisation, and these sources of this culture for most of them were ecclesiastical rather than both ecclesiastical and secular.

That these changes happened at the period AD 570-630 is interesting. In 600 nothing accurate may have been recalled of Roman Britain, 400 representing the threshold of memory even through family storytelling. Most popular memory will have covered a shorter timespan, with a cut-off *c*.475. AD 600 would, then, represent the first point at which the Roman heritage ceased to be a living memory in any accurate fashion: it had passed into history. Perhaps this is one reason why, alongside new forms of kingship and the new role of the Church in eastern Britain and the North, that the late sixth and early seventh century saw rapid change and political upheaval. Aspirations of maintaining or returning to unified British-ruled Britain were no longer supported by memories of a unified Roman Britain, while these were finally crushed in geopolitical terms with the defeat of Cadwallon, king of the strongest surviving British territory, Gwynedd, in 633. Thereafter, as Leslie Alcock rightly noted, the Britons never again attempted to retake Anglo-Saxon eastern England, as it might now be termed.[1]

Memory and generational transformation might also explain why widespread change in material culture, from dress fashions to architectural styles, appears to characterize Britain in the seventh century. Britain ceased to be retrospective and British-dominated, and became integrated with a new Continental culture, then emerging. This culture was focused not on the Empire and Late Roman Church structure, but on the Frankish kingdom and the Papacy at Rome. The same reasons that enabled British survival and the maintenance of political and military supremacy in the fifth and sixth centuries might be seen as inhibiting British participation in this 'new world', and facilitating Anglo-Saxon entry into the new political and cultural community. Thus, Britain's Roman legacy played a central role in preserving British political independence and cultural identity, but it also prevented the British kings from entering the wider network of seventh-century European relations. Through Augustine's mission the 'Anglo-Saxons' became part of this 'world' more swiftly and fully, so that when Bede wrote he quite literally lived in a different period of history — in a sense a different 'world' — from the fifth and sixth century.[2]

Through emulation of Franks and Papal Christian models, Anglo-Saxon kings adopted the trappings of the Frankish state and abandoned the Germanic pagan heritage of their grandparents. By the time of the Anglo-Saxon military and political seizure of the entire British West, with the exception of parts of Wales and Dumnonia, they had entered into a new version of Frankish Romano-Christian culture just as fully as the Britons had been part of the Late Antique form of this. In Britain, new political, religious, cultural and economic relationships in the seventh century resulted from this, and with it the foundation of England, Scotland and Wales as distinct and separate political and cultural entities.

This period is crucial to understanding British history as a whole, but reinterpreting fifth- and sixth-century Britain in this way also has many implications for the study of the end of the Roman Empire more widely. Rather than being the area of the former Roman West in which Late Roman culture was most entirely swept away in the fifth century, and in which exceptional curiously archaic local cultures flourished, quite the opposite would seem to be true. It was within the mainstream, but was the only part of the West in which the descendants of Roman citizens lived under their own rule, with their own Romano-Christian culture and in recognisably Late Roman political units, into the sixth century. It was the most successful western society in Late Antiquity at exporting its own culture to its neighbours. The significance of this was not perhaps lost on those in sixth-century Byzantine Constantinople who sent merchants to Britain to engage in both trade and diplomacy: it should not be lost on us.

Bibliography and references

Abbreviations:

DE	Winterbottom, M. (ed & trans) 1978. *Gildas. The Ruin of Britain and other works*. London/Chichester
Civitas	Dark, K.R. 1994. *Civitas to Kingdom*. London and New York
CMCS	*Cambridge/Cambrian Medieval Celtic Studies*
Discovery	Dark, K.R. 1994. *Discovery by Design*. Oxford
E.Ch.	Edwards, N. & Lane, A. (eds) 1992. *The Early Church in Wales and the West*. Oxford
EC	Dark, K.R. (ed) 1996. *External Contacts and the Economy of Late Roman and Post-Roman Britain*. Woodbridge
IP	Bieler, L. (ed) 1975. *The Irish Penitentials*. Dublin
Landscape	Dark, K. & Dark, P. 1997. *The Landscape of Roman Britain*. Stroud.
OAK	Bassett, S. (ed) 1989. *The Origins of Anglo-Saxon Kingdoms*. London
PRB	O'Brien, E. 1999. *Post-Roman Britain to Anglo-Saxon England: Burial Practices Reviewed*. Oxford
The End	Knight, J.K. 1999. *The end of antiquity archaeology, society and religion AD 235-700*. Stroud
TRAC	*Theoretical Roman Archaeology Conference*

Introduction

1   For the geography of Anglo-Saxon England after 600, see: Hill, D. 1981. *An Atlas of Anglo-Saxon England*. Oxford. For an outline of the history: Campbell, J. 1991. *The Anglo-Saxons*. London

2   Webster, L. and Backhouse, J. (eds) 1991. *The Making of England: Anglo-Saxon Art and Culture AD 600-900*. London. The best recent discussions of dress and burial in seventh- to eighth-century England are: Boddington, A. 1990. 'Models of burial, settlement and worship: the Final Phase reviewed' in Southworth, R. (ed) *Anglo-Saxon cemeteries: a reappraisal*, 177-9. Stroud; Geake, H. 1999. 'Invisible kingdoms: the use of grave-goods in seventh-century England' in Dickinson, T. & Griffiths, D. (eds) *The Making of Kingdoms*. 203-15. Oxford; Geake, H. 1997. *The Use of Grave-Goods in Conversion-Period England, c. 600-c. 850*. Oxford. See also the important discussion of the date of deposition of hanging bowls in Anglo-Saxon burials, by Helen Geake: Geake, H. 1999. 'When were hanging bowls deposited in Anglo-Saxon graves?', *Medieval Archaeology* 43, 1-18. A related and intriguing possibility that has perhaps received less detailed comment than it warrants is that even the famous grave in Sutton Hoo mound 1 was designed to present its occupant as a Roman emperor, not a Germanic king: Filmer-Sankey, W. 1996. 'The "Roman emperor" in the Sutton Hoo ship burial', *Journal of the British Archaeological Association* CXLIX , 1-9

3   Potter, T. & Johns, C. 1992. *Roman Britain*. London; Jones, B. & Mattingly, D. 1990. *An Atlas of Roman Britain*. London; *Landscape*

4   On the period in general and the concept of 'Late Antiquity': Hodges, R. & Whitehouse, D. 1983. *Mohammed, Charlemagne and the origins of Europe*. London; Cameron, A. 1993. *The Mediterranean World in Late Antiquity, A.D. 395-600*. London; Webster, L. & Brown, M. (eds) 1997. *The Transformation of the Roman World AD 400-900*. London; Randsborg, K. 1991. *The First Millennium A.D. in Europe and the Mediterranean*. Cambridge

5   Exemplified by the later chapters in Frere, S. 1967. (1st ed) *Britannia*. London; and by Alcock, L. 1971. (1st ed) *Arthur's Britain*. Harmondsworth and New York

6   Esmonde-Cleary, S. 1989. *The Ending of Roman Britain*. London; *OAK*

7   Casey, P.J. (ed) 1979. *The End of Roman Britain*. Oxford

8   Reece, R. 1980. 'Town and country: the end of Roman Britain', *World Archaeology* 12.1, 77-92; Reece, R. 1989. 'Models of continuity', *Oxford Journal of Archaeology* 8.2, 231-6; Reece, R. *My Roman Britain*. Cirencester; Reece, R. 1992. 'The end of the city in Roman Britain' in Rich, J. (ed) *The city in Late Antiquity*. 136-44. London

9   The principal themes of Higham's 'hypothesis' (his term) are covered in Higham, N. 1992. *Britain, Rome and the Anglo-Saxons*. London; Higham, N.J. 1994. *The English Conquest: Gildas and Britain in the Fifth Century*. Manchester/New York; Higham, N.J. 1995. *An English Empire. Bede and the early Anglo-Saxon Kings*. Manchester/New York; Higham, N. 1999. '*Imperium* in early Britain: rhetoric and reality in the writings of Gildas and Bede', in Dickinson, T. & Griffiths, D. (eds) *The Making of Kingdoms*. 31-6. Oxford; Higham, N.J. 1993. *The Origins of Cheshire*. Manchester/New York, 68-77

10 Jones, B. & Mattingly, D. 1990. *An Atlas of Roman Britain*. London

11 Wacher, J. 1995. *The Towns of Roman Britain* (2nd ed). London; Burnham, B.C. & Wacher, J. 1990. *The 'Small Towns' of Roman Britain*. London; *Landscape*

12 Welsby, D.A. 1982. *The Roman military defence of the British provinces in its later phases*. Oxford; Maxfield, V.A. (ed) 1989. *The Saxon Shore*. Exeter; Cotterill, J. 1994. 'Saxon raiding and the role of the Late Roman coastal forts of Britain', *Britannia* XXV, 227-239

13 *Civitas* 45; Thomas, C. 1981. *Christianity in Roman Britain*. London; Thomas, C. 1986. 'Recognising Christian origins: an archaeological and historical dilemma', in Butler, L.A.S. & Morris, R.K. (eds) *The Anglo-Saxon Church*, 121-5. London; Quensel-von Kalben, L. 1999. 'The British Church and the emergence of Anglo-Saxon kingdoms' in Dickinson, T. & Griffiths, D. (eds) *The Making of Kingdoms*, 89-98. Oxford; *Civitas* 58-9. On portable altars: Thomas, C. 1971. *The early Christian archaeology of North Britain*. Edinburgh, 190-8

14 Painter, K.S. 1999. 'The Water Newton silver: votive or liturgical?', *Journal of the British Archaeological Association* CLII, 1-23

15 *Civitas* 30-6; Casey, P.J. & Hoffman, B. 1999. 'Excavations at the Roman temple in Lydney Park, Gloucestershire', *The Antiquaries Journal* 79, 81-144

16 Watts, D. 1998. *Religion in Late Roman Britain*. London and New York, 40-1 and 58-9, although it is impossible to accept Watts' arguments for the relative fortunes of Christianity and paganism in Roman Britain. We know far too little about the relationship of the known artefacts and structures to Christian practice in fourth-century Britain to use them to assess its rise or decline: archaeologically the growth of Christianity is largely visible in the decline of pagan practice. For Uley, see chapter 3 of this book

17 *Civitas* 30-6; *Landscape*

18 Bohme, H.W. 1986. 'Das Ende der Römerherrschaft in Britannien und die Angelsächsische Besiedlung Englands im 5. Jahrhundert', *Jahrbuch des Römisch-Germanischen Zentralmuseums Mainz* 33, 469-574; Hines, J. 1990. 'Philology, archaeology and the *adventus Saxonum vel Anglorum*' in Bammesberger, A. & Wollmann, A. (eds) *Britain 400-600: Language and History*, 17-36. Heidelberg

19 Contra: Bohme, H.W. 1986. 'Das Ende der Römerherrschaft in Britannien und die Angelsächsische Besiedlung Englands im 5. Jahrhundert', *Jahrbuch des Römisch-Germanischen Zentralmuseums Mainz* 33, 469-574

20 Plouviez, J. 1999. 'Who needs a hypocaust anyway?', *Saxon* 30, 3. I am very grateful to Jude Plouviez for providing further information about the Scole find and other supporting-arm brooches from the area, and for discussing these with me. Pers comm J. Plouviez 2000

21 *Civitas* 47

22 *Civitas* 257

23 Armit, I. 1997. *Celtic Scotland*. London

24 Bohme, H.W. 1986. 'Das Ende der Römerherrschaft in Britannien und die Angelsächsische Besiedlung Englands im 5. Jahrhundert', *Jahrbuch des Römisch-Germanischen Zentralmuseums Mainz* 33, 469-574; Hines, J. 1990. 'Philology, archaeology and the *adventus Saxonum vel Anglorum*' in Bammesberger A. & Wollmann A. (eds) *Britain 400-600: Language and History*, 17-36. Heidelberg

25 Collins, R. 1991. *Early Medieval Europe 300-1000*. London; Goffart, W. 1980. *Barbarians and Romans AD 418-584*. Princeton; Pohl, W. (ed) 1997. *Kingdoms of the empire*. Leiden; Ausenda, G. (ed.) 1995. *After Empire: an ethnology of Europe's barbarians*. Woodbridge; James, E. 1988. *The Franks*. Oxford; *The End,* chapters 2 and 3; Wickham, C. 1981. *Early Medieval Italy*. London/Basingstoke

26 Todd, M. 1995. *The Early Germans*. Oxford; Hedeager, L. 1992. *Iron Age Societies. From Tribe to State in Northern Europe, 500 B.C. to A.D. 700*. Oxford

27 Thompson, E.A. 1968. *The Early Germans*. London; James, E. 1982. *The Origins of France*. London; James, E. 1988. *The Franks*. Oxford

28 Adam, J.P., Aubin, G. et al 1996. *Les Premiers Monuments Chretiens de la France*. Paris; *The End,* chapters 2 and 3

29 Reynolds, P. 1995. *Trade in the western Mediterranean AD 400-700: the ceramic evidence*. Oxford; *The End*, 158; Brogiolo, G.P. & Ward-Perkins, B. 1999. *The Idea and Ideal of the Town between Late Antiquity and the Early Middle Ages*. Leiden

30 This is clearly seen in the Frankish controlled areas of what, in the fourth century, had been Gaul ('Frankia'): Rouche, M. (ed) 1997. *Clovis et son temps/ La bapteme de Clovis*. Paris (2 vols); Perin, P. & Feffer, L.-C. 1987. *Les Francs*. Paris (2 vols); Wood, I. (ed.) 1998. *Franks and Alamanni in the Merovingian period*. Woodbridge; *The End,* chapters 2 and 3; and the works by James cited above: James, E. 1982. *The Origins of France*. London; James, E. 1988. *The Franks*. Oxford. 'Roman' in the sense used in the term 'Romano-Christian' here, refers primarily to what was in Late Roman terms 'provincial' culture, such as 'Romano-Gallic' or 'Romano-British' culture, and this itself showed considerable diversity reflected in regional specifics of these later developments

31 Perin, P. 1980. *La datation des tombs merovingiennes: historique, méthodes et applications*. Geneva; Halsall, G. 1992. 'The origins of the *reihengraberzivilisation*: Forty years on' in Drinkwater, J.F. & Elton, H. (eds) *Fifth-Century Gaul: A Crisis of Identity?*, 196-207. Cambridge; Halsall, G. 1995. *Early Medieval Cemeteries*. Glasgow

32 Heather, P. 1996. *The Goths*. Oxford

33 Collins, R. 1983. *Early Medieval Spain*. London

34 Webster, L. & Brown, M. (eds) 1997. *The Transformation of the Roman World AD 400-900*. London

35 Whether or not 'Celt' (and so 'Celtic') is a valid term in the study of this period, and earlier, has been hotly debated recently. For positive view of the 'Celts' as an historically-extant people: Cunliffe, B. 1997. *The*

Ancient Celts. London, and Green, M. and Howell, R. 2000. *A pocket guide to Celtic Wales*. Cardiff. For a more sceptical approach: James, S. 1999. *The Atlantic Celts: ancient people or modern invention?* London, and Collis, J. 1996. 'The origin and spread of the Celts', *Studia Celtica* 30, 17-34

36 Pohl, W. 1998. 'Conceptions of ethnicity in early medieval studies' in Little, L.K. & Rosenwein, B.H. (eds) *Debating the Middle Ages: issues and readings*, 15-24. Oxford; Pohl, W. 1991. 'Conceptions of ethnicity in early medieval studies', *Archaeologia Polona* 29, 39-49

37 Harries, J. 1994. *Sidonius Appolinaris and the Fall of Rome AD 407-485*. Oxford, 27, 41

38 Anderson, W.B. (ed and trans) 1963-5. *Sidonius Poems and Letters* (vol 2). 'To Lampriddius' (VIII.ix) 447 and 'To Namatius' (VIII.vi) 429-32. London and Cambridge, Mass

Chapter 1

1   *Civitas*, 52-3
2   *Civitas*, 53
3   Cameron, A. 1985. *Procopius and the sixth century*. London
4   Conveniently mapped in Lane, A. 1994. 'Trade, gifts and cultural exchange in Dark Age western Scotland' in Crawford, B.E. (ed) *Scotland in the Dark Ages*, 103-15. St Andrews
5   *Civitas*, 52-3
6   *Civitas*, 68
7   These sources have been usefully summarised in Snyder, C. 1998. *An Age of Tyrants*, 32-7. Stroud. See also: Burgess, R.W. 1990. 'The Dark Ages return to fifth-century Britain: the *Restored* Gallic Chronicle exploded', *Britannia* 21, 185-95
8   Wood, I. 1984. 'The end of Roman Britain: Continental evidence and parallels' in Lapidge, M. & Dumville, D. (eds) *Gildas: New Approaches*, 1-25. Woodbridge
9   *Civitas*, 10; *The End*, 47-9, 54-6
10 Drinkwater, J.F. 1989. 'Patronage in Roman Gaul and the problem of the Bagaudae' in Wallace-Hadrill, A. (ed.) *Patronage in Ancient Society*, 189-203. London; Drinkwater, J.F. 1992. 'The Bacaudae of fifth-century Gaul' in Drinkwater, J.F. & Elton, H. (eds) *Fifth-Century Gaul: A Crisis of Identity?* 208-17. Cambridge. Greg Woolf's observation is reported in his brother's article on British towns: Woolf, A. 1999. '*Adventus, patrocinium* and the urban landscape in late Roman Britain' in Leslie, A. (ed) *Theoretical Roman Archaeology and Architecture*, 33-47. Glasgow
11 *Civitas*, 55-8
12 *Civitas*, 55; Stancliffe, C. 1983. *St Martin and his biographer*. Oxford; *The End*, 117-20
13 *Civitas*, 56-7; *The End*, 135. For a translation of the Letter to Louocatus and Catihernus, dated 509-21: Howlett, D.R. 1995. *Celtic Latin Tradition of Biblical Style*. Dublin, 66-70
14 Brooks, D.A. 1983-4. 'Gildas' *De Excido Britanniae*: its revolutionary meaning and purpose', *Studia Celtica*, 18-19, 1-10
15 *Civitas*, 57-8
16 Drinkwater, J.F. 1998. 'The usurpers Constantine III (407-411) and Jovinus (411-413)', *Britannia* 29, 269-98
17 *Civitas*, 58
18 Dumville, D.N. 1977. 'Sub-Roman Britain: history and legend', *History* 62, 173-92
19 Hood, A.B.E. (ed and trans) 1978. *St Patrick. His Writings and Muirchu's Life*. London/Chichester. The most important recent work of commentary is Dumville, D.N. et al 1993. *Saint Patrick A.D. 493-1993*. Woodbridge
20 Winterbottom, M. (ed and trans) 1978. *Gildas. The Ruin of Britain and other works*. London/Chichester; Lapidge, M. 1984. 'Gildas's education and the Latin culture of sub-Roman Britain' in Lapidge, M. & Dumville, D. (eds) *Gildas: New Approaches*, 27-50. Woodbridge
21 On the location of Gildas: *Civitas*, Appendix 1, see also *DE*, I.21 which says that the Picts, who are elsewhere said to be in the north of Britain (*DE*, 1.14), are at 'the far end of the island'. That is, Gildas was writing in the south of western Britain. On the purpose and character of *DE* see: Lapidge, M. & Dumville, D. (eds) *Gildas: New Approaches*. Woodbridge. The standard discussion of Gildas' chronology is: Dumville, D.N. 1984. 'The chronology of *De Excidio Britanniae*, Book I' in Lapidge, M. & Dumville, D. (eds) *Gildas: New Approaches*, 61-84. Woodbridge. See also the comments in *Civitas*, 158-60, supporting this chronology although suggesting a broader date range 525-60 is possible for the composition of *DE*, and it is just possible that Gildas's death was reliably recorded in Irish annalistic sources, at 570: Dumville, D.N. 1997. 'The origins and early history of Insular monasticism: aspects of literature, Christianity, and society in Britain and Ireland, A.D. 400-600', *Bulletin of the Institute of Oriental and Occidental Studies, Kansai University* 30, 85-107. It is in the latter work that Professor Dumville considers the possibility that Gildas ended his career as an abbot
22 *DE*, 1.14-26
23 On Arthur: Dumville, D.N. 1977. 'Sub-Roman Britain: history and legend', *History* 62, 173-92; Charles-Edwards, T. 1991. 'The Arthur of history' in Bromwich, R. et al (eds) *Arthur of the Welsh*, 15-32. Cardiff

24 Sharpe, R. 1984. 'Gildas as a Father of the Church' in Lapidge, M. & Dumville, D. (eds) *Gildas: New Approaches*, 193-205. Woodbridge; *IP*, 60-9

25 *IP*, 70-95; Dark K.R. 1996. 'Pottery and local production at the end of Roman Britain' in *EC*, 53-56 (54)

26 *Civitas*, 184-91

27 In addition, Mark Corney has pointed out in conversation that the buckles worn by some figures in Vergilius Romanus resemble fifth-century belt sets from Britain. Pers comm 1998. It may or may not be the case that the servants depicted in the feast scene have blond hair — unlike the 'guests' — and a hairstyle somewhat reminiscent of Sidonius' description of the Saxon's characteristic haircut

28 *Civitas*, 184-91

29 James, H. 1997. 'Llandysilio Church and Parish 500-1543: from heartland to borderland', *Carmarthenshire Antiquary* 33, 5-261

30 Wright, N. 1985. 'Did Gildas read Orosius?, *CMCS* 9, 31-42; Wright, N. 1991. 'Gildas' reading: a survey', *Sacris Erudiri* 32, 121-62

31 *Civitas*, 181; Denison, S. 2000. 'Gemstone evidence for late Roman survival', *British Archaeology* 52, 4

32 Dumville, D.N. 1999. *A Palaeographer's Review: The Insular System of Scripts in the Early Middle Ages*, vol 1. Osaka

33 Nash-Williams, V.E. 1950. *The Early Christian Monuments of Wales*. Cardiff; Knight, J.K. 1995. 'Penmachno revisited: the consular inscription and its context', *CMCS* 29, 1-10; Okasha, E. 1993. *Corpus of early Christian inscribed stones in south-west Britain*. London

34 For example: Sims-Williams, P. 1990. 'Dating the transition to Neo-Brittonic: phonology and history, 400-600' in Bammesberger, A. & Wollmann, A. (eds) *Britain 400-600: Language and History*, 217-61. Heidelberg. Thomas' classification is outlined in: Thomas, C. 1994. *And Shall These Mute Stones Speak? Post-Roman Inscriptions in Western Britain*. Cardiff

35 Knight, J.K. 1992. 'The Early Christian Latin inscriptions of Britain and Gaul: chronology and context' in *E.Ch.*, 45-50; Knight, J.K. 1996. 'Seasoned with salt: Insular-Gallic contacts in the early memorial stones and cross-slabs' in *EC*, 109-120; Knight, J.K. 1981. '*In tempore Iustini consulis*: contacts between the British and Gallic Church before Augustine' in Detsicas, A. (ed) *Collectanea Historica*, 54-62. Maidstone

36 Dark, K. 1992. 'Epigraphic, art-historical, and historical approaches to the chronology of Class I inscribed stones' in *E.Ch.*, 51-61

37 *Civitas*, 267-9

38 For examples: Lewis, J.M. 1976. 'A survey of early Christian monuments of Dyfed, west of the Taf' in Boon, G.C. & Lewis, J.M. (eds) 1976. *Welsh Antiquity. Essays mainly on Prehistoric Topics presented to H.N. Savory upon his Retirement as Keeper of Archaeology*, 177-92. Cardiff

39 Howlett, D.R. 1995. *Celtic Latin Tradition of Biblical Style*. Dublin; Howlett, D.R. 1997. *British books in the Biblical style*. Dublin; Howlett, D.R. 1998. *Cambro-Latin compositions: their competence and craftsmanship*. Dublin; Howlett, D. 1998. 'Literate culture in Dark Age Britain', *British Archaeology* 33, 10-11. For a reasoned published assessment of Howlett's work by a leading Latinist: Hood, A.B.E. 1999. 'Review article: lighten our darkness — Biblical style in early medieval Britain and Ireland', *Early Medieval Europe* 8.2, 283-6

40 Macmanus, D. 1991. *A Guide to Ogam*. Maynooth; Swift, C. 1997. *Ogam Stones and the Earliest Irish Christians*. Maynooth. For the excavation at Silchester: Clarke, A. & Fulford. M. 1999. *Silchester Insula IX. Interim Report No 3*. Reading; Silchester Roman Town Project 2000 *The Silchester Ogham Stone*. Reading; Silchester Roman Town Project 2000 *Silchester Roman Town Life Project Insula IX Site Guide*. Reading

41 *Civitas*, 192-3

42 Important recent studies include: Dumville, D.N. 1988. 'Early Welsh poetry: some problems of historicity' in Roberts, B.F. (ed) *Early Welsh Poetry: Studies on the Book of Aneirin*, 1-16 (4-7). Aberystwyth; Dumville, D.N. 1989. 'The origins of Northumbria: some aspects of the British background' in *OAK*, 213-22; Koch, J. (ed.) 1995. *The Celtic Heroic Age* (2nd ed). Malden, Mass; Koch, J.T. (ed.) 1997. *The Gododdin of Aneirin*. Cardiff; Padel, O. 1998. 'A new study of the Gododdin', *CMCS* 35, 45-55; Koch, J.T. 1986. 'When was Welsh literature first written down?', *Studia Celtica*, 20/21 (1985-6), 43-66; Koch, J.T. 1988. 'The Cynfeirdd Poetry and the language of the sixth century' in Roberts, B.F. (ed) *Early Welsh Poetry: Studies in the Book of Aneirin*, 17-41. Aberystwyth

43 Newton, S. 1993. *The Origins of Beowulf and the Pre-Viking Kingdom of East Anglia*. Woodbridge

44 Sims-Williams, P. 1984. 'Gildas and vernacular poetry' in Lapidge, M. & Dumville, D. (eds) *Gildas: New Approaches*, 169-90. Woodbridge

45 For Adomnan's Life of Columba, see: Sharpe, R. (trans) 1995. *Adomnan of Iona: Life of St Columba*. London/New York; *Civitas*, 92. On the dating of these Lives overall: Lapidge, M. & Sharpe, R. 1985. *A bibliography of Celtic-Latin literature 400-1200*. Dublin

46 The dating and problems of the *Vita Prima Sancti Samsonis* is discussed briefly in: Davies, W. 1982. *Wales in the Early Middle Ages*. London, 215; and *Civitas*, 92

47 Dumville, D.N. 1985. 'Late seventh- or eighth-century evidence for the British transmission of Pelagius', *Cambridge Medieval Celtic Studies* 10, 39-52

48 *Civitas*, 209-13

49 On early 'Anglo-Saxon' runes: Hines, J. 1990 'The runic inscriptions of early Anglo-Saxon England' in Bammesberger, A. & Wollmann, A. (eds) *Britain 400-600: Language and History*, 437-55. Heidelberg; A. Bammesberger (ed), *Old English Runes and their Continental Background*. Heidelberg

50 The starting point for any such discussion is: Dumville, D.N. 1977. 'Sub-Roman Britain: history and legend', *History* 62, 173-92. Also note the points made, in a different Insular context, by Hughes, K. 1972. *Early Christian Ireland: an Introduction to the Sources*. Ithaca and London

51 Yorke, B. 1993. 'Fact or fiction? The written evidence for the fifth and sixth centuries AD' in Filmer-Sankey, W. (ed) *Anglo-Saxon Studies in Archaeology and History* 6, 45-50. Oxford

52 Yorke, B. 1999. 'The origins of Anglo-Saxon kingdoms: the contribution of written sources' in Dickinson, T. & Griffiths, D. (eds) *The Making of Kingdoms*, 25-30. Oxford; Yorke, B. 1989. 'The Jutes of Hampshire and Wight and the origins of Wessex' in *OAK*, 84-96

53 Dumville, D.N. 1975/6. '"Nennius" and the *Historia Brittonum*'. *SC* x/xi, 78-95: Dumville, D.N. 1977. 'On the North British section of the *Historia Brittonum*', *Welsh History Review* viii.3, 345-54; Dumville, D.N. 1986. 'The historical value of the *Historia Brittonum*', in Barber, R. (ed) *Arthurian Literature VI*, 1-26. Cambridge

54 The arguments are summarised in *Civitas*, 103-4

55 Davies, W. 1978. *An Early Welsh Microcosm: Studies in the Llandaff Charters*. London; Davies, W. 1979. *The Llandaff Charters*. Aberystwyth; *Civitas*, 140-8

56 Dumville, D.N. 1977. 'Kingship, genealogies and regnal lists' in Sawyer, P. & Wood, I.N. (eds) *Early Medieval Kingship*, 72-104. Leeds; Dumville, D. 1985. 'The West Saxon Genealogical Regnal List and the Chronology of Early Wessex', *Peritia* 4, 21-66; Miller, M. 1975. 'Historicity and the pedigrees of the northcountrymen', *Bulletin of the Board of Celtic Studies* 26, 255-80

57 For Bede's text: Colgrave, B. & Mynors, R.A.B. (ed and trans) (3rd ed) 1991, *Bede's Ecclesiastical History of the English People*. Oxford; McClure, J. & Collins, R. (eds) 1994. *Bede Ecclesiastical History of the English People*. Oxford. For a critical evaluation of the utility of this for understanding the fifth and sixth centuries: Sims-Williams, P. 1983. 'The settlement of England in Bede and the "Chronicle"', *Anglo-Saxon England* 12, 1-41; Goffart, W. 1988. *The Narrators of Barbarian History (A.D. 550-800): Jordanes, Gregory of Tours, Bede, and Paul the Deacon*. Princeton

58 Dumville, D.N. 1989. 'The Tribal Hidage: an introduction to its texts and their history' in *OAK*, 225-30; Davies, W. & Vierck, H. 1974. 'The contexts of Tribal Hidage: social aggregates and settlement patterns', *Frühmittelalterliche Studien* 8, 229

59 Gelling, M. 1978. *Signposts to the Past; Place-Names and the History of England*. London; Gelling, M. 1984. *Place-Names in the Landscape*. London

60 Roberts, T. 1992. 'Welsh ecclesiastical place-names and archaeology' in *E.Ch.*, 41-4; Owen, H.W. 1998. *The Place-Names of Wales*. Cardiff; Padel, O.J. 1985. *Cornish Place-name Elements*. Nottingham; Jones, A. 1992. 'Decoding Cornish churchyards' in *Early Church*, 104-24

61 *Civitas*, 130-3

62 Dark, K.R. 1992 'A sub-Roman re-defence of Hadrian's Wall?' *Britannia* 23, 111-20

63 For lingering pro-imperial sentiment: Wood, I. 1987. 'The fall of the Western Empire and the end of Roman Britain', *Britannia* 18, 251-62

64 Scull, C. 1992. 'Before Sutton Hoo: structures of power and society in early East Anglia' in Carver, M. (ed) *The Age of Sutton Hoo*, 3-24. Woodbridge; Welch, M. 1993. 'The archaeological evidence for federate settlement in Britain during the fifth century' in Vallet, F. and Kazanksi, M. (eds) *L'armée Romaine et les barbares du IVe au VIIe siècles*, 269-77. Paris; Böhme, H.W. 1986. 'Das Ende der Römerherrschaft in Britannien und die Angelsächsische Besiedlung Englands im 5. Jahrhundert', *Jahrbuch des Römisch-Germanischen Zentralmuseums Mainz* 33, 469-574. The chronology of 'Anglo-Saxon' metalwork in this period still depends ultimately upon analogy with Continental material, which can be more accurately dated: Bohme, H.W. 1974. *Germanische Grabfunde des 4. bis 5. Jarhunderts zwischen unterer Elbe und Loire*. Munchen; and Bohme, H.W. 1987. 'Gallien in der Spatantike', *Jahrbuch des Romanischen Germanischen Zentralmuseum zu Mainz* 34, 770-73. This last publication moves the chronology of Bohme's *stufen* (stages) forward, so that *stufe* II starts in the later fourth century, *stufe* III to the middle third of the fifth century, and requires the chronology for Britain proposed in the author's 1986 paper to be adjusted similarly

65 Hawkes, S.C. 1986. 'The south east after the Romans: the Saxon settlement' in Maxfield, V.A. (ed) *The Saxon Shore*, 78-95. Exeter; Williamson, T. 1993. *The origins of Norfolk*. Manchester and New York, 49-54; Warner, P. 1996. *The origins of Suffolk*. Manchester and New York, 60-2

66 Hawkes, S.C. 1986. 'The south east after the Romans: the Saxon settlement' in Maxfield, V.A. (ed) *The Saxon Shore*, 78-95. Exeter; and Ager, B.M. 1996. 'A quoit brooch style belt-plate from Meonstoke, Hants' in Griffiths, D. (ed) *Anglo-Saxon Studies in Archaeology and History* 9, 111-14. Oxford. Current debates regarding quoit brooches themselves are conveniently summarised by Harrison, G. 1999. 'Quoit brooches and the Roman-Medieval transition' in Baker, P. et al (eds) *TRAC* Oxford, 108-120. For more detail: Ager, B.M. 1985. 'The smaller variants of the Anglo-Saxon quoit brooch', *Anglo-Saxon Studies in Archaeology and History* 4, 1-58; Ager, B.M. 1990. 'The alternative quoit brooch: an update' in Southworth, E. (ed) *Anglo-Saxon Cemeteries: a Reappraisal*. Liverpool

67 Corney, M. pers comm 1998

68 Watson, B. 1998. 'A brief history of archaeological exploration in Roman London' in Watson, B. (ed) *Roman London. Recent Archaeological Work*, 13-22. Portsmouth, Rhode Island; Parnell, G. 1982. 'The excavation of the Roman city wall at the Tower of London and Tower Hill, 1954-76', *Transactions of the London and Middlesex Archaeological Society* 33, 85-133; Parnell, G. 1993. *The Tower of London*. London

69 Ward-Perkins, B. 1984. *From Classical Antiquity to the Middle Ages: Urban Public Building in Northern and Central Italy, AD 300-850*. Oxford

70 Milne, G. 1997. *St Bride's church London*. York

71 Jones, M.U. 1980. 'Mucking and the early Saxon settlement in Essex' in Buckley, D. (ed) *Archaeology in Essex to AD 1500*, 82-95. London; Jones, W.T. 1980. 'Early Saxon cemeteries in Essex' in Buckley, D.G. (ed) *Archaeology in Essex to AD 1500*, 87-95. London

72 Steane, K. & Vince, A. 1993. 'Post-Roman Lincoln: archaeological evidence for activity in Lincoln from the fifth to the ninth centuries' in Vince, A. (ed) *Pre-Viking Lindsey*, 71-9. Lincoln; Jones, M.E. 1993. 'The latter days of Roman Lincoln' in Vince, A. (ed) *Pre-Viking Lindsey*, 14-28. Lincoln; Jones, M.J. 1994. 'St Paul in the Bail, Lincoln: Britain in Europe?' in Painter, K. (ed) *'Churches Built in Ancient Times' Recent Studies in Early Christian Archaeology*, 325-48. London

73 *Civitas*, 65, 74; Ottaway, P. 1993. *Roman York*. London, 111-117; Monaghan, J. 1997. *Roman pottery from York*. York, 971-3, 1043, 1050, 1138, 1147-8

74 Darvill, T. & Gerrard, C. 1994. *Cirencester: Town and Landscape*. Cirencester; M. Corney lecture at TRAC 2000

75 It may be relevant that Gildas believed that the mid-fifth century British ruler Vortigern (his *superbus tyrannus* — a pun on the name Vortigern which may be translated as 'over-ruler') presided over a 'council' which established the 'Saxons' in eastern Britain under Late Roman billeting terms (*DE* 1.23). If this relates to a provincial council, then Vortigern might well have been (in 440-90) the last known provincial governor of Maxima Caesariensis

76 Tyers, P. 1996. *Roman pottery in Britain*. London, 78-80

77 Kent J.P.C. 1979. 'The end of Roman Britain: the literary and numismatic evidence reviewed' in Casey, P.J. (ed) 1979. *The End of Roman Britain,* 15-27. Oxford; White, S. 1998. 'The Patching Hoard', *Medieval Archaeology* 42, 88-93

78 *Civitas*, 203, 205-6. For Continental evidence, see also: Gorini, G. 1996. 'Currency in Italy in the fifth century AD' in King, C.E. & Wigg, D.G. (eds) *Coin Finds and Coin Use in the Roman World*, 185-202. Berlin

79 In fact, Roman coins do occur in fifth- and sixth-century 'Anglo-Saxon' graves, but it is unclear whether these derive from contact with coin-using Britons, or wholly from scavenging curios or raw material from deserted Romano-British sites. Some probably represent the latter, but not necessarily all: *Civitas*, 214

80 Bland, R. & Johns, C. 1992. *The Hoxne hoard: an illustrated introduction*. London

81 White, S. 1998. 'The Patching Hoard', *Medieval Archaeology* 42, 88-93

82 Tyers, P. 1996. *Roman pottery in Britain*. London, 78-80; Brown, A. 1994. 'A Romano-British shell-gritted pottery manufacturing site at Harrold, Bedfordshire', *Bedfordshire Archaeology* 21, 19-107

83 Dark, S.P. 1996. 'Palaeoecological evidence for landscape continuity and change in Britain *c*.AD 400-800' in *EC,* 23-51. See also *Landscape*, 143-4

84 *DE* 1.18 suggests that buildings of stone were still considered 'normal' in mid-sixth century Britain. Yet, as few new structures were constructed in stone at this date, this must relate to Roman-period buildings. Croom, A.T. 2000. *Roman clothing and fashion*. Stroud; van Driel-Murray, C. 1987. *Roman footwear: a mirror of fashion and society*. London. I am grateful to Dr van Driel-Murray for discussing footwear in late fourth- and fifth-century Britain with me. Cool, H. 1992. 'Roman metal hair pins from southern Britain', *Archaeological Journal* 147, 148-82 and lecture at London *TRAC* 2000. I am grateful also to Dr Cool for discussing hairdressing and clothing fashions in this period with me

85 *Civitas*, 175

86 Harries, J. 1994. *Sidonius Appolinaris and the Fall of Rome AD 407-485*. Oxford, 131-3

Chapter 2

1 Hills, C. 1993. 'Who were the East Anglians?' in Gardiner, J. (ed) *Flatlands and wetlands,* 14-23. Norwich; Timby, J. 1993. 'Sancton 1 Anglo-Saxon cemetery. Excavations carried out between 1976 and 1980', *Archaeological Journal* 150, 243-365

2 Williamson, T. 1993. *The origins of Norfolk*. Manchester and New York, 67-8

3 *DE,* 1.5. Quensel-von Kalben, L. 1999. 'The British Church and the emergence of Anglo-Saxon kingdoms' in Dickinson, T. & Griffiths, D. (eds) *The Making of Kingdoms*, 89-98, Oxford, supports the view of extensive Late Romano-British Christianity, but supposes that the Anglo-Saxons targetted the British Church in areas they controlled because of its association with British elites. However, there is no evidence that the fifth- and sixth-century Anglo-Saxons associated Christianity with the British elite, or deliberately tried to expunge it from their territory

4 *DE,* 1.24, which paints a picture of widespread late fifth-century devastation, is presumably referring to the situation in eastern Britain as a whole if this is no more than polemic

5 Coates, R. 1991. 'On some controversy surrounding *Gewissae/Gewissei, Cerdic* and *Ceawlin*', *Nomina* 13, 1-12; Blair, J. 1994. *Anglo-Saxon Oxfordshire*. Stroud, 12, 23-7

6 Blair, J. 1994. *Anglo-Saxon Oxfordshire*. Stroud, 12, 23-7; Henig, M. & Booth, P. 2000. *Roman Oxfordshire*. Stroud, 187-92; Hawkes, S.C. 1986. 'The early Saxon period' in Briggs, G. et al (eds) *The Archaeology of the Oxford Region*, 64-108. Oxford; Chambers, R.A. 1987. 'The late- and sub-Roman cemetery at Queensford

Farm, Dorchester-upon-Thames, Oxon', *Oxoniensia* LII, 35-69; White, R.H. 1988. *Roman and Celtic Objects from Anglo-Saxon Graves*. Oxford

7   For examples see: Scott, E. 1993. *A Gazetteer of Roman Villas in Britain*. Leicester; Yorke, B. 1994. *Wessex in the early middle ages*. London, 49

8   Miles, D. 1984. *Archaeology at Barton Court Farm, Abingdon, Oxon*. London

9   Lewit, T. 1991. *Agricultural Production in the Roman Economy A.D. 200-400*. Oxford; Ager, B.M. 1996. 'A quoit brooch style belt-plate from Meonstoke, Hants' in: Griffiths, D. (ed) *Anglo-Saxon Studies in Archaeology and History* 9, 111-14. Oxford; Stedman, M. 1998. 'Three early Anglo-Saxon metalwork finds from the Isle of Wight, 1993-6', *Proceedings of the Hampshire Field Club Archaeological Society* 53, 109-19

10   Fleuriot, L. 1980. *Les origines de la Bretagne*. Paris; Thompson, E.A. 1968. 'Britonia' in Barley, M.W. & Hanson, R.P.C. (eds) *Christianity in Britain 300-700*, 201-5. Leicester

11   Sims-Williams, P. 1983. 'Gildas and the Anglo-Saxons', *CMCS* 6, 1-31

12   Dickinson, T. 1980. 'The present state of Anglo-Saxon cemetery studies' in Rahtz, P., Dickinson, T. & Watts, L. (eds) *Anglo-Saxon Cemetery Studies 1979*, 11-34. Oxford

13   Meaney, A. 1964. *A Gazetteer of Early Anglo-Saxon Burial Sites*. London; *PRB*, ch 5

14   For instance: Hamerow, H. 1992. 'Anglo-Saxon settlements on the gravels' in Fulford, M. and Nichols, L. (eds) *Developing landscapes of lowland Britain: the archaeology of the British gravels*, 39-46. London

15   Rahtz, P.A. 1976. 'Buildings and rural settlement, and Gazetteer of Anglo-Saxon domestic settlement sites' in Wilson, D.M. (ed) *The archaeology of Anglo-Saxon England*, 49-94 and 405-52. Cambridge; Marshall, A. & Marshall, C. 1994. 'Differentiation, continuity and change in Anglo-Saxon buildings', *Archaeological Journal* 150, 364-402

16   West, S. 1985. *West Stow: the Anglo-Saxon village* (2 volumes). Ipswich

17   *Ibid*

18   *Ibid* and Hamerow, H. 1993. *Excavations at Mucking 2: The Anglo-Saxon Settlement*. London; Bell, M. 1977. *Excavations at Bishopstone, Lewes (Sussex Archaeological Collections 115)*; Bell, M. 1978. 'Saxon settlements and buildings in Sussex' in Brandon, P. (ed) *The South Saxons*, 36-53. Chichester; Millett, M. 1983. 'Excavations at Cowdrey's Down, Basingstoke, Hants', *Archaeological Journal* 140, 151-78

19   Welch, M. 1992. *Anglo-Saxon England*. London, ch 2

20   Hamerow, H. 1993. *Excavations at Mucking 2: The Anglo-Saxon Settlement*. London; West, S. 1985. *West Stow: the Anglo-Saxon Village*. Suffolk

21   Hamerow, H. 1991. 'Settlement mobility and the "Middle Saxon shift": rural settlements and settlement patterns in Anglo-Saxon England', *Anglo-Saxon England* 20 1-18; Scull, C. 1999. 'Social archaeology and Anglo-Saxon kingdom origins' in Dickinson, T. & Griffiths, D. (eds) *The Making of Kingdoms*, 17-24. Oxford; Scull, C. 1999. 'Social archaeology and Anglo-Saxon kingdom origins' in Dickinson, T. & Griffiths, D. (eds) *The Making of Kingdoms*, 17-24. Oxford

22   Powlesland, D. 1997. 'The Anglo-Saxon settlement at West Heslerton, North Yorkshire' in Hawkes, J. & Mills, S. (eds) *Northumbria's Golden Age*, 55-65. Stroud; Powlesland, D. 1997. 'Early Anglo-Saxon settlements, structures, forms and layout' in Hines, J. (ed) *The Anglo-Saxons from the Migration Period to the Eighth Century. An Ethnographic Perspective*, 101-116. Woodbridge

23   Nielsen, P.O., Randsborg, K. & Thrane, H. (eds) 1993. *The Archaeology of Gudme and Lundeborg*. Copenhagen

24   Rahtz, P.A. 1999. 'Royal sites' in Lapidge, M. et al (eds) *The Blackwell encyclopedia of Anglo-Saxon England*, 399-401. Oxford

25   Higham, N. 1992. *Britain, Rome and the Anglo-Saxons*. London, 121-126

26   Dixon, P. 1982. 'How Saxon is the Saxon House?' in Drury, P. (ed) *Structural Reconstruction: Approaches to the Interpretation of the Excavated Remains of Buildings*, 275-86. Oxford; James, S., Marshall, A. & Millett, M. 1985. 'An early Medieval building tradition', *Archaeological Journal* 141 (1984), 182-215. The relationship between the British and Germanic populations of eastern England in the fifth and sixth centuries has been the subject of much recent academic interest, for example: Woolf, A. 1994. 'When England turned English', *British Archaeological News* new series 18, 5

27   James, S., Marshall, A. & Millett, M. 1985. 'An early Medieval building tradition', *Archaeological Journal* 141 (1984), 182-215. For the 'Anglo-Saxon' settlement (Catholme) arguably most like the Romano-British site at Dunston's Clump: Losco-Bradley, S. & Wheeler, H. 1984. 'Anglo-Saxon settlement in the Trent valley: some approaches' in Faull, M. (ed) *Studies in late Saxon settlement*, 101-14. Oxford

28   Hamerow, H. 1994. 'Migration Theory and the Migration Period' in Vyner, B. (ed) *Building on the Past. Papers celebrating 150 years of the Royal Archaeological Institute*, 163-77. London; Hamerow, H. 1997. 'Migration Theory and the Anglo-Saxon "identity crisis"' in Chapman, J. & Hamerow, H. (eds) *Migrations in Archaeological Explanation*, 33-44. Oxford; Hamerow, H. 1994. 'The archaeology of rural settlements in early medieval Europe', *Early Medieval Europe* 3.2, 167-79

29   Ford, S. 1997. 'Excavation of Saxon structures and Bronze Age features at Bentley Green Farm, Bentley, Hampshire, 1994', *Proceedings of the Hampshire Field Club Archaeological Society* 52, 59-7; Blair, J. 1994. *Anglo-Saxon Oxfordshire*. Stroud

30   Perkins, D.R.J. & Hawkes, S.C. 1991. 'The Thanet Gas Pipeline Phases I and II (Monkton Parish), 1982', *Archaeologia Cantiana* (1990) 108, 83-114; Mackey, R. 1998. 'The Welton villa — a view of social and economic change during the Roman period in East Yorkshire' in Halkon, P. (ed) *Further Light on the Parisi*,

21-32. Hull; Whitwell, J.B. 1988. 'Late Roman settlement on the Humber and Anglian beginnings' in Price, J. & Wilson, P.R. (eds) *Recent Research in Roman Yorkshire*, 49-78. Oxford. Other Roman-period SFBs were reported on the internet discussion list BRITARCH, by N. Finn on 15 February 2000. These were found at Appleby Magna, Leicestershire, and consisted of three or four late fourth-century rectilinear features, lined with stakes within their cuts

31 Richards, J.D. 1987. *The Significance of Form and Decoration of Anglo-Saxon Cremation Urns*. Oxford; Carver, M. 1989. 'Kingship and material culture in early Anglo-Saxon East Anglia' in *OAK*, 141-58

32 Colgrave, B. & Mynors, R.A.B. (ed and trans) (3rd ed) 1991. *Bede's Ecclesiastical History of the English People*. Oxford, 51; Bremmer, R.H. 1990. 'The Nature of the Evidence for a Frisian Participation the Adventus Saxonum' in Bremmersberger, A. & Wollmann, A. (eds) *Britain 400-600: Language and History*, 353-371. Heidelberg

33 Hills, C.M. 1979. 'The archaeology of Anglo-Saxon England in the pagan period: a review', *Anglo-Saxon England* 8, 297-329

34 Hills, C.M. 1998. 'Spong Hill and the Adventus Saxonum' in Karkov, C.E., Wilham-Crowley, K.M. and Young, B.K. (eds) *Spaces of the Living and the Dead*, 15-26. Oxford

35 For example: Hawkes, S.C. 1986. 'The south-east after the Romans: the Saxon settlement' in Maxfield, V.A. (ed) *The Saxon Shore*, 78-95. Exeter; Yorke, B. 1989. 'The Jutes of Hampshire and Wight and the origins of Wessex' in *OAK*, 84-96

36 Hines, J. 1984. *The Scandinavian Character of Anglian England in the Pre-Viking Period*. Oxford; Hines, J. 1992. 'The Scandinavian character of Anglian England: an update' in Carver, M. (ed) *The Age of Sutton Hoo*, 315-30. Woodbridge; Bremmer, R.H. 1990. 'The Nature of the Evidence for a Frisian Participation in the Adventus Saxonum' in Bremmersberger, A. & Wollmann, A. (eds) *Britain 400-600: Language and History*, 353-371. Heidelberg; Brooks, N. 1989. 'The Creation and Early Structure of the Kingdom of Kent' in *OAK*, 55-74; Brugmann, B. 1999. 'The role of Continental artefact-types in sixth-century Kentish chronology' in Hines, J., Nielsen, K.H. & Siegmund, F. 1999. *The Pace of Change. Studies in Early-Medieval Chronology*, 37-64. Oxford

37 Meaney, A. 1964. *A Gazetteer of Early Anglo-Saxon Burial Sites*. London; Richards, J.D. 1995. 'An archaeology of Anglo-Saxon England' in Ausenda, G. (ed) *After Empire: an ethnology of Europe's barbarians*, 51-74. Woodbridge; *PRB,* ch 5

38 Härke, H. 1997. 'Early Anglo-Saxon social structure' in Hines, J. (ed) *The Anglo-Saxons from the Migration Period to the Eighth Century. An Ethnographic Perspective*, 125-59. Woodbridge; Harke, H. 1992. *Angelsachsische Waffengräber des 5. bis 7. Jahrhunderts*. Cologne; Harke, H. 1989. 'Early Saxon weapon burials: frequencies, distributions and weapon combinations' in Hawkes, S.C. (ed) *Weapons and Warfare in Anglo-Saxon England*, 49-61. Oxford

39 Fisher, G. 1988. 'Style and sociopolitical organisation: a preliminary study from early Anglo-Saxon England' in Driscoll, S.T. & Nieke, M.R. (eds) *Power and Politics in Early Medieval Ireland*, 128-44. Edinburgh, conveniently summarises the relevant data

40 Meaney, A. 1964. *A Gazetteer of Early Anglo-Saxon Burial Sites*. London; *PRB*, ch 5

41 *PRB*, 7, 185

42 James, E. 1980. 'Merovingian cemetery studies and some implications for Anglo-Saxon England' in Rahtz, P. et al (eds) *Anglo-Saxon Cemeteries 1979*, 35-55. Oxford; James, E. 1989. 'Burial and status in the Early Medieval West', *Transactions of the Royal Historical Society* 5.39, 23-40

43 Härke, H. 1992. *Angelsachsische Waffengräber des 5. bis 7. Jahrhunderts*. Cologne; Harke, H. 1997. 'Early Anglo-Saxon social structure' in Hines, J. (ed) *The Anglo-Saxons from the Migration Period to the Eighth Century. An Ethnographic Perspective*, 125-59. Woodbridge

44 Crawford, S. 1999. *Childhood in Anglo-Saxon England*. Stroud; Pader, E.J. 1980. 'Material symbolism and social relations in mortuary studies' in Rahtz, P.A. et al (eds) *Anglo-Saxon cemeteries 1979*, 143-160. Oxford

45 Vierck, H. 1978. 'Trachtenkunde und Trachegeschicte in der Sachsen-Forschung, ihre Quellen, Zile und Methoden and Die anglische Frauentracht' in Ahrens, C. (ed) *Sachsen und Angelsachsen*, 231-44 and 245-53. Hamburg

46 Hills, C.M. 1979. 'The archaeology of Anglo-Saxon England in the pagan period: a review', *Anglo-Saxon England* 8, 297-329

47 The most extensively-excavated and thoroughly-studied 'Anglian' cremation cemetery in England is probably Spong Hill, Norfolk, published in series of substantial volumes: Hills, C.M. et al 1977-84. *The Anglo-Saxon cemetery at Spong Hill, Elmham* as volumes of *East Anglian Archaeology* (6, 11, 24, 34) and McKinley, J.K. 1994. *Spong Hill, Part IV: the cremations* = *East Anglian Archaeology* 69, containing palaeopathological analysis of the cremated bone. Carnegie, S. & Filmer-Sankey, W. 1993. 'A Saxon "cremation pyre" from the Snape Anglo-Saxon cemetery, Suffolk' in Filmer-Sankey, W. (ed) *Anglo-Saxon Studies in Archaeology and History* 6, 107-12. Oxford; Welch, M. 1992. *Anglo-Saxon England*. London

48 McKinley, J.K. 1994. *Spong Hill, Part IV: the cremations* = *East Anglian Archaeology*, 69; Welch, M. 1992. *Anglo-Saxon England*. London

49 That the finding of the 'proper' urn was important is demonstrated by: Richards, J.D. 1987. *The Significance of Form and Decoration of Anglo-Saxon Cremation Urns*. Oxford

50 Down, A. & Welch, M. 1990. *Chichester excavations VII: Appledown and The Mardens*. Chichester

51 On the ships themselves: Haywood, J. 1999. *Dark Age Naval Power* (2nd ed). London

52 Crawford, S. 1997. 'Britons, Anglo-Saxons and the Germanic burial ritual' in Chapman, J. & Hamerow, H. (eds) *Migrations in Archaeological Explanation*, 45-72. Oxford. On the sort of kinship structures that might have lain behind such 'family burial grounds': Charles-Edwards, T. 1993. *Early Irish and Welsh Kinship*. Oxford; Charles-Edwards, T. 1997. 'Anglo-Saxon kinship revisited' in Hines, J. (ed) *The Anglo-Saxons from the Migration Period to the Eighth Century. An Ethnographic Perspective*, 171-203. Woodbridge. On family and its possible implications for status representation in the provision of grave-goods, see Jorgensen, L. 1987. 'Family burial practices and inheritance systems. The development of an Iron Age society from 500 BC to AD 1000 on Bornholm, Denmark', *Acta Archaeologica* 58, 17-53

53 Dickinson, T. 1979. 'On the origin and chronology of the Early Anglo-Saxon disc brooch' in Hawkes, S.C. et al (eds) *Anglo-Saxon Studies in Archaeology and History I*, 39-80. Oxford; *PRB*, 185-6 and ch 5; Philpott, R. 1991. *Burial Practices in Roman Britain*. Oxford

54 Williams, H. 1997. 'Ancient landscapes and the dead: the reuse of prehistoric and Roman monuments as early Anglo-Saxon burial sites', *Medieval Archaeology* 41, 1-32; Williams, H. 1998. 'Monuments and the past in early Anglo-Saxon England', *World Archaeology* 30, 90-108; *PRB*, 186

55 Yorke, B. 1994. *Wessex in the early middle ages*. London, 46

56 *PRB*, ch 5; Eagles, B. 1979. *The Anglo-Saxon Settlement of Humberside*. Oxford; Eagles, B. 1989. 'Lindsey' in *OAK*, 202-12. London; Leahy, K. 1993. 'The Anglo-Saxon settlement of Lindsey' in Vince, A. (ed) *Pre-Viking Lindsey*, 29-44. Lincoln; Leahy, K. 1999. 'The formation of the Anglo-Saxon kingdom of Lindsey' in Dickinson, T. & Griffiths, D. (eds) *The Making of Kingdoms*, 127-34. Oxford

57 The possibility of finding Britons in Anglo-Saxon graves has become widely discussed among archaeologists: Hills, C.M. 1993. 'Where have all the dead Saxons gone?' in Carver, M. (ed) *In search of cult*, 55-9. Woodbridge; Woolf, A. 1994. 'When England turned English', *British Archaeological News* 18, 5; Harke, H. 1995. 'Finding Britons in Anglo-Saxon graves', *British Archaeology* 10, 7; Williams, H.M.R. 1999. 'Identities and cemeteries in Roman and early Medieval Britain' in Baker, P., Forcey, C., Jundi, S. & Witcher, R. (eds) *TRAC 98*, 96-107. Oxford

58 Young, B.K. 'The myth of the pagan cemetery' in Karkov, C.E., Wilham-Crowley, K.M. & Young, B.K. (eds) 1999. *Spaces of the Living and the Dead*, 61-86. Oxford; Young, B.K. 1977. 'Paganisme, christianisme et rites funéraires merovingiens', *Archeologie medievale* 7, 3-81; James, E. 1992. 'Royal burials among the Franks' in Carver, M. (ed) *The Age of Sutton Hoo*, 243-54. Woodbridge

59 Lanciani, R. 1893. *Pagan and Christian Rome*. Boston and New York, 202-4; 'grave-goods' found in St Petronilla's chapel adjacent to St Peter's alone include agate goblets in what may have been Honorius' wife's tomb, glass vessels, jewellery, and clothed burial

60 Hodges, R. 1989. *The Anglo-Saxon Achievement*. London, 29-31

61 Textual evidence for converted 'Anglo-Saxons' prior to 597 is noted by Meens, R. 1994. 'A background to Augustine's mission to Anglo-Saxon England', *Anglo-Saxon England* 23, 5-17

62 For this and the next paragraph: Henig, M. & Booth, P. 2000. *Roman Oxfordshire*. Stroud, 185-6; Tyler, S. 1992. 'Anglo-Saxon settlement in the Darenth valley and environs', *Archaeologia Cantiana* 110, 71-82; Batchelor, D. 1997. 'Darenth Park Anglo-Saxon cemetery, Dartford', *Archaeologia Cantiana* 116 (1996), 35-72; Evison, V.I. 1965. *The Fifth-Century Invasions South of the Thames*. London

63 Evison, V.I. 1994. *An Anglo-Saxon Cemetery at Great Chesterford, Essex*. London; Evison, V.I. & Hill, P. 1996. *Two Anglo-Saxon Cemeteries at Beckford, Hereford and Worcester*. York

64 White, R.H. 1988. *Roman and Celtic Objects from Anglo-Saxon Graves*. Oxford, 100-101

65 *PRB*, 96; White, R.H. 1988. *Roman and Celtic Objects from Anglo-Saxon Graves*. Oxford, 207-9

66 Blair, J. 1992. 'Anglo-Saxon pagan shrines and their prototypes', *Anglo-Saxon Studies in Archaeology and History* 5, 1-28; Wilson, D. 1992. *Anglo-Saxon Paganism*. London/New York, ch 3; Butler, C. 1998. 'Rescue archaeology in mid-Sussex', *Current Archaeology* 156, 464-7

67 Brooks, N. 1984. *The early history of the Church of Canterbury: Christ Church from 597 to 1066*. Leicester, 17-24; Jones, M.J. 1994. 'St Paul in the Bail, Lincoln: Britain in Europe?' in Painter, K. (ed) *'Churches Built in Ancient Times' Recent Studies in Early Christian Archaeology*, 325-48. London; Thomas, C. 1981. *Christianity in Roman Britain*. London, 170-4

68 Blair, J. 1992. 'Anglo-Saxon pagan shrines and their prototypes', *Anglo-Saxon Studies in Archaeology and History* 5, 1-28

69 Hines, J. 1997. 'Religion: the limits of knowledge' in Hines, J. (ed) *The Anglo-Saxons from the Migration Period to the Eighth Century. An Ethnographic Perspective*, 375-400. Woodbridge

70 Wilson, D. 1992. *Anglo-Saxon Paganism*. London/New York, ch 1

71 *Ibid*, ch 2

72 Wilson, D. 1992. *Anglo-Saxon Paganism*. London/New York, 18, 118-9, 143-5; Arnold, C.J. (2nd ed) 1997. *An archaeology of the early Anglo-Saxon kingdoms*. London, 161

73 Hills, C.M. 1983. 'Animal stamps on Anglo-Saxon pottery in East Anglia', *Studien zur Sachsenforschung* 4, 93-110; Wilson, D. 1992. *Anglo-Saxon Paganism*. London/New York; Capelle, T. 1987. 'Animal stamps and animal figures on Anglo-Saxon and Anglian pottery', *Medieval Archaeology* 31, 94-6

74 Richards, J.D. 1987. *The Significance of Form and Decoration of Anglo-Saxon Cremation Urns*. Oxford; Hines, J. 1997. 'Religion: the limits of knowledge' in Hines, J. (ed) *The Anglo-Saxons from the Migration Period to the Eighth Century. An Ethnographic Perspective*, 375-400. Woodbridge

75 Hauck, H. et al 1985-9. *Die Goldbrackteaten der Völkerwanderungzeit*. Munich; Axboe, M. 1999. 'The chronology of the Scandinavian gold bracteates' in Hines, J., Nielsen, K.H. & Siegmund, F. *The Pace of Change. Studies in Early-Medieval Chronology*, 126-47. Oxford

76 Wilson, D. 1992. *Anglo-Saxon Paganism*. London/New York, ch 2; Blair, J. 1992. 'Anglo-Saxon pagan shrines and their prototypes', *Anglo-Saxon Studies in Archaeology and History* 5, 1-28; Babb, L. 1998. 'A corpus of Anglo-Saxon weapons and knives in Buckinghamshire County Museum', *Records of Buckinghamshire* 38 (1996), 139-52 (145). For Walton: Farley, M. 1976. 'Saxon and medieval Walton, Aylesbury: excavations 1973-4', *Records of Buckinghamshire* 20.2, 153-290

77 Wilson, D. 1992. *Anglo-Saxon Paganism*. London/New York, 100-1

78 Hirst, S.M. 1985. *An Anglo-Saxon Inhumation Cemetery at Sewerby, East Yorkshire*. York; Wilson, D. 1992. *Anglo-Saxon Paganism*. London/New York, 77-80; Davidson, H.E. 1992. 'Human sacrifice in the pagan period in north-western Europe 1992. Anglo-Saxon symbolism' in Carver, M. (ed) *The Age of Sutton Hoo*, 93-130. Woodbridge; Wilson, D. 1992. *Anglo-Saxon Paganism*. London/New York, 100

79 Adams, B. & Jackson, D. 1988-9. 'The Anglo-Saxon cemetery at Wakerly, Northamptonshire; excavated by Mr D. Jackson', *Northamptonshire Archaeology* 22, 69-183

80 Wilson, D. 1992. *Anglo-Saxon Paganism*. London/New York, 96-7; Shepherd, D.J. 1999. 'The elusive warrior maiden tradition — bearing weapons in Anglo-Saxon society' in Carman, J. & Harding, A. (eds) *Ancient Warfare. Archaeological Perspectives*, 219-48. Stroud; Leigh, D. 1984. 'Ambiguity in Anglo-Saxon Style I art', *Antiquaries Journal* 64, 34-4; Arnold, C.J. (2nd edn) 1997. *An Archaeology of the Anglo-Saxon Kingdoms*. London/New York, 153. For example, 'button brooches' clearly show a human face, but whether or not this is meant to represent a pagan deity is unclear: Avent, R. and Evison, V.I. 1982. 'Anglo-Saxon button brooches', *Archaeologia* 107, 77-124

81 Crabtree, P. 1994. 'Animal exploitation in East Anglian villages' in Rackham, J. (ed) *Environment and economy in Anglo-Saxon England*, 40-54. York; Welch, M. 1992. *Anglo-Saxon England*. London, 39-42; Murphy, P. 'The Anglo-Saxon landscape and rural economy: some results from sites in East Anglia and Essex' in Rackham, J. (ed) *Environment and economy in Anglo-Saxon England*, 23-39. York

82 Myres, J. 1977. *A Corpus of Anglo-Saxon Pottery of the Pagan Period* (2 vols). Oxford

83 Ford, S. 1995. 'The excavation of a Saxon settlement and a Mesolithic flint scatter at Northampton Road, Brixworth, Northamptonshire', *Northamptonshire Archaeology* 26, 79-108

84 Williams, D. & Vince, A. 1997. 'The characterization and interpretation of early to middle Saxon granitic tempered pottery in England', *Medieval Archaeology* XLI, 214-220

85 Hines, J. 1984. *The Scandinavian Character of Anglian England in the Pre-Viking Period*. Oxford

86 Hamerow, H. 1993. *Excavations at Mucking 2: The Anglo-Saxon Settlement*. London

87 Myres, J. 1977. *A Corpus of Anglo-Saxon Pottery of the Pagan Period* (2 vols). Oxford. The most useful survey of the domestic pottery is in: Hamerow, H. 1993. *Excavations at Mucking 2: The Anglo-Saxon Settlement*. London

88 *Civitas*, 123-4; Hamerow, H., Hollevoet, and Vince, A. 1997. 'Migration-period settlements and "Anglo-Saxon" pottery from Flanders', *Medieval Archaeology* 38, 1-18

89 Darvill, T. 1988. 'Excavations on the site of the early Norman Castle at Gloucester 1983-4', *Medieval Archaeology* 32, 1-49

90 Welch, M. 1992. *Anglo-Saxon England*. London, 111-116

91 Hines, J. 1993. *Clasps Hektespenner Agraffen*. Stockholm; Hines, J. 1997. *A New Corpus of Anglo-Saxon Great Square-Headed Brooches*. Woodbridge

92 Brush, K. 1988. 'Gender and mortuary analysis in Anglo-Saxon archaeology', *Archaeological Review from Cambridge*, 76-89; Harke, H. 1992. *Angelsächsische Waffengraber des 5. bis 7. Jahrhunderts*. Cologne

93 Hamerow, H. 1993. *Excavations at Mucking 2: The Anglo-Saxon Settlement*. London, 90

94 Richards, J.D. 1992. 'Anglo-Saxon symbolism' in Carver, M. (ed) *The Age of Sutton Hoo*, 131-48. Woodbridge

95 For example, Fisher, G. 1988. 'Style and sociopolitical organisation: a preliminary study from early Anglo-Saxon England' in Driscoll, S.T. & Nieke, M.R. (eds) *Power and Politics in Early Medieval Ireland*, 128-44. Edinburgh

96 Dickinson, T.M. 1993. 'Early Saxon saucer brooches: a preliminary overview' in Filmer-Sankey, W. (ed) *Anglo-Saxon Studies in Archaeology and History* 6, 11-44. Oxford; Dickinson, T.M. 1991. 'Material culture as social expression: the case of Saxon saucer brooches with running spiral decoration', *Studien zur Sachsenforschung* 7, 39-70

97 Richards, J.D. 1987. *The Significance of Form and Decoration of Anglo-Saxon Cremation Urns*. Oxford; Harke, H. 1997. 'Early Anglo-Saxon social structure' in Hines, J. (ed) *The Anglo- Saxons from the Migration Period to the Eighth Century. An Ethnographic Perspective*, 125-59. Woodbridge; Ravn, M. 1998. *Germanic social structure — a methodological study in the use of archaeological and historical evidence in migration period Europe*. University of Cambridge PhD

98 Meaney, A. 1999. 'Paganism' in Lapidge, M. et al (eds) *The Blackwell encyclopedia of Anglo- Saxon England*, 351-52. Oxford

99 Carver, M. 1998. *Sutton Hoo: Burial Ground of Kings?* London; Carver, M.O.H. 1992. 'The Anglo-Saxon cemetery at Sutton Hoo: an interim report' in Carver, M. (ed) *The Age of Sutton Hoo*, 343-73. Woodbridge; Denison, S. 1999. 'New Saxon horse burial in Suffolk', *British Archaeology* 50, 5; Meadow, I. 1996. 'Wollaston: the "pioneer" burial', *Current Archaeology* 154, 391-5; Filmer-Sankey, W. 1992. 'Snape Anglo-Saxon cemetery:

the current state of knowledge' in Carver, M. (ed) *The Age of Sutton Hoo*, 39-52. Woodbridge; Wilson, D. 1992. *Anglo-Saxon Paganism*. London/New York, 101

100 *PRB*, 138-9; Anon, 2000. 'New finds at Sutton Hoo', *The National Trust Magazine*, 9; Anon, 2000. 'Sixth-century cemetery points to origins of Sutton Hoo', *British Archaeology* 54, 5

101 Filmer-Sankey, W. 1992. 'Snape Anglo-Saxon cemetery: the current state of knowledge' in Carver, M. (ed) *The Age of Sutton Hoo*, 39-52. Woodbridge; Wilson, D. 1992. *Anglo-Saxon Paganism*. London/New York, 101

102 Scull, C. 1993. 'Archaeology, early Anglo-Saxon society and the origins of Anglo-Saxon kingdoms' in Filmer-Sankey, W. (ed) *Anglo-Saxon Studies in Archaeology and History* 6, 65-82. Oxford

103 Malim, T. 1997. 'New evidence on the Cambridgeshire Dykes and Worsted Street Roman Road', *Proceedings of the Cambridge Antiquarian Society* 85, 27-122; Warner, P. 1996. *The origins of Suffolk*. Manchester and New York, 67-9; Williamson, T. 1993. *The origins of Norfolk*. Manchester and New York, 65-7

104 For potential parallels, see James, E. 1989. 'The origins of barbarian kingdoms: the continental evidence' in *OAK*, 40-54; O Corrain, D. 1972. *Ireland Before the Normans*. Dublin; O Croinin, D. 1995. *Early Medieval Ireland 400-1200*. London/New York

105 Huggett, J.W. 1988. 'Imported grave goods and the early Anglo-Saxon economy', *Medieval Archaeology* 32, 63-96

106 Wood, I.N. 1992. 'Frankish hegemony in England' in Carver, M. (ed) *The Age of Sutton Hoo*, 235-42. Woodbridge

107 Brooks, N. 1989. 'The Creation and Early Structure of the Kingdom of Kent' in *OAK*, 55-74

108 Carver, M. 1998. *Sutton Hoo: Burial Ground of Kings?* London; Carver, M.O.H. 1992. 'The Anglo-Saxon cemetery at Sutton Hoo: an interim report' in Carver, M. (ed) *The Age of Sutton Hoo*, 343-73. Woodbridge; Filmer-Sankey, W. 1992. 'Snape Anglo-Saxon cemetery: the current state of knowledge' in Carver, M. (ed) *The Age of Sutton Hoo*, 39-52. Woodbridge

109 The best discussion of the site yet published is: Wise, P. 1991. 'Wasperton', *Current Archaeology* 126, 256-9. It is further discussed in *PRB*, 93-4

110 Yorke, B. 1985. 'The Kingdom of the East Saxons', *Anglo-Saxon England* 14: 1-37; Warner, P. 1996. *The origins of Suffolk*. Manchester and New York, 65; Rutherford Davis, K. 1982. *Britons and Saxons. The Chiltern Region 400-700*. Chichester

111 The following discussion is based on data in Perring, D. 1991. *Roman London*. London, 128-9; Blackmore, L. 1986. Des res (Close City and Thames). 'Early and middle Saxon buildings in the Greater London area', *London Archaeologist* 5(8), 207-16; Symonds, R.P. & Tomber, R.S. 1992. 'Late Roman London: an assessment of the ceramic evidence for the City of London', *Transactions of the London and Middlesex Archaeological Society* 42, 59-181. For the area north of twentieth-century 'Greater London': Wingfield, C. 1995. 'The Anglo-Saxon settlement of Bedfordshire and Hertfordshire: the archaeological view' in Holgate, R. (ed) *Chiltern Archaeology*, 31-43. Dunstable; *Civitas*, 88

112 Pers comm. Niblett, R. 1999; Faulkner, N. 1997 (for 1996). 'Verulamium: interpreting decline', *Archaeological Journal* 153, 79-103

113 Crummy, P. 1997. *City of Victory*. Colchester, 125-153; Faulkner, N. 1994. 'Later Roman Colchester', *Oxford Journal of Archaeology* 13.1 93-119

114 Rodwell, W.J. & Rodwell, K.A. 1985. *Rivenhall, investigations of a villa, church and village, 1950-77*. London; Millett, M. 1997. 'The question of continuity: Rivenhall reviewed', *Archaeological Journal* 144, 434-8. The critical comments of Millett regarding the overall interpretation of Rivenhall by its excavators do not detract from this particular point

115 *PRB*, 105-110, 118-121, 127-32

116 Hines, J. 1999. 'The Anglo-Saxon archaeology of the Cambridgeshire region and the middle Anglian kingdom' in Dickinson, T. & Griffiths, D. (eds) *The Making of Kingdoms*, 135-50. Oxford

117 Welch, M. 1989. 'The kingdom of the South Saxons: the origins' in *OAK*, 75-83; Down, A. 1988. *Roman Chichester*. Chichester

118 Boon, G.C. 1959. 'The latest objects from Silchester, Hants', *Medieval Archaeology* 3, 79-88

119 The discussion here is based on data in Brooks, D.A. 1986. 'A review of the evidence for continuity in British towns in the fifth and sixth centuries', *Oxford Journal of Archaeology* 5.1, 77-102; Brooks, D.A. 1988. 'The case for continuity in fifth-century Canterbury re-examined', *Oxford Journal of Archaeology* 7.1, 99-114; Darling, M.J. 1987. 'The Caistor-by-Norwich 'massacre' reconsidered', *Britannia* 18, 263-72; Anon, 1998. *Venta Belgarum*. Winchester; Wacher, J. 1995. *The Towns of Roman Britain* (2nd ed). London

120 Wallace, C. pers comm. 2000; Lyne, M. 1997. 'The end of Roman pottery production in south central Britain', *Study Group for Roman Pottery Suffolk Annual Conference abstracts* 6; Tyers, P. 1996. *Roman pottery in Britain*. London

121 Maynard, D.J., Cleary, R., Brooks, I.P. & Price, J. 'Excavations at Foxton, Cambridgeshire 1994' in Price, J., Brooks, I.P. & Maynard, D.J. (eds) 1997. *The Archaeology of the St Neots to Duxford Gas Pipeline 1994*, 21-39. Oxford; Hart, F.A. 1984. 'Excavation of a Saxon *Grubenhaus* and Roman ditch at Kent Road, St Mary Cray', *Archaeologia Cantiana* 101, 187-216

122 Dark, K.R. 1996. 'Pottery and local production at the end of Roman Britain' in *EC*, 53-6 (58-9)

123 Roger White has noted that Roman material in 'Anglo-Saxon' cemeteries often seems as substitutes for 'proper Anglo-Saxon objects' in what could be the poorer graves. This could explain why 'old' Roman

material might be scavenged to be re-used, while 'new' pottery was generally 'Anglo-Saxon'. If one could obtain a new pot, then an 'Anglo-Saxon' one was preferable, perhaps in general, perhaps for burial purposes. For White's argument: White, R.H. 1988. *Roman and Celtic Objects from Anglo-Saxon Graves*. Oxford

Chapter 3

1   The Late Roman material from Hinton St Mary and Frampton is summarised by Thomas, C. 1981. *Christianity in Roman Britain*. London, 181-2

2   Holbrook, N. 1998. *Cirencester. The Roman Town defences, public buildings and shops*. Cirencester; Brown, D. 1976. 'Archaeological evidence for the Anglo-Saxon period' in McWhirr, A.D. (ed) *Studies in the archaeology and history of Cirencester,* 19-46. Oxford

3   Heighway, C. & Bryant, R. 1999. *The Golden Minster*. York (the plan discussed below is shown on fig 1.3, page 5); Darvill, T. 1988. 'Excavations on the site of the early Norman Castle at Gloucester 1983-84', *Medieval Archaeology* 32, 1-49; *Discovery*, 95

4   *Discovery*, 95, 97; Smith, R.J.C., Healy, F., Allen, M.J., Morris, E.L., Barnes, I. & Woodward, P.J. 1997. *Excavations along the Route of the Dorchester By-pass, Dorset, 1986-8*. Wessex

5   Sunter, N. & Woodward, P.J. 1987. *Romano-British Industries in Purbeck*. Dorset

6   Knight, J.K. 1999. 'Late Roman and post-Roman Caerwent: some evidence from metalwork', *Archaeologia Cambrensis* CXLV, 35-66 (36, 45-7); Campbell, E. & MacDonald, P. 1993. 'Excavations at Caerwent vicarage orchard garden: an extra-mural post-Roman cemetery', *Archaeologia Cambrensis* 142, 74-98; Knight, J.K. 1988. 'Caerwent' in Edwards, N. & Lane, A. (eds) *Early medieval settlements in Wales AD 400-1100*, 35-8. Bangor and Cardiff

7   White, R. & Barker, P. 1998. *Wroxeter. Life and Death of a Roman City*. Stroud, 110-12, 126-8

8   This would accurately reflect the description of mid-sixth century western British towns in *DE*, 1.26: 'the towns of our land are not populated even now as once they were; right up to the present they are deserted, in ruins and unkempt'. Note that this implies that towns are still 'populated' to some extent, just 'not as they once were'

9   *Discovery*, 94-97

10   *Discovery*, 95; Cunliffe, B. & Davenport, P. 1988. *The Temple of Sulis Minerva at Bath vol. 1*. Oxford. The bowl is described and illustrated in Cunliffe, B. (ed.) 1988. *The Temple of Sulis Minerva at Bath vol. 2. The Finds from the Sacred Spring*. Oxford, 11-12 fig 6 (no 18), 41 Plate VIII

11   Cunliffe, B. 1995. *Roman Bath*. London, 115-7

12   *Discovery*, 95

13   Timby, J.R. 1998. *Excavations at Kingscote and Wycomb, Gloucestershire*. Cirencester

14   Woodiwis, S. (ed) 1992. *Iron Age and Roman salt production and the medieval Town of Droitwich*, York

15   *Civitas*, 153-4

16   Leach, R. 1982. *Excavation at Catsgore 1970-3: a Romano-British village*. Bristol; Entwistle, R. et al 1994. *Salisbury Plain Project 1993-4 interim report*. Reading, esp. 23-4

17   Leach, R. 1982. 'The Roman interlude in the south-west: the dynamics of economic and social change in Romano-British south Somerset and north Dorset' in Miles, D. (ed) *The Romano-British countryside: studies in rural settlement and economy* (2 vols), 209-67. Oxford

18   *Discovery*, 80-1, 98

19   *Discovery*, 89

20   Heighway, C. 1987. 'Anglo-Saxon Gloucestershire' in Heighway, C. (ed) *Anglo-Saxon Gloucestershire*, 225-247. Gloucester; Selkirk, A. 2000. 'Frocester', *Current Archaeology* 169, 11-19 (18-19); Price, E. 2000. *Frocester*. Gloucester

21   *Discovery*, 98. Pers comm Holinrake, N. & C. 1999

22   The following two paragraphs draw on data in Branigan, K. 1976. *The Roman Villa in South-West England*. Bradford-on-Avon

23   Holbrook, N. 1998. *Cirencester. The Roman Town defences, public buildings and shops*. Cirencester; Barker, P. et al 1997. *The Baths Basilica Wroxeter*. London, 319-23

24   Wilson, D. 1993. *Excavation of a Romano-British Villa at Wortley, Gloucestershire. Ninth Interim Report 1993*. Keele; Wilson, D. 1995. *Excavation of a Romano-British Villa at Wortley, Gloucestershire. Eleventh Interim Report 1995*. Wortley

25   Meates, G.W. 1979. *The Roman villa at Lullingstone Volume 1: the site* (2 vols). Chichester

26   I am grateful to the staff of Chedworth National Trust property, especially Mark George, for discussing the fourth-century and later occupation with me. Pers comm George, M. and Bethel, P. 2000

27   Heighway, C. 1987. *Anglo-Saxon Gloucestershire*. Gloucester

28   Thomas, A. & Holbrook, N. 1996. 'Llandough', *Current Archaeology* 146, 73-7

29   *Discovery*, 50; *Civitas*, 161-2; Pearce, S.M. 1985. 'The Early Church in the Landscape: Evidence from North Devon', *Archaeological Journal* 142, 255-75; Pearce, S.M. 1982. 'Church and society in South Devon', *Proceedings of the Devonshire Archaeological Society* 40, 1-18; Pearce, S.M. 1982. 'Estates and church sites in Dorset and Gloucestershire: the emergence of a Christian society' in Pearce, S.M. (ed) *The early Church in Western Britain and Ireland*, 117-138. Oxford

30   Dark, K.R. 1993. 'St Patrick's *uillula* and the fifth-century occupation of Romano-British villas' in Dumville, D.N. et al 1993. *Saint Patrick A.D. 493-1993*, 19-24. Woodbridge

31   Petts, D. 1998. 'Burial and Gender in Late- and Sub-Roman Britain', *TRAC 97, Proceedings of the Seventh Annual Theoretical Roman Archaeology Conference Nottingham*, 112-124

32   Rahtz, P., Wright, S. & Hirst, S. 2000. *Cannington*. London, 422-3, 427; Watts, L. & Leach, P.J. 1996. *Henley Wood, Temples and Cemetery Excavations 1962-69 by the late Ernest Greenfield and others*. York; *PRB*, 32-4, 38, 30-1; Leech, R. 1981. 'The excavation of a Romano-British farmstead and cemetery on Bradley Hill, Somerton, Somerset', *Britannia* 12, 177-252

33   *PRB*, 32-4, 38, 30-1

34   Petts, D. 1998. 'Burial and Gender in Late- and Sub-Roman Britain', *TRAC 97. Proceedings of the Seventh Annual Theoretical Roman Archaeology Conference Nottingham*, 112-124

35   Penney, S. & Shotter, D.A. 1996. 'An inscribed Roman salt-pan from Shavington, Cheshire', *Britannia* 27, 360-364

36   Barker, P. 1974. 'Two burials under the refectory of Worcester cathedral', *Medieval Archaeology* 18, 146-51; *PRB*, 31, 38

37   *Civitas*, 65-7

38   *Contra:* Painter, K. 1999. 'Natives, Roman and Christians at Uley? Questions of continuity of use at sacred sites', *Journal of Roman Archaeology* 12, 694-703, who fails to explain the post-Roman enclosure bank, grass-tempered pottery and other features at the site. The exact plan of the post-Roman church at Uley might be questioned, but it is simply untrue that Roman-period temples were seldom converted into churches elsewhere, as in Sicily (eg Syracuse) and widely in the eastern Mediterranean (eg Aizanoi and Athens). We are insufficiently informed about the origins and nature of Christian practice in fifth-century Britain to dismiss such parallels as wholly irrelevant. There may also be greater evidence for the re-use of temples as churches in Gaul than Painter allows, see *The End*, ch 3. So, the interpretation of the immediate post-temple phase of Uley as a fifth- to sixth-century church surrounded by an enclosure and encompassing domestic and religious activity (proposed by the excavators) should, in my opinion, stand

39   Rahtz, P.A. & Watts, L. 1979. 'The end of Roman temples in the west of Britain' in Casey, P.J. (ed) *The End of Roman Britain*, 183-210. Oxford

40   Colgrave, B. & Mynors, R.A.B. (ed and trans) (3rd ed) 1991. *Bede's Ecclesiastical History of the English People*. Oxford, 141-2

41   The identification of western British monasteries of this date and these specific sites are discussed in: *Discovery*, ch 2

42   Rahtz, P.A. 1971. 'Excavations at Glastonbury Tor, Somerset, 1964-6', *Archaeological Journal* 12, 71-81; Rahtz, P.A. 1993. *Glastonbury*. London, 54-60

43   Sparey-Green, C. 1996. 'Poundbury, Dorset: settlement and economy in Late and Post-Roman Dorchester' in *EC*, 211-52

44   Rahtz, P. 1993. *Glastonbury*. London, 54-60 (57). Note that the only finds — an iron ferrule and patch of wood ash under the cairn — might possibly have been one or more objects (such as a bishop's crozier or pilgrim's staff) being venerated as relics here. Sites in the vicinity are discussed in: Rahtz, P.A. 1993. *Glastonbury*. London, 54-60, 99-100 and 106-9. An early Byzantine leaded brass censer (for incense), dating to the sixth or seventh century, has been found at Silver Street near the later medieval Abbey, but the significance of this to any fifth- and sixth-century ecclesiastical activity at the site and even whether this is a modern or ancient loss, are unclear

45   Woodward, A. & Leach, P. 1993. *The Uley Shrines. Excavation of a Ritual Complex on West Hill, Uley, Gloucestershire: 1977-9*. London, fig 150 and 202-3

46   *Discovery*, 38-50; *PRB*, 31, 38

47   *Discovery*, 46 and 50

48   Implied by *DE*, 1.12 referring to 'feast days' as part of Christian practice

49   The following discussion is based — where not otherwise referenced — on observations in Campbell, E. 1996. 'The archaeological evidence for external contacts: imports, trade and economy in Celtic Britain AD 400-800' in *EC*, 83-96; Campbell, E. 1988. 'The post-Roman pottery' in Edwards, N. & Lane, A. (eds) *Early Medieval Settlement in Wales AD 400-1100*, 124-36. Bangor/Cardiff; Campbell, E. 1989. 'New finds of post-Roman imported pottery and glass from South Wales', *Archaeologia Cambrensis* 138, 59-66; Fulford, M.G. 1989. 'Byzantium and Britain: a Mediterranean perspective on post-Roman Mediterranean imports in western Britain and Ireland', *Medieval Archaeology* 33, 1-6; Rahtz, P.A. et al 1992. *Cadbury Congresbury 1968-73: a late/post-Roman hilltop settlement in Somerset*. Oxford

50   Williams, D. & Carreras, C. 1995. 'North African amphorae in Britain', *Britannia* XXVI, 231-52, where they cautiously note that, in addition to finds from Tintagel and perhaps Dinas Powys, 'North African amphorae recovered from Bush Lane, London, Market Hall, Gloucester and Mucking may possibly have arrived during the fifth century' (240)

51   Campbell, E. 1996. 'Trade in the Dark Age West: a peripheral activity?' in Crawford, B.E. (ed) *Scotland in Dark Age Britain*, 79-92. Aberdeen; Campbell, E. 1996. 'The archaeological evidence for external contacts: imports, trade and economy in Celtic Britain AD 400-800' in *EC*, 83-96; Fulford, M.G. 1989. 'Byzantium and Britain: a Mediterranean perspective on post-Roman Mediterranean imports in western Britain and Ireland', *Medieval Archaeology* 33, 1-6

52 *Ibid*

53 *Ibid* and Wooding, J. 1996. 'Cargoes in trade along the western seaboard' in *EC*, 67-82; Thomas, C. 1990. '"Gallici Nautae de Galliarum Provinciis" — a sixth/seventh-century trade with Gaul, reconsidered', *Medieval Archaeology* 34, 1-26

54 Morris, C.D., Batey, C.E., Brady, K., Harry, R., Johnson, P.G. & Thomas, C. 1999. 'Recent work at Tintagel', *Medieval Archaeology* 43, 206-15

55 Wooding, J. 1996. 'Cargoes in trade along the western seaboard' in *EC*, 67-82

56 Wooding, J. 1996. 'Cargoes in trade along the western seaboard' in *EC*, 67-82 (81)

57 Bowman, A. 1996. 'Post-Roman imported pottery in Britain and Ireland: a maritime perspective' in *EC*, 97-108

58 Olson, L. 1989. *Early Monasteries in Cornwall*. Woodbridge; Greeves, T. 2000. 'Visions in the fog? Dartmoor in the first millennium AD', *Devon Archaeological Society Newsletter* 76, 10-11

59 Bu'Lock, J.D. 1960. 'The Celtic, Saxon and Scandinavian settlement at Meols in Wirral', *Journal of the Historical Society of Lancashire and Cheshire* 122, 1-28

60 Dickinson, T.M. 1982. 'Fowler's Type G penannular brooches reconsidered', *Medieval Archaeology* 26, 41-68; Youngs, S.M. (ed) 1989. *The Work of Angels*. London; Graham-Campbell, J. 1991. 'Dinas Powys metalwork and the dating of enamelled zoomorphic penannular brooches', *Bulletin of the Board of Celtic Studies* 38, 220-32; Youngs, S.M. 1995. 'A penannular brooch from near Calne, Wiltshire', *Wiltshire Archaeological and Natural History Magazine* 88, 127-31. I am grateful to Susan Youngs for discussing a range of issues concerning metalwork of this period with me at length, and providing copies of her unpublished lecture notes on these subjects and a large amount of unpublished information on this topic specifically for this book, with permission to use this material

61 Youngs, S. 1998. 'Medieval hanging bowls from Wiltshire', *Wiltshire Archaeological and Natural History Magazine* 91, 35-41. See also Brennan, J. 1991. *Hanging bowls and their contexts*. Oxford; Geake, H. 1999. 'When were hanging bowls deposited in Anglo-Saxon graves?' *Medieval Archaeology* 43, 1-18

62 Graham-Campbell, J. 1991. 'Dinas Powys metalwork and the dating of enamelled zoomorphic penannular brooches', *Bulletin of the Board of Celtic Studies* 38, 220-32; Alcock, L. 1995. *Cadbury Castle, Somerset: The Early Medieval Archaeology*. Cardiff

63 *Civitas*, 123-5

64 Carver, M. 1987. *Underneath English towns*. London, 42

65 Cool, H.E.M. 2000. 'The parts left over: material culture into the fifth century' in Wilmott, T. & Wilson, P. (eds) *The Late Roman Transition in the North*, 47-65. Oxford

66 Cool *ibid* argues that new fashions begin in very late fourth-century Britain but leaves open the question of how long these persist into the fifth century. She works from well-dated fourth- and early fifth-century contexts forward. Here the approach is to work from well-dated later fifth- and sixth-century deposits, to argue for the continuation of these fashions (perhaps in modified form) until the mid- or late- sixth century at earliest

67 Burrow, I.C.G. 1979. 'Roman material from hillforts' in Casey, P.J. (ed) *The end of Roman Britain*, 212-29. Oxford. As we saw in the introduction, second-century Romano-British brooches could still be worn in, at earliest, the late fourth century — perhaps a fourth-century brooch might have still been worn in the late sixth century

68 Barker, P. et al 1997. *The Baths Basilica Wroxeter*. London, 369-318 — especially chapters 4 and 7

69 Woodward, A. & Leach, P. 1993. *The Uley Shrines. Excavation of a Ritual Complex on West Hill, Uley, Gloucestershire: 1977-9*. London

70 Campbell, E. 1989. 'A blue glass squat jar from Dinas Powys, South Wales', *Bulletin of the Board of Celtic Studies* 36, 239-45; Campbell, E. 1988. 'Dinas Powys' in Edwards, N. & Lane, A. (eds) *Early Medieval Settlement in Wales AD 400-1100*, 58-61. Bangor/Cardiff; Alcock, L. 1987. *Economy, Society and Warfare among the Britons and Saxons*. Cardiff; Alcock, L. 1963. *Dinas Powys. An Iron Age, Dark Age and Early Medieval Settlement in Glamorgan*. Cardiff

71 Rahtz, P.A. et al 1992. *Cadbury Congresbury 1968-73: a late/post-Roman hilltop settlement in Somerset*. Oxford

72 Esmonde-Cleary, S. 1989. *The Ending of Roman Britain*. London, 155-7; Tyers, P. 1996. *Roman pottery in Britain*. London, 180, 192-3

73 Symonds, R.P., with Hassall, M., Tomber, R. White, R. & Wild, P. 1997. 'Roman pottery' in Barker, P. et al *The Baths Basilica Wroxeter*, 369-318. London (for example, the comments on p316 suggest the use of calcite gritted ware and Nene Valley ware in Phase Z (dated by the excavators to the sixth century)). Pottery mended by rivetting is discussed on pp203, 218

74 White, R. & Barker, P. 1998. *Wroxeter. Life and Death of a Roman City*. Stroud, 110-12, 126-8

75 RCAHMW 1976. *Glamorgan vol. I: pre-Norman*. Cardiff, 115 and 118-9

76 Pretty, K. 1997. 'Vessel glass' in Barker, P. et al *The Baths Basilica Wroxeter*, 319-23. London. In conclusion to her analysis of this material, Pretty remarks 'good fourth-century glass continued in use well into the fifth, and possibly sixth, century' (323)

77 Barker, P. et al 1997. *The Baths Basilica Wroxeter*. London, 319-323 (203)

78 *IP*, 148-9

79 *Discovery*, 67-72

80 Woodward, A. & Leach, P. 1993. *The Uley Shrines. Excavation of a Ritual Complex on West Hill, Uley, Gloucestershire: 1977-9*. London
81 *DE*, 1.14. Higham, who considers that the independent British polities of western Britain were ruled by kings, noted the use of the term 'governor' in Gildas' *De Excido* but believes that this refers to subordinate officials to Anglo-Saxon kings, ruling subservient British populations in the east of Britain: Higham, N.J. 1994. *The English Conquest: Gildas and Britain in the Fifth Century*. Manchester/New York, 134, 141, 173, 193
82 *Civitas*, 102-3
83 *Civitas*, 83-6
84 *Discovery*, 95; *Civitas*, 89
85 Alcock, L. 1995. *Cadbury Castle, Somerset: The Early Medieval Archaeology*. Cardiff
86 Burrow, I.C.G. 1981. *Hillfort and hill-top settlement in Somerset in the first-eighth centuries*. Oxford
87 Eagles, B. 1994. 'The archaeological evidence for settlement in the fifth to seventh centuries AD' in Aston, M. & Lewis, C. (eds) *The Medieval Landscape of Wessex*, 13-32. Oxford
88 Hinton, D.A. 1998. *Saxons and Vikings*. Wimborne
89 *Civitas*, 112
90 *Discovery*, 87, 90
91 Alcock, L. 1995. *Cadbury Castle, Somerset: The Early Medieval Archaeology*. Cardiff
92 Petts, D. 1997. 'Elite Settlements in the Roman and Sub-Roman Period', *TRAC 96. Proceedings of the Sixth Annual Theoretical Roman Archaeology Conference Sheffield 1996*. 101-12
93 *Discovery*, 87, 90
94 *DE*, 2.33. Higham's argument that this phrase in *De Excidio* implies an ultimate 'Anglo-Saxon' over-kingship of sixth-century western Britain is unconvincing, given these possibilities and the possibility of a very large British kingdom contemporary with Gildas, located between the Mersey and Hadrian's Wall (see chapter 5 of this book)
95 This could explain Gildas' otherwise puzzling comment that the only fifth-century British ruler praised by name in his work, Ambrosius Aurelianius, was the last member of a Roman *gens* (family) and had parents who had 'worn the purple' (that is, held senior Roman imperial office), and were killed in the 'Saxon revolt' in the late fifth century (*DE*, 1.25). Perhaps Ambrosius' father was the last governor (assuming this remained an exclusively male post, as in the Late Roman Empire) of one of the British provinces. This is likely to have been the only senior imperial office held by one individual at a time in Britain by the mid-fifth century. Given Gildas' probable location, it may, therefore, be just possible that the last governor of Britannia Prima was a member of the Roman *gens* of the Aurelianii
96 Koch, J.T. 1987. 'A Welsh window on the Iron Age: Manawydan, Mandubracios', *CMCS* 14, 17-52; Petts, D. 1999. 'Christianity and the end of Roman Britain' in Baker, P. et al (eds) *TRAC 98*, 86-95. Oxford
97 *Civitas*, 89-91
98 Wilkinson, P.F. 1995. 'Excavations at Hen Gastell, Briton Ferry, West Glamorgan, 1991-92', *Medieval Archaeology* 39, 1-50
99 *Civitas*, ch 5

Chapter 4
1   *Civitas*, 99, 101-2, 134
2   Hilary Cool Pers comm 2000
3   *Civitas*, 118-19
4   Padel, O.J. 1985. *Cornish Place-name Elements*. Nottingham, especially 226
5   Dark, K.R. 1999. *The early British court*. London
6   *Landscape*, 85-8
7   Johnson, N. & Rose, P. 1982. 'Defended settlement in Cornwall — an illustrated discussion' in Miles, D. (ed) *The Romano-British Countryside: Studies in Rural Settlement and Economy*, 151-207. Oxford
8   *Discovery*, 80-6; Harry, R. & Morris, C.A. 1997. 'Excavations on the Lower Terrace, Site C, Tintagel Island 1990-94', *Antiquaries Journal*, 77, 1-143; Thomas, C. 1993. *Tintagel. Arthur and Archaeology*. London; Nowakowski, J. & Thomas, C. 1990. *Tintagel Churchyard. Excavations at Tintagel Parish Church, North Cornwall, Spring 1990. An Interim Report*. Truro; Nowakowski, J. & Thomas, C. 1992. *Grave News from Tintagel. An Illustrated Account of Archaeological Excavations at Tintagel Churchyard, Cornwall 1991*. Truro; Morris, C.D., Batey, C.E., Brady, K., Harry, R., Johnson, P.G. & Thomas, C. 1999. 'Recent work at Tintagel', *Medieval Archaeology* 43, 206-15; Dark, K.R. 1985. 'The plan and interpretation of Tintagel', *CMCS* 9, 1-17
9   Rahtz, P., Wright, S. & Hirst, S. 2000. *Cannington*. London, 45-57, 407, 414
10 Dark, K.R. 1998. 'Centuries of survival in the west', *British Archaeology* 32, 8-9; Dark, K.R. 1998. 'Centuries of survival in the west', *British Archaeology*
11 The best general work on these inscribed stones is: Okasha, E. 1993. *Corpus of early Christian inscribed stones in south-west Britain*. London. For Lundy: Thomas, C. 1994. *And Shall These Mute Stones Speak? Post-Roman Inscriptions in Western Britain*. Cardiff

12 Rahtz, P., Wright, S. & Hirst, S. 2000. *Cannington*. London; Editor, 1996. 'Ancient cemetery discovered', *Devon Archaeological Society Newsletter* 65, 1-2; Editor, 1997. 'Archaeology in Devonshire', *Devon Archaeological Society Newsletter* 68, 4

13 Mytum, H. 1992. *The origins of early Christian Ireland*. London and New York; Laing, L. 1985. 'The Romanization of Ireland in the fifth century', *Peritia* 4, 261-78. On British missionary work in fifth- and sixth-century Ireland: Sharpe, R. 1989. '*Quator sanctissimi episcopi*: Irish saints before St. Patrick' in O Corrain, D. et al (eds) *Sages, saints and storytellers*. Maynooth; Sharpe, R. 1990. 'Saint Mauchteus, disciplus Patricii' in Bammesburger, A. and Wollmann, A. (eds) *Britain 400-600: language and history*, 85-93. Heidelburg; Dumville, D.N. 1993. 'British missionary activity in Ireland' in Dumville, D.N. et al *Saint Patrick AD 493-1991*, 133-45. Woodbridge; Charles-Edwards, T.M. 1999. 'Britons in Ireland c.550-800' in Carey, J. et al (eds) *Ildanach Ildirech*, 15-26. Andover and Aberystwyth

14 Preston-Jones, A. 1992. 'Decoding Cornish churchyards' in *E.Ch.*, 104-24

15 *DE*, 2.28; Hollinrake, N. & C. pers comm 1998; Olson, L. 1989. *Early Monasteries in Cornwall*. Woodbridge

16 Preston-Jones, A. 1992. 'Decoding Cornish churchyards' in *E.Ch.*, 104-24; Olson, L. 1989. *Early Monasteries in Cornwall*. Woodbridge

17 Petts, D. forthcoming 'The development of enclosed churchyards in western Britain'. I am very grateful to David Petts for allowing me access to the text of this paper prior to publication

18 Boon, G.C. 1991. 'Byzantine and other exotic Ancient bronze coins from Exeter' in Holbrook, N. and Bidwell, P.T. (eds) *Roman Finds from Exeter*, 38-45. Exeter

19 Display in Royal Institution of Cornwall Museum, Truro 1999; Philpott, R.A. 1998. 'Three Byzantine coins found near the north Wirral coast in Merseyside', *Transactions of the Historical Society of Lancashire and Cheshire* 148, 197-202

20 For many of these dedications: Bowen, E.G. 1956. *The settlements of the Celtic saints in Wales*. Cardiff

21 The shrine of St Ia at Constantinople was rebuilt by Justinian I in the early sixth century, according to Procopius 'Buildings' I.ix

22 Dumville, D.N. *The Insular churches in the Age of the Saints*. O'Donnell Lecture, unpublished. I am grateful to Susan Youngs for telling me about Ragnall O'Floinn's work, presented at conferences and awaiting publication by him: S. Youngs, pers comm 2000

23 This is a key theme of *Discovery*. Charles-Edwards, T. 1989. 'Early Medieval kingships in the British Isles' in *OAK*, 28-39

24 *Discovery*, chapters 3 and 4. 'Anglo-Saxon' metalwork has been found at Denbury: J. Hines pers comm 1999

25 *Civitas*, 155-6

26 Hughes, K. 1966. *The Church in early Irish society*. London

27 *Civitas*, 192

28 Dark, K.R. 1999. *The early British court*. London

29 Olson, L. 1989. *Early Monasteries in Cornwall*. Woodbridge, 16

30 Dark, K.R. 1993. 'Roman-period activity at prehistoric ritual monuments in Britain and Armorica', *TRAC* Aldershot, 133-46; *The End*, 140-1; *PRB*, 60

31 Page, W. 1924. *A history of the county of Cornwall* (part 5). London, illustration on page 6. Griffith, F.M. 1986. 'Salvage observations at the Dark Age site at Bantham Ham, Thurlestone, in 1982', *Proceedings of the Devon Archaeological Society* 44, 39-57; Fox, A. 1955. 'Some evidence for a Dark Age trading site at Bantham', *Antiquaries Journal* 35, 55-67; Silvester, R. 1981. 'Excavations on the post-Roman site at Bantham', *Proceedings of the Devon Archaeological Society* 39, 89-118; Thomas, A.C. 1958. *Gwithian Ten Years Work (1949-59)*. Gwithian

32 Thomas, C. 1971. *Britain and Ireland in Early Christian Times AD 400-800*. London, 21

33 Herring, P. 1993. *St Michael's Mount*. Truro; Rose, P. 1999. 'County Archaeologist's Summaries. Cornwall', *CBA South West* 2 (Spring 1999), 36

35 Preston-Jones, A. & Rose, P.G. 1986. 'Medieval Cornwall', *Cornish Archaeology* 25, 135-85; Simpson, S.J., Griffith, F.M. & Holbrook, N. 1989. 'The prehistoric, Roman and early post-Roman site at Hayes Farm, Clyst Honiton', *Proceedings of the Devon Archaeological Society* 47, 1-28; Reed, S. 1997. 'First investigation of a Blackdowns Iron Pit', *Devon Archaeological Society Newsletter* 67, 1; Editor, 1997. 'Possible Dark Age date for Blackdowns iron pit', *Devon Archaeological Society Newsletter* 69, 12

36 First suggested in *Civitas*, 92-4

37 Holbrook, N. & Bidwell, P.T. (eds) 1991. *Roman Finds from Exeter*. Exeter

38 *Landscape*, 82-4

39 *Civitas*, 42-3, 98-9

40 *Landscape*, 82-4; Longley, D. 1998. 'Bryn Eryr: an enclosed settlement of the iron Age on Anglesey', *Proceedings of the Prehistoric Society* 64, 225-73; Kelly, R.S 1990. 'Recent research on the hut-group settlements of North-West Wales' in Burnham, B.C. and Davis, J.L. (eds) *Conquest, co-existence and change*, 102-11. Lampeter

41 Casey, P.J. & Davies, J.L. with Evans, J. 1993. *Excavations at Segontium (Caernarfon) Roman Fort, 1975-1979*. London

42 *Discovery*, 76-9

43 Baynes, E.N. 1908. 'The excavations at Din Lligwy', *Archaeologia Cambrensis* 6.8, 183-210; Baynes, E.N. 1930.

'Further excavations at Din Lligwy', *Archaeologia Cambrensis* 85, 375-93; Fasham, P.J., Kelly, R.S., Masson, M.A. & White, R.B. 1998. *The Graenog Ridge: The Evolution of a Farming Landscape and its Settlements in North-West Wales*. Aberystwyth, 28-9, 93-4, 136-7, 164, 130-5

44 I am grateful to the excavator of Glyn, Mark Redknap, for providing detailed comments and photographs of the site in addition to the published material, for this book

45 Kelly, R.S 1990. 'Recent research on the hut-group settlements of North-West Wales' in Burnham, B.C. and Davis, J.L. (eds) *Conquest, co-existence and change*, 102-11. Lampeter; Dark, S.P. 1996. 'Palaeoecological evidence for landscape continuity and change in Britain *c.* AD 400-800' in *EC*, 23-51. See also *Landscape*, 143-4; Dark, P. 2000. *The Environment of Britain in the First Millennium A.D.* London, 150-4

46 James, H. 1992. 'Early medieval cemeteries in Wales' in *E.Ch.*, 90-103

47 James, H. 1992. 'Early medieval cemeteries in Wales' In *E.Ch.*, 90-103; Denison, S. 1999. 'Christian graves around adapted barrow', *British Archaeology* (September) 5, on which the following account is based

48 Dark, K.R. 1993. 'Roman-period activity at prehistoric ritual monuments in Britain and the Armorican peninsula' in *TRAC*, 133-46

49 *DE*, 2.3; in *DE*, 3.108 there are what may be hints of the use of Roman-style medical practices in mid-sixth century western Britain

50 *Civitas*, 156-7

51 Hogg, A.H.A. 1969. 'Pen Llystyn: a Roman Fort and other Remains', *Archaeological Journal* 125, 101-92; *Discovery*, 99; *The End*, 137-40; Crew, P. & S. 1997. 'Geophysical Survey at Llanfor, Merioneth, 1997', *Archaeology in Wales* 37, 13-20

52 Dark, K.R. 1999. *The early British court*. London

52 *DE*, 2.34; *Civitas*, 76-8, 110-12, 118-9, 130

53 *DE*, 2.33

54 Gruffydd, R.G. 1990. 'From Gododdin to Gwynedd: reflections on the story of Cunedda', *Studia Celtica* 24/25 (1989/1990), 1-14; Gruffydd, R.G. 1994. 'In search of Elmet', *Studia Celtica* 28, 63-79

55 Brassil, K.S., Owen, W.G. & Britnell, W.J. 1992. 'Prehistoric and early medieval cemeteries at Tandderwen, near Denbigh, Clwyd', *Archaeological Journal* 148 (1991), 46-97

56 *Civitas*, 98

57 Burnham, B. 1993. 'I. Wales', *Britannia* 24, 269-76 (71 and 73)

58 Manley, J., Grenter, S. & Gale, F. (eds) 1991. *The Archaeology of Clwyd*. Clwyd; *Discovery*, 76, 141; Gardner, W. & Savory, H. 1964. *Dinorben. A Hillfort Occupied in Early Iron Age and Roman Times*. Cardiff

59 Edwards, N. 1991. 'The Dark Ages' in Manley, J., Grenter, S. & Gale, F. (eds) *The Archaeology of Clwyd*, 129-41. Clwyd; *The End*, 161-2

60 *Civitas*, 98, 118

61 *Discovery*, 76

62 James, T.A. 1985. 'Excavations at the Augustinian Priory of St John and St Teulyddog, Carmarthen 1979', *Archaeologia Cambrensis* 134, 120-61; *Landscape*, 85

63 Campbell, E. 1990. 'Carew Castle', *Archaeology in Wales* 30, 69; Gerrard, S. 1990. 'Excavations during 1990 Bastion', *Carew Castle Archaeological Project Newsletter* 3, 2-5; *Discovery*, 73; Crane, P. 1998. 'Porth y Rhaw, Solva', *Archaeology in Wales* 38, 124-5

64 *Discovery*, 73, 75-6; Williams, G. & Mytum, H. (ed by K. Blockley) 1998. *Llawhaden, Dyfed*. Oxford

65 This and the following paragraph are based on James, H. 1992. 'Early medieval cemeteries in Wales' in *E.Ch.*, 90-103; James, T.A. 1992. 'Air photography of ecclesiastical sites in South Wales' in *E.Ch.*, 62-76; James, H. 1997. 'Llandysilio Church and Parish 500-1543: from heartland to borderland', *Carmarthenshire Antiquary* 33, 5-261. I am grateful to Heather James for providing written comment regarding Welsh cemeteries for this book

66 *Discovery*, 91-3

67 Campbell, E. & Lane, A. 1993. 'Excavations at Longbury Bank, Dyfed, and early medieval settlement in South Wales', *Medieval Archaeology* 37, 15-77

68 Charles-Edwards, T. 1971. 'The seven bishop-houses of Dyfed', *Bulletin of the Board of Celtic Studies* 24, 247-62

69 *DE*, 2.31; Hamp, E. 1996. 'Vortiporis protictoris', *Studia Celtica* 30, 293; Richards, M. 1960. 'The Irish settlements in south-west Wales — a topographical approach', *Journal of the Royal Society of Antiquaries of Ireland* 90, 133-52; *Discovery*, ch 2

70 *Civitas*, 192-3; Evans, D.S. 1979. 'Irish and the languages of post-Roman Wales', *Studies* 68, 19-32

71 James, H. 1987. 'Excavations at Caer, Bayvil 1979', *Archaeologia Cambrensis* 136, 51-76

72 McManus, D. 1991. *An introduction to Ogam*. Maynooth

73 Alcock, L. (2nd ed) 1989. *Arthur's Britain*. Harmondsworth, 123-4

74 *Civitas*, 79-83

75 *Civitas*, 83; Murphy, K. 1993. 'Plas Gogerddan, Dyfed: a multi-period burial and ritual site', *Archaeological Journal* 149 (1992), 1-38

76 *Civitas*, 118

77 *Civitas*, 79-83

247

Chapter 5

1   Ottaway, P. 1993. *Roman York*. London; Bidwell, P. (ed) 1999. *Hadrian's Wall 1989-1999*. Carlisle

2   *PRB*, 62-70; Miket, R. 1980. 'A restatement of evidence for Bernician Anglo-Saxon burials' in Rahtz, P. et al (eds) *Anglo-Saxon Cemeteries, 1979*, 289-305. Oxford; Lucy, S. 1999. 'Changing Burial Rites in Northumbria AD 500-750' in Hawkes, J. & Mills, S. (eds) *Northumbria's Golden Age*, 12-43. Stroud; Sherlock, S.J. & Welch, M.G. 1992. *An Anglo-Saxon Cemetery at Norton, Cleveland*. London

3   Dark, K.R. 1992. 'A sub-Roman re-defence of Hadrian's Wall?', *Britannia* 23, 111-20; Dark, K. & Dark. S.P. 1997. 'New archaeological and palaeoecological evidence for a sub-Roman reoccupation of Hadrian's Wall', *Archaeologia Aeliana* XXIV, 57-72; Dark, K.R. 2000. 'The Late Roman Transition in the North: a discussion' in Wilmott, T. & Wilson, P. (eds) *The Late Roman Transition in the North*, 81-88. Oxford

4   Dark, K.R. 2000. 'The Late Roman Transition in the North: a discussion' in Wilmott, T. & Wilson, P. (eds) *The Late Roman Transition in the North*, 81-88. Oxford

5   Dark, K. & Dark, S.P. 1997. 'New archaeological and palaeoecological evidence for a sub-Roman reoccupation of Hadrian's Wall', *Archaeologia Aeliana* XXIV, 57-72

6   Keevill, G.D., Shotter, D. & McCarthy, M. 1989. 'A *solidus* of Valentinian II from Scotch Street Carlisle', *Britannia* 20, 254-5

7   Dark, K.R. 1992. 'A sub-Roman re-defence of Hadrian's Wall?', *Britannia* 23, 111-20; Dark, K. & Dark. S.P. 1997. 'New archaeological and palaeoecological evidence for a sub-Roman reoccupation of Hadrian's Wall', *Archaeologia Aeliana* XXIV, 57-72. The possible 'bucket binding' found at Goldsborough is illustrated by Cool, H.E.M. 2000. 'The parts left over: material culture into the fifth century' in Wilmott, T. and Wilson, P. (eds) *The Late Roman Transition in the North*, 47-65 (59 and 62). Oxford

8   Dark, K.R. 1992. 'A sub-Roman re-defence of Hadrian's Wall?', *Britannia* 23, 111-20; Dark, K. & Dark. S.P. 1997. 'New archaeological and palaeoecological evidence for a sub-Roman reoccupation of Hadrian's Wall', *Archaeologia Aeliana* XXIV, 57-72; Dark, K.R. 2000. 'The Late Roman Transition in the North: a discussion', in Wilmott, T. & Wilson, P. (eds) *The Late Roman Transition in the North*, 81-88. Oxford

9   Wilmott, T. 2000. 'The Late Roman transition in Birdoswald and on Hadrian's wall' in Wilmott, T. & Wilson, P. (eds) *The Late Roman Transition in the North*, 13-23. Oxford

10   Dark, K.R. 2000. 'The Late Roman Transition in the North: a discussion' in Wilmott, T. & Wilson, P. (eds) *The Late Roman Transition in the North*, 81-88. Oxford

11   Wilmott, T. 1997. *Birdoswald: excavation on a Roman fort on Hadrian's Wall and its successor settlements 1987-92*. London; Wilmott, T. 2000. 'The Late Roman transition in Birdoswald and on Hadrian's wall' in Wilmott, T. & Wilson, P. (eds) *The Late Roman Transition in the North*, 13-23. Oxford

12   For earrings in Roman Britain: Allason-Jones, L. 1989. *Ear-rings in Roman Britain*. Oxford

13   *Civitas*, 65,74; Ottaway, P. 1993. *Roman York*. London, 111-7; Monaghan, J. 1997. *Roman pottery from York*. York, 971-3, 1043, 1050, 1138, 1147-8; Phillips, D. & Heywood, B. 1995. *Excavations at York Minster volume I: from Roman fortress to Norman cathedral*. Swindon

14   *Civitas*, 72-3

15   Dark, K.R. 2000. 'The Late Roman Transition in the North: a discussion' in Wilmott, T. & Wilson, P. (eds) *The Late Roman Transition in the North*, 81-88. Oxford

16   Smith, I. 1996. 'The archaeology of the early Christian Church in Scotland & Man AD 400-1200' in Blair, J. & Pyrah, C. (eds) *Church Archaeology. Research Directions for the Future*. York

17   *PRB*, 62-70. Kenyon, D. 1991. *The origins of Lancashire*. Manchester and New York, 63, notes possible 'sub-Roman cemeteries' at Winnick (overlying a prehistoric barrow), Roosebeck and elsewhere

18   *PRB*, 30-39

19   O'Sullivan, D.M. 1996. 'Six pagan Anglian burials from Cumbria' in Griffiths, D. (ed.) *Anglo-Saxon Studies in Archaeology and History* 9, 15-24. Oxford

20   I am grateful to the excavator, Tove Oliver, for discussing the site in detail and allowing me to examine the relevant finds. The published report is Lambert, J. 1996. *Transect through Time*. Lancaster. Both the account of Fremington and Fremington ware pottery below is based on the published information and my own observations

21   Hutchinson, G. 1979. 'The bar-lug pottery of Cornwall', *Cornish Archaeology* 18, 81-104

22   Baldwin, J. 1997. *Edinburgh, Lothians and the Borders*. Edinburgh; Driscoll, S.T. 1997. *Excavations at Edinburgh castle in 1988-91*. Edinburgh; Alexander, D. 1997. 'Excavation on Arthur's Seat fort, Edinburgh, 1995', *Proceedings of the Society of Antiquaries of Scotland* 127, 595-600

23   Smith, I. 1996. 'The archaeology of the early Christian Church in Scotland & Man AD 400-1200' in Blair, J. & Pyrah, C. (eds) *Church Archaeology. Research Directions for the Future*. York; Thomas, C. 1992. 'The early Christian inscriptions of southern Scotland', *Glasgow Archaeological Journal* 17, 1-10

24   Cowie, T.E. 1978. 'Excavations at the Catstane, Midlothian 1977', *Proceedings of the Society of Antiquaries of Scotland* 109, 166-201; Petts, D. 1998. 'Burial and Gender in Late- and Sub-Roman Britain', *TRAC 97. Proceedings of the Seventh Annual Theoretical Roman Archaeology Conference Nottingham*, 112-124

25   This and the following paragraph draw on data in Smith, I. 1996. 'The archaeology of the early Christian Church in Scotland & Man AD 400-1200' in Blair J. & Pyrah, C. (eds) *Church Archaeology. Research Directions for the Future*. York; *PRB* 40

26 The most recent account of these chains is Breeze, A. 1998. 'Pictish chains and Welsh forgeries', *Proceedings of the Society of Antiquaries of Scotland* 128, 481-4

27 Fowler, E. 1955. 'A catalogue and survey of the metalwork from Traprain Law', *Proceedings of the Society of Antiquaries of Scotland* LXXXIX, 118-221; Smith, I. 1996. 'The archaeology of the early Christian Church in Scotland & Man AD 400-1200' in Blair, J. & Pyrah, C. (eds) *Church Archaeology. Research Directions for the Future*. York

28 Koch, J.T. 1997. (ed) *The Gododdin of Aneirin*. Cardiff, 180

29 Smith, I. 1984. 'Patterns of Settlement and Land Use of the Late Anglian Period in the Tweed Basin' in Faull, M.L. (ed) *Studies in Late Anglo-Saxon Settlement*, 177-96. Oxford; Alcock, L. 1988. (Jarrow Lecture) *Bede, Eddis, and the Forts of the North Britons*; Alcock, L. 1993. *The Neighbours of the Picts: Angles, Britons and Scots at War and at Home*. Dornoch, Rosemarkie; Hope-Taylor, B. 1960. 'Report on Bamburgh excavations', *University of Durham Gazette* (Dec 1960), 11-12; Hope-Taylor, B. 1962. 'Report on Bamburgh excavations', *University of Durham Gazette* (March 1962), 5-6; Alcock, L., Alcock, E.A. & Foster, S.M. 1986. 'Reconnaissance excavations on Early Historic fortifications and other royal sites in Scotland, 1974-84: excavations near St Abb's Head, Berwickshire, 1980', *Proceedings of the Society of Antiquaries of Scotland* 116, 255-79

30 Holdsworth, P. 1991. 'Dunbar', *Current Archaeology* 127, 315-7; Holdsworth, P. 1993. 'Excavations at Castle Park, Dunbar: an interim report on the Anglian evidence', *Transactions of the East Lothian Antiquarian and Field Naturalists Society* 22, 31-52

31 Alcock, L. 1993. *The Neighbours of the Picts: Angles, Britons and Scots at War and at Home*. Dornoch, Rosemarkie, 20-1

32 Smith, I. 1991. 'Sprouston, Roxburghshire: an early Anglian centre in the eastern Tweed Basin', *Proceedings of the Society of Antiquaries of Scotland* 121, 261-94

33 Alcock, L. 1993. *The Neighbours of the Picts: Angles, Britons and Scots at War and at Home*. Dornoch, Rosemarkie, 27, 29-30

34 Alcock, L. 1993. *The Neighbours of the Picts: Angles, Britons and Scots at War and at Home*. Dornoch, Rosemarkie, 24-5; O'Brien, C. & Miket, R. 1991. 'The early medieval settlement of Thirlings, Northumberland', *Durham Archaeological Journal* 7, 57-91

35 Hope-Taylor, B. 1977. *Yeavering: An Anglo-British Centre of Early Northumbria*. London; Scull, C.J. 1991. 'Post-Roman Phase I at Yeavering: A Re-consideration', *Medieval Archaeology* XXXV, 51-63

36 Hill, P. 1997. *Whithorn and St Ninian. The Excavation of a Monastic Town 1984-91*. Stroud

37 *Ibid* 12, 28-9, 260-1

38 Brooke, D. 1999. *Saints and Goddesses: The Interface with Celtic Paganism*. Whithorn

39 *PRB* 39; Lowe, C.E. 1991. 'New light on the Anglian "Minster" at Hoddom', *Transactions of the Dumfriesshire and Galloway Natural History and Antiquarian Society*, 3rd ser, 66, 11-35

40 Longley, D. forthcoming, 'The Mote of Mark: the archaeological context for the decorated metalwork'. I am grateful to David Longley for making this paper available to me prior to publication

41 Cessford, C. 1994. 'Pictish Raiders at Trusty's Hill?', *Transactions of the Dumfriesshire and Galloway Natural History and Antiquity Society* 69, 81-88

43 Stevenson, J.B. 1995. *Glasgow, Clydesdale and Stirling*. Edinburgh; Wilson, A. 1995. 'Roman Penetration in Strathclyde South of the Antonine Wall. Part one: The Topographical Framework', *Glasgow Archaeological Journal* 19, 1-30; Wilson A. 1997. 'Roman Penetration in Strathclyde South of the Antonine Wall. Part two: Romanization', *Glasgow Archaeological Journal* 20, 1-40

44 Alcock, L. & Alcock, E.A. 1990. 'Reconnaissance excavations on Early Historic fortifications and other royal sites in Scotland, 1974-84: excavations at Alt Clut, Clyde Rock, Strathclyde, 1974-5', *Proceedings of the Society of Antiquaries of Scotland* 120, 95-149

45 Pers comm E. Campbell 2000

46 Crone, A. 1991. 'Buiston', *Current Archaeology* 127, 295-7; Crone, A. 1998. 'The development of an Early Historic tree-ring chronology for Scotland', *Proceedings of the Society of Antiquaries of Scotland* 128, 485-493

47 Anderson, M.O. 1982. 'Dalriada and the creation of the Kingdom of the Scots' in Dumville, D., McKitterick R. & Whitelock, D. (eds) *Ireland in Early Medieval Europe*, 106-32. Cambridge; Broun, D. 2000. 'The Seven Pictish provinces and the origins of Alba' in Cowan, E.J. & McDonald, R.A. (eds) *Alba: Celtic Scotland in the Medieval Era*. East Linton; Broun, D. 'The origin of Scottish identity' in Bjorn, C., Grant, A. & Stringer, K.J. (eds) *Nations, nationalism and patriotism in the European past*, 35-55. Copenhagen

48 Foster, S.M. 1992. 'The state of Pictland in the Age of Sutton Hoo' in Carver, M. (ed) *The Age of Sutton Hoo*, 217-34. Woodbridge; Foster, S.M. 1996. *Picts, Gaels and Scots*. London

49 Anderson, M.O. 1987. 'Picts the name and the people' in Small, A. (ed) *The Picts. A New Look at an Old Problem*, 7-14. Dundee

50 Nicolaisen, W.F.H. 1996. *The Picts and their Place Names*. Rosemarkie; Sharpe, R. (trans) 1995. *Adomnan of Iona: Life of St Columba*. London/New York

51 For overviews of the archaeological evidence for the Picts: Foster, S.M. 1992. 'The state of Pictland in the Age of Sutton Hoo' in Carver, M. (ed) *The Age of Sutton Hoo*, 217-34. Woodbridge; Foster, S.M. 1996. *Picts, Gaels and Scots*. London; Small, A. (ed) 1987. *The Picts: a New Look at Old Problems*. Dundee; Friell, J.P.G. & Watson, W.G. (eds) 1984. *Pictish Studies: Settlements, Burial and Art in Dark Age Northern Britain*. Oxford; Carver, M. 1999. *Surviving in Symbols. A Visit to the Pictish Nation*. Edinburgh

52 Foster, S.M. 1996. *Picts, Gaels and Scots*. London, ch 4; Hunter, J. 1997. *A Persona for the Northern Picts*. Rosemarkie; Alcock, L. 1984. 'A survey of Pictish settlement archaeology' in Friell J.G.P. & Watson, W.G. (eds) *Pictish Studies. Settlement, Burial and Art in Dark Age Northern Britain*, 7-41. Oxford; Alcock, L. 1979. 'The north Britons, the Picts and the Scots' in Casey P.J. (ed) *The End of Roman Britain*, 134-42. Oxford

53 Hood, A.B.E. (ed and trans) 1978. *St. Patrick. His Writings and Muirchu's Life*. London/Chichester, *Epistola 2*, 15

54 *PRB*, 40-2

55 Alcock, E.A. 1992. 'Burials and cemeteries in Scotland' in *E.Ch.*, 125-30; Close-Brooks, J. 1984. 'Pictish and other burials' in Friell, J.G.P. & Watson, W.G. (eds) *Pictish Studies. Settlement, Burial and Art in Dark Age Northern Britain*, 87-114. Oxford; Ashmore, P. 1980. 'Low cairns, long cists and symbol stones', *Proceedings of the Society of Antiquaries of Scotland* 110, 346-355

56 Ritchie, A. 1989. *Picts. An Introduction to the Life of the Picts and the Carved Stones in care of the Secretary of State*. Edinburgh; Hicks, C. 1991. 'The Pictish Class I Animals' in Spearman, R.M. & Higgitt, J. (eds) *The Age of Migrating Ideas*, 196-202. Edinburgh; RCAHMS 1999. *Pictish Symbol Stones: an illustrated gazetteer*; Jackson, A. 1984. *The Symbol Stones of Scotland: A Social Anthropological Resolution of the Problem of the Picts*. Kirkwall; Stevenson, R.B.K. 1980. 'Pictish art' in Wainwright, F.T. (ed) *The Problem of the Picts* (2nd ed), 97-128. Edinburgh/Perth; Alcock, E.A. 1988-9. 'Pictish stones Class 1: where and how', *Glasgow Archaeological Journal* 15, 1-21

57 Samson, R. 1992. 'The reinterpretation of Pictish symbols', *Journal of the British Archaeological Association* 145, 29-65

58 This and the following paragraph are based on: Foster, S.M. 1996. *Picts, Gaels and Scots*. London, 75-8

59 Graham-Campbell, J. 1991. 'The Norries Law Hoard and the Dating of Pictish Silver' in Spearman, R.M. & Higgitt, J. (eds) *The Age of Migrating Ideas*, 115-7. Edinburgh

60 Edwards, K.J. & Ralston, I.B.M. 1978. 'New dating and environmental evidence from Burghead fort, Moray', *Proceedings of the Society of Antiquaries of Scotland* 109, 202-10; Small, A. 1969. 'Burghead', *Scottish Archaeological Forum* 1, 61-8; Foster, S.M. 1996. *Picts, Gaels and Scots*. London, 43-4

61 Ritchie, J., Graham, N. & Stevenson, J.N. 1991. 'Pictish cave art at East Wemyss, Fife' in Spearman, R.M. & Higgitt, J. (eds) *The Age of Migrating Ideas*, 203-8. Edinburgh

62 Foster, S.M. 1996. *Picts, Gaels and Scots*. London, 75

63 Alcock, L. & Alcock, E.A. 1990. 'Reconnaissance excavations on Early Historic fortifications and other royal sites in Scotland, 1974-84: 5A, Excavations & other fieldwork at Forteviot, Perthshire, 1981; B, Excavations at Urquhart Castle, Inverness-shire, 1983; C, Excavations at Dunnottar, Kincardineshire, 1984', *Proceedings of the Society of Antiquaries of Scotland* 122, 215-87; Hughson, I. 1997. 'Horses in the Early Historic Period: Evidence from the Pictish Sculptured Stones' in Davies, S. & Jones, N.A. (eds) *The Horse in Celtic Culture: Medieval Welsh Perspectives*, 23-42. Cardiff

64 For this and the following two paragraphs: Trench-Jellicoe, R. 1998. 'The Skeith stone, Upper Kilrenny, Fife, in its context', *Proceedings of the Society of Antiquaries of Scotland* 128, 495-513; Proudfoot, E. 1996. 'Excavations at the long cist cemetery on the Hallow Hill, St Andrew's, Fife, 1975-7', *Proceedings of the Society of Antiquaries of Scotland* 126, 387-454; Foster, S.M. 1996. *Picts, Gaels and Scots*. London, 79

65 Alcock, L., Alcock, E. & Driscoll, S.T. 1989. 'Reconnaissance excavations on early historic fortifications and other royal sites in Scotland, 1974-84: 3: Excavation at Dundurn, Strathearn, Perthshire, 1976-77', *Proceedings of the Society of Antiquaries of Scotland* 119, 189-226; Close-Brooks, J. 1986. 'Excavations at Clatchard Craig, Fife', *Proceedings of the Society of Antiquaries of Scotland* 116, 117-84; Alcock, L. 1981. 'Early historic fortifications in Scotland' in Guilbert, G. (ed) *Hill-fort Studies*, 150-81. Leicester; Alcock, L. 1984. 'A survey of Pictish settlement archaeology' in Friell, J.G.P. & Watson, W.G. (eds) *Pictish Studies. Settlement, Burial and Art in Dark Age Northern Britain*, 7-41. Oxford; Foster, S.M. 1998. 'Before *Alba*: Pictish and Dal Riata power centres from the fifth to the late ninth centuries AD' in Foster, S., Macinnes A. & Macinnes, R. (eds) *Scottish Power Centres from the Early Middle Ages to the Twentieth Century*, 1-31. Glasgow; Ralston, I. 1980. 'The Green Castle and the promontory forts of north-east Scotland' in Thomas, L.M. (ed) *Settlements in Scotland 1000 BC-AD 1000*, 27-40. Edinburgh; Ralston, I. 1987. 'Porthknockie: promontory forts and Pictish settlements in the north-east' in Small, A. (ed) *The Picts: A New Look at Old Problems*, 15-26. Dundee

66 Sharples, N. 1998. *Scalloway: a broch, Late Iron Age settlement and medieval cemetery in Shetland*. Oxford; Armit, I (ed) 1990. *Beyond the brochs*. Edinburgh

67 For this and the following paragraph: Forsyth, K. 1997. *Language in Pictland*. Studia Hameliana 2; Forsyth, K. 1995. 'Language in Pictland, Spoken and Written' in Nicoll, E. (ed) *A Pictish Panorama*, 7-10. Balgavies, Angus; Forsyth, K. 1995. 'The ogam-inscribed spindlewhorl from Buckquoy: evidence for the Irish language in pre-Viking Orkney', *Proceedings of the Society of Antiquaries of Scotland* 125, 677-96

68 Anderson, M.O. (rev ed) 1980. *Kings and kingship in early Scotland*. Edinburgh; Bannerman, J. 1974. *Studies in the History of Dalriada*. Edinburgh/London; Duncan, A. 1975 *Scotland. The making of the kingdom*. Edinburgh, ch 3

69 Ritchie, A. 1987. 'The Picto-Scottish interface in material culture' in Small, A. (ed) *The Picts. A New Look at and Old Problem*, 59-67. Dundee

70 Ritchie, G. & Ritchie, A. 1991. *Scotland: Archaeology and Early History*. Edinburgh

71 Ritchie, G. (ed) 1997. *The Archaeology of Argyll*. Edinburgh; Ritchie, G. & Harman, M. 1996. *Argyll and the*

Western Isles. Edinburgh; Campbell, E. 1999. *Saints and Sea-kings. The First Kingdom of the Scots*. Edinburgh; Ritchie, G. 1996. *Argyll and the Western Isles* Edinburgh; Armit, I. 1996. *The Archaeology of Skye and the Western Isles*. Edinburgh

72   Campbell, E. & Lane, A. 1991. 'Celtic and Germanic Interaction in Dalriada: The Seventh-Century Metalworking Site at Dunadd' in Spearman, R.M. & Higgitt, J. (eds) *The Age of Migrating Ideas*, 52-63. Edinburgh; Nieke, M.R. & Duncan, H.B. 1988. 'Dalriada: the establishment and maintenance of an early historic kingdom in northern Britain' in Driscoll, S.T. & Nieke, M.R. (eds) *Power and Politics in Early Medieval Britain and Ireland*, 6-21. Edinburgh; Campbell, E. & Lane, A. forthcoming. *Excavation at Dunadd: an early Dalriadic capital*. Oxford

73   Scott, J.G. 1961. 'The excavation of a crannog at Loch Glashan, Mid Argyll', *Archaeological News Letter* 7.1, 20-1

74   This account of the site is based on Sharpe, R. (trans) 1995. *Adomnan of Iona: Life of St Columba*. London/New York; MacDonald, A. 1997. 'Adomnan's Monastery at Iona, 24-44' and McCormick, F. 'Iona: the archaeology of the early monastery, 45-68' both in Bourke, C. (ed) *Studies in the cult of Saint Columba*. Dublin

75   Fisher, I. 1997. 'Early Christian archaeology of Argyll' in Ritchie, G. (ed) *The Archaeology of Argyll*. Edinburgh; Ritchie, G. & Harman, M. 1996. *Argyll and the Western Isles*,181-20. Edinburgh; Foster, S.M. 1996. *Picts, Gaels and Scots*. London, 84-5; Fisher, I. 1996. 'The west of Scotland' in Blair, J. & Pyrah, C. (eds) *Church Archaeology. Research directions for the future*, 37-41. York

76   Laing, L. & Longley, D. 1998. 'The early Christian and later medieval ecclesiastical site at St Blane's, Kingarth, Bute', *Proceedings of the Society of Antiquaries of Scotland* 128, 351-565

77   Foster, S.M. 1996. *Picts, Gaels and Scots*. London, 36

Conclusion

1   Alcock, L. 1971. *Arthur's Britain*. New York
2   Campbell, J. 1991. *The Anglo-Saxons*. London

Index

This index lists only places mentioned in the text.
Places mentioned in figures are shown in **bold**.